THE PACIFIC ECONOMY
Growth and External Stability

THE PACIFIC ECONOMY

Growth and External Stability

Edited by

Mohamed Ariff

ALLEN & UNWIN
In association with
The Pacific Trade and Development Conference Secretariat
The Australian National University
and The Institute of Strategic and International Studies (ISIS)
Malaysia

© Mohamed Ariff, 1991

First published in 1991
Allen & Unwin Pty Ltd
8 Napier Street, North Sydney NSW 2059

HC
681
.P2885
1991

National Library of Australia
Cataloguing-in-Publication entry:

The Pacific economy: growth and external stability.

  Bibliography.
  Includes index.
  ISBN 1 86373 036 2.
  ISBN 1 86373 035 4 (pbk.).

  1. Pacific Area — Economic conditions. 2. Pacific Area — Foreign economic relations. 3. Pacific Area — Economic policy. I. K. A. Mohamed Ariff, 1940-   . II. Pacific Trade and Development Conference. Secretariat. III. Pacific Trade and Development Conference (18th : 1989 : Kuala Lumpur, Malaysia). IV. Institute of Strategic and International Studies (Malaysia).

330.91823

Set in 10.5/11.5 Plantin by Excel Imaging, St Leonards NSW
Printed by Kim Hup Lee Printing, Singapore

Contents

Tables		vii
Figures		ix
Contributors		xi
Foreword		xiii
Noordin Sopiee		
Preface		xv
Mohamed Ariff		
1	Introduction	1
	Mohamed Ariff	
2	Economic stability and growth in the Pacific: an overview	11
	Ross Garnaut	
3	Pacific growth and macroeconomic performance: models and issues	27
	Anne O. Krueger	
4	The United States in the world economy	44
	Barry P. Bosworth	
5	The Japanese economy and Pacific development	60
	Heizo Takenaka	
6	The current account and economic policy: the Australian experience in the 1980s	71
	R. G. Gregory	
7	Macroeconomic development and prospects in East Asia	93
	Yung Chul Park	
8	Macroeconomic management in the ASEAN countries	121
	Mari Pangestu	
9	Exchange rate regimes and practices: Malaysian perspectives	155
	Lin See Yan	
10	Resource gaps and external financing in the Asia–Pacific countries	176
	Manuel F. Montes	

11	Commodity trends and policy responses with reference to the Pacific *Ronald C. Duncan*	192
12	Evolving patterns of comparative advantage in the Pacific economies *Ippei Yamazawa, Akira Hirata and Kazuhiko Yokota*	213
13	The Pacific and the world economy: inter-relations *Lawrence B. Krause and Mark Sundberg*	233
14	The role of multilateralism and regionalism: a Pacific perspective *H. Edward English and Murray G. Smith*	253

APPENDIXES

5A	A long-term economic forecast for the Asia–Pacific region	276
9A	Supplementary data	277
12A.1	Index of trade intensity	288
12A.2	Index of revealed comparative advantage	288
12A.3	Index of trade complementarity	288
12A.4	Regression analysis of trade flows	289
12A.5	Trade statistics	290
13A	Outline of the Asia-Pacific MSG model	290
14A.1	Statement on trade policy by PECC Standing Committee	295
14A.2	Joint statement ministerial-level meeting, 5–7 November 1989, Canberra	297
Notes		299
Bibliography		304
Index		313

Tables

1.1　Asia–Pacific key macroeconomic indicators, 1980, 1985, 1987　6
3.1　Per capita incomes and growth performance of the Asian high flyers, 1965–87　31
3.2　Investment breakdown for Korea in the 1980s　38
4.1　Net saving and investment as a share of net national product, United States, 1951–89　45
4.2　Projections of baseline federal deficits, 1980–94　51
4.3　Alternative measures of inflation, 1985–90　57
5.1　Contribution to Japan's economic growth by individual demand items　61
5.2　Interdependence coefficients　64
5.3　Impact of changes in American and Japanese GNP　65
5A.1　Relative GNP: case 1　276
5A.2　Relative GNP: case 2　277
7.1　Economic performance of East Asia and Japan　94
7.2　Contribution of internal and external demand growth　95
7.3　Trade account in Japan, Korea and Taiwan, 1987–93　95
7.4　Volume and prices of imported oil　102
7.5　Current account, savings and investment　102
8.1　Comparative inflation rates, current account balances, real GDP growth, central government deficit/surplus by region, 1971–88　122
8.2　ASEAN countries, macroeconomic performance, 1971–88　128
8.3　ASEAN countries, growth rate of broad money, 1971–88　128
8.4　ASEAN countries, deposit rate, external debt outstanding, debt-service ratio　129
8.5　ASEAN countries, gross domestic saving and gross investment, 1971–89　130
9A.1　Malaysia, macroeconomic indicators　277
9A.2　Malaysia, financial and monetary indicators　279
9A.3　Balance of payments　281
9A.4　Exchange rate arrangements as of 31 March 1989　282
9A.5　US dollar vis-à-vis other currencies　284

9A.6   Appreciation/depreciation of the US dollar   284
9A.7   Exchange rates of ringgit against selected currencies   285
9A.8   Inter-bank money market rates, 3-monthly   287
9A.9   Current account   287
10.1   Debt indicators   177
10.2   Savings, investment, resource gap   179
10.3   Average incremental capital–output ratios   180
10.4   Average annual capital inflows   182
10.5   Average annual financial disbursements from OECD and OPEC economies   184
10.6   Direct investment flows   186
10.7   Korea's overseas investment by region   188
10.8   Japanese investment and manufacturing advantage, cumulative approvals   191
11.1   Growth trends in agricultural production   193
11.2   Shares of non-fuel primary commodities in developing country merchandise exports, 1971–86   194
11.3   Growth rates of agricultural commodity exports of developing countries by region, 1970–85   195
11.4   World shares of agricultural commodity exports by developing country regions   195
11.5   Annual changes in export earnings, developing countries, 1979–88   197
11.6   Growth in meat consumption, selected countries, 1975–88   201
11.7   Calories per capital per day from vegetable fats and oils and from all sources, average for 1979–81   202
11.8   Wholesale Indian vegetables oil prices, 1981–82 to 1986–87   202
12.1   Trade matrix of the Asia–Pacific countries, 1987, 1980 and 1987/80 ratio   214
12.2   Matrix of trade intensity indexes, 1980 and 1987   218
12.3   Changes in R C A Xs of selected products in the Pacific countries, 1980 and 1987   226
12.4   Matrix of complementarity indexes, 1980 and 1987   228
12.5   Determinants of Asia–Pacific trade flows, 1970, 1980 and 1987   230
13.1   Gramm–Rudman–Hollings deficit reduction in the United States with targeting   249
13.2   Current account balancing act with employment targeting   251
13A.1 Regional trade matrix, 1987   295
13A.2 Structure of Asian NIE exports, 1986   295

Figures

4.1 Retirement and non-retirement saving 46
4.2 Ratio of household wealth to income, with and without capital gains, 1960–88 47
4.3 The current account and the trade balance, 1960–88 53
4.4 Real and nominal exchange rates, 1970–88 54
4.5 Trends in merchandise trade, 1960–1988 54
6.1a Traded and non-traded goods production 74
6.1b Traded and non-traded goods production 74
6.1c Traded and non-traded goods production 74
6.2 Male real wages, actual and predicted 76
6.3 Ratio of corporate gross operating surplus (GOS) to GDP 77
6.4 Ratio of net lending overseas to GDP 78
6.5 Ratios of government net savings and net overseas lending to GDP 81
6.6 Ratios of private net savings and net overseas lending to GDP 81
6.7 Ratios of government and private sector net savings to GDP 82
6.8 Ratios of government net savings and the statistical discrepancy to GDP 83
6.9 Ratios of government and private net savings (including statistical discrepancy) to GDP 83
6.10 Competitiveness index 84
6.11a Ratio of gross operating surplus (GOS) to wage bill index, farm and non-traded good sector 86
6.11b Ratio of gross operating surplus (GOS) to wage bill index, manufactured and non-traded goods sector 87
6.11c Ratio of gross operating surplus (GOS) to wage bill index, export and non-traded goods sector 88
6.12 Ratio of exports to GDP, current and constant prices 89
6.13 Ratio of manufacturing value added and imports to GDP 89
6.14 Moving average ratios of overseas borrowing (two-year lag) and household savings 91
7.1 United States trade deficit with Japan, Korea and Taiwan 96

7.2	Change in unit labour cost in manufacturing	98
7.3	The won and the US dollar and the won/yen exchange rate	99
7.4	The NT dollar, the US dollar and the NT dollar/yen exchange rate	100
7.5	Real effective exchange rates of Japan, Korea and Taiwan	101
7.6	United States imports from East Asia	115
8.1	ASEAN countries, terms of trade	124
8.2a	ASEAN countries, GDP growth rates	125
8.2b	ASEAN countries, inflation rates	126
8.3a	ASEAN countries, quarterly nominal exchanges rates	131
8.3b	ASEAN countries, quarterly real effective exchange rates	132
10.1	Asia–Pacific direct investment flows	189
10.2	Japan and United States direct investment flows	189
11.1	Income terms of trade of non-fuel primary commodities by developing country regions, 1965–85	197
12.1	'Flying geese' in the Pacific: transfer of industries in East and Southeast Asian countries	224

Contributors

Mohamed Ariff	Faculty of Economics and Administration, University of Malaysia, Kuala Lumpur, Malaysia
Barry P. Bosworth	The Brookings Institution, Washington DC, United States
Ronald C. Duncan	International Commodities Market Division, World Bank, Washington DC, United States
H. Edward English	Department of Economics, Faculty of Social Sciences, Carleton University, Ottawa, Canada
Ross Garnaut	Department of Economics, Research School of Pacific Studies, Australian National University, Canberra, Australia
R.G. Gregory	Department of Economics, Research School of Social Sciences, Australian National University, Canberra, Australia
Akira Hirata	Institute of Developing Economies, Tokyo, Japan
Lawrence B. Krause	Graduate School of International Relations and Pacific Studies, University of California, San Diego, United States
Anne O. Krueger	Department of Economics, Duke University, Durham, United States
Lin See Yan	Bank Negara Malaysia, Kuala Lumpur, Malaysia
Manuel F. Montes	Department of Economics, University of the Philippines, Quezon City, Philippines
Mari Pangestu	Centre for Strategic and International Studies, Jakarta, Indonesia
Yung Chul Park	Department of Economics, Korea University, Seoul, Korea
Murray G. Smith	Centre for Trade Policy and Law, Carleton University and the University of Ottawa, Ottawa, Canada
Noordin Sopiee	Institute of Strategic and International Studies, Kuala Lumpur, Malaysia
Mark Sundberg	World Bank, Washington DC, United States

Heizo Takenaka	Institute of Fiscal and Monetary Policy, Ministry of Finance, Tokyo, Japan
Ippei Yamazawa	Department of Economics, Hitotsubashi University, Tokyo, Japan
Kazuhiko Yokata	Institute of Developing Economies, Tokyo, Japan

Foreword

It was Leon Trotsky who said at the beginning of this century that anyone who yearned for the quiet life had no right to be born in the twentieth century. Certainly, anyone who wishes to be spared a period of momentous change could be said to have no right to live in this exciting decade. The gale-force winds of change that swept us into the 1990s will sweep us through into the next century.

In this context, any present-day conference that sets out to study issues and, by extension, attempts to predict future trends, runs the risk of being overtaken by events before the first participants arrive.

The Pacific Trade and Development Conference Series, started in Tokyo in 1968, has to its credit remained intact, contemporaneous *and* relevant. Over the past twenty years, PAFTAD has not only widened the breadth and scope of topics covered but also remained highly sensitive to the current-day scenarios.

The theme for this PAFTAD Conference, 'Macroeconomic management in the Pacific: growth and external stability', is highly topical in the light of what can be safely deduced as some clear trends for the future, notwithstanding the unpredictability of our times. There is, for instance, the decline of the age of ideology and the ascendance of economics. In this age of increasingly managed international economics, 'macroeconomic management' becomes a highly topical and important subject for debate.

We at the Institute are proud to have been a part of PAFTAD 18. We believe that the Conference has contributed much intellectual capital on trade and development issues, and are confident that its deliberations, as always, will receive the attention of policy scholars and practitioners in the Asia-Pacific region.

Noordin Sopiee
Director-General
Institute of Strategic and International Studies
Kuala Lumpur
October 1990

Preface

This volume presents the papers written for the Eighteenth Pacific Trade and Development Conference, held in Kuala Lumpur on 11–14 December 1989 on the theme 'Macroeconomic management in the Pacific: growth and external stability'.

The PAFTAD Conference Series has always addressed issues of current importance and responded to the demands of the Pacific circumstances. Accordingly, it was considered opportune for PAFTAD to take a hard look at the Pacific macroeconomic experience at the tail end of the decade and to draw lessons from it. This volume pays attention to issues that arise in relation to macroeconomic management in so far as it has a bearing on the economic growth and external stability of the region. The critical message that runs throughout the volume is that macroeconomic management of each country has considerable externalities for others in the region, given the growing economic interdependence among them. It is hoped that this volume, in keeping with the PAFTAD tradition of providing data and analysis on policy issues, will be useful to policymakers in the region.

The approach employed here was to take the papers presented at the Conference, suggest changes in the light of discussion at the meeting, and then adapt revised papers for inclusion in the volume. The exception to this is the paper by Manuel Montes (Chapter 10), who was commissioned after the Conference to write a paper to fill a gap that was left open due to totally unforeseen circumstances.

The volume begins with an overview and a general review of models and issues that relate to Pacific growth and macroeconomic performance. Five papers examine individual country experiences of the 1980s, including those of developed, developing and advanced developing countries in the region. Three papers follow which discuss specific issues relating to exchange rates, financial interdependence and commodity trends. A further three papers deal with broader issues of economic inter-relations.

The Conference was organised by the Eighteenth PAFTAD Conference Organising Committee under the leadership of Dr Noordin Sopiee as Chairman and Professor Mohamed Ariff as Secretary-General, in association with the Institute of Strategic and International Studies (ISIS) Malaysia, Kuala

Lumpur. The Committee was, of course, assisted by the advice and support of the International Steering Committee of the conference series, and the PAFTAD Conference Secretariat at the Australian National University.

We are especially grateful for the work undertaken by Dr Muthi Semudram in summarising the Conference discussion. This provided essential background to the overview of Conference themes provided in Chapter 2 by Professor Ross Garnaut.

The editorial process was facilitated by many people. Special thanks are due to Professor H. W. Arndt for his help as editorial consultant. Gary Anson edited the manuscript for accuracy and consistency of style and it was wordprocessed by Kim-Lan Ngo, Minni Reis and Maxine Fulton.

We are grateful for financial support from the following organisations: the Ford Foundation, the Rockefeller Brothers Fund, the Henry Luce Foundation, the Taiwan Institute of Economic Research, the Asian Development Bank, the Foundation of International Education, the International Development Research Center, and the Australian National University.

Mohamed Ariff
October 1990

1 Introduction

MOHAMED ARIFF

The dynamics of the Pacific economy are such that the Asia–Pacific region has outpaced all other regions in terms of economic growth over the last two decades. This is hardly surprising, since the region is the home, not only for major players like the United States and Japan and 'high flyers' like Korea and Taiwan, but also for eclectic developing countries on the fast track like Malaysia and Thailand. The region has also become increasingly interdependent over the years, thanks to substantial increase in intra-regional trade and investment flows. Over one-half of the region's merchandise exports is directed at regional markets, and a slightly smaller proportion of the region's capital exports go to regional destinations. Several Asia–Pacific countries also maintain high profiles outside the region, especially in Western Europe.

Significant industrial restructuring is continually taking place in the region, in response to the shifting patterns of comparative advantage, with some productions and production processes being phased out or relocated, and some others being upgraded. Rapid technological changes, thanks to heavy investments in research and development, are also contributing substantially to the restructuring process and hence to the dynamism of the region.

Important structural adjustments are also underway in the region in the face of serious macroeconomic imbalances that have arisen. These imbalances pose a threat, not only to intra-regional economic relations and external stability, but also to the open trading system of the world at large. Conscious of such dangers, the major Asia–Pacific economies have resorted to serious macroeconomic adjustments.

Impressive economic performances of individual Asia–Pacific countries notwithstanding, some worrying signs have appeared on the horizon. The surge in economic growth has apparently caused stresses and strains in the system which may consequently break it down unless timely and appropriate corrective measures are taken. Much of the problem revolves around the bilateral trade gaps between the United States and Japan, giving rise to looming fears of a nasty trade war between the two economic giants. It is in the interest of not only these two rivals, but others as well, that such a trade war is averted. As Korea and Taiwan are no longer marginal players in the field, their policy actions do have greater externality than is usually supposed. These NIEs are also doing their bit, along with others, to help diffuse the tension in the region.

It is pertinent to take a closer look at the United States and Japan, since they play central roles. It is indeed remarkable that the United States economy has been expanding non-stop since 1982. It is also noteworthy that this impressive growth has not led to any overheating of its economy, as inflation and unemployment rates have remained amazingly low. The expansion of the United States economy is attributed in no small measure to expansionary fiscal policy, with soaring federal budget deficits which peaked at US$213 billion or 5 per cent of GDP in 1986. As domestic savings have been insufficient to finance domestic investments, foreign borrowings have increased sharply. In addition to the huge domestic resource gap, the United States also faces persistent current account deficits in the balance of payments. Consequently, United States interest rates have risen significantly, providing incentives for the inflow of foreign funds. High interest rates seem to have had a dampening effect on domestic investment, as the ratio of investment to GDP has not risen over this period despite the inflow of foreign funds. Private investments may have been crowded out in the process.

It appears that the United States has been living beyond its means, underproducing and over-consuming. It would then follow that the United States must increase production and/or reduce consumption. As United States capacity utilisation is already at a very high level and unemployment at a very low level, the scope for increased production is rather limited, barring significant productivity improvements. The burden of adjustment will therefore have to fall largely on consumption. Increased government expenditures being a major source of consumption expansion for the United States in the 1980s, a substantial proportion of any reduction in consumption may have to be accounted for by reduced government expenditures. To close the domestic resource gap, savings will have to increase. As the decline in national savings has been associated with the expansion of the public sector deficit, a reduction in that deficit is necessary to bring about an increase in the national saving rate. Hopefully, government deficits will decline yearly within the framework of the Gramm-Rudman-Hollings balanced budget act. It is noteworthy that United States budget deficits have come down from over US$200 billion to about US$150 billion annually.

The trade deficits of the United States have been a major source of concern, not only for the country itself but also for others for whom the United States represents the largest export market. While some ascribe this trade deficit to a loss of United States export competitiveness, and others blame it on 'unfair' trade practices by the rest of the world, there appears to be a general consensus that the problem is structural and not cyclical. Be that as it may, there is little doubt that the solution to the problem must include a correction of the budget deficit and the exchange rate. It cannot be denied that exchange rate depreciation of the dollar has helped improve the United States trade balance, after some initial misgivings apparently due to the J-curve effect. Although the United States trade deficit is declining, it is still running at a level of US$120 billion annually. It appears that exchange rate adjustments alone are not sufficient to redress the external imbalance and that a correction of the budget deficit is also in order.

The manner in which the United States brings about such corrections will have important global and regional repercussions. Rapid adjustments will lead to a drastic contraction of world demand, adversely affecting many export-oriented economies. Gradual adjustments, on the other hand, will pave the way for a soft landing, but prolonged trade deficits may spur protectionist measures in the United States. In either case, the implications are not favourable, especially for those countries which rely heavily on the United States market.

It is not certain that Japan, the other major actor in the Pacific region, will be able to take up the slack left by the United States correction process. Japan is the opposite of the United States in that it enjoys internal and external surpluses. There is a need to synchronise corrections taking place in the United States with appropriate structural adjustments on the Japanese side so that the net external impact is not negative. Japan can facilitate the process by reducing its external surplus through expansion of domestic demand and internationalisation of its economy. More specifically, Japan needs to make its market more accessible to imports by dismantling its non-tariff barriers.

Seen from this perspective, the appreciation of the yen represents an important move in the right direction, as it has helped reduce Japan's external surplus. At the same time, increased government expenditure on public works has helped stimulate domestic demand in Japan. It is remarkable that Japan has adjusted itself rapidly and smoothly to the high yen (*endaka*) phenomenon and was able to register high growth rates in 1987 and 1988 of 4 per cent and 6 per cent, respectively. It is also encouraging to note that Japan's economic growth in recent years has been fuelled strongly by domestic demand expansion rather than export expansion. In the wake of the rising yen, recent years have also witnessed significant industrial restructuring in Japan, increased sourcing of components and parts by Japanese industries from outside Japan, increased Japanese capital outflows, both direct and portfolio, and visible changes in Japanese consumer behaviour. While all this does augur well, the fact remains that Japan cannot be a substitute for the United States market, not only because it is substantially smaller in size, but also because the Japanese propensity to import has been notoriously low. It is unlikely that the rapid domestic expansion in Japan will translate itself into increased imports, unless Japan seriously mounts a major domestic policy reform that will include substantial deregulation.

Japan is increasingly assuming the role of the leading power in the region, without fully accepting the responsibilities that come with such a role. Preserving the multilateral and open basis of trade is one such responsibility and Japan needs to set good examples by opening up its own market first. The responsibilities also include a commitment to contribute greater shares of official development assistance and private capital to the development of less developed countries.

Australia and New Zealand have continued the process of closer integration with the Pacific, following the reorientation forced by the accession of the

United Kingdom to the European Community. The latter's common agricultural policy, in particular, has hurt these economies, where primary products still constitute as much as three-fourths of exports. Australia and New Zealand have been running substantial external deficits exacerbated by terms of trade deterioration, which was particularly severe in the first half of the 1980s. In response to all this, they have been diversifying their exports and export markets but their high inflation rates have eroded the competitiveness of their exports despite significant exchange rate adjustments. It is noteworthy that both Australia and New Zealand have undertaken domestic policy reforms, including unilateral trade liberalisation, in addition to moving to complete free trade with each other.

Canada has been more successful in adjusting and reorientating its economy in the wake of reduced access to the European Community market for its agricultural products, thanks mainly to its proximity to the United States. Canadian exports to the United States have increased sharply in recent years, resulting in sizeable bilateral trade surplus for Canada. It is of interest to note that the two-way trade between the United States and Canada exceeds that of any other pair of countries. The recent Canada–United States Free Trade Agreement has boosted the prospects of increased trade and capital flows between the two countries. However, Canada is saddled with accumulated external debts, the service of which has contributed to its growing current account deficits.

The NIEs of the region are the star performers, registering high, often double-digit, growth rates. All of them have benefitted from the yen appreciation, which has served to strengthen the competitiveness of their exports, especially in the United States market. The NIEs are also emerging as important importers in the region. It is interesting to observe that the NIEs have been importing more from the region than Japan since 1988. Taiwan has been running a substantial current account surplus for many years, while Korea achieved a modest current account surplus for the first time in 1986.

Pressure from the United States, which has sizeable deficits with both Korea and Taiwan, has led to revaluation of the Korean won and the New Taiwan dollar, the latter appreciating more sharply than the former. The United States pressure also led Taiwan to liberalise its imports. Although Korea has followed suit by eliminating import licensing for many products and reducing tariffs, there has been a strong Korean political resistance to the United States pressure. There has been much less United States pressure on Hong Kong and Singapore, not only because they already have very liberal trade and foreign investment regimes, but also because their trade surpluses with the United States are not as large as those of Korea and Taiwan. In any case, their impact on the region is somewhat marginal because of their very small size.

Indonesia, Malaysia, the Philippines and Thailand (ASEAN-4) have recovered from the prolonged slump in commodity prices in the first half of the 1980s. The slump forced these countries to make important policy shifts. Indonesia, in particular, has implemented spectacular policy reforms which included repeated devaluation of the rupiah, fiscal austerity, and trade and financial liberalisation, in an attempt to avert a major debt crisis. Malaysia adopted more liberal policies towards foreign investments, allowed the ringgit to depreciate drastically, de-emphasised the role of the public sector and imposed curbs on government expenditure. As a result, Malaysia was able to register high growth rates of 7.6 per cent, 8.7 per cent and 8.5 per cent in 1987, 1988 and 1989 respectively, compared with a negative growth of -1.2 per cent in 1985.

The Philippines has also been rebounding and its economic performance would have been better had it not been for the unfortunate domestic political uncertainties. Major economic reforms have been postponed for political reasons. Nevertheless, a transition from consumption-led growth to investment-led growth is underway in the Philippines. The Philippines has to simultaneously service its staggering external debts and increase investments in new industries, a very tough task for any debilitated economy.

Thailand is the most promising of all ASEAN-4 countries. It is the fastest growing economy in the subregion, with double-digit growth rates. All indications are that Thailand is well on its way to NIE status. Its manufacturing sector is doing extremely well, with manufactured exports growing rapidly. At the same time, Thailand also mounted successful diversification in agriculture. Thailand has been so successful in attracting foreign investments that it is already suffering from what may be termed 'investment indigestion'. Rapid growth has led to the emergence of serious problems, including severe infrastructural bottlenecks, excessive industrial concentration around the Bangkok metropolitan region, growing shortages of skilled labour and rapid environmental deterioration. There are already signs of the economy overheating with an inflation rate of 7-8 per cent, which is high compared with Malaysia's 3-4 per cent.

China, the biggest economy in the Pacific in terms of population, has made considerable strides in the 1980s with output growth averaging almost 10 per cent. Its impressive economic performance is attributed largely to the bold economic reforms which it mounted during the decade. China's increased participation in international trade was made possible by the massive inflow of foreign investment into the special economic zones which are located along the Pacific coast. It is not clear whether China will extend the economic reforms and continue further to open up its economy. Internally, there are signs that the decentralisation process, which seemed so promising a while ago, is reversing itself as the authorities at the centre tighten their grip on the provinces. Externally, China has suffered a major setback as a result of its crackdown on the pro-democracy movement. In short, the future outlook of China is somewhat hazy.

The above picture, painted with broad brush-strokes, is intended to serve as backdrop to the papers presented in this volume (see also Table 1.1, which provides data relating to key macroeconomic indicators). The contents of this volume cover a wide range of issues and policies of relevance and importance to the Pacific economies. Although the main concern of the volume revolves

Table 1.1 Asia–Pacific key macroeconomic indicators, 1980 (per cent)

Economic indicators	United States	Japan	Canada	Australia	New Zealand	Korea
1980						
Real GDP growth over previous year	-0.1	4.4	1.5	1.5	1.9	-3
Manufacturing share in GDP	24	29	19	19	23	28
Export growth	13	18	-0.5	-0.3	13	10
Import growth	8	-3	-3	7	2	-9
Export/GNP ratio	8	14	26	18	28	15
BoP current surplus (deficit)/GNP	0.1	-1	-0.04	0.6	-4	-9
Total external debt/GNP	30.4	52.9	55.5	18.9	54.2	48.8
Debt servicing/exports	2.1	3.2	7.2	5	4.7	12.3
Budget surplus (deficit)/GNP	-3	-4.4	-3	-2	-7	-0.2
Inflation rate	9	4	11	12	14	25
Unemployment rate	7.2	2	7.4	6	2.7	5.2
International reserves/imports	51	23	19	21	5	5
Gross National Savings/GNP	17	32	23	23	23	49
1985						
Real GDP growth over previous year	3.3	4.9	3	1.4	1.8	5.4
Manufacturing share in GDP	20	30	16	17	24	28
Export growth	-0.5	6	2	2	14	0.4
Import growth	10	-0.1	5	1	-2	30.5
Export/GNP ratio	5	13	24	12	23	40
BoP current surplus (deficit)/GNP	-3	4	-0.3	-5	-5	-1
Total external debt/GNP	40	68	64.8	31.6	61.3	56.3
Debt servicing/exports	2.5	2.2	2.1	15.7	1.3	21.7
Budget surplus (deficit)/GNP	-3.5	-1.4	-6.1	0.7	-5	-1
Inflation rate	3	1	3	6	10	5
Unemployment rate	7.2	2.6	10.5	8.2	3.6	4
International reserves/imports	33	27	14	32	27	10
Gross National Savings/GNP	14	33	20	20	24	31.1
1987						
Real GDP growth over previous year	3.2	4.7	4.8	4.4	-2	11.1
Manufacturing share in GDP	20	29	19	17	21	30
Export growth	17	0	12	17	11	36.4
Import growth	2	11	4	2.3	9	29.2
Export/GNP ratio	6	12	24	14	28	48
BoP current surplus (deficit)/GNP	-4.5	-4.1	-2	-5	-5	8
Total external debt/GNP	51.6	65.5	69	40.1	63.3	27.5
Debt servicing/exports	2.3	4.4	8.4	19.8	5.5	21.9
Budget surplus (deficit)/GNP	-3.5	-2.7	-4.2	0.7	-12.1	-1
Inflation rate	3	-0.2	1	8	13	4
Unemployment rate	6.2	2.8	8.8	8	4.1	3.1
International reserves/imports	38	63	18	43	45	8
Gross National Savings/GNP	13	34	20	20	27	37

Source: International Economic Data Bank, Australian National University.

INTRODUCTION

(Table 1.1 cont'd)

China	Taiwan	Hong Kong	Singapore	Indonesia	Malaysia	Philippines	Thailand
6.6	7.8	10.9	9.7	7.9	7.4	5.3	4.7
35	36.3	27	28	9	23	26	20
23	23	19	10	-3	-1	19	12
12	33	15	11	16	14	3	9
7	48	70	223	30	63	23	27
-1	2.2	-6	1	4	-1	-5	-6
1.6	—	—	18.3	27.9	13.7	49.4	25.9
4.6	—	—	1	7.9	2.5	7.1	5
-3.6	-0.04	1.8	0.8	-3.96	-8.3	-1.3	-2.7
4	8	15	11	12	7	16	13
4.9	1.2	4.3	3	1.7	5.6	4.8	0.8
42	9	—	25	35	38	38.4	28
29	32	27.5	34	34	30	26	20
12.7	4.4	-0.1	-1.6	2.4	-1.1	-4.5	1.3
37	24	24	14	18	25	20	20
5	0.2	6.6	-5	-10.7	-7.8	-14.1	-3.8
13.5	32.1	88.6	125.3	14.9	37	15.5	22.5
10	50.8	91	110.8	21.7	48.5	14.1	18.9
-4	15.3	6	-0.02	-2.3	-2	-0.1	-4.1
5.9	4.8	—	18.6	44.1	—	81.9	47.8
6.3	-0.2	—	3.5	24.9	28.9	19	25.3
-6.8	3	0.6	2	-3.8	-7.4	-1.8	-4.4
2.6	3	3	-1.8	6	-1	19	0.6
1.8	2.9	3.6	4.1	2.1	6.9	6.1	—
41	121	—	44	26	46	13	25
34.4	31.9	27.3	41	25	27	15	20
9.4	11.2	13.6	8.8	3.6	5.5	5.3	6.8
34	40	22	29	14	25	25	24
17.8	34.8	36.8	27.8	19.5	29.2	18.1	31.7
4.3	45.8	37.1	27.4	6.5	14.7	33.6	42.4
14	54.7	102.5	136.7	24.7	55.3	16.7	24.2
0.1	18.7	5.9	2.7	-3.1	7.6	-1.6	-1.1
10.4	8.8	—	21.9	79.7	74.8	86.5	44.2
13.2	3.2	—	2.4	27.9	20	22.7	13.6
-0.7	1.4	3.2	0.5	-5.4	-7.6	25.2	-0.7
6	-3	6	1	9.3	5	8	4
2	2	1.8	4.7	3.6	8.7	9.1	—
56	245	—	42	33	46	22	34
37	38	—	41	25	32	17	23

revolves around the macroeconomic management of the Pacific economies, its scope is stretched somewhat to consider other related issues which have a bearing on the region's economic resilience.

Chapter 2, by Garnaut, provides an overview and a succinct synthesis of various issues addressed in the Eighteenth Pacific Trade and Development Conference, from which the present volume emanates. This chapter provides an analytic context for focusing on the models, lessons and issues that emerge from the macroeconomic experiences of Pacific countries.

In Chapter 3, Krueger takes a hard look at the development models that have been prevalent over the past several decades and scrutinises their relevance in the light of the growth experience of the 'high flyers' of the Pacific region (Korea, Taiwan, Hong Kong and Singapore). She pays particular attention to the role of the trade regime, and that of government, in these economies and factors in the lessons from all this in her assessment of the Pacific outlook for the 1990s.

The macroeconomic management of the United States economy and its implications for the rest of the world in general, and the Pacific region in particular, is the main concern of Chapter 4, in which Bosworth focuses on the United States fiscal and trade deficits. He drives home the point that United States policy adjustments must include fiscal restraint and argues that the depressive effect of such restraint can be offset by an easy monetary policy. The main thrust of the discussion centres on the restructuring of the United States economy away from domestic consumption towards the tradeable goods industries without a recession.

The role of Japan in the development of the Pacific economy is the object of a critical analysis by Takenaka in Chapter 5. The discussion of the externalities of Japan's macroeconomic policies, both positive and negative, is instructive, but the most interesting part of the analysis relates to the role that Japan must play as an 'absorber' in the event of a declining American demand and the sort of domestic economic reform that Japan must undertake consistent with such a role.

In Chapter 6, Gregory deals with Australian macroeconomic experiences of the 1980s and the ways in which macroeconomic adjustments have been used to promote structural reforms which were apparently designed not only to correct short-term macroeconomic imbalances but also to stimulate long-term growth. The major thrust of the chapter, however, lies in its attempt to pin down the determinants of the current account. Its main concern is to provide reasons for current account outcomes rather than policy prescriptions.

In Chapter 7, Park discusses macroeconomic developments in Korea and Taiwan and examines their prospects. The discussion centres to a considerable extent on the United States as the main market for their manufactured exports and on Japan as the major source of capital and technology for their development. It is argued that export-oriented industrialisation in East Asia has led to an increased dependence on Japan for supplies of parts, components and industrial materials, which in turn has contributed to their growing trade imbalances with Japan. Considerable skepticism is also expressed about Japan as an alternative to a shrinking United States market.

Macroeconomic management and policies of the ASEAN-5 (Brunei excluded) in the wake of the various external shocks experienced in the 1980s are discussed by Pangestu in Chapter 8. The discussion revolves mainly around macroeconomic imbalances caused by external changes and domestic policies. Although there are considerable variations among the ASEAN-5, one gets the impression that they have all performed fairly well and have coped with the recessionary influences of global slowdown in the early 1980s. Macroeconomic adjustment policies, notably fiscal restraint and exchange depreciation, and structural changes through deregulation and liberalisation, are highlighted as the major policy instruments that proved to be helpful.

Chapter 9 deals with exchange rate regimes and practices focusing on the Malaysian experience, with somewhat peripheral references to the exchange rate policies of other developing countries in the region. In this chapter Lin discusses at length the ways in which the Malaysian ringgit was managed in the 1980s. It has been shown that the shift in Malaysia's exchange rate policy in the face of a prolonged recession contributed significantly to the recovery of the Malaysian economy. Although the bulk of the analysis is Malaysia-specific, it is relevant to other countries in that it underscores the importance of exchange rate corrections as a policy instrument. There are lessons that others can learn from the Malaysian experience about the dangers of serious exchange rate distortions.

In Chapter 10, Montes discusses the role of external financing in filling the domestic resource gaps. Asian countries, with the exception of the Philippines, were able to avoid a debt crisis, although their level of indebtedness was not very different from that of the Latin American countries. Montes attributes this mainly to the better export base and higher investment ratios of Asian countries. The role of Japan as a resource surplus country and the emergence of the NIEs as net financing suppliers are also highlighted as manifestations of growing financial interdependence in the Asia–Pacific region.

Commodity trends and policy responses in the Pacific context are examined by Duncan in Chapter 11. The analysis shows that variable commodity prices will continue to be an important source of external shock to developing countries. The scope and limitations of such policies as a hedge against price risks and the use of fiscal and monetary measures to manage the terms of trade shocks are also discussed. An important conclusion that one may draw from the analysis is that bad macroeconomic policies (for example, overvalued exchange rates) can be more costly for primary producers than industry specific interventions (such as export taxes).

An attempt is made in Chapter 12 by Yamazawa, Hirata and Yokota to quantify changes in trade relationships among the individual Pacific countries and to identify the underlying forces generating new patterns of comparative advantage. The study points to a general increase in the degree of complementarity among the Pacific countries, which represents an important explanatory variable of trade flows. Their regression analysis suggests that physical proximity and macroeconomic factors are also important as determinants of the Pacific trade flow.

Krause and Sundberg have made an effort in Chapter 13 to identify the key factors which are likely to influence the global economic environment and to examine the ways in which these are likely to impact on economic growth and external stability in the Pacific. The authors present a number of alternative scenarios, but argue that the world economic system is moving towards a dual structure, with Europe on the one side and the rest of the world, focused on the Pacific countries, on the other. They then go on to simulate the corrections of the United States external deficit in such a world, using a policy mix that would avert a 'hard landing' and a contraction in world demand.

Finally, in Chapter 14, English and Smith examine the current trends in the multilateral economic system and in regionalism and arrive at the conclusion that multilateral and regional efforts are necessary to maintain the world trading system. It is argued that neither multilateralism nor regionalism can perform the whole task single-handedly: regionalism in the Pacific is seen as a supplement to, and not as a substitute for, the multilateral trading system.

2 Economic stability and growth in the Pacific: an overview

ROSS GARNAUT

The Pacific experience through the 1980s reinforces the old knowledge that economic stability is necessary for rapid growth to be sustained over long periods. Through the 1980s, the sustenance of growth in Pacific countries had to overcome recurrent challenges to stability, from home and abroad. To a considerable extent, Pacific economies have met these challenges effectively, although major imbalances remain as threats to the continuation of growth through the 1990s.

The sustained dynamism of the Pacific economies has had its origins in the internationally-oriented industrialisation of East Asia—at first in Japan, Hong Kong and Taiwan, later joined by Singapore and the Republic of Korea, and more recently other Southeast Asian economies. Macroeconomic instability through the 1980s has threatened this growth directly in several economies. It has also threatened growth indirectly, through its effects on the trading system that has supported internationally-oriented growth.

This overview selects for discussion several of the major issues linking macroeconomic stability and growth in Pacific economies, as they are raised in other chapters in this volume, and as they emerged in the discussion of these papers at the Eighteenth Pacific Trade and Development Conference in Kuala Lumpur.

INTERNATIONAL FINANCIAL INTEGRATION

The macroeconomic experience of Pacific economies in the 1980s was profoundly affected by the progress of international financial integration from the late 1960s.

The increased integration of world capital markets transformed Japanese and United States payments imbalances, and the relationship between them (Bosworth, Chapter 4; Takenaka, Chapter 5). The large, sustained United States current account deficits of the 1980s could not have been supported by international capital markets in earlier decades. Neither could Japan have placed such large quantities of capital onto international markets: Japan in earlier decades would have been forced earlier into fundamental domestic economic adjustment.

Increasing financial integration is an important part of the background to Australia's capacity to finance through the late 1980s an investment boom and a huge and increasing current account deficit and foreign debt, without being forced into early retrenchment and adjustment (Gregory, Chapter 6).

Increasing financial integration is important to the viability of the new instruments that are being developed to finance the maintenance of export incomes through fluctuations in commodity prices (Duncan, Chapter 11). The new hedging instruments which Duncan and his colleagues at the World Bank have been encouraging—commodity bonds, commodity swaps, currency commodity swaps—depend on a high degree of international financial integration and intermediation. The new instruments depend on participating countries being closely integrated into international financial markets.

International financial integration is important background to the ASEAN experience of the 1980s: variations in income associated with large fluctuations in the terms of trade were financed (with varying implications for domestic stability) through a variety of mechanisms, some of which were not available in earlier decades.

The Pacific experience of increasing international financial integration through the 1980s contrasts with that of other developing regions. The countries that are the subject of this volume, with the sole exception of the Philippines, are closely integrated into an international financial system. Most developing countries in Latin America and Africa, and a number elsewhere in Asia, have through the 1980s moved further from the international financial system. Some have been completely separated from international credit. A number of countries which have been closely and increasingly linked into external financial markets have been able to sustain rapid growth over lengthy periods. Other countries have not been able to sustain rapid growth.

Montes (Chapter 10) demonstrates the crucial role that open financial markets have played in sustaining investment and growth in the Pacific region. He notes that East Asian developing countries' access to international markets freed investment levels from constraints imposed by domestic savings. This was important to the rapidly rising and, in the 1980s, high rates of investment in Indonesia and Malaysia. It was crucial to relatively good growth performance in these economies through the 1980s. For Australia, New Zealand, Canada and the United States, continued access to international financial markets allowed investment rates to be maintained despite large reductions in savings rates. International financial integration allowed gradual absorption in Japan, Taiwan and Korea of the structural implications of higher savings rates (Taiwan and Korea) and lower domestic investment rates (Japan and Taiwan).

Thus, through much of the Pacific region, international financial integration allowed internationally-oriented growth to proceed more smoothly than would have been possible in earlier decades, in the face of large changes in savings and investment behaviour in individual economies. Access to international markets itself influenced savings and investment behaviour.

The Philippines alone of countries discussed in detail in this volume was affected substantially by limitations on access to international finance. The fall in Philippines domestic savings rates was reinforced by a large decline in capital inflow. The consequence was investment rates in the 1980s dramatically lower than in the preceding decade, contributing to catastrophically weaker growth performance.

Table 10.2 highlights the contrast between increasing international financial integration in most Pacific economies, and international disintegration affecting most Latin American economies. In this context, the Philippines experience is Latin American rather than Pacific. The contrast in growth performance between those countries which have retained access to international financial markets, and those which have not, highlights the importance of effective macroeconomic management.

WHAT IS EXTERNAL STABILITY?

Increasing financial integration has raised challenging questions about the appropriate definition of 'external stability' or 'external balance' in economies which are closely integrated into international financial markets. These are addressed in some contributions to this volume—notably those of Pangestu (Chapter 8), Bosworth (Chapter 4) and Gregory (Chapter 6)—and were the subject of discussion at the Kuala Lumpur conference.

Is the divergence of savings and investment rates in Pacific economies, reflected in growing current account deficits in some countries and surpluses in others, evidence of increasing 'external imbalance'? Or is it rational adjustment to expanded opportunities for international financial exchange raising welfare in all countries? Neoclassical welfare economics would suggest the latter, in the absence of major market imperfections (such as might be introduced by government regulation which distorts prices and incentives for investment and savings). But this approach sits uneasily alongside political concern in many countries about large current account imbalances and some of their consequences.

The issue seemed simpler in the days of fixed exchange rates, in the first two decades after Bretton Woods. The central issue was then thought to be whether a current account surplus or deficit was sustainable without an adjustment of currency parities.

The textbooks of the 1960s distinguished between 'autonomous' and 'accommodating' capital flows. There was 'external stability' when autonomous (generally long-term) capital flows were equal in magnitude and opposite in sign to the current account balance. 'Accommodating' capital flows—generally short-term flows initiated by the authorities for balance of payments management purposes—could be utilised for long enough to allow the correction of a payments deficit or surplus through variations in expenditure policy. 'Fundamental disequilibrium' or external imbalance existed when the balance between the current account and long-term capital flows could only be restored with exchange rate adjustment. The simplicity of this treatment was undermined by the floating of exchange rates and the vast expansion in the scale and variety of international capital flows.

Bosworth's chapter on the recent United States experience raises in a particularly challenging way the question of what constitutes external stability in contemporary circumstances. The United States expansion of the 1980s has been based on a powerful expansion of consumption, financed by heavy borrowing both domestically and abroad, and by the sale of assets to foreigners. The benefits of higher consumption to the current generation carry a potentially high cost of reduced standards of living in the future.

Uncomfortable though this outcome may be to Americans and others, it is not necessarily unsustainable over a lengthy period. It was suggested in the discussion at the conference that the United States has US$15 trillion of marketable assets, and that the absolute value of assets under American ownership has actually expanded over the period of high current account deficits. Foreign ownership of American assets can expand at the late 1980s rate of around US$150 billion per annum for a considerable time without generating a crisis in financial markets.

The continuation of large deficits may be thought undesirable, or threatening, by Americans, but in modern international financial markets it is not necessarily 'unstable'.

The American polity's discomfort with sustained deficits has precipitated intense debates about their origins, and about appropriate policy responses to them. It has been accepted by economists that the current account deficit is domestic in origin. However, the political argument has been won by those who argue that the external deficit results from foreigners' restrictions and 'unfair practices' in trade and industry policy. The strength of the latter view has generated serious discussion of interventions that have the capacity to damage substantially American economic welfare and the international trading system. Early reduction of the external and domestic deficits is therefore important to avoid the implementation of trade-destroying policies, even if they are not required to avoid retribution on world financial markets.

Within this context, there are attractive elements in the definition of external balance that Pangestu applied to her analysis of the ASEAN experience. For Pangestu, an economy has 'external stability' for as long as it retains the capacity to make necessary adjustments, in time to avoid bankruptcy or major distortions in resource allocation.

This definition depends on the propensity of governments (more or less strongly influenced by community opinion) to introduce distorting policies to 'correct' payments imbalances. Or, to look at it from the other side, it depends on the capacity of governments to take prompt, effective and efficient policy action in response to the emergence of payments imbalances that require correction. By this definition, external balance is to some extent determined by what governments (or their polities) think it is, and partly by the ability of governments to respond when these limits are breached, up to objective limits represented by the loss of international creditworthiness.

Helpful though the Pangestu definition is in bringing out the policy dimensions of 'external balance', it would be useful for some purposes to be able to define the concept in a less open-ended and more objective manner. I have favoured a definition that draws attention to issues of inter-generational distribution: that an economy is in 'external balance' if currency convertibility is maintained at all stages of the international business cycle without recourse to external borrowings that are so large that their servicing requires absolute reductions in average living standards at some future time (Garnaut and Baxter, 1983).

The discussion of macroeconomic adjustment in this volume tells us that 'external balance' by both the Pangestu and the Garnaut and Baxter definitions is consistent with much larger current account deficits and levels of foreign debt, as a proportion of GDP, in rapidly growing economies and in flexible economies. It is consistent, for example, with much larger deficits in most Pacific economies than in Latin America. Montes comments that in 1983, Malaysia, the Philippines and Korea had similar ratios of debt to GNP to Brazil, Mexico and Peru. That Malaysia and Korea, but not the others, escaped the debt crisis, and the consequences of international financial disintegration, reflects their greater capacity for structural adjustment. Montes observes that this is itself partly the result of greater international orientation in foreign trade. But it also reflects the relatively higher priority accorded to macroeconomic stability, and the greater autonomy of government from pressures and vested interests that seek to resist adjustment.

Gregory's discussion of the Australian case raises the definitional questions in an unusual form. In Australia there is now a large current account deficit alongside a federal budget surplus. The high external deficit is entirely the result of private borrowings. Unlike the United States, Australia has not been pressed into trade-distorting policies, and shows no current tendency in this direction. There is no external imbalance by Pangestu's definition.

But private decisions on investment and borrowing may still be inconsistent with the maintenance of living standards over time. These circumstances may amount to external imbalance which requires correction by policy action. Australia may be experiencing external imbalance by the Garnaut and Baxter definition.

By any definition, large deficits amount to external imbalance if their continuation is likely to lead to substantial deterioration in the terms of access to international financial markets. Despite the origins of Australian deficits in private sector decisions and behaviour, Australia would seem to be closer to external imbalance than the United States in this most fundamental sense.

EXTERNAL STABILITY AND GROWTH

There are several causal links, in both directions, between external stability and growth. At the crudest level, economies that are insolvent internationally do not grow. Thus cautious macroeconomic management is an essential component of the 'East Asian growth model'. Conversely, economies that are achieving high levels of growth on a sustained basis find it easier to maintain external stability: countries that are growing fast have been able to manage relatively easily levels of debt that have crippled others.

Krueger (Chapter 3) emphasises the crucial roles of high and increasing international orientation to both growth and stability. High ratios of exports to production have helped to keep East Asian developing economies out of the debt crisis, even when their ratios of foreign debt to output have been very high, as in Korea and Indonesia in the early 1980s.

Manufactured export growth in the East Asian style contributes to diversification of exports away from heavy concentration in primary commodities. This reduces fluctuations in the terms of trade. At the same time, external orientation unleashes pressures to reduce and to remove growth-inhibiting distortions in the domestic economy. As growth proceeds to higher levels of productivity and incomes, the continuation of growth is increasingly less tolerant of regulatory distortions. Regulatory distortions become progressively more damaging to growth, amounting to a 'shifting bottleneck', requiring progressively more far-reaching deregulatory initiatives if strong growth is to be sustained.

Conversely, macroeconomic instability has at times triggered the introduction of growth-inhibiting microeconomic distortions, as recently in the United States, and more severely in China. But not always: as suggested in the discussion of Indonesia, Malaysia, Thailand, Australia, New Zealand, Japan, Taiwan and Korea, macroeconomic crisis has in some circumstances served to focus attention on the need for efficiency-increasing structural reform.

Krueger also notes the importance of governments' considerable and increasing use of indirect rather than direct interventions in the economy in securing successful economic development in the Pacific.

Krueger's assessment is that government intervention in resource allocation decisions has been less important, intrusive and distorting than in other developing countries and regions—even in Korea, the most intrusive of the NIE governments.

Macroeconomic policy, Krueger says, is not fiscal and monetary policy alone, but the whole range of policies that affect the prices at which goods, services and factors of production are exchanged, and the ease with which resources are able to move from less to more productive uses. Structural flexibility associated with heavy reliance on markets for allocation of factors of production and distribution of goods and services has facilitated adjustment to macroeconomic shocks from home and abroad.

High savings rates also distinguish the 'East Asian growth model'. High savings support high levels of domestic investment without generating problems of external stability.

Krueger attributes high private savings partly to policies which keep after-tax returns to savings high in real terms. Bosworth is not so sure about the United States, where much private saving is undertaken by institutions, such as some superannuation funds, with 'target' rates of accumulation. When savers have absolute targets for balances at some future point in time, higher interest rates can cause reduction in current rates of savings. Bosworth also draws attention to the perverse response of American private savings to fiscal measures taken in the early 1980s to raise after-tax returns on savings. It is impossible to avoid the conclusion that the relationship between incentives and savings rates depends on the local institutional environment.

There is also considerable evidence of endogeneity of savings rates in relation to rates of growth (Park, Chapter 7). Rapidly growing incomes in East Asia have facilitated high savings rates. The converse relationship seems to have been important in a period of slow growth in incomes in the United States and Australia.

PUBLIC SAVINGS AND THE BALANCE OF PAYMENTS

Krause and Sundberg (Chapter 13), Bosworth (Chapter 4) and Montes (Chapter 10) all discussed the standard national accounting identity relating the various components of domestic revenue and expenditure, and the current account of the balance of payments.

Among the Pacific economies can be found all the possible combinations of budget and current account outcomes. There are budget deficits associated with current account deficits in the United States. On the other side of the coin are surpluses in budgets and current accounts in the late 1980s in Korea, Singapore and Taiwan. Japan has twin surpluses now, but earlier ran payments surpluses with budget deficits. There are examples of budget deficits being associated with current account surpluses (Malaysia), and combinations of budget surpluses and current account deficits (Australia).

In East Asia, savings rates have been so high in recent years that substantial public deficits have been consistent with surplus in external payments. This has been dramatically the case with Malaysia, where external accounts were in deficit when the budget deficit reached 19 per cent of GDP early in the decade, but have recently been in surplus with the budget deficit around 6 per cent of GDP. Japan, too, carried a budget deficit and external payments surplus for much of the past two decades. Now that the Japanese budget is in surplus, it has joined Taiwan and Korea with twin surpluses.

Japan's budget turnaround in recent years has run counter to the requirements of the widely accepted (if questionable) objective of reducing the current account surplus. It has been driven by attitudes to fiscal prudence that had their origin in times when Japanese private savings were smaller.

The New Zealand case, and that of the United States with increasing twin deficits through the fiscal expansion of the 1980s, fit neatly into the conventional view of the relationship between budget outcomes and the balance of payments.

Some doubts were expressed about whether declines in the United States budget deficit would exercise such powerful leverage over the current account. Krause and Sundberg, modelling historical experience, suggested that X reduction of the budget deficit would reduce the current account deficit by only 0.2X within three years, and 0.33X within five years. Others thought this outcome depended on what was assumed about changes in relative prices to maintain activity growth through the period of adjustment to a stronger fiscal outcome.

The Australian case provided the one conundrum. In Australia a few years ago, as in the United States, the budget was seen as the starting point for an attack on the two deficits. But as the budget moved strongly into surplus over recent years, the current account deficit increased.

Heinz Arndt suggested that higher real taxation levels might have reduced private savings. Gregory noted the contribution of declining savings (the extent of which was obscured by weaknesses in the national accounts), but emphasised high levels of private investment. It was noted in discussion that high current account deficits were less likely to generate large adjustment problems where they were associated with high levels of private investment, economic liberalisation and high rates of immigration.

UNITED STATES IMBALANCES WITH JAPAN AND THE NIES

There was much discussion at the Kuala Lumpur conference of the payments imbalances across the North Pacific. It has been conventional wisdom that the failure of coordination of Japanese and United States macroeconomic policies in the early 1980s led to serious problems. The discussion at the conference questioned that wisdom in a fundamental way.

The story of payments imbalances across the North Pacific in the early 1980s is well known: the co-incident loosening of fiscal policy and tightening of monetary policy in the United States, and inverse policies in Japan, led to a strong dollar and a weak yen, to larger current account surpluses in Japan and deficits in the United States, and to great tension in the bilateral trade relationship. Certainly, the trade tensions and the rise of protectionist sentiment in the United States are costly, and to be avoided in a perfect world.

But, looking at the whole experience, we may even have had a fortuitous coincidence of diverging policies. The international financial system would have experienced much greater strain if the Reagan experiment with deficit budgeting, tax cuts and military expenditure had occurred at a time when Japan was not making the opposite adjustment. Even with close international financial integration, if Japan had not embarked on fiscal contraction after the late 1970s oil crisis, and so increased its current account surplus, the financing of the United States deficits would have placed even greater pressure on international financial markets. There would have been a much larger increase in real interest rates around the world and a much larger problem for international development.

The divergence of policy was certainly not costless. In a perfect world, some form of joint financing of increased defence expenditure would have led to less tension over trade relations. Alternatively, if the United States had been able to do without the tax cuts, and Japan had not tightened fiscal policy so much, external payments imbalances would have been smaller. But, given that the United States was committed to implementation of the fiscal policies that were in fact followed in the 1980s, then there would have been greater international macroeconomic problems—a greater shortage of funds for investment and higher interest rates—if Japan had not tightened policy.

Krause and Sundberg, Bosworth and others saw the end of the Cold War as providing a favourable environment for reducing the budget deficit in the United States, and therefore for easing imbalances in external payments.

The Kuala Lumpur conference paid considerable attention to the relationship between reduction in the budget deficit and reduction in United States GDP, and the impact of reduced United States activity on East Asian growth.

Takenaka and Park went close to suggesting that lower United States budget deficits would mean lower United States output. Analytically, if policies to reduce demand were combined efficiently with policies to switch production towards, and demand away from, tradeable goods and services, there is no reason why a reduction in the budget deficit should be associated with a decline in total United States production. Parallel to that, on the other side of the Pacific, there is some combination of switching of production and demand, and reduction in total expenditure, that would allow the maintenance of the sustainable historical trend in economic growth.

It is a common but erroneous view that reduction of net imports into the United States must diminish opportunities for ASEAN, other East Asian and other economies seeking to grow through exports.

Any increase in net exports from the United States must be matched by declines in net exports from somewhere else. This is simply a matter of accounting identities. If that somewhere else is in the Western Pacific, say in Japan or Taiwan, with higher intensity of trade with ASEAN and Asian NIEs, then the overall adjustment process may even provide a net stimulus to exports from developing countries in the Western Pacific region.

The big question is whether the macroeconomic adjustments are made efficiently. Big mistakes can be made in the process of adjustment. There is no need for the United States to go into recession in the process of reducing its budget deficit, but if there is an important miscalculation, it may. If it does, then the terrible multipliers that are presented in both the Takenaka and Park chapters start to apply: United States output falls by 2 per cent, Japanese output falls another 1 per cent as a result, and then Korean and ASEAN output decline even more. All countries share a large interest in macro-adjustments being promoted smoothly and successfully in the United States and Japan.

This analytic perspective is confirmed by the experience of the ASEAN and other East Asian economies in the second half of the 1980s. These were years in which the United States and Japan began to make fiscal and external adjustments. The shifts in budget and payments outcomes from the mid-1980s were very substantial. In the United States, expenditure ceased expanding, there was substantial easing of total public expenditure growth, and there were no more unfunded tax cuts. The trend changed decisively in Japan as well in an expansionary direction. For a number of years now, American net imports have not contributed to expansion of demand for exports from developing countries in the Western Pacific.

These times of adjustment have seen the most buoyant expansion of ASEAN and Chinese manufactured exports. During these years, for the first time, manufactured exports became a majority of total exports in Malaysia, Thailand and China, and non-oil exports became the majority of exports in Indonesia. These good years for trade expansion have seen the early stages of the adjustment that needs to continue through the 1990s.

EXTERNAL STABILITY AND COMMODITY PRICE FLUCTUATIONS

Mohamed Ariff and other Malaysian hosts firmly directed the conference's attention to the links between primary commodity exports, fluctuations in the terms of trade and macroeconomic instability.

A decade before the Kuala Lumpur conference—or eight months after—a conference on macroeconomic instability in the Pacific would have focused strongly on the oil price, as a major factor affecting both natural resource exporting and importing economies. It was, after all, the payments deficits following the oil price increases of the later 1970s that precipitated the fiscal tightening, the lower real exchange rates, the slowing of domestic structural adjustment, and the tendency towards increasing payments surpluses in Japan, Korea and Taiwan in the early 1980s. The collapse of oil prices through the mid-1980s added powerfully to the tendency to surplus.

Duncan's chapter, and comments on it by Soesastro, are reminders that instability in the world oil price could return in future. Duncan gave us reasons to expect a return to high oil prices for a period in the 1990s. This would again place pressure on external payments throughout the region. This possibility provides one reason for caution in current adjustment policies in Japan and Taiwan, directed at reducing surpluses.

But memories are short, and the Kuala Lumpur conference focused on the price fluctuations of commodities other than oil which are important in the exports of the ASEAN and Oceanian economies.

Instability in the terms of trade has been a major source of macroeconomic management problems in Indonesia, Malaysia, Thailand, the Philippines and Australia through the 1980s.

It was noted that internationally-oriented general trade policies can diminish fluctuations in commodity prices and in individual countries' terms of trade.

More complete integration of international food markets would diminish the importance of fluctuations in export prices. Food markets in the European Community, the United States, Japan and many developing economies are constrained by interventions which insulate domestic producers and consumers from world price fluctuations. Thus adjustment to variations in market conditions is concentrated in a relatively small part of the world market.

Duncan thought that closer integration of international food markets would diminish the frequency and scale of major price movements, but that the primary commodity stock cycle would still generate periodic price 'spikes'.

This was noted with concern by Yamazawa, who said that the spectre of unstable prices was an important argument in Japanese domestic debate over agricultural protection. Others observed that world price fluctuations would be somewhat less severe if Japan entered world food markets in an open way, and that particular food commodities would represent such a small part of Japanese household income after liberalisation that concerns about price fluctuations affecting welfare were groundless.

The stabilising effect of more integrated world food markets would be of great value if in future the world economy had to adjust to large changes in climatic conditions over relatively short periods. Poor countries, in particular, would then find much greater food security in integration into international markets in advance of change than in policies of self-sufficiency.

The East Asian growth style, with strong growth in manufactured exports, is itself effective in reducing vulnerability to fluctuations in prices of primary commodities. All of the East Asian economies began their periods of rapid growth with strong export specialisation in primary commodities. High international orientation facilitated manufactured exports, now in all of the major ASEAN economies as well as in Northeast Asia. Malaysia had once been more vulnerable than most economies to fluctuations in the terms of trade, but by the late 1980s no commodity contributed more than 15 per cent to total exports.

Krause, with the Australian and Malaysian experience in mind, noted that fluctuations in the real exchange rate in a primary commodity exporting economy inhibited expansion of manufactured exports. For this and other reasons, efforts should be made to stabilise the real exchange rate through the commodity price cycle.

Australia's floating exchange rate in the 1980s had delivered unusually strong and stable growth in domestic employment and activity, at the expense of wide fluctuations in the real exchange rate.

The ASEAN economies provide rich experience with attempts to stabilise the real exchange rate. The Indonesian case cautions against use of nominal exchange rate depreciation to improve competitiveness. Each of the oil shocks led to a large appreciation of Indonesia's real exchange rate. Twice, some time after the shocks, in 1978 and 1983, large rupiah devaluation was meant to bring the real exchange rate back towards levels prevailing before the price increases. On each occasion, the exchange rate devaluation was overwhelmed by inflation, although less completely on the latter occasion.

The devaluation of the late 1980s appears to be generating a more sustained improvement in Indonesian competitiveness because real economic conditions, especially the lower terms of trade, but also more liberal trade policy, support the lower real exchange rate.

Any measure which delays expenditure of income from temporarily higher terms of trade supports stabilisation of the real exchange rate, whether the nominal rate is set by the authorities or in a market. Variations in the budget outcome are the most reliable means of effecting stabilisation, but there are institutional limits to the use of fiscal policy for short-term stabilisation.

Krueger commended the use of fiscal and export income stabilisation funds in Papua New Guinea, to effect counter-cyclical variation in the economy's savings.

Malaysia sought to combat the macroeconomic effects of low terms of trade in the early 1980s by holding up the exchange rate, expanding government expenditure, and increasing borrowing. In the end, the attempt failed, because the authorities were too ambitious in their approach to stabilisation, leading to a rate of increase in indebtedness that was judged to be unsustainable.

Duncan focused attention on a range of new stabilisation instruments that are available to the authorities or private exporters, to hedge against price fluctuations. These involve the sale of risk to outside parties that are in a better position to bear it. The outside parties may wish to accept the risk speculatively, or to balance opposite risks (as users of commodity imports may wish to do). These instruments are effective only in an economy that is closely integrated into international markets.

Thailand through the 1980s provided an intriguing case of attempted stabilisation of the real exchange rate through controls on capital flows. Krause endorsed this approach in principle, although the experience of the early 1970s made Australians skeptical. Thailand's limited success through the 1980s seems to have depended, at least to some extent, on the government's influence over the borrowing of state enterprises, and in any case could be expected to become less successful over time. Among other costs, controls on capital and other foreign exchange flows would make Duncan's hedging instruments less effective.

My own reading of the Pacific primary exporting economies' experience in the 1980s is that the first line of defence against instability in the real exchange rate should be through internationalisation and export diversification. The second line of defence should be countercyclical fiscal policy, at least to the extent of holding expenditure growth on a steady course as revenue fluctuates cyclically with the terms of trade. This is properly supported by extensive private and public use of international hedging mechanisms. These actions reduce vulnerability to instability without causing distortions in resource allocation. They can be similarly effective under fixed and floating exchange rate regimes. But attempts at stabilisation should not be too ambitious: some instability is inevitable in the face of uncertainty about future terms of trade, if the Malaysian error of unsustainable rates of increase in indebtedness is to be avoided.

MACROECONOMIC STABILITY AND STRUCTURAL REFORM

Macroeconomic problems have undoubtedly been a source of pressure for microeconomic distortion in the United States. However, in the Western

Pacific, especially in the late 1980s, perceptions of macroeconomic crisis have been used to promote structural reforms that are favourable to growth. This is true whether the 'crisis' has been associated with adjustment to payments surpluses (Taiwan, Japan and Korea) or to deficits (Australia, New Zealand, Indonesia, Malaysia and Thailand).

The recent use of macroeconomic crisis to promote liberalisation contrasts with earlier experience of many of these same economies, when payments deficits provided occasions for raising protection and tightening exchange controls.

Is there any natural or logical association between macroeconomic adjustment and either increased distortion or efficiency-increasing microeconomic reform? Adjustments to a payment surplus are generally favourable to liberalisation, although in Australia in the early 1970s and Thailand recently they have been associated with controls on capital movements.

Adjustments to payments deficits often encourage popular support for trade and payments controls, although the controls are always less effective than other instruments. The contrasting reality is that microeconomic liberalisation and reform, including reduction in protection, can be expected to contribute to increased productivity and living standards, offsetting the fall in living standards associated with reduction in real absorption. Microeconomic reform is desirable at any time, but arguably more compelling when the alternative is even larger reductions in living standards at a time of adjustment to a payments deficit.

The recent experience of the Pacific tells us that whether economic crisis helps or hinders efficiency-raising reform depends on relevant elite or community opinion on the desirability of liberalisation. Western Pacific governments, leaning towards liberalisation at this time in history, have been able to turn macroeconomic problems to their cause.

EXTERNAL ADJUSTMENT AND INCOME DISTRIBUTION

Introductory remarks by Dato Raja Ariffin brought the conference's attention to one complex set of connections between macroeconomic management and sustainability of East Asian style growth: the links between macroeconomic adjustment, income distribution and political stability.

Narongchai noted that strong internationally-oriented growth in Thailand in recent years has generated tension associated with changes in the distribution of income and wealth. The rapid growth in the import-oriented manufacturing sector has increased inequality, as measured by the Gini coefficient.

The Park and Takenaka chapters emphasise that one important constraint on domestic demand expansion and adjustment in Japan, Korea and Taiwan, particularly Japan and Taiwan at present, was its effect on income distribution, asset inflation and therefore political stability.

This linkage needs to be addressed systematically, together with the question of what types of policies are helpful in reducing the distributional strains of adjustment.

For countries having to make the opposite adjustment, involving falling real expenditure and real wages, there are pressures of another kind. Distributional issues seem to have been important to the United States and Australian experiences (see the Bosworth and Gregory chapters) with budget adjustment. American Congressional disputes over budget deficit reduction have centred on the varying distributional effects of competing packages. Australia's more successful efforts to reduce a large budget deficit were facilitated by emphasis on distributional equity in taxation and expenditure reforms.

Adjustment to both surpluses and deficits generates large changes in the distribution of income and wealth. Adjustment in both directions is eased by fiscal policies that are associated with an equitable distribution of the burden of change.

EXTERNAL STABILITY AND THE INTERNATIONAL TRADING SYSTEM

The failures of macroeconomic adjustment in the United States in the 1980s have been associated with an historic change of political attitudes to the international trading system. United States leadership has sustained the liberal system in the postwar period, but the domestic political basis of that leadership has now been lost. The United States is no longer willing to lead alone.

This dangerous development has been accompanied by another threat to the postwar system: a Western Europe concerned with its own internal integration has been diverted further from concern with the international system by the need to accommodate the dramatic recent developments in Eastern Europe. No contribution to filling the vacuum left by the United States withdrawal from leadership can be expected from Europe. And the United States cannot be expected to take the lead in combatting breaches of the international rules in the European Communities' dealings with Eastern Europe.

The assessments, asserted strongly by Americans at the conference, led to sober judgements about the future of the trading system. Krause and Sundberg thought it likely that the global system would deteriorate, and that the best prospects for the international system lay in a dual system that left Germany to exercise leadership in Europe while the Asia-Pacific economies together sought to maintain an open system for the rest of the world. Krueger thought that there was a possibility of a major breakdown of the system through the introduction of trading blocs, but not a high probability. More hopeful assessments by English and Smith (Chapter 14) and Holmes depended on the willingness and capacity of Western Pacific economies to play a major role, through their own leadership in trade liberalisation, in maintaining the open international system.

The prospects of favourable outcomes for the international trading system would be better if the United States made faster progress on its macroeconomic problems, particularly in reducing the budget deficit. The 'peace dividend' from the end of the Cold War would help.

The interest of large debtor and deficit economies, such as Australia and the United States, would be served best by Northeast Asian surplus. While trade liberalisation would do most for Northeast Asian, North American and world welfare, it would exert less leverage on payments surpluses than measures to expand domestic expenditure. In its current mood on trade policy, the American polity would require action on liberalisation as well as expenditure, whatever the contributions of each to external payments adjustment. Northeast Asian stalling on liberalisation would lead the region into the worst possible outcome: increased American protection, and stronger pressure for increased expenditure in surplus economies.

Thus much hangs on the capacity of Japan and Taiwan (and Korea, although—probably temporarily—not now a surplus economy) to maintain momentum in trade liberalisation. Interestingly, Japanese and especially Korean economists were skeptical about the likely future pace of liberalisation in Northeast Asia. The skepticism was strongest in relation to farm products, which become the main political test of progress in the eyes of the United States Congress. Park and Hong were deeply skeptical about the likelihood of momentum being maintained in Japan, seeing the 1989 voluntary export restraints on Korean knitwear as the beginnings of corrosion of liberal Japanese approaches to manufactures trade.

The data before the Kuala Lumpur conference nevertheless provided evidence of huge recent progress in Japanese, Korean and Taiwanese import expansion and liberalisation. Japan had quickly emerged in the late 1980s as an importer of processed foodstuffs of comparable absolute size to Europe and the United States. Imports of manufactured goods had increased rapidly, especially from East Asia. Momentum would be sustained by imports from Japanese subsidiaries abroad, and by the lagged impact of earlier changes in relative prices on institutions involved in import and distribution. The new pattern of import trade would change the balance of political forces operating on trade policy, in directions favourable to further liberalisation.

There was no doubt about the liberal directions of trade policy in ASEAN (Indonesia, and to some extent in Thailand and Malaysia), Australia and New Zealand. Progress in these countries would be helpful to American perceptions of fairness in the international system, but only marginally so in the absence of strong progress in Northeast Asia.

Thus, at this dangerous time, the maintenance of the liberal international trade system which has sustained unprecedented growth in the Pacific region depends on American progress in overcoming macroeconomic imbalances. Even in the best of circumstances, the transition will take a number of years. The dangers of rupture of the international system during this period of transition are substantial.

The best chance of preserving the liberal system lies in Western Pacific governments committing themselves now to further large steps in trade liberalisation by recognising the critical weakness of the system at this time and reinforcing each other's resolve, including through the scheduled meetings of APEC on trade policy. This is necessary for a successful conclusion to the

Uruguay Round. Nothing else is likely to shore up leadership of the international system at a time of United States disillusionment and European distraction.

3 Pacific growth and macroeconomic performance: models and issues

ANNE O. KRUEGER

This chapter aims to assess the development of the Pacific region in light of models of growth and development, and to analyse the adequacy of those models for evaluating the challenges of growth in the coming decade. To accomplish such a task within the confines of a single chapter, however, requires that details and also many important issues be ignored in order to focus on key parameters.

To achieve this task, the first section starts with a consideration of the domain of macroeconomic policy, focusing on those elements that appear to have most relevance for Pacific growth, and provides a short overview of the entire Pacific region in the context of that framework. The overview in turn provides a context for focusing on the models, lessons and issues that emerge from consideration of the 'high flyers' of the Pacific region: Hong Kong, Korea, Singapore and Taiwan. In the second section of the chapter, some key aspects of their astonishing growth experience and the lessons they hold for the rest of the Pacific region are examined. Section three then relates that experience to development models that have been prevalent over the past several decades, while the fourth section assesses the two key issues—the role of the trade regime and the role of government—on which the experience of the four high flyers (and other countries around the world) sheds light relevant to the course of the 1990s. A fifth section then considers the lessons that appear to be relevant in assessing the outlook for the 1990s, while a final section places these prospects in international context.

GROWTH IN THE PACIFIC REGION

Until the 1980s it was conventional to regard macroeconomic policy in developed and developing countries as covering almost exclusively monetary and fiscal policy. The experience of the 1980s, however, has taught an important lesson: macroeconomic policy covers not only monetary and fiscal policy, narrowly defined, but also exchange rate policy, trade policy, financial policy and wages policy. In part, this broadened definition of macroeconomic policy arises from the recognition that controls and economic inefficiencies in the major goods and factor markets inevitably spill over, and affect, macroeconomic policy. In part, it stems from the fact that the focus of concern for macroeconomic policy is the economic environment within which private decisions are made. While large fiscal imbalances can result in inflation with consequent high levels of distortion, so too can credit rationing, distortions in agricultural pricing policies, overvalued exchange rates propped up by import licensing, and interventions in the labour market that drive up the cost of hiring labour.

Appropriately understood, therefore, macroeconomic policy is really concerned with the entire set of governmental decisions that affect the incentives confronting private decisionmakers within the economy.[1]

When asked to consider macroeconomic policy in the Pacific region, therefore, in principle, the entire thrust of governmental policies significantly impacting on decisions governing resource allocation should be reviewed. Fortunately, despite huge diversities among the Pacific countries—to which attention turns shortly—there appears to be a reasonably common range of issues which will be crucial to growth prospects for the 1990s. Despite the differences among countries, the Pacific region does have some similarities vis-à-vis other parts of the world: some countries are indebted, but only one or two (the Philippines being perhaps the most notable) have levels of debt so high that it is a major macroeconomic problem; the problem of inflation, which dominates economic policy formulation in some parts of the world, does not appear presently or prospectively to be a serious issue affecting growth prospects; agriculture is little discriminated against in most of the countries of the region; and labour markets do not in general appear to be so highly distorted as to affect growth prospects.

There are, therefore, several key areas of policy that are crucial to growth of the Pacific region. Broadly, they all fall under the heading of liberalising markets and streamlining incentives, and are the issues covered in this chapter. Before turning attention to them, however, it is worthwhile to note the similarities among countries of Asia and the Pacific, as well as differences.

There are three broad bases on which it is useful to categorise the countries of the Pacific. One is the level of development, which is roughly reflected by estimates of per capita income. The second is the rate of economic growth. The third is the trade and payments orientation of the country. Using these criteria, five groups of countries may be distinguished: the industrial giants (the United States and Japan), whose economic growth is moderate and whose large economic base results in a very diversified structure of trade with considerable emphasis on manufactures; the land-rich developed countries of the region (Australia, New Zealand and Canada), which also have high per capita incomes and moderate growth but whose pattern of trade conforms more to their highly favourable endowment of land; the four rapidly growing NIEs (Hong Kong, Korea, Singapore and Taiwan), whose per capita incomes and level of development are well above those of the fourth and fifth groups but well below those of the first two and whose exports are heavily concentrated in manufactures because of their relatively poor endowment of natural resources; the near-NIEs (Thailand, Malaysia, the Philippines and Indonesia), who are far better endowed with raw materials than the rapidly-growing NIEs, whose rates of growth have generally been moderately high (except for the Philippines) and other developing countries (China, Burma, Vietnam, Kampuchea, Papua New Guinea and the small Pacific islands), whose per capita incomes are significantly lower than the fourth group, whose growth rate has been much slower, and for whom trade is of lesser importance. Of course, there are large differences among countries within each group, but they are not as large as the differences between groups, and, in any event, if focus is to be on prospects for the region, some generalisations are inevitable.

Although the growth prospects of all of these countries are inter-related, the relative importance of various macroeconomic factors differs considerably, depending on their present stage of development and current economic policies. Here, we review the broad characteristics of each group, focusing to some degree on the NIEs. In the final section of this chapter, the factors most crucial to each group's growth are reviewed in light of the analysis in the section preceding it.

The stylised facts about these countries and country groups are well known. Japan and the United States are clearly the dominant economies in the region. Of course, their economies and their growth are important determinants of the prosperity of the entire world economy, and key factors influencing their performance will be crucial to the region in the 1990s. Those factors are therefore considered in a later section. Both have high levels of per capita income, and both appear to have exhausted most of the potential for growth through shifting resources from agriculture to industry and from increasing labour force participation: future growth will hinge largely on macroeconomic management and the ability of each to find policies that reduce structural rigidities and enhance factor productivity. For the United States, key macroeconomic issues focus on: one, changing the domestic saving–investment balance and, in that context; two, resolving the problem of the American fiscal deficit; and three, increasing the openness of the American economy, or, at the least, resisting protectionist pressures. For Japan, key issues probably centre more around resolving structural rigidities, especially in home goods industries. These issues are dealt with at considerable length in other chapters in this volume and are not addressed in depth here.

Australia, Canada and New Zealand are smaller industrialised countries and differ from the United States and Japan not only in size but in the extent to which their relatively abundant land resources affect their economic structure. Their growth prospects depend primarily on their success in increasing efficiency within their economies and they will be strongly affected by the growth of the international economy and the openness of markets. In the Canadian case, the Canada–United States Free Trade Agreement may also affect future growth.

All of the countries in the first two groups had experienced a long period of development prior to the Second World War. Japan, of course, grew exceptionally rapidly in the first several decades after 1945, partly because there was still scope for productivity gains through shifts of resources from agriculture to industry. By the 1980s, however, that opportunity had been largely exploited, although there appear significant opportunities for further productivity gains in agriculture and some services.

The third group of countries has provided the world with an astonishing growth performance over the past three decades. It is this group which has provided the world with new models of development, to which attention turns in a later section. As late as 1960, all of them had very low per capita incomes, and none was regarded as having outstanding prospects for development. All have experienced growth at rates well in excess of any other developing (or developed) countries. It is this group of countries, whose experience is unique in the entire world, that has challenged traditional growth models and provided important lessons for other developing countries. In the following section, therefore, some stylised facts regarding their growth performance are quickly reviewed.

The fourth group of countries sustained above-average rates of growth in the first three decades of development effort, but their performance did not reach the levels of achievement that the third group attained. There is considerable evidence that the lessons of the East Asian NIEs have been well learned by the fourth group of countries and that growth rates in some of this group are currently accelerating. For present purposes, however, this group of successful developing countries can be regarded as something of a 'follower' group. They have benefitted from the experiences of the East Asian NIEs and Japan, both in being able to observe and learn from them, but also in having a rapidly expanding regional market.[2]

The final group of countries is not yet in the 'newly industrialising' category. While growth rates have differed significantly among them, all have yet to find ways of achieving rates of growth of per capita income significantly above that of other developing countries. In a sense, they are potential beneficiaries of the rapid growth of the others, but they have not as yet attained the proper mix of ingredients to reach above-average growth. For them, the lessons from the East Asian NIEs have not yet been translated into domestic economic policy, but they are crucially relevant for their future prospects.

THE COMPARATIVE GROWTH OF THE FOUR 'HIGH FLYERS'

The data in Table 3.1 vividly illustrate the success of the four high flyers. The first four columns give individual data for Hong Kong, Korea, Singapore and Taiwan. For purposes of comparison, the last column gives the average for all middle-income countries.[3] By 1987 each of the four had per capita incomes well above the average of middle-income countries. Indeed, Singapore and Hong Kong's per capita incomes are high enough so that one could arguably justify regarding them as newly developed countries! In each case, except Singapore, export growth dramatically exceeded the growth of real GNP by a

Table 3.1 Per capita incomes and growth performances of the Asian high flyers, 1965–87

	Hong Kong	Korea	Singapore	Taiwan	All middle-income LDCs
Population (millions) 1987	5.6	42.1	2.6	19.7	1 038
Per capita income 1987 (US dollars)	8 070	2 690	7 940	4 989	1 810
Average annual growth rates:					
Real GDP:					
1965–80	8.6	9.5	10.1	na	5.7
1980–87	5.8	8.6	5.4	na	2.1
Real per capita GNP,					
1965–87	6.2	6.4	7.2	7.2	2.5
Exports:					
1965–80	9.5	27.2	4.7	19.1	2.4
1980–87	11.4	14.3	6.1	13.5	5.5
Investment:					
1965–80	8.6	15.9	13.3	15.8	8.6
1980–87	1.3	10.0	3.2	3.4	-1.6
Private consumption:					
1965–80	9.0	7.8	8.0	8.4	6.7
1980–87	6.9	5.5	3.9	6.1	2.4

Notes: na—not available.
US Department of Commerce data were used for Taiwan's per capita income. If, instead, Taiwanese domestic data are used at the official exchange rate prevailing at the end of 1987, the estimate would be a per capita income of US$5,537, contrasted with US$4,989 as estimated by the US Department of Commerce.

Sources: All data except for Taiwan: World Bank, *World Development Report*, 1989; for Taiwan: *Taiwan Statistical Databook*, 1988; US Department of Commerce, *Foreign Economic Trends and Their Implications for the U.S.*, March 1989; and World Bank, *World Development Report*, 1989, for exports.

factor of more than 2:1, and even exceeded the rate of growth of investment. By contrast, the average for all middle-income countries was for export growth to lag the growth of real GNP prior to 1980. The higher growth rate for exports from all middle-income countries after 1980 reflects in part the payoff from policy reforms, as policymakers have increasingly recognised the lessons emanating from the high flyers: an import-substitution strategy severely penalised exports and resulted in slow growth of the entire domestic economy.

As the data further demonstrate, the four high flyers were affected by the worldwide recession, as were all middle-income countries. However, their ability to withstand the downturn in the international economy (and, in the case of Korea, the heavy debt-servicing burdens of the early 1980s) was considerably greater than that of other, more inner-oriented countries. Consequently, the real rates of growth of the high flyers, while lower than in the 1965–80 period, nonetheless remained impressive.

Although the growth of exports outpaced even that of investment in the high flyers, the growth rates of investment and of savings were also impressive. In part, these high rates of growth reflect the profitable opportunities that accompanied the outer-oriented development strategies. In part, also, they resulted from high growth rates themselves and the realignments of savings incentives. Shifting to positive real interest rates for domestic savers was among the policy reforms instituted in each during the course of their growth. As with all middle-income countries, the rate of growth of investment fell in the early 1980s. However, the high flyers experienced growth in real investment, albeit at slower rates than had earlier occurred, while the average for all middle-income developing countries was for real investment to decline over the first seven years of the decade.

Although until 1980 investment grew more rapidly than private consumption for the high flyers, their overall growth was so rapid that they could also experience growth of consumption well above the average for all middle-income countries. Moreover, all were able to sustain to some degree the growth of consumption above that of real income throughout the 1980s. Citizens were thus to some extent buffered from the full impact of the worldwide recession.

Space limitations preclude even superficial consideration of many other major aspects of the successful performance of the four East Asian economies. A few, however, deserve brief mention. First, the natural rate of population growth fell off sharply in all four countries, thus enhancing the rate of growth of per capita income resulting from rapid overall growth. Second, non-agricultural employment and real wages grew rapidly in all four economies, and declining levels of unemployment generally accompanied their rapid growth. Third, as is well known, estimates of the income distribution of Korea and Taiwan for the early 1960s and the late 1970s all suggest that income distribution was, and has remained, considerably more equal than that of most other developing countries (see Kuznets, 1988: 515).[4] Fourth, import growth was virtually as rapid as export growth in all cases: what was happening was a structural shift in the economy as the shares of both imports and exports in GNP rose. In Korea, for example, the trade ratio (defined as the ratio of exports plus imports to GNP) rose from 12 in 1953 to 20 in 1963, to 62 in 1973 and to 85 in 1983. Taiwanese performance was similar: starting from a trade ratio of 22 in 1953, the number rose to 101 by 1983 (Kuznets, 1988: 513).

The reasons that an outer-orientation contributed to rapid growth, and the role of government and government policy in affecting economic performance, are considered in the next section. Here, it suffices to note a few of the differences among the four. First and most obvious, Singapore and Hong Kong have virtually no agricultural sector, which is regarded by some as a drag on development.[5] Second, the industrial organisation of the four has differed in a variety of ways. On the one hand, Singapore and Taiwan actively encouraged private foreign investment throughout their period of rapid growth. By contrast, Hong Kong's policy was one of strict neutrality, while Korean policy was fairly restrictive with respect to foreign direct investment until 1980.[6] On the other hand, most enterprises in Hong Kong and Taiwan were small-scale, while Korean *chaebol* were very sizeable. Singapore's industrial structure appears to have been somewhere in between.

Third, Hong Kong experienced considerable continuing immigration, as did

Singapore and Taiwan to a lesser extent. By contrast, migration was an insignificant factor in Korea. None of these similarities or differences, however, are crucial to assessing the two key issues arising out of the experience of the four for development models, or for assessment of prospects for the 1990s. Consideration, therefore, turns to an analysis of the inter-relationships between an outer-oriented trade strategy and overall development, on the one hand, and of the role of government in development, on the other. Table 3.1 provides some indicators of the spectacular growth performance of the four 'supergrowth' economies.

THE CHALLENGE OF THE HIGH FLYERS TO EARLIER DEVELOPMENTAL THOUGHT

In the early years of developmental efforts, it was thought that developing countries were poor because they had very little capital stock per person; they had very little capital stock per person, in turn, because savings rates were low due to poverty. Further, because of 'underdevelopment', as it was then called, it was believed that markets failed to function and that governments would therefore have to accept a leading role in developmental efforts.

The prescription for development, therefore, was twofold: additional capital would have to be accumulated, and governments would have to take a major role in assuring the appropriate allocation of that capital (and other resources).

It was further thought that, although other aspects of the development process would be challenging, finding ways to increase capital accumulation would be the key issue. It was assumed that if additional resources could be obtained for capital accumulation (through increasing the domestic public or private savings rate or through foreign aid), other problems would be secondary. For purposes of analysing the lessons that have been learned, only one aspect of this assumption needs noting now: little or no attention was given to the determinants of the efficiency with which capital, once resources were available, would be used. It was implicitly assumed that government controls could readily assure the efficiency of resource use.

As a corollary to the conclusion that a shortage of capital was the key bottleneck to development, most analysts of development concluded or assumed that the heavily agricultural structure of developing countries was a consequence of capital shortage, and that additional savings (or foreign resources) would be allocated largely towards 'industrialisation'. Since most developing countries were predominantly agricultural, while developed countries appeared to be predominantly industrial, it was natural to believe that 'development' would be accompanied by an increasing share of output and employment in non-agricultural, and especially in industrial, activities. What was not so natural, and turned out to be mistaken, was the additional assumption that industrial development could precede, or at least take place, independently of agricultural development. Most developing countries learned that

that was a mistake in the course of the subsequent two decades. However, for present purposes, that lesson is not central to models of East Asian growth and development, because almost all Asian economies have long since learned the crucial role that agriculture plays.[7]

What is central is that policymakers and development economists concluded that, given underdevelopment, the growth of domestic industry would have to take place in a hothouse, or protected, environment. There were several intellectual underpinnings for this view. First, the infant-industry argument had long since been recognised as a legitimate basis for encouraging domestic industry. To be sure, it was recognised that there would be short-term costs, and that the infant would eventually have to lower costs significantly. Costs would have to fall enough so that long-term societal profitability of the infant in the absence of protection would later earn a rate of return adequate both to compensate for past losses and to provide a return on capital equal to that available in other investments. Second, many analysts believed that imports of capital equipment would be needed in fixed proportions to investment in industry, given that there was little industrial equipment produced in developing countries. They further believed that the market for developing countries' exports of primary commodities was unlikely to exhibit rapid growth, and that therefore protection should be put in place in order to 'save scarce foreign exchange' for investment purposes. The view held by Nurkse (1958), that 'balanced growth' would be essential, was an outcome of that 'elasticity pessimism'.

In the event, almost all developing countries experienced balance of payments difficulties during the 1950s, and then imposed foreign exchange controls and import limitations more restrictive than anything contemplated by Nurkse or other balanced growth advocates. In most developing countries, when this happened, protection of new industries was extended indiscriminately to virtually any 'foreign-exchange saving' activity, often at exceedingly high costs.

By the late 1950s most developing countries had highly restrictionist trade regimes and were encouraging industrial growth through 'import substitution'. Indeed, the situation was serious enough so that Chenery and Strout (1966) developed their famous 'two-gap' model, in which either a foreign exchange bottleneck or inadequate savings might prove the critical limitation on growth.

A first, and important, lesson emerging from East Asia, and one which will be discussed below, was that there were alternatives to the import-substitution model. In many regards, this is the foremost contribution of the East Asian economies to the world's understanding of the development process. Certainly, an understanding of how and why outer-oriented growth out-performs an import-substitution based strategy is a key to analysing the prospects for growth and development in the 1990s.

However, the second leg of the presumptions of the 1950s also requires discussion, especially if one is looking forward to the 1990s; that is, the appropriate role of government in development. As already mentioned, early development thought *assumed* that markets were functioning highly imperfectly in developing countries and that, therefore, governments had to undertake many of the roles filled by markets in developed countries. Although it was recognised that governments would play a key role in providing essential infrastructure, without which there would be severe constraints on growth of any type of economic activity, focus was, by and large, much more on non-traditional governmental roles.[8]

Although the precise combination of governmental interventions varied from country to country, a usual set of controls and regulations resulted in the establishment of governmentally-owned manufacturing and distribution activities (parastatal enterprises), often with prohibitions upon private sector activities in competition with parastatals. In addition, controls over private economic activity were pervasive: in most countries, a new investment could not be undertaken without some imports, and an import licence was required. Often that licence, in turn, could not be obtained without a prior investment licence, granted by another governing body. Then, too, there were price controls, regulations governing the conditions of work for employees which went far beyond the avoidance of employer monopsony power, and credit rationing administered by banks but regulated by governments, to name the most frequently encountered interventions.

In almost all countries in which there was an import-substitution strategy, government controls of the type mentioned above were pervasive. In most of them, analysts sooner or later demonstrated the inefficacy of these controls.[9] However, because these controls were imposed in the context of import-substitution regimes, the issues arising as to the role of government could not be resolved independently of the experience of countries adopting other trade strategies. Thus, if one is to consider the experience of East Asia and the models of development that emanate from it, two issues are paramount: that of the appropriate trade regime and that of the role of government. These issues are addressed in the next section.

OUTER-ORIENTED DEVELOPMENT AND THE ROLE OF GOVERNMENT

Outer-oriented trade strategies and development

When Chenery and Strout (1966) formulated their two-gap model of economic growth, they actually had a now almost-forgotten 'third' gap—absorptive capacity. They assumed that, in addition to any constraint imposed on the rate of growth by savings and by foreign exchange availability, there was simply an upper limit as to the rate at which an economy could grow for any significant period of time. In their numerical work, they put this limit at around 8–10 per cent annually, and dropped it from further consideration, asserting that such a rate was not in any event witnessed for any period of time. The success of the outer-oriented East Asian countries demonstrated that faster growth was certainly possible, and further, that contrary to what had earlier been thought, it was possible through an outer-oriented trade strategy.

There is little need to demonstrate that an export-oriented trade strategy was an important contributing factor to rapid growth. As Table 3.1 demonstrates, export growth exceeded the growth of real GNP in all the high flyers but Singapore. Korea sustained an average annual growth rate of exports of 27 per cent over a two-decade period. Perhaps even more remarkable, three of the four achieved double-digit export growth during the 1980–87 period. In addition to the direct evidence, a number of authors, including Balassa (1978), Bhagwati (1988), Krueger (1978) and Michaely (1977), have elsewhere analysed the subject extensively (see also World Bank, 1987) and demonstrated the importance of export growth. There is thus no question as to its prominence.

The important question is *why* an outer-oriented trade strategy has contributed so much to growth. For purposes of analysing lessons and prospects for the 1990s, a number of paths of influence of the trade strategy on growth rates can be identified. First, an outer-oriented trade strategy provides a setting for economic activity in which there is a competitive environment, with adequate incentives for economic performance at appropriate scales of economic activity that approximately reflect the social returns to these activities. The competitive environment is the world economy, and its role as an impartial arbiter of performance cannot be overestimated. Simultaneously, the world economy is a very large market, and economic activities can be undertaken at an appropriate scale of economic activity. Moreover, since export incentives tend to be fairly uniform across potential exporting activities, there is considerably less divergence between private and social profitability under an outer-oriented trade strategy than can occur in highly protected markets when effective rates of protection can range from negative numbers to hundreds, and occasionally even thousands, of per cent.

As contrasted with import substitution, an outer-oriented trade strategy provides advantages considerably greater than earlier recognised: competition appears to induce much greater attention to costs, and considerably greater efforts towards reducing them, than does a sheltered domestic environment.[10] In most developing countries, the size of the domestic market is far too small for effective competition among producers of similar products, even when import licensing practices do not virtually automatically allocate market shares among domestic firms. If investment licences are issued to a sufficiently large number of firms to permit domestic competition, individual production runs are too small to overcome the high costs of machinery and equipment. Even with only one firm, the size of production runs can be too small to realise economic production, and simultaneously, monopoly power is conveyed to the single producer.[11]

In addition to the role of competition, the ability to obtain needed inputs from low-cost sources and to operate production runs and plants at efficient scale, and to concentrate production in lines for which domestic factor prices are reasonably advantageous, there are a number of political and economic reasons why an outer orientation may permit better overall economic performance.

Clearly, governments that encourage export-led growth usually do so with reasonably uniform across-the-board incentives, thus giving rise to less variation in effective protection rates across activities than occurs in most import-substitution regimes.[12] Even when governments do intervene, there are more obvious and visible limits to the extent of intervention, and relatively quicker feedback as to policy mistakes. This was certainly true in the Korean case, as discussed below.

The role of government

Whereas it is almost universally agreed that exports played an important, if not a crucial, role in the rapid growth of the high flyers, there is somewhat less agreement as to the role of government in the development process. Since crucial questions about the role of government in the economy generally, and in developing countries' economies in particular, will probably be a central issue for the 1990s, it is well to review what evidence there is with regard to this issue.

The interpretations of the governmental role in Korea and Japan have been numerous, with different analysts focusing on the extent to which 'governmental guidance' of one sort or another affected resource allocation and managerial decisions.[13]

The empirical evidence seems to support the view that the government played a smaller role in the economies of the high flyers than it did in that of other developing countries. While the government was certainly active in monitoring economic activity, there was less direct parastatal production and less overall size of government than was the case in most developing countries.[14]

Almost all analysts would agree that Hong Kong was or is an instance of virtual laissez-faire, that Singapore intervened primarily in the market for factors of production (land, credit and labour), and that Taiwan was less interventionist than Korea, which is regarded as the most interventionist country of the group.

For concreteness, therefore, I shall focus on the Korean case. Whatever government intervention there may have been, it seems clear that incentives for exporting were fairly uniform, at least in contrast with incentives for import-substitution in most developing countries. Likewise, it seems evident that Korean officials regarded their function as expediting the flow of goods and services to port, and that procedures regarding the compensation of exporters were fairly well administered and did not involve long bureaucratic delays.

By the 1980s, at least, the role of the public sector in investment was limited by any standard. Table 3.2 presents data for Korea on the breakdown of investment for the 1980s (see Tanzi, 1987: 39).

Public expenditure, as a percentage of GNP, fluctuated just above 20 per cent over the same time period. This contrasts with 33 per cent for India, 35 per cent and over for Malaysia, 25 per cent for Pakistan, 24 per cent for Thailand and 30–33 per cent for Sri Lanka (Tanzi, 1987, Table 1).

Table 3.2 Investment breakdown for Korea in the 1980s (percentage of GNP)

	1981	1982	1983	1984	1985
Public	4.3	4.6	4.7	4.8	4.7
Private	26.0	24.0	25.2	27.1	26.4

Source: Tanzi (1987).

However, data on public expenditures do not provide an indication of the total impact of the government on economic activity and resource allocation. Controls over private sector activities, and sector or even firm-specific controls, can also have a significant effect on resource allocation.

In the Korean case, these direct interventions were, as already mentioned, gradually replaced by more uniform across-the-board incentives, for exports in the 1960s and for credit in the 1980s. Even so, there seems little doubt that the government made several efforts to determine which industries should be promoted. In so doing, it made, and recognised, major mistakes in attempting to direct the flow of resources into particular lines of activity. In contrast to other countries, where high-cost industries once established are protected indefinitely, there was a fairly rapid shift in policies in Korea when this occurred. Certainly, this was true of the decision to move towards heavy industry in the late 1970s. Within Korea, there seems to be widespread agreement that the policies of the late 1970s were economically disastrous; this was the time when the government was consciously attempting to guide resources into the industries it had targeted. Some observers of the Korean scene use this episode as evidence of the interventionist stance of the government.[15] In fact, it was probably this episode that convinced most policymakers in Korea that their more advanced economy required further liberalisation, more reliance upon indirect controls and less on direct controls, if development was to continue.

Further still, it can be argued that the very fact of an outer-oriented strategy limits considerably the extent to which governments can employ direct controls over private sector activity, both formally and effectively. At a formal level, the ability of a firm to export is already proof of a sort of performance: as such other bureaucratic controls and inspections seem somewhat less necessary to policymakers. Moreover, no genuinely outer-oriented strategy has succeeded in the context of highly restrictive import controls.[16]

However, for present purposes, what may be most important is that Korean growth, like that of Taiwan and Singapore, was accompanied by continuing liberalisation. For example, the authorities initially encouraged exports by a combination of export subsidies, tax rebates, 'wastage allowances' which facilitated imports of intermediate goods and raw materials to be re-exported, and credit rationing. Over time, increasing reliance was placed upon the exchange rate, and the relative and absolute importance of export subsidies and tax remissions diminished. Likewise, the nominal interest rate, which had been well below the rate of inflation in the late 1950s and early 1960s, was above the rate of inflation by the 1980s: to the extent that credit rationing still existed at all, it nonetheless was a much less potent allocator of resources than it was when the real rate of interest was significantly negative.

Import liberalisation started in the early 1960s, as the import regime was liberalised greatly, simply because of the greater availability of foreign exchange. By the mid-1960s the positive list (of permitted imports) was switched to a negative list (of prohibited imports), itself a significantly liberalising move (see Frank, Kim and Westphal, 1985). Later on, tariff rates were lowered and quantitative restrictions have continued to be removed; they now apply only to a few commodities.

Moreover, policy reforms also liberalised other markets. In particular, there were major budgetary reforms in the early 1960s, and financial liberalisation has been occurring at various intervals. Indeed, financial reform was the focus of the Structural Adjustment Loans extended by the World Bank in the early 1980s. By the 1980s, real returns to savers were highly positive, and Korea's savings rate reached 38 per cent of GNP in 1988.

Thus, even if the Korean economy has not been laissez-faire, there has been a continuous trend towards increasing liberalisation of the economy, and removal of controls over private sector activity as uniform incentives increasingly replaced quantitative, sector-specific, regulations. In the next section, it will be suggested that continuing liberalisation of markets and provision of increasingly uniform incentives is a necessary condition for sustaining rapid growth, and that the ability of the governments of Asia to pursue this objective will be an important determinant of economic growth in the region in the 1990s.

Before turning to that, however, one last point should be noted. All of the successful East Asian economies have been ones in which there has been a great deal of attention by governments to infrastructure and social development. Attention had to be paid to provision of adequate power, port capacity, telephone lines, domestic transport capacity, and other infrastructure services that are prerequisites for a successful export-oriented strategy. While government policy with regard to direct controls was essentially one of gradual liberalisation, government policy with regard to infrastructure was to avoid congestion and bottlenecks and to provide economically efficient services that would permit private firms to export. Simultaneously, resources were allocated for education and social services in order to provide an increasingly skilled labour force.

THE GROWTH MODEL FOR THE 1990s

Possibly the most important lesson to emerge from the experience of the East Asian high flyers is that development is a continuing process, and that continuing liberalisation, and removal of efficiency-inhibiting controls, is an essential part of that process. In the context of a truly poor country, with classic Arthur Lewis dimensions of 80 per cent in agriculture, and 20 per cent in other activities, a first prerequisite is undoubtedly to stimulate growth of agricultural productivity. That doubtless requires the provision of adequate incentives for farmers, as Schultz (1961) so forcefully demonstrated. In addition, of course, strong governmental support through infrastructure services, research and extension, irrigation and other means is necessary.

When industrial growth begins accelerating, heavy-handed direct controls initially have two effects: they may result in resource misallocation but they may also stimulate faster development, at least for a while. However, after the initial relatively straightforward industrial activities are well launched, further rapid industrial growth results in an increasingly complex industrial structure. As it does so, the disadvantages of small market sizes, lack of competition and other phenomena described above increase, and the stimulus to further growth diminishes. Simultaneously, the costs of attempting to administer an economy through direct controls rise sharply as the number of individual activities, the degree of interdependence between them (and between them and the international economy), and the sophistication of the business community all increase. Growth decelerates increasingly rapidly unless measures are taken for liberalisation; for a while, that deceleration may be overcome by rising investment rates, increasing education of the labour force, and other phenomena, but the underlying pressure is there.

At least in the East Asian economies, labour markets were fairly unregulated throughout the period of rapid growth. Attainment of a realistic exchange rate, and of means to assure the maintenance of real proceeds for exports, was achieved early in the period of rapid growth. Import liberalisation proceeded gradually after that, and financial liberalisation also began, and has continued into the 1980s. If that pattern can be taken as a lesson, it would suggest that continuing liberalisation will be desirable for further growth as the economies of the East Asian high flyers become increasingly complex. Should they fail to continue liberalising, it is likely that their growth rates will decline significantly in the 1990s. Particularly for Korea and Taiwan, it is likely that the costs of maintaining existing agricultural policies will mount sharply in the 1990s; labour market conditions will tighten sharply if rural out-migration rapidly slows down. Existing price support and other programs appear likely to result in just such an outcome.

To a degree, the same pattern has been occurring in the United States and Japan, with tax reform leading the supply-side moves that have been carried out. In Japan, considerable financial liberalisation has also occurred, while in the United States deregulation of transportation and other services has also taken place. Although those economies are more advanced than those of the East Asian high flyers, the mandate for further liberalisation may be equally important precisely because of their greater advancement and complexity. Certainly, New Zealand and Australia have had their own brand of deregulation and liberalisation. As this study is being written (September 1989), it would appear that efforts to liberalise the Australian labour market are coming to the fore. While the process of liberalisation itself is far from easy, it seems clear that informed opinion in those countries is that those policy reforms are essential for further growth.

For the second tier of NIEs, the resource-rich Southeast Asian countries, there is every evidence that their acceleration of growth can continue if they proceed to liberalise their economies. The more buoyant the world economy is, the better their prospects are. But, with the exception of Indonesia, it would appear that the NIEs of Southeast Asia have passed the point where their dependence on natural resources significantly alters the growth model for them. To be sure, productivity increases in agricultural and in extractive industries will help accelerate growth, and deterioration in the terms of trade for major primary commodity exports will reduce the realised rates of economic growth. Nonetheless, Thailand and Malaysia by now have sufficient diversity of exports, both primary commodity and other, that it would appear that their growth will be contingent upon the degree to which incentives remain appropriate and the government provides support for development through appropriate investments in infrastructure.

We are thus confronted with a picture of Pacific growth in which the challenges facing each group of countries over the next decade are to find ways to identify and remove the next tier of constraints to efficient resource allocation and growth. With the possible exception of some of the islands, means seem to have been found for spurring agricultural growth. In most, industrial development has also begun. For the countries where significant protection of industrial imports is still a major factor in resource allocation (primarily the fourth and fifth group of countries), it is likely that success in removing protection and shifting towards a more outer-oriented trade regime will be the key to their growth in the 1990s. For Taiwan and Singapore, liberalisation of agriculture, finance and services will be at the top of the list. For the developed countries of the region, the priorities will vary significantly from country to country, but those that fail to achieve further liberalisation and integration of markets are likely to experience slower growth.

GROWTH PROSPECTS IN THE 1990s

The Pacific region is such a large part of the world economy that it is impossible to consider regional prospects in the absence of global prospects, or vice versa. Moreover, there are some global issues currently on the policy agenda whose resolution will significantly affect the economic prospects of all nations. Policies adopted by Japan and the United States will significantly affect the outcome, while those adopted by other countries in the region will also have an impact, but to a lesser degree.

The crucial issue, of course, is the form and substance of the international trading system. Its evolution matters, and matters greatly, for the prospects of all countries in the world. For small countries, the impact of the international economy is greater because of their crucial dependence on trade for adequate size of market and supply of the myriad of complex goods that constitute the output of modern industrial activities. For relatively small countries whose growth prospects depend on their successful reform of trade policies, the evolution of the international economy will make the task harder or easier: the likelihood that their reforms can be carried out will be greater, the more rapid the growth of the international economy; moreover, the payoff from reforms in terms of higher living standards and more satisfactory growth is greater when the international economy is experiencing more rapid growth.

It is well known that the growth of the international economy has been rapid throughout the era since 1945, and that it was spurred in part by liberalisation of trade first by Europe, then by Japan, and now by the NIEs. Trade liberalisation was successful to the extent that tariffs were virtually eliminated on industrial commodities; the trading nations still wishing to protect found themselves resorting to measures other than tariffs to achieve their goals. Currently, protection is centred in non-tariff measures, and especially in barriers to trade in agriculture and services.

The Uruguay Round of trade negotiations under GATT is currently underway, and trade negotiators are attempting to grapple with the difficult issues involved in agreeing to ways of reducing these barriers to trade. The task of negotiating mechanisms for mutual reduction of these barriers is difficult, but given the extent to which future growth opportunities appear to lie in non-commodity areas, it is clearly of utmost importance for the world trading system.

Simultaneously, the United States has signed a bilateral free trade agreement with Canada, while the European Community is engaged in vigorous negotiations to achieve a unified internal market by 1992. There are significant dangers that a failure to reach satisfactory agreement in the Uruguay Round could push Europe and North American more towards bloc-farming free trading arrangements and away from the multilateral, non-discriminatory trading system that has, by and large, served the world so well over the past four decades.

Although there are strong economic forces pushing for greater integration of the international economy, there is a risk that the centripetal forces associated with the formation of trading blocs could undermine the trading framework of the past four decades. Should that happen, the longer-term growth prospects of the entire global economy would diminish. Over the shorter run, however, it would be those who were left out of the blocs that might suffer most. For Japan and the countries of the Western Pacific region, this threat to continued growth is serious, although not probable.

Because such an outcome could seriously impair the growth prospects of most Asian countries, a crucial policy issue affecting the course of the decade will arise at its very beginning. The activism and stance of those countries towards the Uruguay Round will affect its outcome, and thus the likelihood of the degeneration into trading blocs.

Assuming that that outcome can be avoided, there are strong reasons to believe that the 1990s could represent a prosperous period for the international economy: there are large productivity gains to be achieved by exploiting existing knowledge in communications and information technology, and there is reason to hope that biotechnology breakthroughs may form a second basis for productivity advances.[17] Those potential gains, combined with the gains from liberalisation of controls, constitute the basis on which significant advances in productivity and living standards could be achieved.

If the international economy grows at a satisfactory rate, then the countries of the Pacific that continue to liberalise their economies, and support private economic activities with appropriate infrastructure and an educated labour force, will probably realise rapid growth. If the imbalance between monetary and fiscal policy in the United States can be satisfactorily corrected, and the American and Japanese economies remain open, there is considerable basis for optimism that their growth rate in the 1990s can equal or exceed that of the 1980s. Canada, Australia and New Zealand will benefit by the growth of the international economy, although the process of liberalisation in those countries will be crucial to their growth.

There is every reason to believe that the high flyers can continue their growth at rapid rates if their process of liberalisation continues, although the growth rate will probably diminish somewhat as the gap between their productivity levels and those of the developed countries shrinks.[18] Simultaneously, the Southeast Asian countries whose trade regimes and protectionist structures are not highly restrictive may be ready to achieve accelerated growth through further trade liberalisation and shifts towards an outward-orientation. For them, the challenge will be to liberalise other markets and remove protection for imports. That would leave the fifth group of countries, discussed at the outset, with an opportunity to accelerate their growth. Whether they are able to do so will depend on the situation, policies and programs of each individual country. But it is likely that, by the year 2000, there will be few, if any, countries left in the fifth category, and that most of those now regarded as being in the fourth category will themselves be high flyers.

4 The United States in the world economy

BARRY P. BOSWORTH

This chapter discusses the economic outlook for the United States for the 1990s, focusing on domestic economic developments over the medium term and some potential implications for the world economy.

THE CURRENT SITUATION

The United States is enjoying one of its longest periods of economic expansion since the Second World War. Inflation, unemployment and interest rates have all declined dramatically from the levels that existed at the beginning of the 1980s. Most American families have also enjoyed substantial gains in their standards of living, at least as measured by their consumption. Yet the whole decade was marked by strong criticisms of government economic policies by economists and unusually dire predictions that recession lay around the corner. This contrast between the strong current performance of the overall economy and the negative predictions of the future results from the unbalanced nature of economic growth in the 1980s. The economic expansion has been based on an unprecedented expansion of consumption supported by heavy borrowing, both domestically and abroad. There have been major benefits to the current generation, but with a potentially high cost of reduced standards of living in the future.

The consumption orientation of the expansion is highlighted by an examination of the trends in the saving-investment balance shown in Table 4.1. The national saving rate, which averaged 7–8 per cent of national income in prior decades, has plunged in the 1980s, reaching a low of 2 per cent in 1986–87. This shift towards consumption is evident in both the private and public sectors. The private saving rate declined to 6 per cent in 1987, and the government budget deficit soared to over 5 per cent of national income by the mid-1980s. Throughout the decade the government budget deficit consistently absorbed more than half of private saving, leaving very little to finance investments in housing and business plant and equipment. On the other side, the domestic rate of investment has been held down by high interest rates, but at 5–6 per cent of national income it has exceeded domestic saving by substantial amounts.

Table 4.1 Net saving and investment as a share of net national product, United States, 1951–89

	\multicolumn{8}{c}{Percentage of net national product}
Item	1951–60	1961–70	1971–80	1981–85	1986	1987	1988	First half of 1989
Net saving:[a]								
Private saving[b]	8.7	9.4	9.7	8.2	7.4	6.0	6.8	7.2
Government saving	-0.7	-1.0	-2.0	-4.6	-5.3	-4.3	-3.8	-3.9
Total national saving-investment:	8.0	8.4	7.7	3.6	2.1	1.7	2.9	3.3
Net foreign investment	0.3	0.7	0.3	-1.3	-3.8	-3.7	-2.7	-2.2
Net domestic investment	7.7	7.7	7.5	5.0	5.6	5.3	5.4	5.2

Notes: a Net saving and investment equal the gross flow minus capital consumption allowances (the depreciation of existing capital). Net national product equals GNP minus capital consumption allowances. The sum of the investment components does not add to total because of statistical discrepancy.
b Business and household saving. Employee pension funds of state and local governments are allocated to household saving to match the treatment of private pension funds.

Sources: Bureau of Economic Analysis, US Department of Commerce, *National Income and Produce Accounts*, July 1989; and author's calculations.

The problem for international economic relations is evident in a comparison of a current rate of national saving of about 3 per cent with a rate of domestic investment of nearly 6 per cent. To fill the gap, the United States has been borrowing overseas at a rate equal to about 3 per cent of national income. The 3 per cent can be taken as a rough measure of the extent to which the nation is living beyond its means—borrowing abroad to support a level of domestic spending in excess of the nation's productive capacity. The result has been to shift the United States from being a net creditor to being the world's largest debtor nation. Furthermore, the low level of domestic investment effectively refutes the argument of some that the foreign financing is being used to support a surge of investment in a revitalised American economy—clearly the borrowing is financing a surge of consumption, not investment.

SOURCES OF CHANGE IN NATIONAL SAVING

Returning to the data of Table 4.1, the overall United States saving rate has declined from an historical average of 7–8 per cent of national income in the decades prior to 1980 to a low of less than 2 per cent in 1986 and 1987 before recovering to the current average of about 3 per cent. Throughout the early part of the decade the focus of attention was on the government budget deficit as the primary factor behind the decline, but discussion tended to overlook an equally important reduction in the private saving rate. At present, the 4 percentage points of the decline in the national saving rate can be divided about equally between a reduced rate of private saving and an increase in the structural budget deficit of the government.

Figure 4.1 Retirement and non-retirement saving (percentage of disposable income)

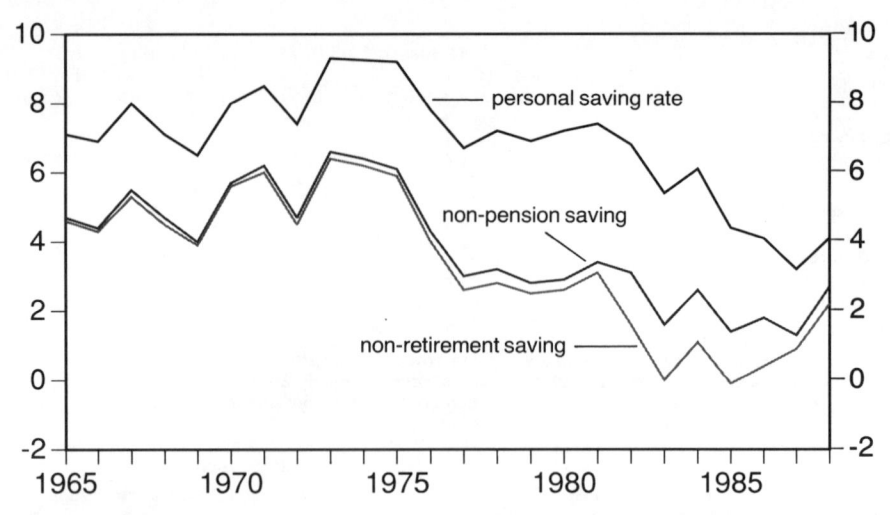

Note: Non-retirement saving excludes employer-financed pension accumulation and IRA and Keough contributions.
Source: As for Table 4.1.

Private saving

In the international comparisons, the United States has long been notable for its low private saving rate; but, at least, that rate had been extremely stable with no apparent evidence of a trend in either direction. That is no longer true and there is evidence of a secular fall in the 1980s.

In accounting for the decline in the saving rate, I would like to emphasise two short-run factors that influence the conclusion about the timing of the decline—when it began—and a third factor as the major cause of the secular decline. First, a very large proportion of household saving is in the form of formal pension plans operated by employers. Prior to the mid-1970s, a large proportion of those plans were underfunded. The passage of a new law, ERISA, in the 1970s set minimum funding requirements for private pensions and forced private firms to increase their contributions. The increased inflow of funds into the pension programs added to the private saving rate throughout the last half of the 1970s.

In the 1980s, however, the dramatic rise in market interest rates, used in computing the present value of future pension liabilities, led many of these funds to be classified as overfunded. Since current tax laws do not allow firms to deduct as a tax expense contributions to an overfunded plan, the inflow of new funds fell off dramatically (see Bernheim and Shoven, 1985: 85–113). The implication of excluding pension fund accumulations is that non-pension saving fell sharply after 1975 with only a modest further decline in the 1980s (see Figure 4.1).

Capital gains and losses have been another major source of fluctuation in the

Figure 4.2 Ratio of household wealth to income, with and without capital gains, 1960–88

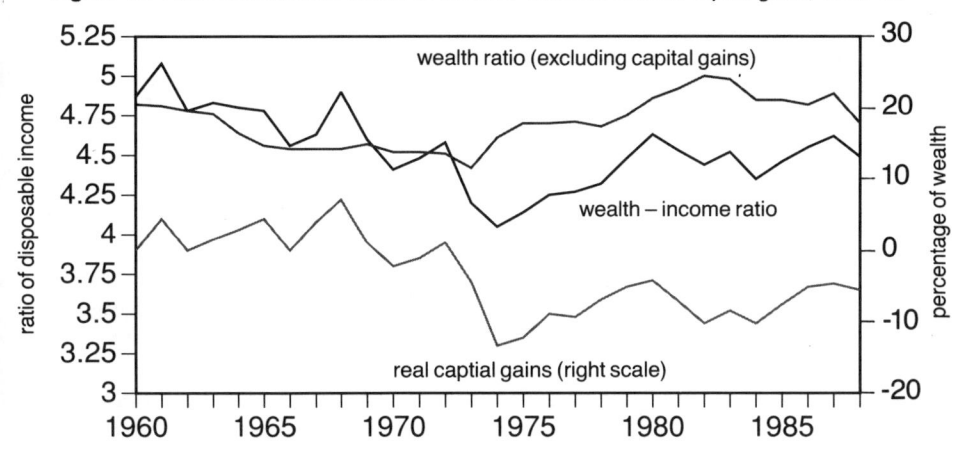

Note: Wealth excluding real capital gains is computed as the cumulative sum of private saving in constant prices.

Sources: Board of Governors of the Federal Reserve System, *Balance Sheets for the U.S. Economy 1949–88*, October 1989; and author's calulations.

saving rate. In the United States, about 60 per cent of corporate stock is held by households and there is an observable historical correlation between changes in the market value of wealth and household consumption. The crash of the United States stock market in 1974 dramatically reduced household wealth by nearly 10 per cent, and it is reasonable to argue that the event should have had a positive effect on saving in future years as households sought to restore their previous wealth position. The importance of capital gains and losses are shown in Figure 4.2, where I have computed a measure of wealth that excludes all *real* capital gains and losses since the 1960s, and compared it to the published market value.[1]

It is evident that the wealth/income ratio, exclusive of capital gains, actually rose after 1975, and that much of the prior loss was restored by 1980. However, a second decline in the stock market in 1981 and large losses in farmland and commercial real estate further depressed wealth in the early 1980s. Only after 1983 did a recovering stock market begin to dominate and add a positive impetus to consumer spending. Again, the adjustment for capital gains and losses on wealth would suggest that the fundamental break in the underlying pattern of saving occurred in the mid-1970s rather than in the 1980s.

The observed pattern of the wealth/income ratio in Figure 4.2 also provides important evidence on the source of the longer-term fall in the saving rate. Even though the saving rate has declined, the ratio of wealth to income has not. The reason, of course, is that income is growing far less rapidly than in the years prior to 1973. Most theories of consumption behaviour emphasise a target wealth/income ratio that, although it depends on demographics and other factors, is supposed to be invariant to the level of income. Thus, the saving rate as the measure of wealth accumulations should be directly proportional to the rate of growth of permanent income, Y^P:

$W_t = \beta Y_t^P,$
$S = W_t - W_{t-1} = \beta (Y_t^P - Y_{t-1}^P)$
$S/Y^P = \beta \Delta Y_t^P/Y^P.$

We would expect a sustained slowing of income growth to lower the saving rate and that appears to be what happened in the period after the first oil crisis. Since income growth is expected to remain low in the 1990s, the private saving rate will also be low.

Much of the international discussion on the outlook for private saving has placed greater emphasis on demographic factors rather than income growth. And, an emphasis on demographic trends does provide a more optimistic outlook for United States saving in the 1990s, because the large bulge of postwar 'baby-boom' generation will be in the age brackets where saving rates are typically high. However, I am concerned that such projections are too optimistic for a very simple reason: there is no historical correlation between the change in private saving rates and a demographic index that reflects the lifecycle profile of saving.

If demographics were important, the private saving rate should have fallen in the United States throughout the period of 1950 to the mid-1970s when the number of retired persons was rapidly rising and the baby-boom generation was very young; yet it was constant or increasing. The reversal of the demographic index after the mid-1970s was, in fact, associated with a fall in the private saving rate. The pattern appears to be that saving declined for all age groups and that it was not due to a shift of income among groups with differing saving rates. I conclude that demographics is a thin reed on which to support expectations of a future rise in the saving rate.

The above review is discouraging in that it does not support an explanation of the current low saving rate that would lead to expectations of a rise in the future. I have emphasised the low growth of income as the primary factor behind the decline in saving rates. And in a sense this same perspective suggests that the current saving rate is not low. For example, it is relatively easy to calculate the rate of saving needed to maintain today's wealth/income ratio. The wealth measure shown in Figure 4.2, including consumer durables, has averaged 4.5 times income in recent years. In addition, income growth has averaged 2.5 per cent annually since 1973. The implied saving rate of 11 per cent (4.5 x 2.5) is very close to the corresponding actual rate (inclusive of consumer durables) of 11-12 per cent in 1988-89. Thus, from the perspective of wealth accumulation, the current saving rate is not low, unless a future acceleration of income growth is to be anticipated.

Incentives for private saving

Incentives for saving are always politically popular, as they hold out the promise of a further tax cut and appear to be a politically painless solution to the lack of national saving. Past experience, however, has not been encouraging. During the 1980s, rates of return in financial markets rose substantially above historical levels, deregulation extended access to those rates to a much larger number of potential savers, and changes in tax laws dramatically lowered marginal tax rates and made it possible to avoid taxation entirely on most saving. Yet the private saving rate fell.

Recently, some studies of cross-sectional data have suggested that tax-exempt Investment Retirement Accounts (IRAs) did add to private saving, even though economic theory would have suggested that such plans would be dominated by substitution with other forms of retirement saving. This type of cross-sectional analysis is severely constrained, because the participation in an IRA plan is likely to serve as a particularly good identifier of individuals who are prone towards saving. In addition, the utilisation of the accounts was concentrated among income and age groups who would have been expected to be saving amounts close to the US$2,000 annual limit on such contributions, even without the program.

Without delving fully into the issue of IRAs, it is interesting to note their impact on private saving, if we accept the argument that they did represent a net addition to saving. The annual flow of contributions to IRAs and Keough plans reached US$45 billion by 1986.[2] It then fell to less than US$20 billion in 1987–88 when the program was cut back. Even if we ignore the annual accumulation of interest income within those accounts, it would be necessary to believe that non-retirement saving fell from 6 per cent of disposable income in the mid-1970s to zero by 1985 and then suddenly turned around and increased at the same time as the IRA program was cut back (see Figure 4.1). While it is possible that such a drop in non-retirement saving did occur for independent reasons, it is surprising that the decline is so heavily correlated with the pattern of annual change in IRAs. At the same time, the loss of government tax revenue, estimated at US$16 billion in 1986, increased the government budget deficit, reducing the national saving rate.

In part, the problem may be that the increased incentives to young households that have not yet accumulated significant wealth are overwhelmed by the increased consumption that results from the capital gains that tax changes provide to holders of existing wealth. But, if that is true, tax incentives for saving are likely to have a low 'bang-for-the-buck' for many years to come: they would not provide an effective means of increasing the national saving rate over the next decade. Furthermore, the behaviour of private defined-benefit pension funds does provide a vivid example of target saving, where increases in the rate of return actually reduce net saving.

Government budget deficit

Primary responsibility for the decline in national saving must lie with the expansion of the public sector deficit, and the reduction of that deficit is the only practical means of increasing the national saving rate. In the early part of the decade, it was common to project a quick adjustment of either taxes or expenditures, and the passage of the Gramm–Rudman–Hollings balanced budget act seemed to imply some political commitment to reducing the deficit. That act mandated specific numerical targets for reducing the budget deficit in future years. And some progress was made in the middle of the decade to reduce the overall budget deficit from in excess of US$200 billion to about US$150 billion annually. Today, however, the continuation of a large future deficit seems deeply ingrained in the budget process; and the Administration and the Congress have consistently found means of avoiding the targets of the balanced budget act.

To understand the debate over the budget deficit, it is important to recognise that it does not reflect major disagreements over economic policy. Instead, the budget deficit has got caught up in an ideological debate about the appropriate size and role of government. No-one argues that the budget deficit is economically desirable; but conservatives see it as an effective tool to restrain liberal pressures of new government programs, and they remain adamantly opposed to any tax increases. That is, in their efforts to restrain the growth of government, they focus on taxes: the budget deficit is bad, but even worse would be a tax increase. At the same time, liberals are unwilling to accept cuts in their expenditure programs as part of an effort to reduce the deficit. There is no evidence of the emergence of any political compromise, and the lack of any economic crisis has reduced any urgency to address the problem.

Both political parties have become convinced that the first to propose a tax increase will be voted out of office. Americans do not seem prepared to accept the sacrifices in their current consumption that any resolution of the budget issues would require. They like the arguments of both parties—no tax increase and no cut in expenditures. It is increasingly common to hear both extremes in the political debate—liberals opposed to expenditure cuts and conservatives opposed to tax increases—argue that the budget deficit simply is not a problem.

The most recent projections of the budget deficit, made by the Congressional Budget Office, are shown in Table 4.2. A continuation of current programs and taxes implies that the overall budget deficit would remain in the range of about US$125 to US$150 billion, and the inevitable pressures for some new programs will probably drive it slightly higher. It will, however, represent a slowly falling percentage of national income. That improvement results only because of a growing surplus in the government administered retirement accounts, which are financed by employment taxes that fall heavily on workers in the lower end of the income distribution. These surpluses exist temporarily because the large baby-boom generation is now in the workforce, but these surpluses are needed to finance future retirement costs. At present, the government borrows from the retirement accounts to finance what is a growing deficit in the operating budget.

Finally, large overall deficits in the 1980s led to a tripling of the public debt and large increases in government interest payments. Thus, the current deficit of US$150 billion can be traced entirely to the increased interest payments on debt issues since 1980. If it was hard to obtain public support for taxes to finance expenditure programs which provide some benefits to taxpayers, it will be doubly difficult to induce the public to support an increase in taxes to pay the interest on old debt.

Table 4.2 Projections of baseline federal deficits, 1980–94 (billion US dollars)

	1980	1989	1990	1991	1992	1993	1994
CBO federal deficit	-74	-161	-141	-144	-141	-143	-128
less surplus in:							
social security (OASDI) (off-budget)	-1	54	65	75	86	99	113
CBO on-budget deficit	-73	-215	-206	-219	-227	-242	-241
less surplus in:							
Medicare (HI)	1	21	23	21	17	15	13
Fed. Employ. Retirement[a]	10	35	35	37	39	41	44
Non-retirement budget targets[b]	-84	-271	-264	-277	-283	-298	-298
Gramm–Rudman–Hollings targets[b]	na	-136	-100	-64	-28	0	na

Notes: na—not available.
   a Includes civilian and military retirement trust funds.
   b Sequestration is not required if the projected deficit exceeds the target but by less than US$10 billion.
   Numbers for 1980 through 1989 are actual. Numbers for 1990 through 1994 are the Congressional Budget Office baseline projections from August 1989.

Sources: Congressional Budget Office, *The Economic and Budget Outlook: An Update*, August 1989, pp.31–61; and author's calculations.

Increasingly, it is evident that projections of future economic trends in the United States should incorporate a continued large budget deficit, camouflaged somewhat by borrowing from the public-sector retirement accounts, and a continued low national saving rate.

The loss of budget policy as a tool for economic stabilisation has also placed enormous pressures on monetary policy. In effect, the ideological debate over the budget deficit has forced the monetary authorities to take on the major responsibility for managing both domestic and external economic balance. In the 1980s they have been very successful in doing so by avoiding the ideological battles and adopting a pragmatic approach that emphasised gradual adjustments of policy with an effort to avoid frequent reversals—what has sometimes been characterised as 'leaning against the wind'. For much of the decade this was not difficult, as the economy was emerging from a very severe recession with very high levels of excess capacity both domestically and in the world economy. With the return to conditions of near 'full employment' in recent years, however, the monetary authorities have become increasingly concerned about the risk inflation. Thus, it has attempted to maintain economic growth within a narrow band of 2 to 3 per cent annually, which it hopes will provide an acceptable compromise between avoiding an acceleration of inflation and rising unemployment. Finally, the external imbalance has not been a major constraint on policy because of the continuing willingness of foreigners to finance the current account deficits.

INTERNATIONAL IMPLICATIONS

The emergence of the United States as a major debtor country is one of the most striking developments of the 1980s. It is surprising from several perspectives. First, we do not normally think of wealthy countries needing to borrow to support consumption in excess of their own income: the historical pattern has been for capital to flow from capital-rich to capital-poor countries. Second, we have been surprised by the ability of international financial markets to support that flow on a sustained basis. What was discussed as a temporary condition in the early 1980s, with widespread fears of financial crisis, now seems likely to last well into the next decade. A large United States current account deficit is emerging as an integral part of most longer-term forecasts of the world economy. Third, the existence of large trade imbalances, between the United States and other major industrial countries, has greatly changed the atmosphere for future negotiations to further reduced trade barriers.

In seeking the causes for the development of a large United States current account imbalance in the 1980s, the public debate has been between those who see it as something done to the United States by foreigners and those who point to developments in the United States. The first group perceives the trade deficit as being forced on the United States against its wishes by the unfair trade practices of other countries. While such an explanation is certainly possible in theory, there are several aspects of the current situation that make such an argument implausible. First, we would have to explain the timing, the suddenness of the emergence of an imbalance in the 1980s. The United States consistently had a small current account surplus in prior decades and, outside of oil, its share of world export markets was rising during the 1970s (Figure 4.3). It would also require belief in a coordinated conspiracy, since by 1985 the United States had a large trade deficit with every region of the globe and the change in the balance with each region was roughly proportionate to the total volume of our prior trade.

Second, if the trade deficit reflected a cutting off of American export markets and the dumping of imports in the domestic market, we would expect to observe an economy mired in recession and high unemployment. In fact, the United States has experienced six years of continuous economic expansion and a steady decline in unemployment. Today, the major economic threat appears to be inflation, as the growth of domestic demand has begun to strain the nation's economic capacity.

Some groups maintain that the trade deficit reflects an inability to compete with cheap foreign labour, and argue that a continued opening of world markets would drag down American real wages and standards of living. Yet the proportion of United States imports coming from countries whose wages are less than half those of the United States has steadily declined. Today, if the United States has a competitiveness problem, it is in comparison with countries whose wage rates are equal to or higher than American wages.

The alternative explanation of most economists emphasises the decline in

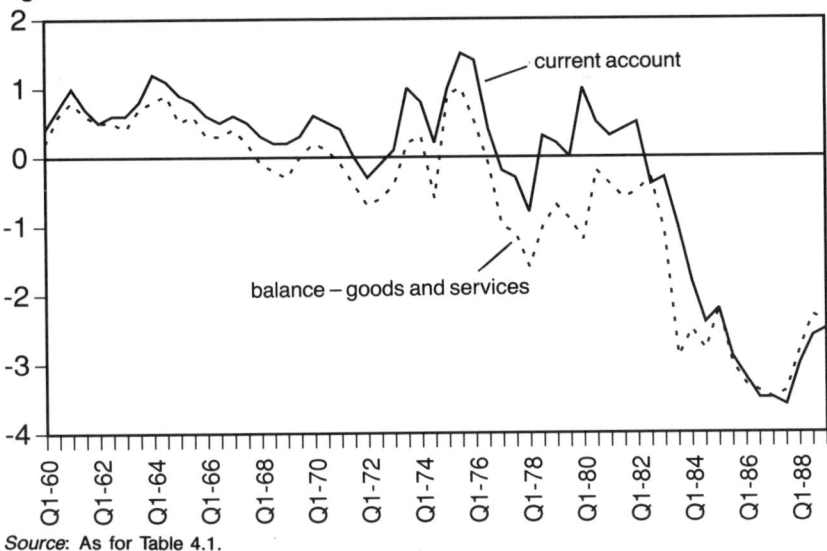

Figure 4.3 The current account and the trade balance, 1960–88 (percentage of GNP)

Source: As for Table 4.1.

national saving as the driving force behind the emergence of a current account deficit. Thus the trade deficit is perceived as a symptom, but not a cause, of domestic economic developments. From an aggregate perspective, a nation's current account balance is simply a measure of the gap between its saving and its investment, or the extent to which its spending exceeds its income—necessitating borrowing from abroad. Simple arithmetic suggests that a nation that saves 3 per cent and invests 6 per cent of its income will have to borrow abroad—import more than it exports.

The drop in national saving has impacted on United States trade through increases in the exchange rate (Figure 4.4). Prior to the 1980s, heavy government borrowing in capital markets would have driven up interest rates and crowded out domestic investment—particularly homebuilding. But with the emergence of more open international capital markets, foreign investors were attracted to United States markets by interest rates far in excess of those available in their home countries. In addition, there was a sharp reversal of the previous net flow of capital from the United States to Latin America. The increased demand for dollars drove up the exchange rate, pricing American goods out of world markets. Thus the financial inflow was matched by an equal current account deficit—reduced exports and increased imports. The United States traded pieces of paper for the goods and services required to support a level of spending in excess of its own income.

Contrary to the public perception of a country flooded with imports, the major change was on the export side (Figure 4.5). With an underlying trend towards more open international markets, both exports and imports have been a rising share of income in all of the industrial countries since the Second World War. While the United States share continued to rise in the 1980s at the historical rate, the share of exports fell off dramatically in the first half of the

Figure 4.4 Real and nominal exchange rates, 1970–88 (1980–82 = 100)

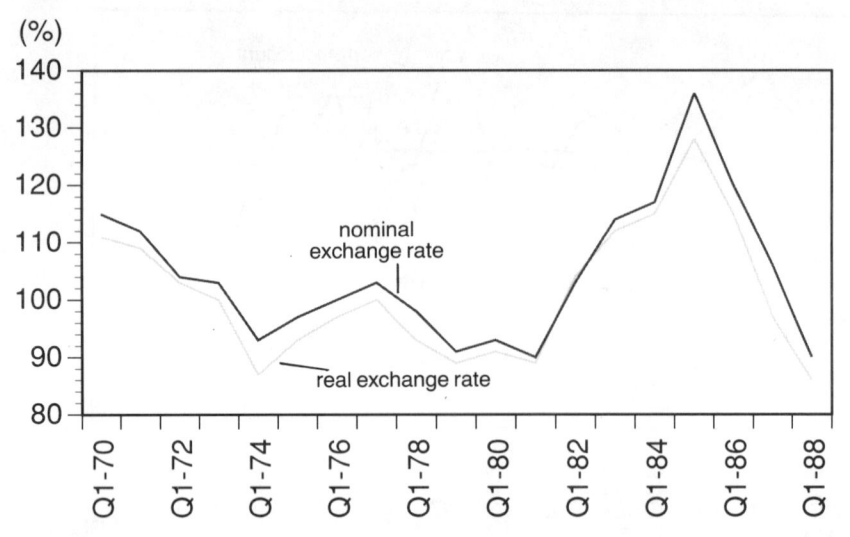

Note: Quarterly averages.
Source: Morgan Guarantee Trust Company, *World Financial Markets*, July 1989, and prior issues.

decade and has begun to recover only slowly in recent years.

The ease with which the shortfall of national saving is being financed by overseas borrowing has been a surprise to most economists. And, in contrast to

Figure 4.5 Trends in merchandise trade, 1960–88 (percentage of GNP)

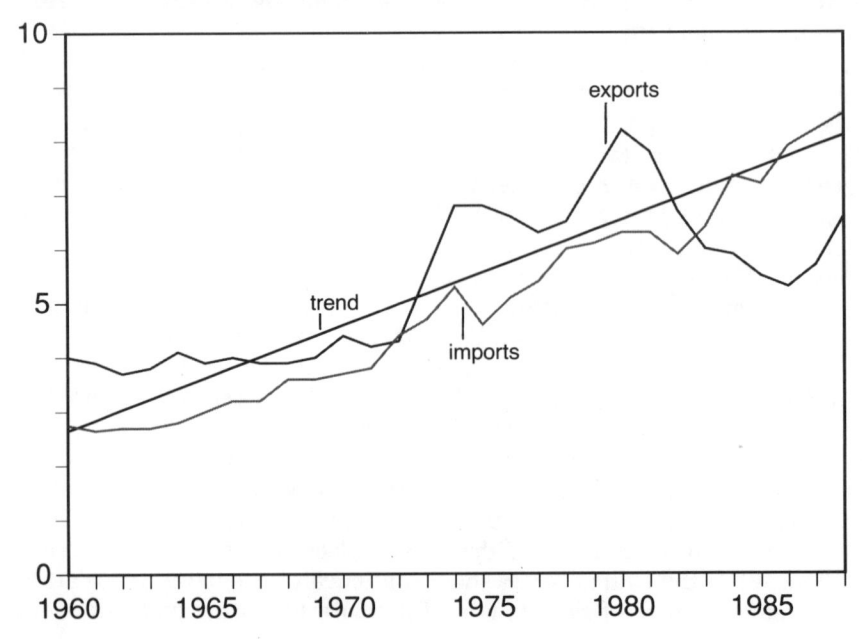

Source: As for Table 4.1.

the situation of a few years ago, a growing number now argue that the pattern could continue for many years into the future. There is nothing in economic markets that prevents an individual from selling inherited assets to support consumption; and, apparently, in the newly expanded system of international capital markets, nations can do the same. Certainly, it will be many years before foreign investors become seriously concerned about the ability of the United States to repay its debts. They do face a risk of exchange rate declines; but current interest rate differentials suggest that they are being compensated for those risks, and they have moved to diversify their portfolios in ways that minimise future exchange rate losses.

Furthermore, the large United States current account imbalance has become an integral part of the world economy, critical to continued expansion. A United States deficit allows a large number of other countries to follow a policy of export-led growth, and many industrial countries have used the opportunity to reduce their own budget deficits and expand the relative size of their tradeable goods industries. Thus, they have become a major backstop to the American policy as private investors can anticipate that foreign governments will intervene to support the dollar, if it should fall rapidly, in order to protect their own tradeable goods industries.

Finally, despite the economic argument that the trade deficit is domestic in origin, the political argument has been won by those who present it as the product of foreign trade discrimination. Even to economists, foreign restrictions on American goods are a serious problem. The United States should act aggressively to open up the markets of other countries. The only difference of view is in the issues of whether such actions will reduce the size of the total deficit as opposed to its composition. In the absence of actions to raise the national saving rate, success in reducing foreign trade barriers will change the pattern of United States trade, an issue of great importance to individual industries; but any effects on the overall trade balance will be offset by changes in exchange rates so as to leave the overall current account deficit equal to the gap between national saving and investment.

Frustration over the trade issues seems to be leading the United States increasingly away from an emphasis on an open international trading system. While the United States rails against foreign restrictions, it tends to ignore the myriad restrictions of its own and has moved to protect a growing number of American import-competing industries. The public policy debate has turned increasingly in the direction of advocacy of some system of managed international trade with specific targets for trade with individual countries. Perversely, such a system of state control of trade seems designed to maximise the disadvantages of the United States political system relative to the countries with whom the United States competes. The notion that the United States could out-manage the Japanese and the Germans boggles the imagination.

As we look ahead towards the 1990s, the stability of the current arrangement, whereby the United States continues to slowly sell off its assets in world markets to support its consumption, is surprising. The budget deficit still generates substantial political concern, but doing something to reduce it is even less attractive because that would mean tax increases and cuts in favourite expenditure programs. Americans are unlikely to undertake the painful reductions in living standards required to increase the national saving rate unless they are forced to do so because of an economic crisis. But forecasts of such a crisis in the near future seem increasingly unlikely. The governments of other industrial countries also have a large stake in the current situation because they have come to rely on the United States trade deficit to sustain the growth of their own economies. And as long as the developing countries are faced with the overhang of existing debt, they are unlikely to expand or provide a significant outlet for international capital. To foreign investors, the United States is a far more attractive investment location than any Latin American country.

If adjustment should come, however, and ultimately it would seem that it must, it would be very good for American exporters. A higher rate of saving in the United States means lower interest rates, a reduction in the attractiveness of foreign capital inflows, a reduced demand for dollars, a lower exchange rate, and a lower price of American goods in world markets. Of course, a lower exchange rate, a fall in the terms of trade, will reduce American standards of living through higher imported goods prices; but when we remember that 90 per cent of American consumption is produced domestically, the loss on the terms of trade will be small relative to the increased revenues from export sales. Consumers will lose, but the producers of tradeable goods will gain.

THE ECONOMIC POLICY OPTIONS

United States economic policy stands at an important crossroads with major differences in the implications for the economy of the decisions that must be made by a new President and the Congress. On the one hand, it could refuse to adjust and continue to borrow overseas—generating a current account deficit—to sustain current levels of consumption. Alternatively, it could undertake an adjustment policy, reducing domestic consumption to the point that higher domestic saving would eliminate the need to borrow overseas. The later policy implies a significantly more restrictive budget policy.

Procrastination

Too often, economists have been quoted as warning that the current economic imbalances will lead to a recession. While it is possible that some sort of financial crisis may precipitate such an event, the more standard view of an economy spending beyond its means is that the future will be one of inflation as demand outruns supply, or high interest rates if the central bank acts to restrain the inflation pressures.

Currently, the United States is trying to meet the demands of a rapidly expanding export market and high levels of domestic demand. The result is growing strains on capacity. In the last two years, raw material prices, exclusive of food and fuel, have increased 16 per cent, and intermediate goods

Table 4.3 Alternative measures of inflation, 1985–90

	Year ending				Quarterly at annual rates					
	1985:4	1986:4	1987:4	1988:4	1988:1 to 1988:2	1988:2 to 1988:3	1988:3 to 1988:4	1988:4 to 1989:1	1989:1 to 1989:2	1989:2 to 1989:3
Measures of actual inflation rate:										
Consumer price index	3.5	1.3	4.5	4.4	4.5	4.7	4.4	5.4	6.4	2.4
Producer price index	1.6	-2.0	2.6	3.4	3.2	4.7	3.5	9.1	6.6	-0.6
Measures of underlying inflation rate:										
CPI less food and energy	4.1	4.2	4.0	4.6	5.4	3.7	5.6	5.3	4.2	2.5
PPI less food and energy	2.6	2.7	2.1	4.0	2.9	5.1	3.8	5.6	3.5	3.8
Average hourly earnings	3.1	2.3	2.8	3.5	3.8	2.9	4.1	3.6	4.3	4.0
Employment cost index (private):										
Compensation	3.9	3.2	3.3	4.9	4.9[a]	4.1[a]	4.1[a]	5.1[a]	4.8[a]	5.0[a]
Wages and salaries	4.1	3.1	3.3	4.1	4.5[a]	4.1[a]	4.1[a]	4.4[a]	4.0[a]	4.9[a]

Note: a Not seasonally adjusted.

Source: Bureau of Labor Statistics, US Department of Labor, *Monthly Labor Review*, December 1989, and prior issues.

prices are up 11 per cent. The rate of consumer goods price inflation has moved up above 5 per cent annually (Table 4.3).

The surprise has been the continued moderate size of nominal wage increases, despite a major erosion of real wages (nominal wage rates adjusted for inflation), which are 4 per cent below the level of 1986. However, unemployment is now down to about 5 per cent, which together with declining real wages is expected to lead to a modest acceleration of wage increases in future years.

The potential growth rate of the United States economy, consistent with a constant utilisation of resources is currently estimated at about 2–2.5 per cent annually—composed of a labour force growth of 1–1.5 per cent and productivity growth of 1 per cent. Growth in excess of that amount will, from the perspective of the central bank, threaten an intensification of inflation pressures. They will respond with a tightening of credit and higher interest rates. If United States interest rates again rise relative to those of other countries, the exchange rate could again head back up as a widening interest rate differential would overcome investors' fears of a future exchange rate decline. The result would be to choke off the recovery of the trade sector and to continue the reliance on a trade deficit to meet domestic spending demands.

It is just such an episode of tightening credit in response to inflation fears that dominated economic developments in the first half of 1989. However, it now appears that the Federal Reserve has succeeded in slowing the economy and relieving some of the inflation pressures. Thus, there is room for some modest decline in United States interest rates and the exchange rate.

I do not believe that current economic analysis is sufficient to answer the question of how long this situation of continued reliance on foreign borrowing to balance domestic demand and supply can continue. Certainly, there is nothing in markets that prevents a society from selling off its assets to support current consumption—individuals do it all the time. There will come a time when the magnitude of debt relative to the nation's wealth will force an adjustment, but for a country as rich as the United States that date is far in the future. There is a special problem created by the exchange rate risk born by investors that lend to the United States—thus the pressures for an ever-widening interest rate differential between the United States and other countries. However, much of this risk can be covered by diversifying into the ownership of tradeable goods firms, which would benefit from a fall in the exchange rate. Furthermore, there is an increasing temptation for the United States government to begin to borrow in foreign currencies—gaining a reduction in short-run interest costs.

The economics of adjustment

The essence of an adjustment policy is to engineer a reduction in domestic consumption so as to eliminate the need to borrow abroad and to provide the resources for an expanded effort to increase productivity and living standards at home. From a practical perspective, that means a reduction in the government budget deficit. A higher rate of private saving would be desirable, but no-one knows how to engineer such an objective short of coercion. The elimination of foreign borrowing means an increased foreign demand for American products, and that demand can only be met by freeing up resources now being used to supply domestic demand, which would represent a more restrictive fiscal policy.

A policy of fiscal restraint will, of course, have a depressive effect on the domestic economy, but, if the policy adjustment is spread over several years, the private economy, with the assistance of an easier monetary policy, can accomplish the restructuring away from domestic consumption towards the tradeable goods industries without a recession. The offset will be reflected in lower interest rates and higher domestic investment; but, more importantly, lower interest rates will lead to a fall in the exchange rate and improved price competitiveness in world markets.

One practical question is the speed at which the restructuring could be expected to occur. That question has been examined in some detail as part of the process of establishing the Gramm–Rudman–Hollings targets for the budget. The consensus was that annual deficit reductions in the range of US$30–50 billion appear to present no serious problem. An important caveat is that the policy does require the active cooperation of the monetary authorities, since budget deficit reductions without sharply lower interest rates and exchange rates imply a recession.

A second interesting issues is the magnitude of the required decline in the real exchange rate. Forecasts of the overall current account balance depend on projections of income growth in the United States and abroad, and the real exchange rate (the relative price of American versus foreign goods). Obviously, if income growth is low in the United States or high abroad, the required decline in the exchange rate would be smaller. However, let us assume a continuation of United States growth in the range of 2–3 per cent annually and foreign growth of about 3 per cent. Under these assumptions, a real exchange rate at today's level would imply a leveling out of the United States current account deficit at about US$125 billion, or about 2–2.5 per cent of GNP, throughout the first half of the 1990s.

In addition, nearly all the studies of United States trade find that the price elasticity of both exports and imports is near unity. The implication is that a 10 per cent decline in the real exchange rate will ultimately reduce the trade deficit by about 1 per cent of GNP. Thus, it is easy to obtain estimates of a decline in the real exchange rate of about 25 per cent, if the United States were to return to current account balance.

The magnitude of the projected decline may seem large, but there are several reasons for it. First, prior to the 1980s the United States was a large creditor nation, earning about 1 per cent of GNP on net income from foreign investments. That surplus is now gone and the United States will need to generate a surplus of trade over and above the levels of the 1970s to finance the deficit on interest income. That changed investment position accounts for more than 10 percentage points of the projected exchange rate decline.

Second, the United States has in the past experienced a secular erosion in the real exchange rate associated with any given trade balance. This trend might be associated with a loss of share in world markets because of a decline in quality or a catchup in the technologies of other countries, but it can also be attributed to a much higher income elasticity of imports than for exports and a pronounced slowing of income growth outside the United States. In either case, this trend amounted to about 10 per cent each decade in the 1950–80 period.

I conclude that it would take a remarkable set of events to raise the possibility of the United States returning to current account balance within the next decade. The real problem is the magnitude of decline in the national saving rate. That decline is understated if we focus only on the budget deficit, because there has also been an erosion of private saving. Similarly, the trade deficit understates the decline, because some of the shortfall has been absorbed in a reduced rate of domestic investment. I do not see the economic basis for projecting a recovery of the private saving rate, since the reasons for its decline are not well understood; and a reversal in the public sector deficit sufficient to eliminate the foreign imbalance would require an enormous shift in the political debate. That seems very unlikely. Finally, elimination of the United States current account deficit would imply changes in the patterns of world trade and exchange rates that would be strongly resisted by other governments.

5 The Japanese economy and Pacific development

HEIZO TAKENAKA

INTRODUCTION

This chapter seeks to evaluate Japan's economic performance in the context of its role in the economic development of the Asia–Pacific region. The growing economic strength of the region has produced frequent and laudatory comment in Japan. Along with many other observers, I anticipate that the Asia–Pacific region will be a major centre of world economic growth in the future.

However, the recent optimistic view of the economy of the Asia–Pacific region has tended to focus only on the region's successes and to largely overlook its demand-side problems. These problems deserve greater attention, especially in view of the fact that the future of the Asia–Pacific region's economy will depend in large part on Japan's management of its macroeconomic and structural adjustment policies. Optimism about the region's economic prospects is not misplaced, but sufficient attention must be paid to Japan's progress in making necessary changes to its domestic economy.

This chapter first briefly examines the Japanese economy, focusing in turn on the positive and negative aspects of its recent pattern of economic development and performance. There follows an economic analysis of the Pacific region, and after an initial overview of the supply and demand structure of the economies of the region, attention turns to demand-side problems, considering what policy changes must be made, particularly in view of the large and continuing United States current accounts deficit.

Finally, this study considers the role Japan should play as a market for exports from the Asia–Pacific region, arguing that innovative policies are needed to address the continuing economic distortions which threaten to create a new dual structure in the Japanese economy.

JAPAN'S RECENT ECONOMIC PERFORMANCE

Positive aspects

Despite the substantial appreciation of the yen in recent years, the Japanese economy appears to be sustaining the long-term economic expansion which

Table 5.1 Contribution to Japan's economic growth by individual demand items (per cent)

	1985	1986	1987	1988
Real economic growth rate	4.9	2.5	4.5	5.7
Domestic demand contribution	3.8	3.9	5.1	7.6
Private demand	4.1	2.9	4.8	7.0
Private final consumption demand	1.6	1.8	2.4	2.8
Private housing	0.1	0.4	1.1	0.8
Private fixed investment	2.1	1.0	1.5	3.1
Private stock increase	0.3	-0.3	-0.2	0.3
Public demand	-0.3	1.0	0.3	0.6
External demand contribution	1.1	-1.4	-0.6	-1.9
Exports etc.	1.1	-1.0	0.7	1.4
Imports etc.	0.0	-0.4	-1.3	-3.3

Note: Quarterly data shows seasonally-adjusted, annualised rate against same item, previous year.
Source: Economic Planning Agency, *National Account Statistics*, various issues.

has characterised it since the end of the Second World War.

Although the appreciation of the yen following the Plaza Agreement of 1985 forced corporate profits down in 1985–86 and raised concerns about a drop in income and consumption, the Japanese economy adjusted smoothly to the stronger yen in 1987 and later years, which saw a revival of economic growth based on strong domestic demand.

In evaluating the performance of the Japanese economy in recent years, we should note not only this sustained economic growth but also the presence of several very significant economic changes. These changes include, for instance, the growing proportion of manufactured goods in Japan's total imports (which have themselves risen substantially) and the expansion of Japanese foreign direct investment. These changes, in turn, are causing very important structural shifts in the Japanese economy.

Table 5.1 displays trends in Japan's economic growth rate and the contributions of major demand items to overall economic growth in the aftermath of the 1985 Plaza Agreement. Japan's economic growth rate was a high 4.1 per cent in 1985, of which 1.1 per cent was attributable to external demand.

External demand fell in 1986 in response to the appreciation of the yen, lowering the growth rate to 2.5 per cent, despite an increase in government expenditures. Economic growth revived in 1987, led by strong private final consumption demand and heavy private fixed investment. This pattern continued in 1988. Though import growth turned the external sector into a drag on the economy, producing a 1.4 per cent contraction, the continued rapid expansion of domestic demand raised the overall economic growth rate to 5.7 per cent.

Trade figures also improved as the yen appreciated. Imports rose by US$15.4 billion between 1986 and 1987 and surged further by US$36.6 billion between 1987 and 1988. Although dollar-denominated exports continued to rise in nominal terms, exports were stable in volume terms, reducing Japan's accounts surplus from US$87 billion in 1987 to US$79.6 billion in 1988.

Within the context of these macroeconomic developments, the strong yen environment produced a number of more specific shifts in the Japanese economy. The proportion of manufactured goods in total imports rose rapidly. Whereas such products accounted for just 22.8 per cent of Japanese imports in 1980 and only 31 per cent of total imports in 1985, manufactured products represented 49 per cent of Japan's total import intake in 1988, reflecting the fact that imports from the Asian NIEs doubled between 1986 and 1988.

Japanese foreign direct investment also expanded rapidly, increasing at an annual rate of US$10 billion and reaching US$47 billion in 1988. Roughly half of this direct investment was directed to the United States, with substantial investment also committed to Europe in anticipation of the European Community's 1992 initiative. Investment in Asian countries, primarily in assembly and processing operations, also rose steadily, accounting for about 20 per cent of total foreign direct investment.

As a result of this expansion in foreign direct investment, output from foreign operations now accounts for 5 per cent of total output by Japanese corporations. This level is still lower than the 10–20 per cent levels typical of American and West German firms, suggesting that a further increase can be expected.

Negative aspects

As discussed in the preceding section, Japan's economy has performed well in recent years, producing roughly 5 per cent growth at 2 per cent inflation levels. The 1989 *White Paper on the Economy*, published by Japan's Economic Planning Agency, evaluates Japan's recent economic performance very favourably, focusing on three trends: the increasing sophistication of the Japanese industry, the globalisation of Japan's businesses, and the expansion of capital stocks in the Japanese economy. The *White Paper* also gives a positive evaluation of Japan's efforts to implement the structural adjustment measures advocated in the Maekawa Report.

Despite these positive developments, however, a number of negative aspects which are implicit in the recent changes in the Japanese economy make the evaluation of the overall Japanese economy more problematic.

First, the value of assets, especially land, has inflated rapidly in recent years. This asset inflation has not only produced substantial distortions in income distribution but has also strongly influenced movements in domestic demand.

In particular, asset appreciation has fuelled increased consumption by property owners. In 1987, this increased consumption was estimated to be in the order of ¥6 trillion, representing 60 per cent of total growth in individual consumption. There is, however, a strong possibility that this rise in consumption also reflects a short-term jump in consumption by asset-poor Japanese who have been priced out of the housing market.

Insofar as the present increase in consumption expenditures reflects this latter phenomenon, it suggests a future drop in housing investment and may have a negative long-term impact on domestic demand. The inflation in asset values may thus have caused a one-time expansion in domestic demand, possibly raising Japan's economic performance above the level which could otherwise have been attained.

The second factor to consider is the appreciation of the yen. Though the view is widespread in Japan that the recent improvement in Japan's external imbalances reflects progress in structural adjustments, my estimates indicate that 80 per cent of the recent shrinkage in Japan's trade surplus can be explained by the appreciation of the yen (Takenaka, 1988). Similarly, the recent surge in foreign direct investment by Japan can be attributed to the revaluation of the yen (Takenaka, Chida, Watanabe and Hiraoka, 1989).

However, the yen has fallen back against the dollar since 1988, suggesting that exchange rate movements may once again produce an expansion in Japan's trade surplus from 1990 onward.

Although the Japanese economy has adjusted smoothly to the appreciation of the yen and turned in a good overall performance in the late 1980s, a slowdown in the Japanese (as well as the American) economy can be expected in the early 1990s. To ensure continued favourable economic performance, Japan will have to promote further structural adjustment through deregulation.

THE STRUCTURE OF THE ASIA-PACIFIC ECONOMY

Japan as a supplier and the United States as an 'absorber'

In discussing economic issues, it goes without saying that one must strike a consistent balance between supply-side and demand-side concerns. However, in discussions of the United States and other industrialised economies, attention is usually focused primarily on demand-side issues, typically from an effective demand perspective.

Similarly, discussions of developing countries' economies generally concentrate on supply-side issues. Since a major concern regarding developing economies is whether they have reached the 'take-off' stage, it is of course important to consider the supply-side of their economies. However, in examining the rapidly industrialising economies of the NIEs and some of the ASEAN countries, it is also necessary to take into account demand-side issues, just as in the case of industrialised nations.

Watanabe (1988) has made a clear analysis of the fundamental supply and demand structure of the Asia-Pacific region. Japan supplies capital and intermediate products to the NIEs and ASEAN countries. This facilitates technology transfer and increases the economic competitiveness of the region, strengthening the supply side of these economies. The products which the NIEs and ASEAN economies produce with Japanese capital and technology are then exported, primarily to the United States. In other words, Japan fills the role of a supplier, while the United States fills that of an export 'absorber'.

Let us examine in detail this pattern of reliance on American demand. Table 5.2 shows changes during the 1980s in the coefficient of interdependence for major countries of the Asia-Pacific region. The interdependence coefficient for

Table 5.2 Interdependence coefficients

	1981	1986
United States–Japan	1.46	1.77
United States–South Korea	0.35	0.47
United States–Malaysia	0.10	0.09
Japan–South Korea	0.73	0.78
Japan–Malaysia	0.40	0.24
South Korea–Malaysia	0.60	0.75

Note: The interdependence coefficient of country A and country B is calculated as follows:
   c = (MAB+MBA) / (GNPA+GNPB),
   where MAB: country A's imports from country B
   MBA: country B's imports from country A
   GNPA: the GNP of country A
   GNPB: the GNP of country B.

each pair of countries is derived by dividing the value of trade between the two by their combined GNP. Thus, the size of the interdependence coefficient indicates the size of bilateral trade in comparison to overall economic scale.

Though these results indicate an increase in economic interdependence in the Asia–Pacific region, they more clearly point to a rise in the region's dependence on the American economy, at least on the demand side. In contrast, there has been little apparent growth in economic interdependence between Japan and other Asian countries in the 1980s. Over the same period, economic linkage between South Korea and some ASEAN countries has also shown remarkable growth.

In the first half of the 1980s, the economies of the Asia–Pacific region achieved strong export-driven economic growth, largely due to supply-side developments, especially capital accumulation and rising technological levels in the NIEs and part of ASEAN. Viewed solely from a demand-side perspective, this growth depended almost entirely on increased exports to the United States. In 1987, 40 per cent of the American trade deficit was attributable to trade with Japan, 20 per cent to trade with NIEs, and 5 per cent to trade with ASEAN. Further, while the overall American trade deficit was declining, the bilateral trade deficit with the NIEs was still expanding. Indeed, it is seldom recognised how extensively economic development in the Asia–Pacific region has depended on the expansion of external imbalances in the United States and other industrialised countries.

The impact of a decline in American demand

This pattern of dependence on American demand for economic growth is unsustainable (Takenaka, 1989). Though the American trade deficit is declining, it is still running at a level of US$120 billion annually. Also, the United States government projects that its net foreign debt will rise above US$1 trillion within several years. In order to stabilise the world capital market, the United States must take measures to reduce its external deficits, primarily by reducing its budget deficit, increasing savings, adjusting its exchange rate and strengthening its supply side.

Our concern here is with the effects of such American policies on the

Table 5.3 Impact of changes in American and Japanese GNP (per cent)

	2 per cent decline in American GNP	2 per cent increase in Japanese GNP	c.f. 1981–86 average growth rate
United States	-2.0	+0.1	2.6
Japan	-1.0	+2.0	3.7
South Korea	-4.6	+1.0	8.3
Singapore	-3.4	+0.2	5.3
Indonesia	-1.4	+1.2	4.3
Malaysia	-4.4	+2.4	4.4
Thailand	-2.6	+0.4	4.7

Asia–Pacific region. I have used a small-scale econometric model of the global economy[1] to simulate the effects of a 2 per cent drop in American GNP on the economic growth rates of nations in the Asia–Pacific region. The results appear in Table 5.3.

In the simulation, Japan's economic growth drops by 1 per cent. This contraction, combined with a 2 per cent drop in United States GNP, has a strongly deflationary effect on other Asian nations. South Korea, which depends on the United States as the destination for 40 per cent of its exports and on Japan as a market for 11 per cent of its exports, sees its GNP plummet by 4.6 per cent. Malaysia, which sends two-thirds of its total exports to Japan, the United States and the Asian NIEs, experiences a 4.4 per cent drop in GNP. The economic consequences for the other nations of the Asia-Pacific region are equally severe.

To test the effectiveness of multilateral policy coordination, the effects of simultaneous deflation in the United States and expansion in Japan were also projected. As shown in Table 5.3, a 2 per cent rise in Japanese GNP has little impact on American economic performance, indicating an asymmetry in the relative effect of American and Japanese economic policies on each other.

A 2 per cent expansion of the Japanese economy does, however, have a substantial impact on other Asian nations. For those countries such as South Korea and Malaysia which depend rather heavily on Japan as an export market (and have rather high income elasticities for exports), economic expansion in Japan has a relatively strong positive effect.

Japan, however, cannot be expected to compensate entirely for a decline in American demand. The first, and most obvious, reason is that, despite its growth, Japan's economy is still less than two-thirds the size of the American economy. Second, Japan's economic structure is such that GNP growth is not strongly linked to an increase in imports. With its current economic structure, Japan would find it difficult to substitute for America as an export market, even if its domestic demand were to expand.

Currently, Japanese imports from the countries of the Asia–Pacific region, especially of finished goods, are rising rapidly, with products from the NIEs in particular finding strong acceptance. This import growth appears to be attributable primarily to the price effect of the upward revaluation of the yen. Though the question of how effective Japan can be as an 'absorber' of Asian exports is an important one, it must be recognised that the Japanese market can provide only a narrow base for stable economic growth in the Asia–Pacific region.

JAPAN AS AN EXPORT 'ABSORBER'

Short-term factors governing economic growth

How will Japanese domestic demand develop in the future and what implications will these changes have for the nations of the Asia–Pacific region? Several factors, among which fiscal policy and private investment in plant and equipment are frequently cited, will determine whether or not the current pattern of economic growth will remain stable in the future.

The active fiscal policy pursued by Japan since 1987 is widely viewed as expansionary in effect, but this interpretation is persuasively challenged by Noguchi (1988). Noguchi argues that the expansionary effect of increased public works spending and specific tax cuts was negated in 1987 by a large overall increase in tax revenues.

Given the current size of Japan's government budget deficit, an expansionary fiscal policy could not be supported without increasing the current tax burden on the private sector. In any case, such a fiscal expansion would have negative effects on the economy in the long run. Consequently, a real increase in domestic demand must be sought from a different source.

Due to its substantial influence on economic conditions, private investment in plant and equipment is also a key element in demand. The present expansion of both overseas and domestic investment may well contribute to a structural shift towards a domestic demand-oriented economy.

However, private investment in plant and equipment is ultimately determined by the consumption patterns of individual consumers. Without dramatic changes in the behaviour of Japanese consumers and a drop in the savings rate, investment in plant and equipment should soon enter a stock adjustment phase. Indeed, it is to be expected that a rapid rise in imports such as the current one will soon produce pressure for inventory adjustment and will exert downward pressure on private investment.

Our understanding of the economic mechanism which governs expansion of domestic demand can perhaps be deepened by borrowing the concept 'hysteresis' from the natural sciences. 'Hysteresis' refers to the tendency of the past history or treatment of a material to determine its response to a present stimulus. Baldwin (1988) has suggested that hysteresis may explain why the drastic realignment of the yen/dollar exchange rate has produced only a limited improvement in bilateral trade imbalances. Baldwin argues that when the strong dollar of the early 1980s increased the international competitiveness of Japanese products, Japanese corporations made irreversible investments; that is, increased their sunk costs, in order to expand exports. Thus when the dollar fell against the yen, dollar-denominated prices for Japanese products changed much more slowly than they historically have in response to exchange rate realignments.

To supplement this analysis of how historical levels of fixed capital affect price shifts, I propose another application of the hysteresis concept to the current economic situation. The strength of the dollar in the early 1980s reduced the return on corporate investment in the United States, pushing the capital/labour ratio down to levels much lower than it would otherwise have reached. Further, assuming that investment incorporates technological advances, this drop in the return on investment would have fed through into a decline in technological progress.

This phenomenon suggests that presence of a hysteresis effect on the supply side could explain the failure of the drop in the dollar to increase the international competitiveness of the United States products and could indicate that a much more drastic decline in the dollar would be required to revive the competitiveness of American industry.

While historical exchange rates greatly influence the level of imports and exports in Japan's Gross National Expenditure (GNE) at any given time, investment in plant and equipment is influenced by future exchange rates. Thus, foreseeing a future increase in the value of the yen, Japanese corporations are reorienting their investment towards the satisfaction of domestic consumer demand, though, as discussed below, there are grounds for some pessimism as to how stable this will be.

The point to note here is that both lagging and leading factors—namely, both past and future economic variables—have presently combined to promote GNP growth. Through a quirk of hysteresis, a complex combination of future expectations and fixed investment in plant and equipment has produced greater growth in the Japanese economy than its actual strength would seem to warrant.

The new dual-level economic structure: barrier to imports?

The degree to which the Japanese market will be able to function as an absorber of exports from the nations of the Asia–Pacific region will depend both on how fast Japanese consumer demand grows and the degree to which this added demand is directed towards goods produced by Asian countries. In more abstract terms, the scope of Japan's role as an export market will depend on the success of structural adjustment measures affecting both movements in consumption and the consumer market. Three specific points should be noted concerning the nature of this needed structural adjustment.

First, a substantial decrease in average working hours will increase leisure time intensive consumption. This shift should produce a drop in the Japanese savings rate. Early steps towards this change, such as the shift to a five-day working week, should produce a smooth transition to this new consumption pattern.

I expect an increase in leisure time to have a larger expansionary effect on consumption than is generally predicted. In Japan, the hours of operation of larger retailers are strictly limited by the Large-Scale Retail Outlet Law and by neighbourhood retailer's councils. Given the current working hours in Japan, the requirement that large retailers close at six or seven o'clock is tantamount to preventing employed Japanese from shopping at all. Therefore, shorter working hours will lead to not only increased consumption of leisure or hobby-related products but also higher volume of overall consumption.

The second factor which will determine the scope of Japan's role as an absorber market for Asian products is the non-tariff barriers (NTBs) which limit market access, as currently represented by the controversy over Japanese business practices. A durable and currently highly visible issue, NTBs are a frequent preoccupation of foreign governments and corporations and are a favourite topic in the mass media. From an economist's perspective, however, the question of whether Japanese business practices are really economically irrational deserves a highly critical appraisal.

Typical Japanese business practices, such as reducing risk by establishing long-term business relationships and diversifying client bases, are also followed by corporations in other countries. Further, many necessary changes are already occurring in response to the rapid market adjustment caused by the appreciation of the yen. A good example of such changes is provided by the consumer electrical products market. Once dominated by small stores effectively controlled by major manufacturers, this market is now being transformed. As competition intensifies and prices fall, products from the NIEs are finding greater acceptance and large discount stores are gaining a larger share of the market. Reflecting the adjustment capacity of its companies, Japan is experiencing strong market-driven change in this sector of the economy.

The final factor bearing on Japan's role as an export market is government regulation, especially as represented by import regulations. In this area, a new type of dual-level economic structure appears to be emerging. The phrase 'dual-level economic structure' of course refers to the well known bifurcation of the Japanese economy during the high-growth 1960s into a modern and a highly productive sector dominated by large corporations and a backward sector composed of smaller companies which suffered from low productivity and under-capitalisation. However, this earlier dual structure is no longer a major issue. More versatile small companies are prospering in the new economic environment created by the shift towards a service and information-based economy, rendering the term 'dual structure' almost obsolete in its older meaning.

Instead, the term is now better applied to the serious divergence between the increasingly active deregulated markets and those markets which are still subject to government regulations. This divergence is creating a deepening public sense of inequality and injustice as incomes in deregulated sectors lag those earned by persons employed in sectors, such as air transportation, which are still sheltered from price competition by government regulation.

The importance of this issue was addressed in an unusually trenchant manner by the Economic Planning Agency's 1988 *White Paper on the Economy*, which based an analysis of structural problems in the Japanese economy on an international comparison of price levels in a number of specific sectors. As most Japanese consumers would have expected, the survey showed that

Japan's overall price level was higher than those of other industrialised nations, with particularly large price differentials in heavily regulated sectors.

The *White Paper* noted that if Japan's price level were to fall to the same level as America's, consumption at current per capita levels would cost only about 70 per cent as much as it does today. Though of course not all price differentials are due purely to government regulation, it is clear that changes in Japan's social and economic systems could effectively produce a substantial increase in real income. A drastic relaxation of government regulations and a broad decline in prices would increase the prosperity of the Japanese people and enable Japan to absorb effectively exports from Asian countries. The critical missing ingredient is political leadership.

The importance of domestic economic reform in Japan

The economic growth which has occurred in the countries of the Asia–Pacific region in the 1980s represents fundamentally unbalanced development because of its dependence on an expansion of the American trade deficit. This situation bears similarities to the way in which the Korean War provided economic stimulus for Japan's postwar economic development through extraordinary demand associated with procurement in that the extraordinary demand created by the United States budget deficit has powerfully encouraged economic development in Asia.

The pressing real world question is whether the economic momentum the Asian countries have picked up can be sustained and transformed into a new and stable pattern of growth as the United States begins to reduce its external deficits. As the econometric simulations discussed earlier in this chapter indicated, this path will not be an easy one, especially in view of the extremely deflationary effect of a contraction of the United States economy. To prevent this, there is no alternative to an unprecedented and drastic reformation of Japan's domestic economy by means of substantial deregulation. If Japan does not make the policy breakthrough which is needed to ensure continued economic development in these countries, it will have failed in its responsibility as the most highly industrialised nation in Asia.

Protectionist measures antithetical to this needed reform are already being taken in Japan. In June 1989 the South Korean government announced the imposition of voluntary export restraints on shipments of knitwear products to Japan. The fact that Japan, which itself has a long history of voluntary restraint agreements with the United States covering such products as textiles, steel and automobiles, has already sought a restraint agreement from South Korea is convincing proof that the NIEs are following rapidly in Japan's footsteps.

Given Japan's reliance on an open international community, however, its hasty refusal to bear some burdens of its own casts a blot on its efforts to achieve structural economic reform. The damage which Japan's voluntary restraint agreement has caused to the long-term competitiveness of American industry and to the economic welfare of its consumers is unmistakable.

Japanese consumers must keep a wary eye on developments to prevent further proliferation of such mistaken measures as the voluntary restraint agreement with South Korea.

As the scope of external imbalances and protectionism expands in the industrialised countries, increasing expectations will be focused on the countries of the Asia–Pacific region as a source of economic vitality in the world economy. However, if there is no adequate 'absorber' or consumer for the products of these countries, they will crowd out other suppliers, creating a new source of economic imbalance and friction. Ultimately, whether the Asia–Pacific region becomes a source of economic vitality or economic friction will depend on the success of Japan's efforts to reform its domestic economy.

6 The current account and economic policy: the Australian experience in the 1980s

R. G. GREGORY

INTRODUCTION

Economic policy usually twists and turns as perceived problems change, but there has been remarkable stability and consistency over the six years of the Labour government elected in 1983. Although inevitably a simplification, the key elements of economic policy focused on two major policy instruments: moderation or real wage growth, through an Accord agreement between the Labour government and Australian Council of Trade Unions (ACTU), and reductions in government claims on national savings through tax increases and expenditure reductions. These instruments were primarily assigned to two major objectives: the Accord to employment growth (internal balance) and reductions in the government deficit to an improvement in the current account of the balance of payments (external balance).[1]

The government's ability to control these instruments has been extraordinary. The Accord has remained intact and real wages have been reduced 3 to 5 per cent during 1983–89. The net Public Sector Borrowing Requirement (PSBR) has changed over the six years from a deficit of 6.7 per cent of GDP to a surplus of 1 per cent, the largest turnaround in the OECD area.

The effects of the policy instruments, however, have been mixed. The Accord–employment link has been a great success and will not be discussed in any depth (see Chapman, Dowrick and Junankar, 1989; Chapman and Gruen, 1990). The anticipated PSBR–current account link has not eventuated, however, and an analysis of this failure is the main concern of this chapter. Over the last eight years current account deficits have been larger than normal and accompanied by an increase in the overseas debt to GDP ratio from 6.2 per cent in 1981/82 to 31.7 per cent in 1986/87. After a pause the debt ratio began to increase again, and depending on exchange rate outcomes, it may be as high as 40 per cent in the early 1990s. Among OECD countries Australia's debt service/GDP ratio is exceeded only by that of New Zealand, and no OECD country is accumulating debt as fast.

Not everyone believes that current account deficits, and high and increasing levels of overseas debt, necessarily matter (Pitchford, 1989), but there is no doubt that the balance of payments is presenting a serious policy dilemma

(Reserve Bank of Australia, 1989) and is being treated as a matter of concern among financial commentators. On 28 August 1989 Moody's Investment Service downgraded the ratings of Australian long-term debt from Aa1 to Aa2. In late October 1989 Standard and Poors also downgraded Australia's long-term credit rating from AA+ to AA.

In this discussion of the PSBR–current account link, an attempt is made to bring together two strands of analysis that are usually kept apart: macro analysis of the current account as the outcome of savings and investment decisions, and micro analysis which suggests that important considerations are the special characteristics of our trade structure and the changing environment faced by import-competing and export sectors. The key question can be posed as follows: does recent experience suggest that in the medium term it is more productive to think of current account outcomes predominantly in terms of structural shocks to import-competing and export sectors (a micro analysis), or is it better to analyse current account outcomes in terms of government and private sector savings and investment decisions (a macro analysis)?

The next section outlines a simple model of internal–external balance to help organise the discussion, while the section after that briefly discusses links between policy instruments and objectives. The final section arranges the data to support the analysis of current account changes, from which the following interesting facts and conjectures emerge:

- over the past five years there appears to be no relationship between changes in the net PSBR and reductions in the current account deficit, mutatis mutandis. Changes in the PSBR are closely correlated with changes in the statistical discrepancy;
- there is a close relationship between changes in the current account deficit and private sector savings and investment;
- recent real exchange rate history does not suggest that the current exchange rate will lead to a sustainable reduction in the current account deficit. There seems to be little relationship between real exchange rate changes and account deficits, or between real exchange rate changes and relative profitability of the traded goods sector; and
- although the dominant academic view is that domestic savings and investment drive the current account, there seems to be some evidence to suggest that there is a significant causation flow in the other direction and that current account outcomes are contributing significantly to changes in household savings.

A SIMPLE MODEL OF THE BALANCE OF PAYMENTS

There are many possible models within which to analyse balance of payments outcomes. For our purposes, perhaps the simplest and most productive is that of Swan–Salter. Salter (1959) assumes three goods, two traded and one non-traded, and exogenous terms of trade (the small country assumption) so that exports and imports can be aggregated. There is a transformation curve link-

THE CURRENT ACCOUNT AND ECONOMIC POLICY 73

ing production possibilities of traded and non-traded goods and an indifference map indicating consumption preferences of domestic consumers. Figure 6.1a shows an economy at point A in long-run equilibrium. The price ratio between traded and non-traded goods (the slope of 11), and the expenditure level (the position of 11), place 11 so that it is tangential to the transformation and indifference curves. Production and consumption of both goods are equal; there is balance of payments equilibrium and no net capital transfers.

The economy could be represented by two points, such as A and B as in Figure 6.1b and be in equilibrium with net capital transfers. In these circumstances, there is full employment—the economy is on the transformation curve at A—but domestic expenditure is greater than production. At this level and pattern of expenditure, non-traded goods production is equal to demand—B is directly above A. Traded good production, however, is less than demand and there is a current account deficit equal to AB. As domestic expenditure exceeds production, the community is spending more than it produces and consequently domestic savings is less than investment. The current account deficit AB measures the shortfall between domestic savings and investment. Domestic savings are being supplemented by borrowing abroad. To achieve current account balance, a necessary condition is that domestic savings and investment be equal and expenditure and production lines should lie on top of each other.

The diagram can also be used to represent a situation where resources are not fully utilised. If B and C were not directly above and below point A, there would be either excess demand or supply of non-traded goods and the economy would not be in internal balance. For example, if the tangency point B were above and to the left of A, then demand for non-traded goods would be less than supply. To achieve full employment equilibrium, the price of non-traded goods would need to decrease relative to traded goods (the slope of the expenditure and production lines would need to be flatter). In response, the production point A would move to the left, and the consumption point B to the right until B was directly above A. The price ratio between traded and non-traded goods is referred to as the real exchange rate.

Over the early years of Labour government, production was thought to be at a point similar to D in Figure 6.1c. There were unemployed resources in both sectors. At prevailing relative prices and expenditure levels domestic consumers chose to be at E. Expenditure exceeded production and the current account deficit could be measured as DE. It was commonly believed that resources were unutilised because real wages were too high and the profit share too low.

The policy response was thought to require at least two steps. First, policies would be needed to increase production and employment. The production line, labelled as 11 in Figure 6.1c, should be shifted outwards to be tangential to the transformation curve so that resources were fully utilised. Any production increase, however, would be associated with domestic expenditure increases and it was generally believed, at prevailing relative prices, that the marginal expenditure–production relationship would involve an unacceptable change in

Figures 6.1a, 6.1b, 6.1c Traded and non-traded goods production

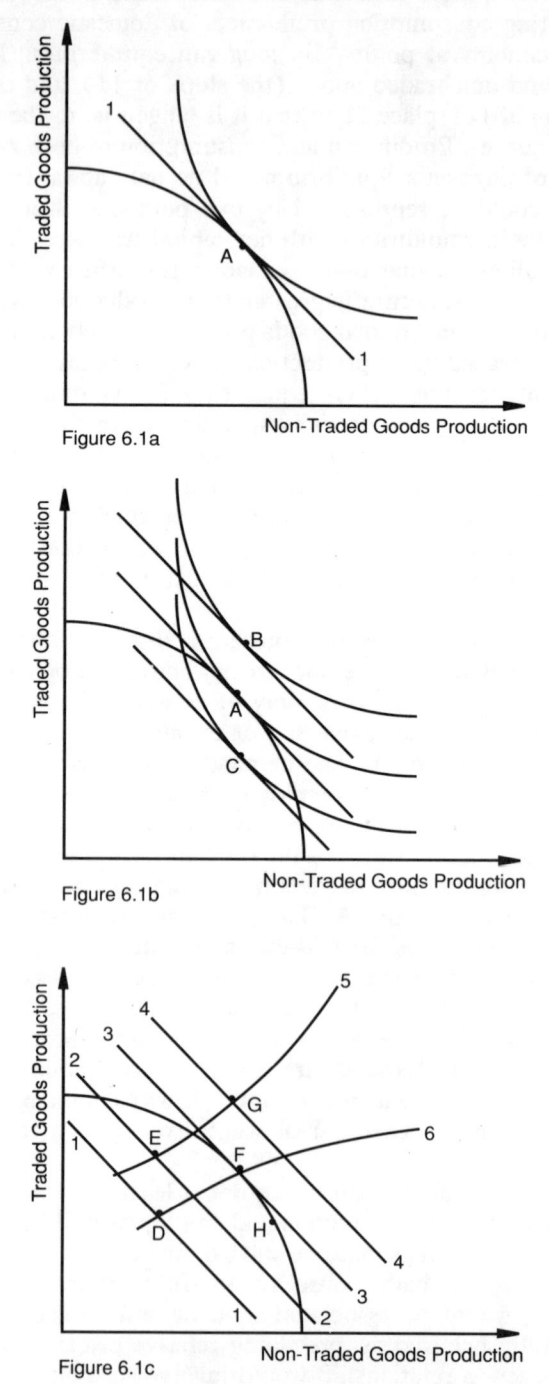

Figure 6.1a

Figure 6.1b

Figure 6.1c

Sources: Reserve Bank of Australia, *Occasional Papers*, 'Australian Economic Statistics 1949–50 to 1986–87', by W.E. Norton and C.P. Aylmer; *Average Weekly Earnings*, States and Australia, ABS Cat. No. 6302.0; *Consumer Price Index*, ABS Cat. No. 6401.1

the current account deficit as the economy moved outwards along the paths labeled 5 and 6 (consumption following path 5 and production tracing path 6). Prevailing price relativities and full employment would imply production at point F, on the production line 3, but, to generate consumption patterns consistent with full employment, the expenditure pattern and level would need to be represented by point G on line 4. The current account deficit would worsen, as the new gap between production and expenditure, FG, exceeds DE.

The second policy step therefore was to change relative prices to encourage production and discourage consumption of traded goods so that the expansion paths 5 and 6 would be drawn together in order to enable the economy to move towards a point such as H, which would be compatible with full employment and current account balance. To achieve two objectives—internal and external balance—the position and slope of the expenditure and production lines would need to be changed.

The policy instrument to achieve production increases (the first step) was the Accord, which provided for wage decisions to be centralised in the Commonwealth Arbitration Commission (now the Industrial Relations Commission). The government and trade union leadership believed they could control and moderate wage outcomes better within the official regulatory system than under the system of partial centralisation that had occurred during 1973–75 and 1979–81 when nominal and real wages increased quickly. The Accord was to restrain inflation and allow faster economic growth without wage breakouts and the contractionary fiscal and monetary policy response that had occurred in the past (Gregory, 1986). It was also to reduce real wages, or at least moderate their growth, so that the profit share could be increased, leading to increased investment, production and employment. In return for wage moderation the ACTU would be consulted on a range of economic policy issues.

The policy instrument to change relative prices and decrease the current account deficit (the second step) was the reduction in government borrowing requirements which would reduce demands on national savings and thus reduce interest rates. The increased government savings would bring the production and expenditure lines close together. The lower interest rates would make the Australian dollar less attractive and lead to exchange rate devaluations, thereby changing relative prices to encourage production and discourage consumption of traded goods. The change in the PSBR would increase savings, alter relative prices, and thus alter the marginal expenditure-production relationship so that as the economy expanded in response to the Accord the current account could improve by increasing production more than expenditure. The expansion paths 5 and 6 in Figure 6.1c would be drawn together.

This model is a static and not fully articulated representation of the economy, and when analysing the actual adjustment we need to be conscious of two influences not yet mentioned. First, there will be lags in the private sector response to policy. For example, if consumption and production decisions are slow to respond to relative price changes but investment in the non-traded goods sector responds quickly to real wage moderation, then the Accord arm of policy, leading to economic growth, may be more successful more quickly than

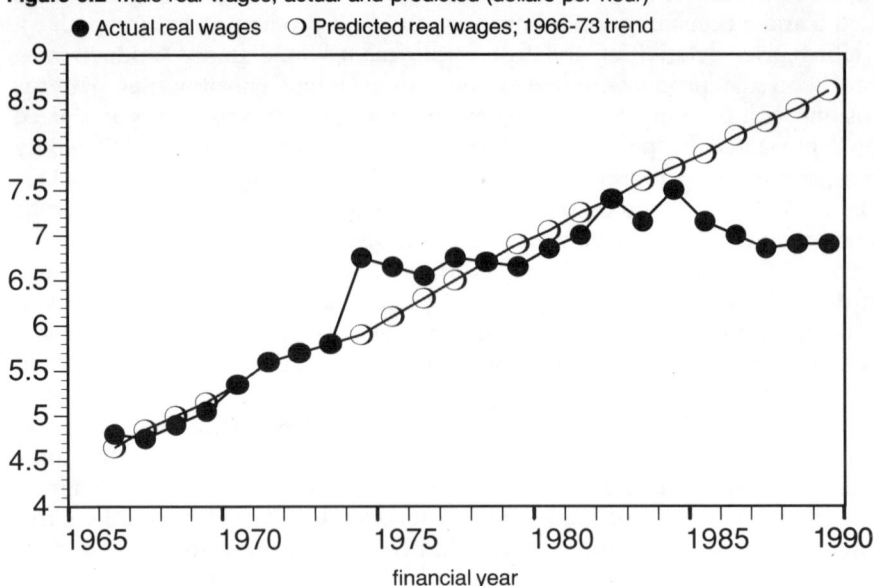

Figure 6.2 Male real wages, actual and predicted (dollars per hour)

● Actual real wages   ○ Predicted real wages; 1966-73 trend

financial year

Sources: Reserve Bank of Australia, *Occasional Papers* No. 8A, 'Australian Economic Statistics 1949-50 to 1986-87', by W.E. Norton and C.P. Aylmer; *Average Weekly Earnings, States and Australia*, ABS Cat. No. 6302.0; *Consumer Price Index*, ABS Cat. No. 6401.1.

the current account–PSBR arm. Indeed, the very success of the Accord may initially increase the current account deficit as investment goods are imported. Second, the position and slope of expenditure and production lines are not fully under the authorities' control. For example, if for exogenous reasons foreign desire to invest in Australia were to increase over the adjustment path the gap between production and expenditure would widen, increase the current account deficit, and thus work to prevent the devaluation needed to reduce the current account deficit.

THE 1983-89 ADJUSTMENTS

The Accord and economic growth

The Accord led to reduced real wages, unprecedented over the last forty years. Real wages are currently somewhere around 20 to 30 per cent below levels projected on the basis of fifties and sixties experience and despite rapid employment growth over the last few years have not increased relative to 1983 levels (Figure 6.2). The moderation of real wage growth has increased the profit share, which for 1988/89 was the highest for at least three decades (Figure 6.3). If the new factor shares are maintained, they should have fundamental effects on investment and growth.

Since 1982-83 the average annual growth rate of GDP, 3.6 per cent, has been 60 per cent greater than the previous decade. The employment increase has been even more spectacular, averaging 2.8 per cent annually, and is the

THE CURRENT ACCOUNT AND ECONOMIC POLICY   77

Figure 6.3 Ratio of corporate gross operating surplus (GOS) to GDP (per cent)

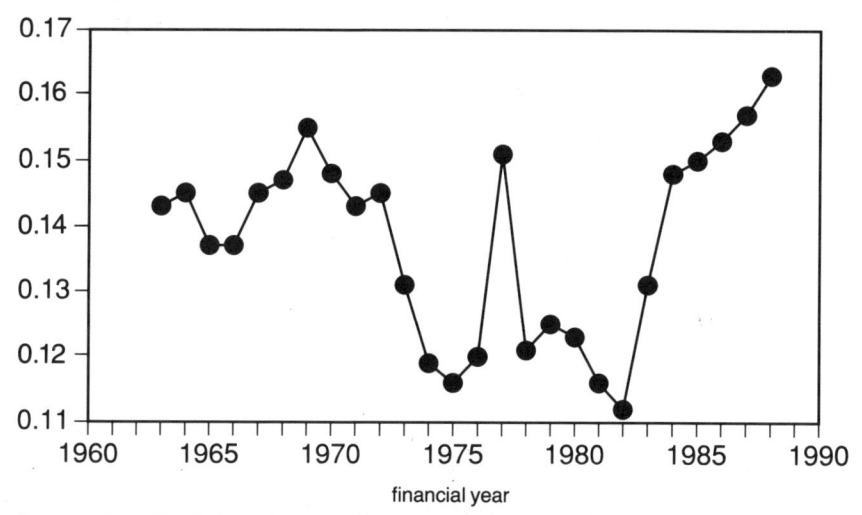

Sources: Australian National Accounts, National Income and Expenditure 1987–88, ABS Cat. No. 5204.0; Australian National Accounts, National Income and Expenditure, June quarter, 1989, ABS Cat. No. 5206.0.

highest in the OECD area, although primarily focused on part-time and female employment. Investment has been slow to respond to the increased profit share, but for 1989/90 private investment was at its highest level for at least three decades. Production has moved closer to the transformation surface. The links between real wages, profits and employment growth seem to have worked in the way suggested by proponents of the Accord.

There has been one disappointment. As a result of the emphasis on almost full cost-of-living adjustments, nominal wage increases have been only marginally below the average of the previous decade. However, model simulations suggest that the Accord has given lower nominal wage outcomes in the economic environment of the late 1980s than those predicted on the assumption of no Accord (Chapman and Gruen, 1989).

Fiscal policy and the current account

The government has also been extraordinarily successful at achieving its fiscal objectives. The Commonwealth fiscal outcome has been transformed from a deficit of 4.1 per cent of GDP for 1983/84 to a projected surplus of 2.5 per cent for 1989/90, the largest fiscal turnaround in the OECD area. For the total government sector, including trading enterprises, the net PSBR has fallen from a deficit of 6.7 per cent of GDP to a projected surplus of 1.0 per cent.

As the economy began to recover from the 1982–83 recession the current account deficit widened from 4 to 6 per cent of GDP (Figure 6.4). Then, following upon a 15 per cent deterioration of the terms of trade, the exchange rate devalued in real terms by approximately 30 per cent during 1985 and

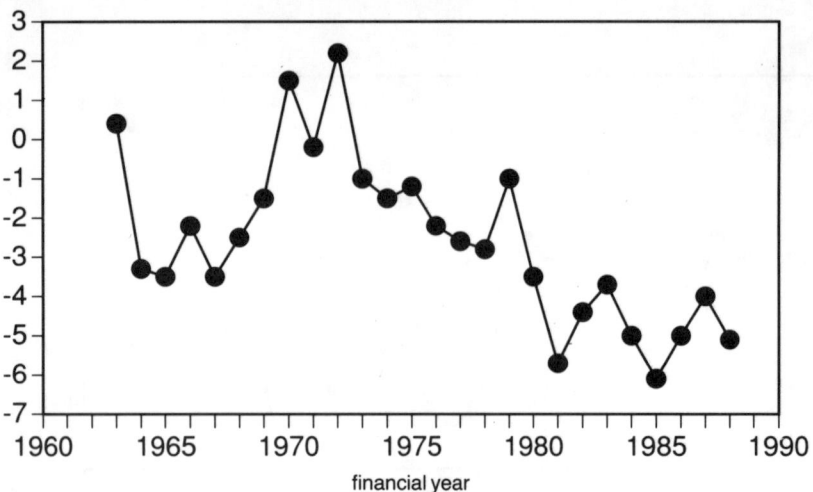

Figure 6.4 Ratio of net lending overseas to GDP (per cent)

financial year

Source: DX Data Base.

1986, changed relative prices, increased profitability of traded goods production and established the precondition for a reduction in the current account deficit. Over the next two years the current account deficit narrowed by 2 percentage points of GDP, responding to expenditure restraint generated by tight monetary policy, the rundown of export stocks and perhaps devaluation effects. In the 1988/89 budget, the Treasury forecast a further 1 percentage point improvement over the next year. After the event, the forecast was in error by 3 percentage points as the current account deteriorated to 6 per cent of GDP. What went wrong?

There were two common responses to this question. The first emphasised short-run considerations and did not question the broad policy stance. It began by pointing out that in 1988 economic forecasters were too pessimistic as to world economic growth and Australian terms of trade and within Australia they misjudged the surprisingly weak effect of tighter fiscal and monetary policy. There was a strong private sector investment boom, not matched by an increase in private savings, and by definition the current account deteriorated. The suggested solution was to reign back expenditure growth. The second response focused on longer-run structural issues that are hindering import replacement and manufactured exports and began to question the underlying rationale of current policy by arguing for more direct intervention into the traded goods sector. It is this response that is assessed in the next section.

THE CURRENT ACCOUNT: SOME ISSUES TO BE RESOLVED

It is always true, as illustrated by the Swan–Salter model, that a current account deficit implies excess demand for traded goods. Consequently, the change in the current account could be thought of as being *primarily* determined by changes in demand and supply conditions for exports and imports. Since the current account must be equal to the capital account, but of opposite sign, it could be that capital inflows or outflows are essentially passive and accommodate demand and supply changes for traded goods. The mechanism would operate as follows. When there is excess demand for traded goods in Australia, and pressure for a current account deficit, the exchange rate would devalue and foreign capital inflows would be attracted by higher interest rates and lower asset prices measured in foreign currency.

An alternative viewpoint is that current account changes could be primarily determined by capital flows to which demand and supply of traded goods adjust. For example, large exogenous foreign capital inflows lead to exchange rate appreciations and falls in traded goods prices so that production is discouraged and consumption encouraged.

Whichever mechanism is driving the current account, the demand and supply of traded goods and international capital flows are inextricably linked[2] but the relative importance placed on each view affects interpretation of recent history and the desirability of particular policy responses. If the current account is determined predominantly by structural factors, relating to demand and supply of traded goods, then measures to influence international capital flows are indirect policy instruments unlikely to change the current account quickly. Policies directed towards the structural problems may be more effective. Conversely, if the current account is determined predominantly by capital flows then trade policy interventions affecting particular export or import competing industries to influence the current account are unlikely to be effective (Forsyth, 1989).

The next few pages adopt a fairly ad hoc approach to investigate more closely the factors underlying the current account deficit. Discussion begins by emphasising the capital account and then returns to an analysis more in the spirit of the Swan-Salter model with its focus on traded goods production and consumption.

The current account and government borrowing requirements

The assignment of the government deficit to the current account is based on the belief that capital flows are the fundamental influence on the current account. This link is usually discussed in terms of the well known accounting identity:

(1) $(T-G)+(S-I)=(X-M)$

where the variables are government revenue (T), government expenditure (G), private savings (S), private investment (I), exports (X) and imports (M). The first and second terms on the left-hand side are government and private net savings respectively. If total domestic net savings are negative, the current account will be in deficit and Australia will be borrowing overseas, either in the form of equity or debt. The identity makes clear that net international capital flows $(X-M)$ are equal to the imbalance of domestic savings and investment. Consequently, the discussion as to whether international capital flows are the driving or passive force involved in balance of payments adjustments has as its counterpart a similar discussion with respect to domestic savings and investment.

Although economic commentators are well aware that (1) is an identity, and does not imply any direct causal links between variables, it has become an increasingly common framework within which to discuss policy (Pitchford, 1989; Harper and Lim, 1989). For example, it has been argued by the Treasury that if government could reduce its demands on national savings, (T-G), there would be less need to draw savings from overseas and the trade account (X-M) should improve. The implicit working rule they seem to have adopted is a significant association between increases in government net savings and reductions in the current account deficit; private sector investment and savings being largely unaffected by the government deficit change. This is the well known twin deficits hypothesis whereby government deficits create current account deficits. Of course, changes in government and private sector net savings could offset each other and the current account remain unaffected by government actions. This is the spirit of Barro (1974), who stresses substitution possibilities between government and private sector spending and savings. Other possibilities also exist. Additional government net savings could affect expectations and increase private investment sufficiently for the current account to move further into deficit.[3]

The basic data underlying (1) for 1975/76 to 1988/89 are presented in the next few figures, measured in current prices and expressed as a proportion of GDP. There are two adjustments to (1) that need to be noted. Net government savings have been defined to exclude public trading enterprises, which for reasons of national accounts data classification have been grouped with the private sector. In addition, the statistical discrepancy has been included as an additional independent term.[4]

Figure 6.5 compares government net savings, (T-G), with net overseas borrowings, (X-M). Despite large changes since 1983/84, there is no obvious evidence that increases in government net savings reduce current account deficits (mutatis mutandis). The widening of the current account deficit, evident over 1979–81, is not accounted for by a reduction in government net savings and after 1981/82 there is no clear relationship between the series. Figure 6.6 compares private net savings, (S-I), with net overseas borrowings, (X-M). The 1979–81 deterioration in the current account was associated with a large decrease in private net savings (predominantly the mining investment boom) and, in general, there is a close relationship between the two series. Figure 6.7 compares government and private sector net savings, and there is some evidence of an inverse relationship but it has not been close over the last five years.

Data after 1983/84 present an obvious puzzle. Despite identity (1) the increase in government net savings seems neither to have reduced the current account deficit (Figure 6.5) nor been offset by changes in private sector net savings (Figure 6.7). The Labour government demands on national savings

THE CURRENT ACCOUNT AND ECONOMIC POLICY 81

Figure 6.5 Ratios of government net savings and net overseas lending to GDP (per cent)

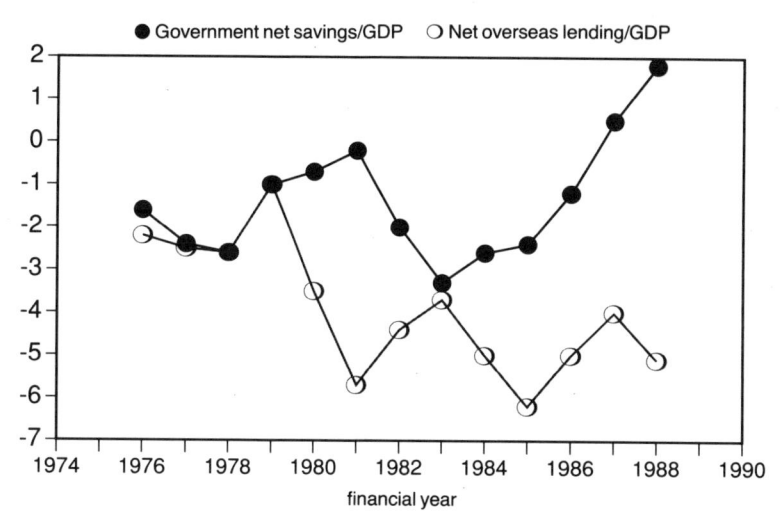

● Government net savings/GDP ○ Net overseas lending/GDP

Sources: Australian National Accounts, National Income and Expenditure 1987–88, ABS Cat. No. 5204.0; *Australian National Accounts, National Income and Expenditure*, June quarter, 1989, ABS Cat. No. 5206.0.

have been reduced by 5 percentage points, the private sector demands increased by 3 percentage points, and the current account, instead of improving by 2, deteriorated by 1.5 percentage points.[5] There is a missing 3.5 percentage points, equal to two-thirds of the current account deficit.

Figure 6.6 Ratios of private net savings and net overseas lending to GDP (per cent)

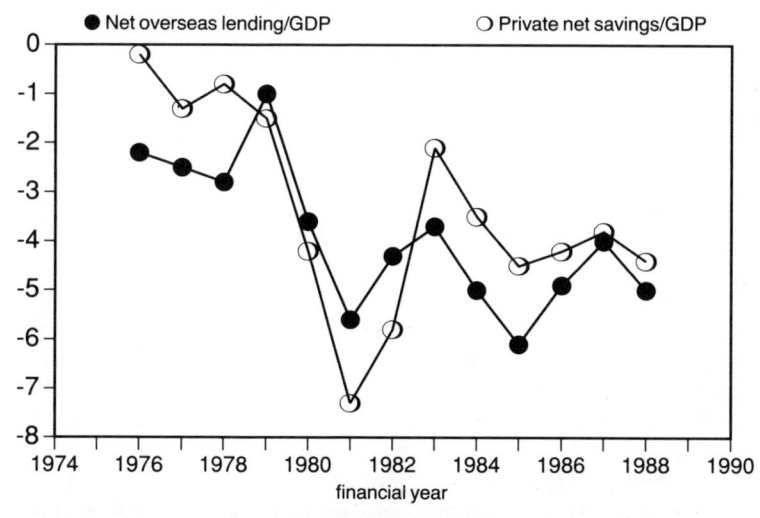

● Net overseas lending/GDP ○ Private net savings/GDP

Sources: Australian National Accounts, National Income and Expenditure 1987–88, ABS Cat. No. 5204.0; *Australian National Accounts, National Income and Expenditure*, June quarter, 1989, ABS Cat. No. 5206.0.

Figure 6.7 Ratios of government and private sector net savings to GDP (per cent)

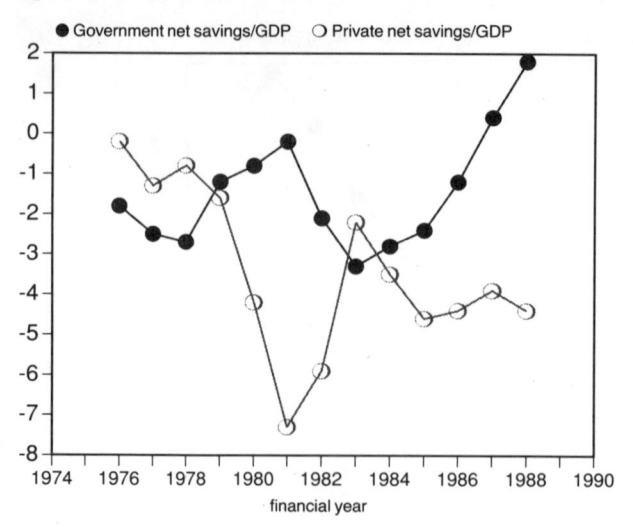

● Government net savings/GDP   ○ Private net savings/GDP

Sources: Australian National Accounts, National Income and Expenditure 1987–88, ABS Cat. No. 5204.0; Australian National Accounts, National Income and Expenditure, June quarter, 1989, ABS Cat. No. 5206.0.

The solution to the puzzle is evident in Figure 6.8, which indicates that since 1983/84 virtually all the reduction in government demands on national savings have been associated with changes in the statistical discrepancy. Contrary to the Treasury hypothesis, there has not been a close association between current account and government net saving outcomes unless all the statistical discrepancy is of private domestic origin. If so, and we allocate the statistical discrepancy to private sector savings, then virtually all government net savings changes have been offset by private net savings changes (Figure 6.9). This implies the opposite working rule to that adopted by the Treasury. Government and current account deficits are not closely related. Government and private sector net savings have been linked together so that changes in one have been offset by changes in the other.

Why are private and government net savings so closely and inversely related? Perhaps in the short run the current account is largely exogenous.[6] If, as suggested earlier, production and consumption of traded goods were slow to respond to government savings, or primarily determined by other variables, then, because of identity (1), government and private sector net savings would necessarily be offsetting. Other possible answers turn on links between PSBR changes and relative prices. These include: one, the reductions in the PSBR did not lead to sufficient relative price changes between traded and non-traded goods; two, relative prices changed as expected, but producers and consumers did not respond; or three, relative prices changed, producers and consumers responded, but there were other exogenous factors bearing upon the current account, such as world demand for exports and terms of trade changes, which offset the expected responses. These issues are discussed in the next section.

THE CURRENT ACCOUNT AND ECONOMIC POLICY 83

Figure 6.8 Ratios of government net savings and the statistical discrepancy to GDP (per cent)

Sources: Australian National Accounts, National Income and Expenditure 1987–88, ABS Cat. No. 5204.0; *Australian National Accounts, National Income and Expenditure*, June quarter, 1989, ABS Cat. No. 5206.0.

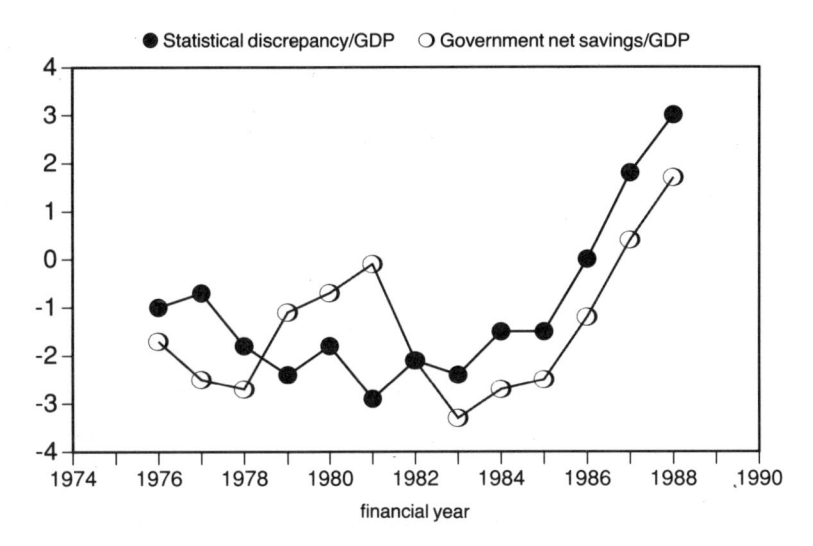

Figure 6.9 Ratios of government and private net savings (including statistical discrepancy) to GDP (per cent)

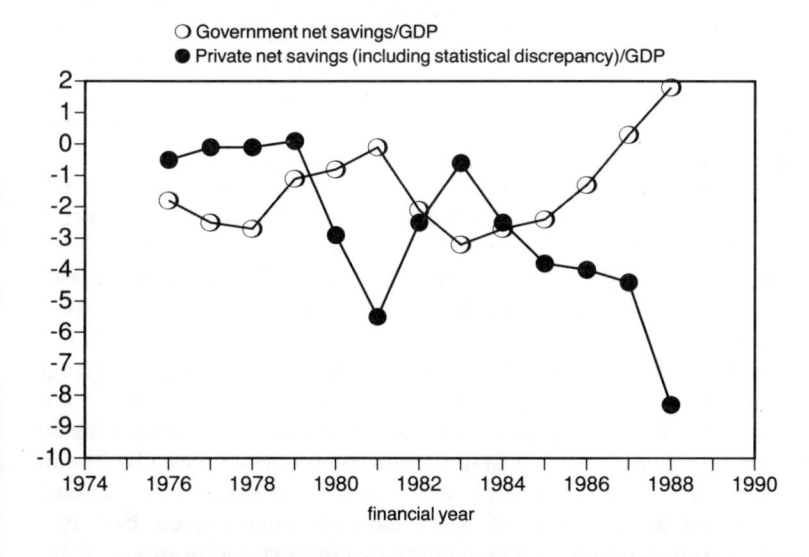

Sources: Australian National Accounts, National Income and Expenditure 1987–88, ABS Cat. No. 5204.0; *Australian National Accounts, National Income and Expenditure*, June quarter, 1989, ABS Cat. No. 5206.0.

Figure 6.10 Competitiveness index (1984/85 = 100)

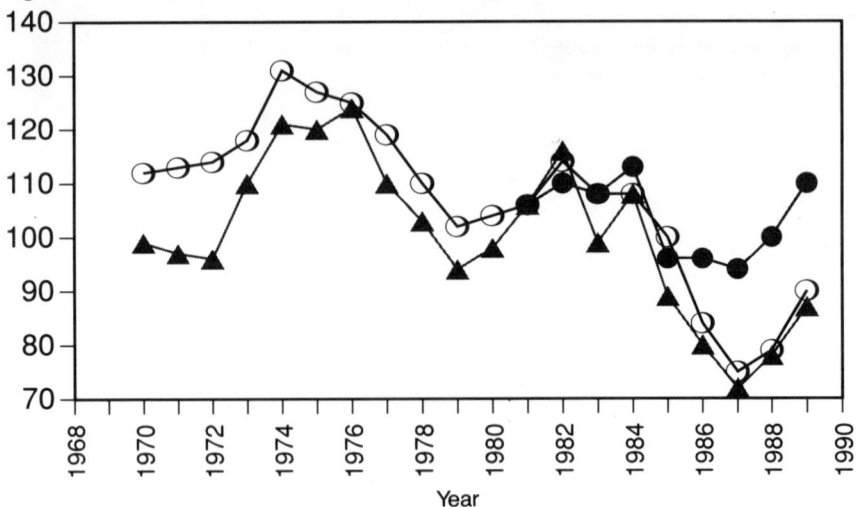

Key: ① Ratio of manufacturing to import prices adjusted for exchange rare changes (data supplied by the Bureau of Industry Economics).
▲ Unit labour costs adjusted for exchange rate changes.
○ CPI adjusted for exchange rate changes.

Source: *Economic Roundup*, The Treasury, AGPS, Canberra.

The demand and supply of traded goods

Relative prices

To what extent have relative prices and profitability changed in response to PSBR reductions? If relative prices are unchanged the current account cannot be improved except by reduced economic activity in all sectors of the economy. It is usual to approximate the ratio to non-traded goods prices by competitiveness indexes which compare Australian cost and price conditions with overseas countries. Figure 6.10 presents three measures.

Since the 1982/83 recession, consumer price inflation in Australia has not moderated as much as in our competitors, and if exchange rates are adjusted for these price indexes (series A) there were substantial real devaluations during 1985 and 1986, approximately equal to the nominal exchange rate changes at the time. The real devaluations have gradually dissipated, however, and the competitiveness index is almost back to early 1970 levels. About a third of the loss of competitiveness has arisen because the nominal exchange rate has appreciated over 1989, despite foreign debt accumulation. Some commentators, such as the Treasury, prefer to adjust the nominal exchange rate for changes in relative unit labour costs; that is, nominal wages adjusted by labour productivity (series B). This series also indicates large real devaluations and, although being eroded, about half of the gains have been maintained. Finally, a partial measure of competitiveness which compares import and domestic manufacturing prices also suggests that there were significant real devaluations which have been completely eroded (series C).

This history presents us with a number of important considerations. First, there is no obvious link between PSBR changes and exchange rates; the reduction in the PSBR has been fairly smooth and continuous since 1983/84 and yet the change in the real and nominal exchange rate has been erratic, devaluing in 1985 and 1986, before half of the adjustment in the PSBR had been completed, and appreciating since.

Second, there is no obvious relationship running from the current account deficit to the real exchange rate. What is to be made of the 1989 appreciations of nominal and real exchange rates? (Gruen and Smith, 1989).

Third, if the exchange rate is devalued, can the improvement in competitiveness be maintained. Recent experience suggests that for a 20 per cent devaluation the economy gains a 3-4 years improvement in competitiveness, but at the price of a 4-5 per cent greater rate of inflation (Figure 6.10). Some economists have argued that sustained real devaluations required even further real wage reductions. If so, there seem to be significant problems for Australian economic management, as it is very difficult to imagine that more could have been done to contain real wages over the period of the Accord.

There are two ideas being discussed which might improve our ability to maintain a real devaluation. The first is labour market deregulation. It is argued that wage bargaining should move to the enterprise level and away from nationwide determinations. The procedure would be to change from predominantly craft to enterprise unions. This is not a radical idea as many enterprise wage agreements now exist. In addition, the national union leadership publicly supports the change and is already arguing for union amalgamations and more local bargaining. In practice, however, the union leadership has sought centralised control of the wage process under the Accord. Short-term actions therefore conflict with rhetoric which seems directed to longer run issues. It seems unlikely, however, that a move towards a deregulated system focused on the enterprise will deliver substantial real wage reductions when the exchange rate devalues. The United Kingdom's experience over 1983-89 suggests that real wages are not more responsive to economic conditions when labour market deregulation is attempted.

The second suggestion relates to the monetary and fiscal mix. Over the last few years nominal and real interest rates in Australia have exceeded OECD averages by a wide margin, particularly at the short end of the market, and it must be true that a significant part of the real exchange rate appreciations of 1988 and 1989 was generated by tight monetary policy. This line of argument would suggest that not enough was done to use fiscal policy to reduce demand. There is a serious policy problem here. The political realities of the late 1980s seemed to be that taxes could not be increased to depress demand. Furthermore, Commonwealth government expenditure had already fallen from 30.0 to 24.5 per cent of GDP and serious economic and political decisions would have been involved in further expenditure reductions.

Figure 6.11a Ratio of gross operating surplus (GOS) to wage bill index, farm and non-traded goods sector (1962/63 = 1)

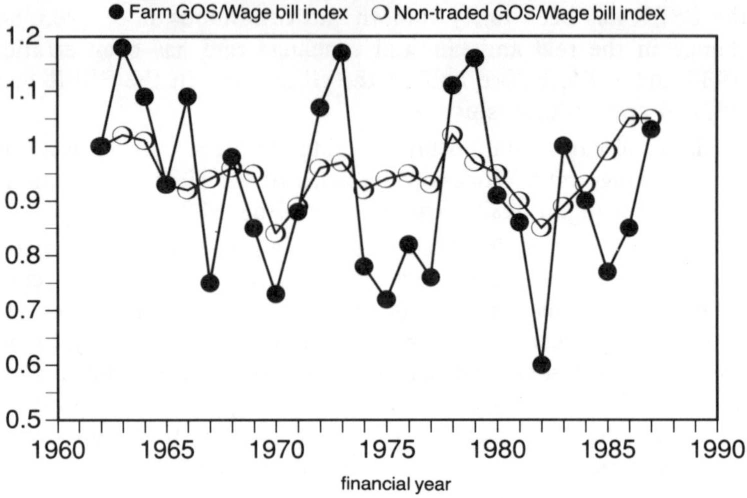

● Farm GOS/Wage bill index   ○ Non-traded GOS/Wage bill index

Sources: *Australian National Accounts, National Income and Expenditure 1987–88*, ABS Cat. No. 5204.0; *Australian National Accounts, National Income and Expenditure*, June quarter, 1989, ABS Cat. No. 5206.0.

Relative profitability

Perhaps, changes in relative profitability of sectors suggest a different prognosis for resource shifts than the real exchange rate history. In the non-traded sector (GDP less mining, agriculture and manufacturing) our profitability index (the ratio of gross operating surplus to wages) has been relatively stable, varying between 85 and 105 per cent (Figure 6.11a). The 1970/71 and 1981/82 recessions are evident in profit dips, but the sector appears to have maintained profitability during the eight years of low growth after 1974/75. Since the Accord there has been a rapid increase in profitability, which is now at its highest level for twenty-five years.

The two main components of the export sector have behaved differently. For agriculture, there is no trend but for mining there is a large lift in profitability at the end of the 1960s, indicating the beginning of the mining boom; there is a marked downturn during the 1981/82 recession but a quick recovery.

The profitability pattern for manufacturing is particularly interesting (Figure 6.11b). After declining gently during the 1960s the profitability index suddenly falls to 60 per cent in 1974/75 and remains around this level for nine years. Since the Accord the increase in profitability is quite exceptional, almost doubling in eight years.

Despite the strong tradition in Australia to discuss incentives for resource shifts between traded and non-traded goods sectors in terms of real exchange rates changes, the relative profitability of sectors appears to bear little relationship to real exchange rate variations. Export sector profitability and real exchange rates are not closely related, but this might be expected since

Figure 6.11b Ratio of gross operating surplus (GOS) to wage bill index, manufactured and non-traded goods sector (1962/63 = 1)

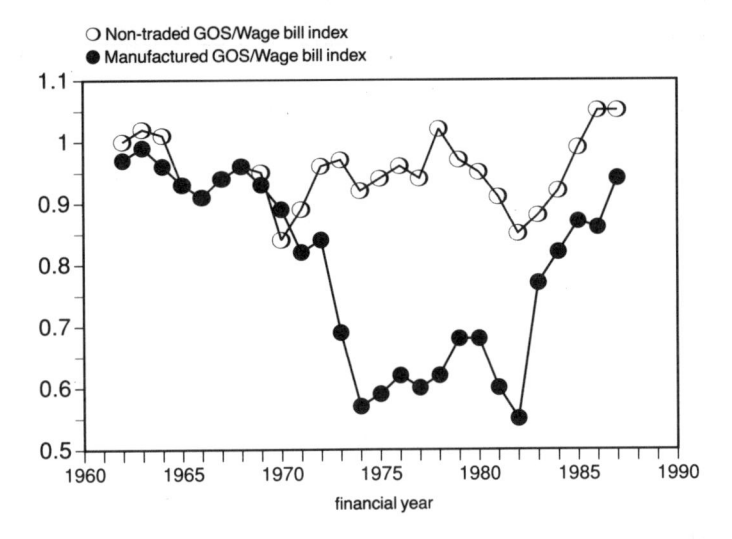

Sources: Australian National Accounts, National Income and Expenditure 1987–88, ABS Cat. No. 5204.0; *Australian National Accounts, National Income and Expenditure*, June quarter, 1989, ABS Cat. No. 5206.0.

exchange rate movements are positively correlated with export price changes (Figure 6.11c). More surprising is the lack of association between manufacturing profitability and the real exchange rate. It is worth pausing on this profitability–exchange rate puzzle for a moment.

The indexes suggest that the large differences in profitability behaviour between manufacturing and the non-traded goods sector are confined to three specific years—1972/73, 1973/74 and 1983/84. The first period, 1972–74, during which there was a substantial loss of manufacturing profitability, coincided with large real wage increases, an appreciating exchange rate and tariff reductions. The data therefore are consistent with traditional views that link manufacturing profitability to real exchange rate changes. It is the second period that is puzzling. Manufacturing profitability increased relative to the non-traded goods sector before the devaluation of the real exchange rate in 1985 and 1986, but when the real exchange rate devalued there is no further marked improvement (Figure 6.11b). Where does this leave the traditional analysis, with its emphasis on the real exchange rate changes and resource shifts? There are a number of conjectures that could be explored. The most promising would seem to be: one, have import quotas for footwear, clothing, textiles and motor vehicles changed the relationship between exchange rate changes and profitability for the manufacturing sector in aggregate?; two, have imported inputs increased in importance and reduced the protective effects of devaluations?; and three, has the structure of the manufacturing sector changed so that it is now less sensitive to import competition?

Figure 6.11c Ratio of gross operating surplus (GOS) to wage bill index, export and non-traded goods sector (1962/63 = 1)

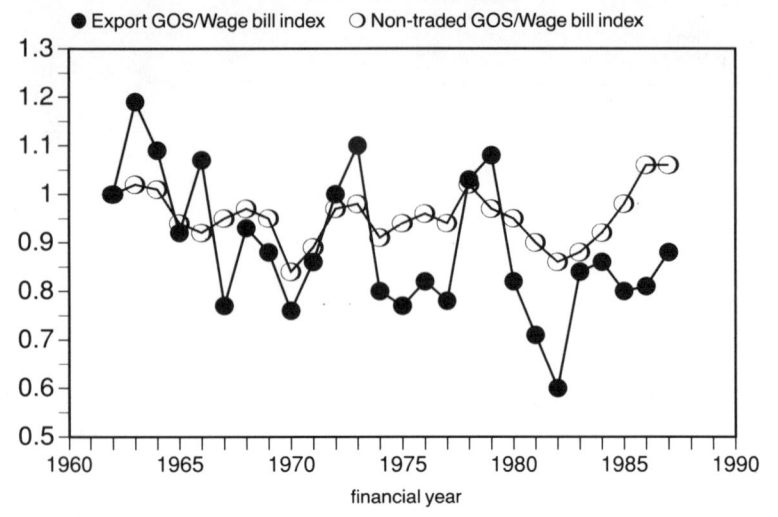

● Export GOS/Wage bill index   ○ Non-traded GOS/Wage bill index

Sources: Australian National Accounts, National Income and Expenditure 1987–88, ABS Cat. No. 5204.0; Australian National Accounts, National Income and Expenditure, June quarter, 1989, ABS Cat. No. 5206.0.

To conclude, the resource responses to changing profitability will receive some brief attention. To measure export production responses, exports are expressed as a ratio of GDP in current and constant prices (Figure 6.12). The importance of export prices is immediately apparent. The Australian economy seems to have experienced little difficulty in increasing export volumes as a share of GDP by about 50 per cent over the last two and a half decades, but in current value terms the export ratio has not significantly changed, whereas for the rest of the OECD export shares have been increasing. Against the long-term trend the export response to the large devaluations of 1985 and 1986 must be judged disappointing.

Figure 6.13 plots indexes for manufacturing value added and imports as a share of GDP. The response to changed profitability is very clear. Since the early 1970s the manufacturing share of GDP, measured in current prices, has steadily fallen to 65 per cent of its earlier level. Over the same period imports have increased as a ratio of GDP by about 20 per cent. Before the mid-1970s, the import and production series tended to move together but, at the time profitability fell, the import penetration ratio began to increase fairly steadily along with the growth of world trade while domestic manufacturing production stagnated. There was until 1989 no clear response of manufacturing output to the devaluations of 1985 and 1986 or to the increased profitability, although perhaps the rate of increase of imports has slowed. It is obvious that much of the current account deficit is related to the rapid decline in the manufacturing sector, but should this be attributed to structural factors and savings and investment behaviour?

THE CURRENT ACCOUNT AND ECONOMIC POLICY

Figure 6.12 Ratio of exports to GDP current and constant prices (1963/64 = 1)

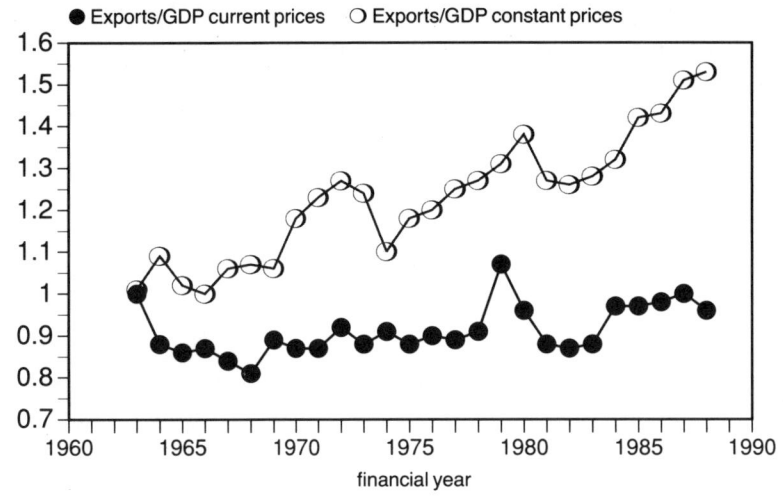

● Exports/GDP current prices   ○ Exports/GDP constant prices

Sources: *Australian National Accounts, National Income and Expenditure 1987–88*, ABS Cat. No. 5204.0; *Australian National Accounts, National Income and Expenditure*, June quarter, 1989, ABS Cat. No. 5206.0.

There have been major changes in structural factors over the last two decades. During the 1950s and most of the 1960s, manufacturing was encouraged behind a tariff wall to serve the domestic market, but since the mid-1960s tariff protection has been reduced considerably. The average effective rate of

Figure 6.13 Ratio of manufacturing value added and imports to GDP (1963/64 = 1)

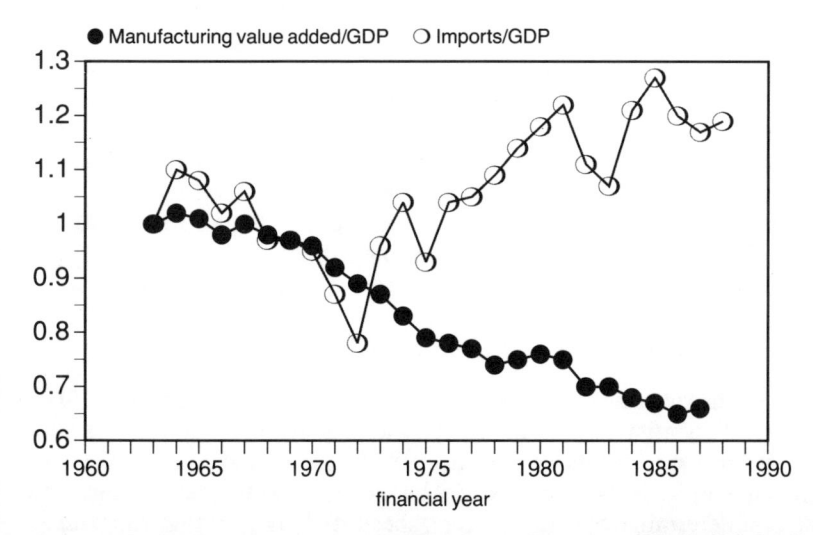

● Manufacturing value added/GDP   ○ Imports/GDP

Sources: *Australian National Accounts, National Income and Expenditure 1987–88*, ABS Cat. No. 5204.0; *Australian National Accounts, National Income and Expenditure*, June quarter, 1989, ABS Cat. No. 5206.0.

protection has fallen from 36 to 17 per cent and current industry plans call for further reductions. As protection has been reduced, the sector has contracted and there has been no significant sign of restructuring towards greater export capability or import replacement. The general pessimism created by tariff reductions has been reinforced by periodic exchange rate appreciations and significant real wage increases, especially during the 1972–74 period. As a result, manufacturing has seen only limited opportunities for growth and capacity has been reduced. Despite current boom conditions, the production of motor vehicles and steel are still less than in the peak years of the 1970s.

It is possible that manufacturing will reverse the trend and become more important in the tradeable goods sectors. The optimism would stem partly from the investment boom of 1989, partly from the belief that some of the real devaluations are still in place, and partly from high profit levels. If profitability can be maintained, the current investment boom may last longer than otherwise and the next decade may be one of more manufacturing investment.

However, there are a number of factors operating in the opposite direction which may adversely affect manufacturing. The rapid growth of expenditure over 1988 and 1989 and the real devaluations of 1985 and 1986 have protected some industries from a faster rate of structural change. For industries subject to Industry Plans, the government has used the changed environment to reduce protection. Motor vehicle quotas have been abolished and the tariff is to be phased down to 35 per cent by 1994. It was only six years earlier that the tariff was 57.5 per cent and import quotas were selling for a tariff premium of around 100 per cent, giving a nominal tariff at the margin of well over 150 per cent. Similarly, for clothing and footwear the long-run tariff has now been set at 55 and 45 per cent respectively and quota allocations liberalised. Two years ago the nominal tariff equivalent of the protection offered by quotas was estimated to be around 135 per cent. As indicated in Gregory (1989), these Industry Plans cannot be sustained without further large devaluations or acceptance of a greater degree of structural change than previously tolerated.

The devaluations have also provided an opportunity to introduce across-the-board tariff reductions. Apart from imports which fall under Industry Plans, all tariffs above 15 per cent will be reduced to that level in five annual steps. Similarly, tariffs between 10 and 15 per cent will be reduced to the lower bound and so on for tariffs between 5 and 10 per cent and 0 and 5 per cent. These adjustments should not lead to large-scale structural changes.

Savings, current account deficits and terms of trade

I now return to the two questions posed at the beginning of this section. First, in the context of identity (1), is it sensible, as has become common in academic circles (Forsyth, 1989; Pitchford, 1989; Harper and Lim, 1989), to place so much emphasis on the balance between domestic net savings and investment as a determinant of the current account? It is true that the widening current account deficit has been associated with a decline in the household saving ratio, but could we adopt the opposite position and argue that the

Figure 6.14 Moving average ratios of overseas borrowings (two-year lag) and household savings (per cent)

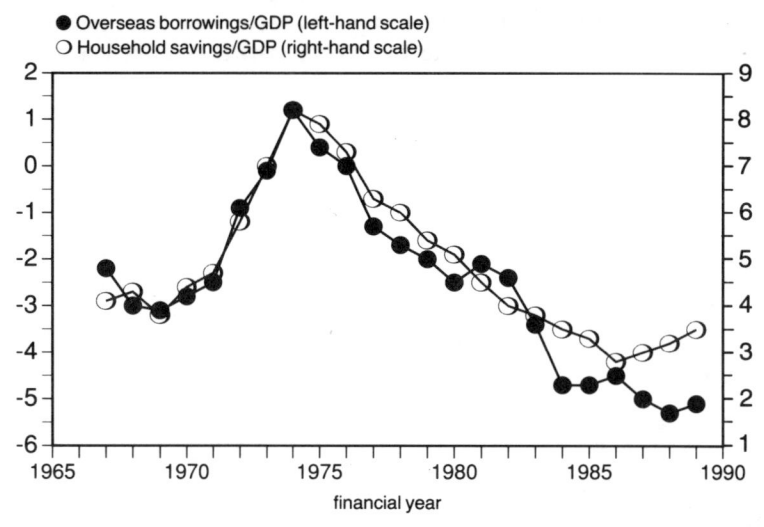

- Overseas borrowings/GDP (left-hand scale)
- Household savings/GDP (right-hand scale)

Source: DX Data Base.

causality runs from current account outcomes to household saving decisions? Figure 6.14 plots a two-year moving average of the current account against a two-year moving average of the household savings ratio two year *later*. A constant is subtracted from the savings ratio to place the data on a similar scale and the moving average is applied to smooth year-to-year fluctuations. The association between the series is remarkably close. Can it be said that changes in the current account deficit *cause* changes in the household saving ratio in subsequent periods? It could be argued, for example, that terms of trade changes positively affect both the current account and inflation—two obvious examples are the Korean War period and 1973-75—and then inflation positively influences savings (Anstie, Gray and Pagan, 1982).

A simple test of the hypothesis that savings are affected by exogenous factors which affect the current account would be to regress the savings ratio against the terms of trade:

$$(2) \frac{HS}{GDP} = -0.11 + \underset{(3.24)}{1.03} \text{T/T} + \underset{(2.55)}{0.81} \text{T/T}_{-1} \quad R^2 = 0.63 \quad DW = 1.31$$

where HS is household savings, GDP is gross domestic product and T/T the terms of trade of goods and services lagged one year.

This regression fits the data well and the coefficient linking terms of trade to the savings ratio is very significant. Obviously, this is not a sophisticated analysis and it is not meant to suggest that saving changes cannot affect the current account balance. In any fully articulated model causality is likely to flow both ways. However, this simple regression suggests that causation could run from the current account to savings and investment.

Second, is a new policy approach to the current account needed? It is clear that an agnostic consideration of the data—the recent history of the real exchange rate, the lack of a clear association between real exchange rate changes and relative profitability of the traded goods sector, the poor performance of manufacturing and the slow rate of export growth—must leave one uncertain as to the success of the current policy stance.

CONCLUDING REMARKS

The growth of overseas debt and widening of the current account deficit has raised many questions as to the functioning of the Australian economy. While there is no doubt that the restrictive monetary policy of 1989 will reduce the current account deficit in the short run by reducing expenditure and economic activity, there seems to be reasonable doubt as to the answers to the following important questions:

- Will the current account deficit be reduced in the longer term without a lengthy period of low resource utilisation? Or will the present investment boom generate an exceptional rate of exports and import replacement?

- Is it sensible to think of the current account, over the medium term, as being driven by savings and investment imbalances? Or is it better to focus directly on those factors which seem to bear most directly on exports and imports such as improvements in the terms of trade, destruction of manufacturing capital stock in response to recessions, and so on?

- Why has the reduction in the PSBR had so little effect on the current account? Should we accept the evidence on face value which, to date, suggests that current account changes are largely independent of PSBR changes?

- Is a substantial and sustained real devaluation a necessary precondition for a reduction in the current account deficit? If so, how can a real devaluation be effected if monetary policy is directed towards moderating domestic demand? Furthermore, once the devaluation is in place how can it be maintained?

- Why is relative profitability of manufacturing so loosely connected to real exchange rate changes? Does this suggest that real exchange rate changes are not so important as a determinant of the current account and therefore the nominal exchange rate might be assigned to moderating inflation?

7 Macroeconomic developments and prospects in East Asia

YUNG CHUL PARK

For the past three years, the countries in Pacific Asia[1] have continued to post an impressive economic performance of rapid growth with stable prices and a substantial accumulation of trade surpluses. As Table 7.1 shows, Japan recorded an almost 6 per cent GNP growth in 1988. For a large country, this constituted rapid growth indeed. Among the East Asian NIEs, economic growth ranged from 7.3 per cent in Taiwan to 12.2 per cent in South Korea. All of the ASEAN economies registered higher rates of growth in 1988 than in 1987. Although the current expansion has entered its fourth year, the Pacific Asian economies have not experienced any serious inflationary threats and the surplus economies like Japan, Taiwan and Korea have seen only a small decline in their trade imbalances relative to GNP.

Exports have been, and will continue to be, the engine of growth in many countries in Pacific Asia, with the ASEAN states having joined the East Asian NIEs as new entrants pursuing export-led development strategies. Among the region's more developed countries, however, there has been a change in the pattern of growth from export-led to internal demand-oriented economic expansion. Table 7.2 shows that Japan's strong growth has been powered by a marked increase in domestic demand including housing investment since 1986. The contribution of net external demand to economic growth turned negative in Taiwan from 1987, with a similar development taking place in Korea in 1989.

Indeed, movements in major macroeconomic indicators in the first half of 1989, and practically all forecasts, suggest that Japan, Korea and Taiwan will in coming years depend more on domestic consumption and investment than before for growth and employment. The three countries have made policy adjustments in an effort to reduce their trade imbalances by stimulating domestic demand and reorienting investment to non-manufacturing industries. Should this trend continue, it will help ease the trade tensions between Pacific Asia and rest of the world that have worsened in recent years. This chapter analyses recent economic developments in the three Northeast Asian economies—Japan, Korea and Taiwan—with the focus on developments in their current accounts, largely because these have been primarily responsible

Table 7.1 Economic performance of East Asia and Japan

	1981–84	1985	1986	1987	1988[b]	1989[c]
GNP growth rates:						
Korea	8.8	7	12.9	12.8	12.2	7.5–8.0
Taiwan	6.9	5.1	11.7	11.9	7.1	7.3
Japan	3.8	4.9	2.5	4.5	5.7	4.2
Hong Kong[a]	6.9	0.8	11.8	13.5	7.4	5.0
Singapore[a]	8.1	-1.6	1.8	8.8	11.0	7.5
Malaysia[a]	6.7	-1.0	1.2	5.2	8.1	7.0
Philippines[a]	-0.2	-4.1	2	5.7	7.0	6.3
Thailand[a]	5.5	3.2	3.5	6.3	11.0	8.5
Indonesia[a]	5.1	1.9	4	3.6	4.7	5.5
Real export growth rate:						
Korea	11.6	4.3	25.6	23.9	15.5	
Taiwan	10.0	4.9	32.2	40.3	12.2	
Japan	7.8	4.2	39.6	16.3	19.3	
Singapore	-1.9	-4.3	54.6	23.5		
Malaysia	11.1	8.8	26.5	4.8		
Philippines	-0.2	-2.2	16.8	8.6		
Thailand	8.7	7.7	16.0	20.4		
Indonesia	3.2	3.7	16.8	21.8		
Hong Kong	0.2	5.8	14.8	32.0		
Price inflation (GNP deflator):						
Korea	8.2	4.2	2.7	3.4	4.3	5–7
Taiwan	4.6	0.2	3.5	0.5	0.8	2.8
Japan	1.8	1.6	1.8	-0.3	1.0	2.5
Hong Kong[a]	8.5	5.6	2.3	5.8	7.5	6.5
Singapore[a]	3.9	-1.2	-3.7	0.9	1.7	2.2
Malaysia[a]	3.6	-1.5	-8.4	7.7	2.7	3.5
Philippines[a]	20.2	18.2	1.6	7.9	8.5	8.0
Thailand[a]	4.0	2.1	1.9	3.9	4.9	4.5
Indonesia[a]	13.5	6.5	-2.7	15.3	9.0	8.5

Notes: a Refers to GDP instead of GNP.
b GDP growth rates and price inflation for 1988 for the ASEAN-4 are the estimates provided by the Economic and Social Commission for Asia and the Pacific. Inflation figures for 1988 for ASEAN are changes in the consumer price index.
c Forecasts for Korea: The Bank of Korea; Japan: Japan Center for Economic Research; Taiwan: Directorate General of Budget, Accounting and Statistics; other countries: Economic and Social Commission for Asia and the Pacific.

Sources: *Major Statistics of the Korean Economy*, Korea Foreign Trade Association, 1988; *International Financial Statistics Yearbook*, IMF, 1988; *International Financial Statistics*, IMF, April 1989; *Taiwan Statistical Data Book*, Republic of China, 1988; *Hong Kong Monthly Digest of Statistics*, Hong Kong, various issues.

for the region's trade imbalances and hence conflicts with North America and Europe.

DECLINE IN THE TRADE SURPLUS OF THE EAST ASIAN NIES: WILL IT CONTINUE?

During 1986–88, Japan, Taiwan and Korea ran a combined surplus of almost US$120 billion a year in their trade account (see Table 7.3). Although a small amount, the ASEAN-4 countries have added to this figure. Adjusting for the trade deficits of Hong Kong, Singapore and China, the Pacific Asia region as a

Table 7.2 Contribution of internal and external demand growth (per cent)

	1981–84	1985	1986	1987	1988
Taiwan:					
GNP growth rate	6.9	5.1	11.7	11.9	7.1
External demand	3.6	4.5	7.3	-1.0	-6.8
Internal demand	3.3	0.7	4.3	12.8	13.8
Japan:					
GNP growth rate	3.8	4.9	2.5	4.5	5.7
External demand	1.2	1.1	-1.4	-0.6	-1.9
Internal demand	2.6	3.8	3.9	5.1	7.6
Korea:					
GNP growth rate	8.7	7.0	12.9	12.8	12.2
External demand	1.0	1.7	3.3	2.2	1.7
Internal demand	7.8	5.3	9.7	10.5	10.5

Note: As a percentage of real GNP in the previous period.

Sources: National Income, Directorate General of Budget, Accounting and Statistics, Taiwan, Republic of China, 1988; *Japanese Economic Indicators Quarterly 1988 4/4*, Japan Economic Planning Agency; *Statistical Yearbook*, Bank of Korea, 1989.

whole accumulated more than US$120 billion on both the trade and current account during the three-year period. Unless policy adjustments are undertaken by both sides of the Pacific, as many forecasts show, the current trend is likely to continue for some years to come. Figure 7.1 shows that the three countries as a group have also been responsible for more than 50 per cent of annual United States trade deficits since 1980. Japan, of course, has accounted for a lion's share. What developments—both external and internal—have led to such a large accumulation of trade surpluses? What policy adjustments have been made to reverse this trend in these countries?

To answer these questions, this section first attempts to identify and then analyse the effects of some of the major economic forces that have brought about the trade surplus expansions and corresponding net domestic saving.[2] During the 1985–88 period, three easily identifiable major macroeconomic variables that have displayed large movements and which are likely to have

Table 7.3 Trade account in Japan, Korea and Taiwan, 1987–93 (billion US dollars)

	Actual			Forecast				
	1986	1987	1988	1989	1990	1991	1992	1993
Japan	92.8	96.4	94.8	93.0	91.8	85.2	74.0	70.6
Korea	4.2	7.7	11.5	7.5	6.0	6.0	6.0	6.0
Taiwan	16.5	18.6	12.1	11.1	8.9	8.0	6.9	6.8
Total	113.5	122.7	118.4	111.6	105.9	99.2	86.9	83.4

Sources: Japan: Actual —*Economic Statistics Monthly*, Bank of Japan, March 1989.
Forecast—*Five-Year Economic Forecast*, Japan Center for Economic Research, February 1989.
Korea: Actual —*Monthly Bulletin*, Bank of Korea, March 1989.
Forecast—For 1989: Korea Development Institute;
For other years: *Revised 6th Five Year Economic and Social Development Plan*, Economic Planning Board, 1988.
Taiwan: Actual —*Financial Statistics Monthly*, Accounting and Statistics, Republic of China, March 1988.

Figure 7.1 United States trade deficit with Japan, Korea and Taiwan

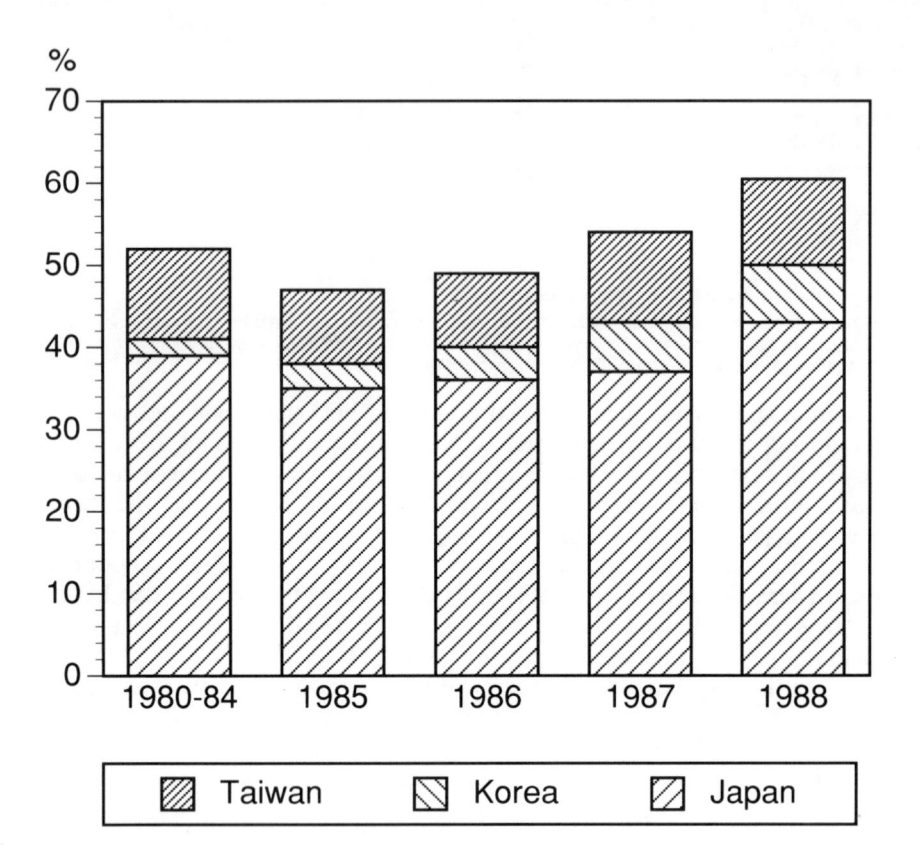

Source: Monthly Statistics of Foreign Trade, OECD, May 1989

dominated changes in the trade accounts of all three countries are: a massive increase in export earnings; terms of trade gains, in particular the large fall in oil prices; and a sharp real exchange rate appreciation. In the following, it is argued that the confluence of changes in these variables have affected both the saving–investment and trade balance, resulting in persistent trade imbalances in all three countries.

South Korea

Throughout much of the postwar period, Korea suffered from a chronic trade deficit. Beginning in the early 1980s, Korea's current account began to improve gradually. By 1986 it recorded a surplus that rose to 8.4 per cent of GNP within two years. This section focuses on developments in the current account for the past four years (1985-88).[3]

During the 1985-87 period, exports grew in real terms on average by 18 per cent, while imports managed a 7.5 per cent growth, in the face of sharply rising unit labour costs caused by the won currency appreciation and wage increases (see Figure 7.2). These cost increases appear to have been offset by a strong United States demand for East Asian manufactures and a larger appreciation of the yen and New Taiwan (NT) dollar vis-à-vis the US dollar than the Korean won (see Figures 7.3 and 7.4), which provided a competitive edge for Korean exporters in the United States market. According to the estimates made by Morgan Guarantee (see Figure 7.5), Korea's real effective exchange rate in fact depreciated by 5.6 per cent, while Japan was struggling with a 29 per cent appreciation and Taiwan saw little change between 1985 and 1987. As a result, Korea was gaining on both Japan and Taiwan in export competitiveness. At the same time, Korean exporters were absorbing as much as possible the cost increases internally at the expense of short-term profits in order to maintain their export market shares.[4]

On the import side, the slow growth of the volume of imports largely reflected the massive decline in oil prices (see Table 7.4) and relatively low income and price elasticities of imports. The government maintained, and still does, a high domestic oil price policy and enforced energy conservation. These factors have lowered the growth of the demand for crude oil so much that the share of crude oil in Korea's total imports declined, as shown in Table 7.4, from 25.3 per cent in 1980 to less than 10 per cent since 1987. In addition to these developments, the J-curve effect, which in Korea lasts almost four quarters after an initial change in the exchange rate, generated larger trade imbalances than otherwise (Park, 1989).

From the end of 1987 to the end of 1988, the value of the won went up further against the US dollar, resulting in a real appreciation of more than 10 per cent. The effect of the currency appreciation on Korea's export earnings was reinforced by wage cost increases. Nominal wages in manufacturing rose almost 20 per cent, while industrial relations were deteriorating with the occurrence of almost 2,000 strikes. Clearly, Korea was losing out to other export competitors including Japan. Despite these unfavourable developments in the domestic economy, Korea managed a 15.5 per cent increase in the volume of exports by absorbing cost increases and taking advantage of Japan's market opening.[5] Benefitting from a further decline in oil prices, in 1988 Korea registered its highest level ever of current account surplus as a proportion of GNP.

Turning to the saving and investment balance, it is argued here that the exogenous shocks which have affected the course of the trade account development have also been responsible for the growing net savings. A visual

Figure 7.2 Change in unit labour cost in manufacturing

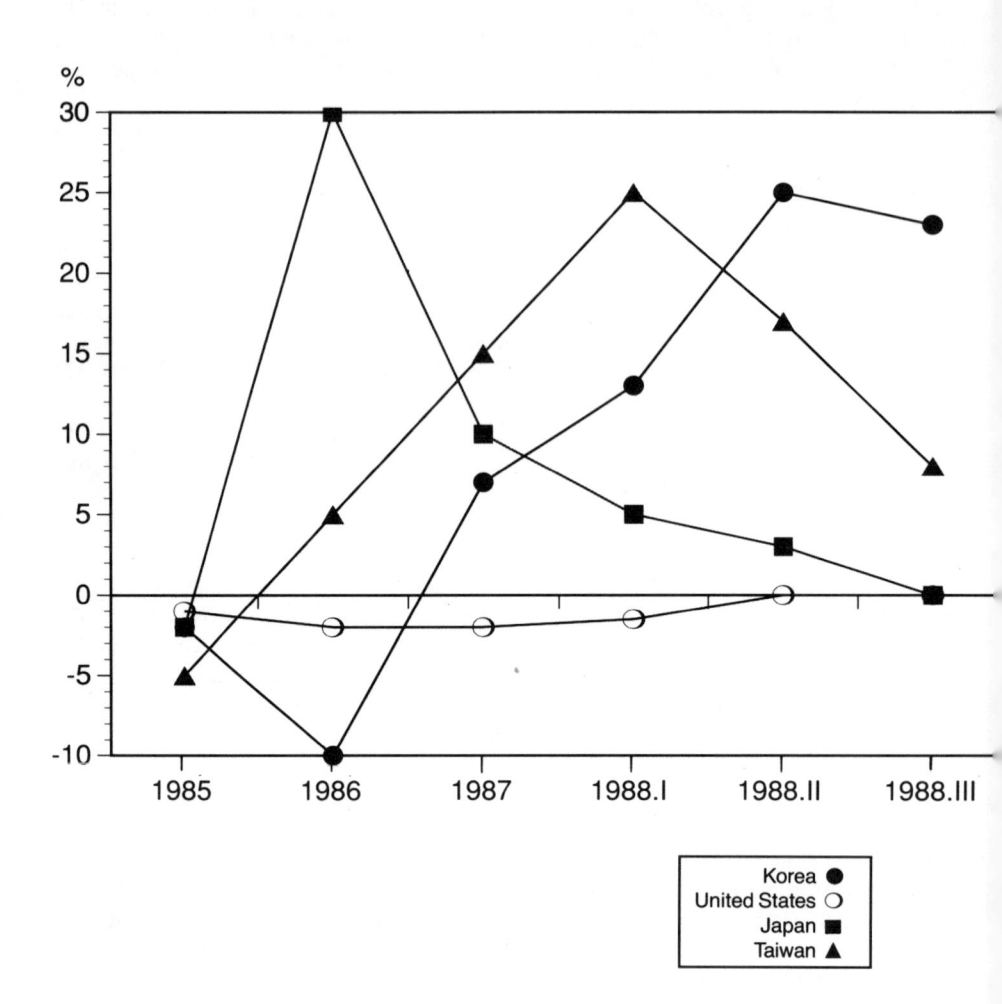

Note: Output divided by the number of people employed in manufacturing.

Sources: Korea Labour Institute; US Department of Labor, Monthly Labour Review, December 1988; Japan Statistics Bureau, Monthly Statistics of Japan, January 1989.

inspection of gross fixed investment in Table 7.5 shows that as a percentage of GNP it has remained remarkably stable, fluctuating between 29.6 per cent and 30.9 per cent between 1982 and 1988, whereas gross savings relative to GNP displayed a steep increase, up from around 23 per cent in the early 1980s to

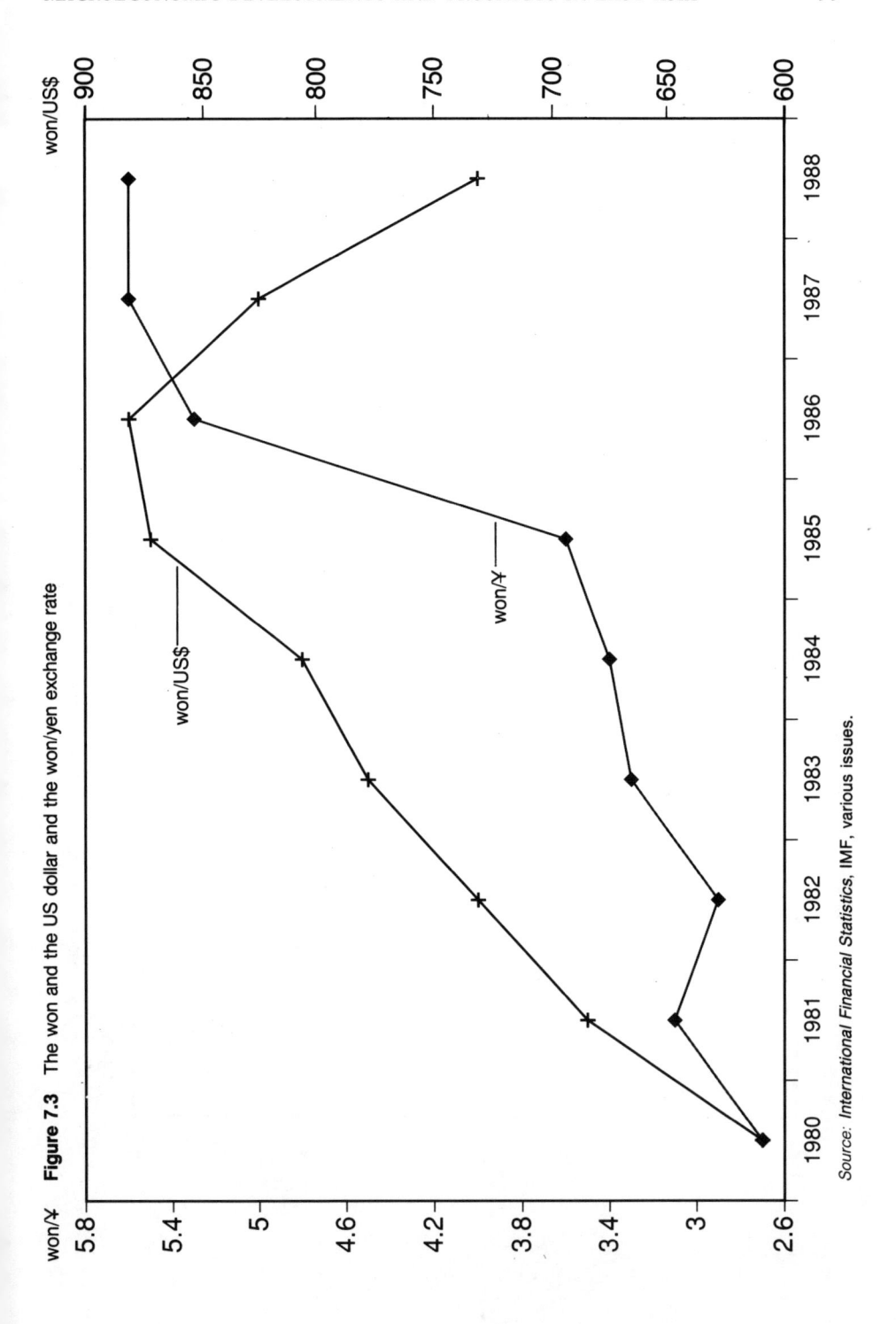

MACROECONOMIC DEVELOPMENTS AND PROSPECTS IN EAST ASIA 99

Figure 7.3 The won and the US dollar and the won/yen exchange rate

Source: *International Financial Statistics*, IMF, various issues.

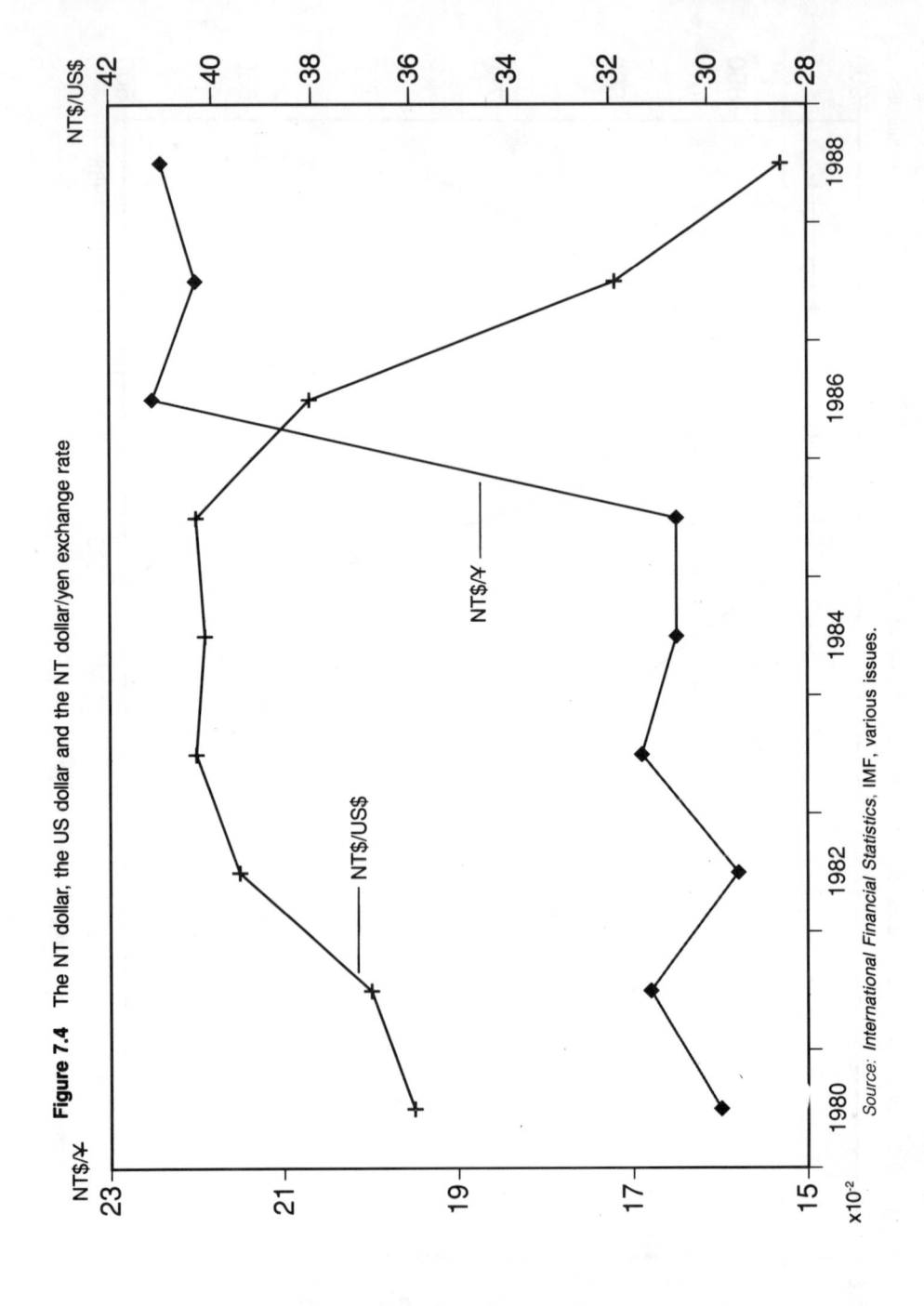

Figure 7.4 The NT dollar, the US dollar and the NT dollar/yen exchange rate

Source: *International Financial Statistics*, IMF, various issues.

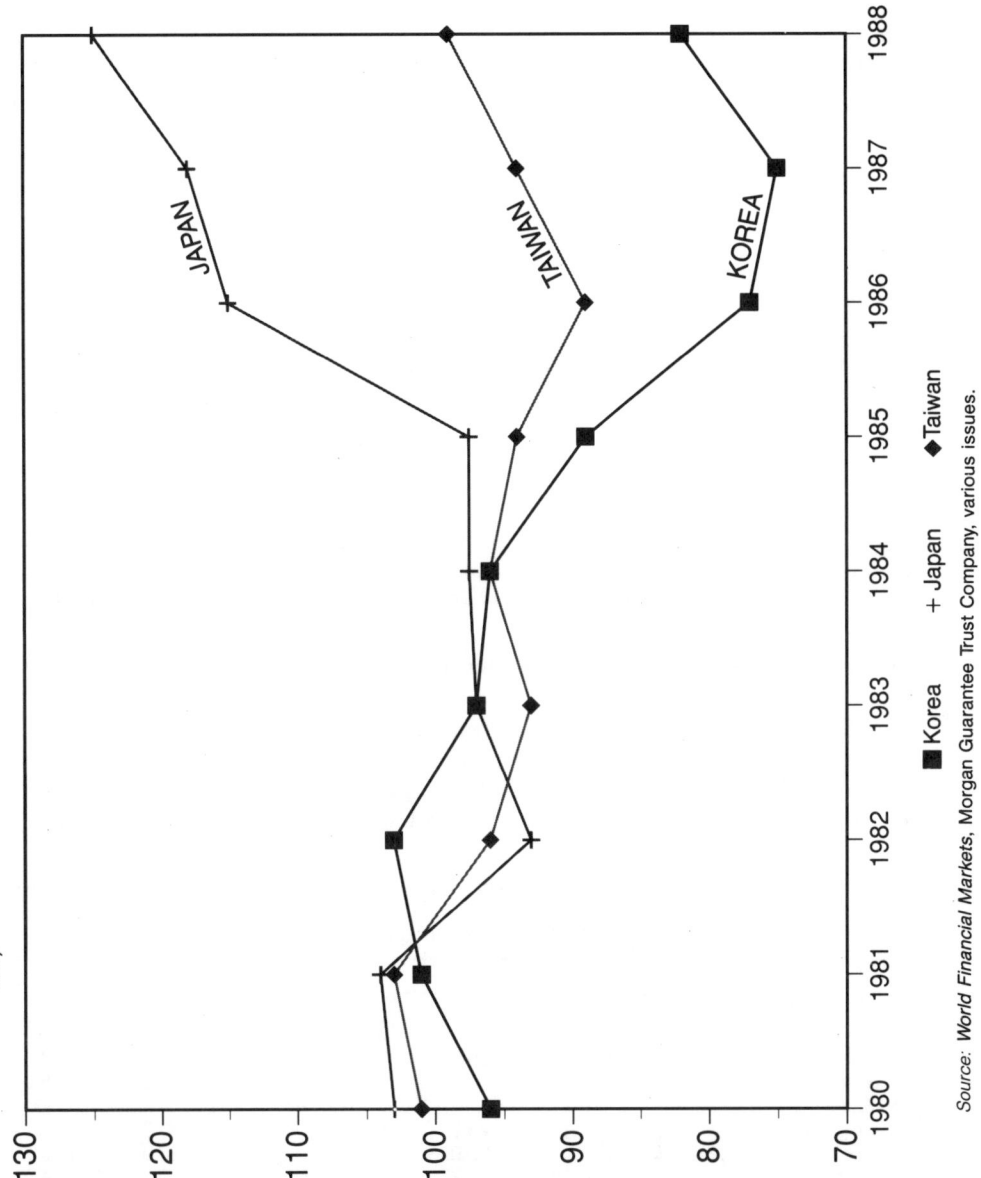

37.7 per cent in 1988. A surplus on the current account, which emerged first in 1986 and which has continued to increase, has therefore been closely related to the large increase in domestic savings.

How then is one to explain the 10 percentage point increase in the propen-

Table 7.4 Volume and prices of imported oil (per cent)

	1980	1981	1982	1983	1984	1985	1986	1987	1988
Korea:									
Volume index[a]	8.5	88.1	89.1	96.5	100.8	100.0	117.6	118.9	136.3
Change in the average of import prices of oil	72.2	15.1	-4.3	-12.2	-2.7	-4.6	-45.5	17.4	-20.0
Crude oil as a percentage of total imports	25.3	24.4	25.2	21.3	18.9	18.0	10.7	9.0	7.1
Japan:									
Volume index[a]	129.9	116.1	108.3	105.6	108.8	100.0	96.4	94.3	98.1
Change in the average of import prices of oil	70.1	7.1	5.7	-13.8	-5.5	-2.8	-52.5	-14.7	-20.0
Crude oil as a percentage of total imports	37.5	37.1	35.0	31.7	28.8	26.7	15.9	13.9	10.0
Taiwan:									
Volume index[a]	98.5	102.3	97.1	89.9	105.7	100.0	91.9	97.0	108.7
Change in the average of import prices of oil		15.9	0.5	-7.9	-4.4	-3.2	-41.1	-8.6	-25.9
Crude oil as a percentage of total imports	20.8	21.0	20.5	20.2	17.2	16.6	8.5	7.3	4.5

Note: a 1985 = 100.

Sources: Monthly Statistics of Japan, Statistics Bureau, March 1989; *Monthly Statistics of Exports and Imports*, Ministry of Finance, Republic of China, January 1989; *Statistical Yearbook*, Bank of Korea, various issues.

sity to save in just over a six-year period? While there are many hypotheses about savings in developing countries, empirical studies using Korean data have failed to identify any set of determinants other than income variables that are of statistical significance in explaining changes in saving behaviour in Korea. Using a variant of the lifecycle model, Nam (1988) shows that of the variables that are statistically significant, a high rate of growth has exerted the strongest influence on saving behaviour in recent years.

It is clear that the savings upsurge was closely correlated with the rapid

Table 7.5 Current account, savings and investment (per cent)

	1980–84	1985	1986	1987	1988
Japan:					
Savings/GNP	31.1	32.0	32.3	32.6	33.6
Gross fixed investment/GNP	29.6	27.8	27.7	28.8	30.4
Current account/GNP	0.9	3.7	4.4	3.6	2.8
Korea:					
Savings/GNP	25.2	29.1	33.1	36.3	37.7
Gross fixed investment/GNP	30.0	30.2	30.8	30.9	29.8
Current account/GNP	-4.7	-1.0	4.5	7.7	8.4
Taiwan:					
Savings/GNP	32.1	33.2	37.7	38.5	34.9
Gross fixed investment/GNP	26.1	18.8	18.1	19.5	20.3
Current account/GNP	4.9	15.1	21.8	18.1	8.5

Sources: Economic Statistics Yearbook, Bank of Korea, various issues; *Annual Report on the National Account*, Economic Planning Agency, Government of Japan, 1988; *Industry of Free China*, Republic of China, March 1989.

growth and the oil price fall during 1986–88. In 1986, when the rate of growth accelerated to 12.9 per cent from 7.9 per cent a year earlier, the saving rate shot up by 4 percentage points. The following two years saw a further increase in the savings propensity to 37.7 per cent, which was again accompanied by double-digit growth. It appears that much of the increase in income for the last two years was unexpected, considered transitory, and hence saved. One possible reason for this is that actual incomes were higher than the forecast and government target levels. Another is that the political transition marked by social and political unrest and uncertainties since 1986 generated pessimistic expectations that an economic slowdown would be inevitable in the process of political democratisation.

Rapid growth and a high domestic oil price policy have also contributed to a large increase in government savings, and rapid growth has resulted in budgetary surpluses as it has pushed taxpayers up into higher tax brackets. In an effort to restrain oil consumption, the Korean government has not fully adjusted domestic prices of oil and petroleum products, though import prices of oil have been declining since the early 1980s. The price differential has provided the government with a large source of revenue and saving. Over the past two years, the government has made successive adjustments of domestic oil prices in line with the falling international prices of crude oil, but the decline in oil prices has by and large been perceived as temporary, because many conflicting forecasts have made firms and households uncertain about the future oil prices. The bulk of income gains from the oil price decline thus appear to have been saved.

Under normal circumstances, the booming economy sustained by the surge in exports would have induced a strong domestic investment. However, the political and social turbulence that has followed democratisation reforms has increased uncertainties in future profits and rates of return on investment. While these uncertainties may have induced households to save more, they have certainly discouraged business investment. In particular, higher wages with a decline in labour productivity and expectations of further deterioration in labour–industry relations have made the outlook for the Korean economy rather pessimistic and held back any major expansion in business investment. The expected won currency appreciation and trade protectionism have obviously complicated what was already a difficult situation.

Taiwan

Unlike Korea, Taiwan has been running a surplus on its trade account consistently for more than two decades except for the three oil-crisis years of 1973, 1974 and 1980. In 1986 the surplus rose to almost 22 per cent of GNP. However one defines a structural surplus, there is little doubt that Taiwan has developed a persistent structural surplus which has proved to be unresponsive to policy changes including a large real appreciation. This section focuses on recent macroeconomic developments to identify some of the sources of Taiwan's trade imbalances.

Following the two years of double-digit growth, the Taiwan economy slowed down considerably and managed a 7 per cent growth in 1988. Much of the slowdown could be traced to a sharp drop in the growth of the volume of exports (see Table 7.1). As in 1987, net exports made a negative contribution to growth in 1988. There was no inflationary pressure to speak of, but trade surpluses as a proportion of GNP plunged to 8.5 per cent from 18.1 per cent in 1987 (Table 7.5). Does this fall mean that Taiwan has been successful in making policy adjustments aimed at correcting the huge trade imbalance?

While domestic demand contributed more to Taiwan's growth in 1988, the actual trade surplus could have been higher depending upon whether the purchase of monetary gold amounting to US$3 billion and commercial gold worth US$2 billion is included in total imports. Subtracting the gold component from total imports, the trade account would look much worse than it is, and the current account to GNP ratio would rise to 12.4 per cent in 1988. Even then, one must be fairly impressed with Taiwan's trade account adjustment.

As in the case of Korea, Taiwan's success in promoting its exports during the 1985–87 period was largely due to favourable external developments and also to structural characteristics unique to East Asian economies. The strong United States demand was perhaps the most important factor, considering the dominance of the United States as Taiwan's export market. Another factor was the NT dollar's weakening vis-à-vis the yen, which strengthened the competitiveness of Taiwanese exporters over Japanese producers in the United States and other markets (see Figure 7.4). In addition, the pass-through ratio is also low and labour productivity in manufacturing has been high (Liang and Liang, 1988). Along with these factors, the falling oil prices brought about a growing imbalance on the trade account during the 1985–87 period.

The volume of exports took a nosedive to 12 per cent in 1988 from more than 40 per cent a year before. Much of the sharp drop was claimed to have been caused by the lagged effect of the NT dollar appreciation against the US dollar in 1986–87 (Lee and Yu, 1988). Declining domestic prices of imported goods and further trade liberalisation stimulated import demand, and together with the export growth deceleration produced a large decline in the ratio of trade surpluses to GNP in 1988.

On the saving–investment balance, domestic savings as a percentage of GNP scaled up to 38.5 per cent in 1987 from about 30 per cent in the early 1980s before declining to 35 per cent in 1988. That the Taiwanese, like the Japanese and Koreans, tend not to consume very much has puzzled many researchers, but the upsurge during 1985–87 was largely the short-term effect of rapid growth and the terms of trade gains (oil). While savings have continued to grow relative to GNP, investment demand has remained depressed. As Table 7.5 shows, the investment/GNP ratio fell to 18.1 per cent in 1986 from a high of 31.2 per cent in 1980. The ratio has recovered somewhat since then, but is still well below that of saving to GNP. From the saving–investment side, the current account movements have been closely associated with declining investment, a problem that has troubled the Taiwanese authorities for some time.

Many reasons, most of them structural, have been given to account for the fact that such a dynamic economy has been unable to find ample investment opportunities in the home market. The anticipation of political and social instability during the political transition following the passing of President Chiang has apparently dampened the investment climate. The deterioration in labour–industry relations, the shortage of labour with wage increases, the market-opening pressures from the United States, and public concern about environmental protection, have created such an unfavourable environment that private investors have sought to undertake capital expansion in the foreign rather than domestic market.

While the government could of course step in to lead investment in social and physical infrastructure and housing to compensate for the sag in private investment, despite the apparent need for this type of investment, it has been reluctant or unable to push through public works projects. Although policymakers have implemented incentive measures for private investment, and over the last two years investment has responded, Lee and Yu (1989) believe that these efforts have not been enough to lift the sagging investment climate in Taiwan.

ADJUSTMENT THROUGH EXCHANGE RATE CHANGES?

For several years now, the United States has applied strong pressure on both Taiwan and Korea to appreciate their currencies against the US dollar with the expectation that such an exchange rate adjustment would help reduce its burgeoning trade imbalances with the two countries. The United States has succeeded in forcing both real as well as nominal appreciation of the two currencies against the US dollar. Contrary to expectations, however, movements in the trade account seem to suggest that the effect of the real appreciation on trade balance has been small in both countries, either because exports and imports are insensitive to changes in the exchange rate or because the effect of the real appreciation has been swamped by other developments.

In both Taiwan and Korea, empirical studies on the effect of exchange rate changes on the trade balance have produced conflicting results depending on the time period and methodology chosen. Nevertheless, it appears that exports are relatively more elastic with respect to changes in both prices and income than real imports are, at least in the long run. In the short run, prices and income elasticities are very small: hence the J-curve effect.

A recent study using Korean data (Park, 1989) shows that in the short run the price elasticity is 0.3 per cent for real exports and 0.2 per cent for real imports. In the long run, however, the price elasticities rise to 2.1 per cent for exports and 1 per cent for imports, and the income elasticities to 2.8 per cent and 1 per cent, respectively. These results suggest that, at least in Korea's case, changes in the exchange rate could generate a powerful long-run effect on the trade account. However, another recent study using Taiwanese data presents a different picture. According to Yu and Ho (1989), a 15 per cent appreciation of the NT dollar against the US dollar over a one-year period (1989 as the baseline) generates a reduction of US$809 million in the merchandise trade account, or a 2.1 per cent reduction from a baseline figure two years later.

The relatively low price and income elasticities of imports are in general related to the commodity structure of imports of the two countries, dominated by raw materials, crude oil and capital goods for which there are only a limited number of domestic substitutes. The high price and income elasticities of exports are in turn associated with the commodity structure of exports, which consists mostly of consumer products with many substitutes from other countries.

Exchange rate policy poses a serious dilemma to both Taiwan and Korea because of a trilateral trade relationship they maintain with Japan: they depend on the United States market for their exports and on Japan for imports of capital and intermediate goods. As long as they stay with the dollar, a unilateral real appreciation strengthens Japan's relative position in the world market and trade is diverted to Japan.

Japanese, Taiwanese and Korean exports are substitutable even at the low end of the product line and will become more so in the future as Taiwan and Korea catch up with Japan. Furthermore, Japan rather than the United States is the major exporter to the East Asian NIEs. These structural characteristics suggest that a unilateral appreciation on the part of Taiwan and Korea will produce little gain for the United States but substantial benefits for Japan. For this reason and the ambiguous effect of exchange rate changes on trade, Taiwan and Korea have resisted United States pressure and only grudgingly adjusted the values of their currencies against the US dollar.

DOMESTIC MARKET ORIENTED GROWTH IN JAPAN

Between 1985 and 1988, the yen/dollar exchange rate appreciated 57 per cent and the real effective exchange rate for Japan almost 56 per cent (see Figure 7.5). Despite such a massive increase in the value of the yen, Japan's current account failed to respond and trade surpluses rose to 4.4 per cent of GNP in 1986 from 3.7 per cent in 1985. The ratio declined to 2.8 per cent in 1988 but has begun to rise again. Many of the recent studies of macroeconomic developments in Japan have focused on the causes of Japan's consistent current account imbalances in the face of a strong yen. Some of these studies have emphasised the importance of the divergent fiscal policy between the United States and Japan as the major cause of the imbalance. These studies essentially reflect the Mundell-Flemming view of internal and external adjustments.

According to what has become a standard explanation, the large increase in United States federal deficits raised United States real interest rates in the early 1980s, which in turn induced capital inflows from abroad. The incipient capital inflow then weakened the dollar against the yen and other major currencies. The dollar appreciation undermined United States competitiveness and generated current account deficits. At the same time, Japan was cutting its budget deficits, leading to lower real interest rates and a weaker yen, which in turn contributed to an expansion of its current account surplus. Financial deregulation and opening up of the capital account transactions in Japan have also increased the depth of the market and in so doing have raised the effective risk tolerance of the market or reduced the risk premium required to induce private asset owners to hold risky foreign securities (Fukao and Okina, 1988). The financial integration has therefore facilitated the capital outflows from Japan and hence the financing of the United States trade deficits.

Fukao and Okina (1988) also argue that the Mundell–Flemming model, when expanded by incorporating a risk element, describes fairly well the movements in the real exchange rates and the real interest rate differential and current account imbalances between Japan and the United States. In the early 1980s the rapid progress in financial market integration offset the effect of a growing trade imbalance on the real exchange rate so that the large real interest rate differential led to a stronger dollar than otherwise, despite the fact that the United States was running a massive trade deficit.

Is the Mundell–Flemming model as useful for analysing the bilateral economic developments between Japan and the United States, characterised by a strong yen and Japan's huge trade surpluses since mid-1985? The Mundell–Flemming view is not as persuasive here as it is in explaining the episode of the early 1980s. One could argue that the continuing increase in the accumulated current account surpluses of Japan has become so large and persistent that it has overwhelmed the effect of financial integration and hence has brought down the real value of the dollar relative to the yen. At the same time, the real interest rate differentials between Japan and the United States have narrowed considerably in recent years. These developments, according to Fukao and Okina, explain the uneasy combination of a growing Japanese trade surplus with a real appreciation of the yen. However, this argument is based on a visual inspection of the raw data and does not necessarily provide any credible evidence to support the validity of the Mundell–Flemming interpretation of Japan's trade account behaviour since 1985.

While the Mundell–Flemming interpretation could not be taken seriously, Fukao and Okina suggest another reason why the dollar will decline further or at least remain weak in the future. In Japan, a large part of foreign securities are held by institutional investors such as banks, insurance companies and investment trusts. In particular, life insurance and non-life insurance companies, which make investments in foreign securities without cover or have no matching foreign liabilities, have played a crucial role in recycling Japan's current account surpluses. These institutions already hold more foreign securities than perhaps optimal, well above 10 per cent of their total assets. As a result, unless the yield differential between the dollar and yen assets rises significantly, Japanese foreign investors will no longer buy dollar assets. This means that the dollar may fall even if the United States current account improves.[6]

Ueda (1988) disputes the Mundell–Flemming interpretation of changes in the dollar/yen real exchange rate and the increase in the United States current account deficits vis-à-vis Japan in the 1980s by showing empirically that exports and imports are not responsive to changes in the real exchange rate and that savings are insensitive to changes in the real interest rate in Japan. As an alternative framework, he suggests an income expenditure model in which the exchange rate determination is ignored.

During 1980–85, according to an income expenditure interpretation, the increase in trade surpluses in Japan could be explained by the following two factors which affected both the trade account and saving–investment balance. One is the increase in United States spending relative to Japan's. Since the income elasticity of Japan's exports is more than twice the size of its income elasticity of imports, the expansion in the United States demand provided a major stimulus to Japan's export industries and fuelled rapid growth. Another factor was the decline in oil prices between 1980 and 1985 (see Table 7.4). The price elasticity of Japan's imports is estimated to be low and less than one. Partly due to this low elasticity, the decline in oil prices reduced the value of Japan's oil imports to about 10 per cent of total imports in 1988 from more than 37 per cent in 1980 (see Table 7.4). On the question of the effect of exchange rate changes, several studies found that the yen appreciation exerted a very small effect on the trade account during the period. A further analysis of this result is taken up in the subsequent discussion.

On the saving–investment side, consumption was lagging behind high growth of income and hence savings relative to GNP rose. Higher incomes also resulted in a large increase in tax revenues, and this together with a spending cut raised net savings of the government sector in the early 1980s. The income gains from the oil price decrease were considered temporary and were saved.

While savings were rising, the ageing of the population appears to have triggered a sharp decline in housing investment. Largely for this reason, the investment/GNP ratio did not move, giving rise to a huge surplus on the trade account. As in the Mundell–Flemming model, the income-expenditure approach identifies fiscal policies of the United States and Japan as having been the major cause of Japan's surplus build-up, but through different channels. The income–expenditure approach, at least during the 1980–85 period, assigns no significant role to the real interest rate and real exchange rate. Instead, the approach works through changes in real income, disregarding the supply side constraint.

In 1986 the strong growth in the United States appeared to have more than offset much of the effect of the massive yen appreciation. This together with a 50 per cent fall in oil prices produced a current account surplus that climbed up to 4.3 per cent of GNP. These two exogenous shocks, particularly the decline in oil prices, were also operating to generate a corresponding excess saving over investment. Despite the booming economy, business investment was sluggish and relative to GNP remained unchanged, mainly because of the further anticipated yen appreciation.

For the last two years (1987–88), the trend in aggregate spending in Japan and the United States has been reversed. Japan grew on average 5.4 per cent whereas the United States managed a 3.7 per cent growth. Oil price declines have been moderate while the yen has appreciated further. These developments have been largely responsible for a fall in Japan's trade surplus for two consecutive years. At the same time, expansionary monetary and fiscal policies have stimulated business and housing investment and also increased public works expenditure. Domestic savings have inched up as a proportion of GNP, mostly because of the rapid growth, but this has been followed by a larger investment expansion, resulting in a smaller net savings both in 1987 and 1988. The investment spurt may indicate that Japan's manufacturing sector completed its adjustment to the yen appreciation by 1987 and has begun undertaking new capital investment to take advantage of growing domestic demand.

Among the several factors that may have directly and indirectly influenced Japan's trade account movements, most controversial has been the effect of the real appreciation of the yen. Trade equations estimated by various authors and institutions show that Japanese exports and imports are not very responsive to changes in the relative prices. Estimation results indicate that the long-run (six years) partial price elasticity of exports lies somewhere within the range of 0.92 per cent and 1.4 per cent. For imports, the partial elasticity lies between 0.32 per cent and 0.66 per cent. Thus, in the long run the Marshall–Lerner condition is met for Japan, although in the short run the sum of the two elasticities is likely to be less than one; hence the J-curve effect.

According to the partial simulation results of Japan's Economic Planning Agency model with 1.38 per cent and 0.32 per cent export and import price elasticities, a sustained exchange rate of 10 per cent would reduce trade imbalances by more than 1 per cent of GNP for the United States and by more than 1.5 per cent for Japan on an annual average over a six-year period at constant prices. At current prices, the effect decreases to one-third to half of the volume effect, but the value effect is still relatively large. A full equilibrium model simulation, in which incomes and prices other than exports and imports are also exogenous, provides a drastically different and pessimistic picture. Because the dollar depreciation generates domestic inflationary pressure and deflationary impact on the world trade and causes higher nominal United States interest rates, the volume effect of the same 10 per cent sustained change declines to 0.24 per cent of United States GNP and 0.69 per cent of Japanese GNP. The value effects with current prices would be even smaller at 0.04 per cent of United States GNP and 0.4 per cent of Japanese GNP (Yoshitomi, 1989a).

There are other explanations why Japan's trade account has been so resilient to the yen appreciation. These include the low pass-through ratio, the 'hysteresis' argument, and the oligopolistic and monopolistic structure of Japan's major export markets. Added to this list, there is Japan's ability to adjust to the yen appreciation in a speedy manner. If the view that the large appreciation of the yen has not affected Japan's exports and imports as much as was anticipated for the last several years is accepted, what then would be the most effective policy prescription for the correction of the trade imbalance between

Japan and the United States? This question is addressed in the following section.

PROSPECTS OF MACROECONOMIC ADJUSTMENTS IN EAST ASIA

Japan

In the first quarter of 1989, the Japanese economy grew 9 per cent compared to the same quarter in 1988. A super-economy like Japan cannot obviously maintain such a high rate of growth for very long, but one cannot fail to notice a transformation of Japan—it has become supremely confident and optimistic about its future. Practically all forecasts, private or government, show that Japan is entering another phase of rapid growth with stability. Unlike other periods, however, Japan will for the next several years power its rapid growth through a domestic demand expansion.

As Table 7.5 shows, Japan's savings propensity has been one of the highest in the world, and despite its rising per capita income and wealth, shows no visible sign of decline in the near future. Since 1983 household savings as a percentage of GNP have remained at around 16 per cent. Since 1986 this ratio has in fact started to go up again. Japan's high propensity to save has been a subject of intense research and debate but still remains an enigma. The tax incentive for household savings, the primitive social security system, high land prices, and other hypotheses have failed to be borne out empirically. The ageing of the population may eventually bring down the saving rate, but such a drop is unlikely to be realised in the coming decade. Japanese workers are still working more than 43 hours a week compared to 38 hours in the United States, and this is unlikely to change for some foreeable time.

Insofar as Japan will not experience any decline in its savings rate, it could sustain a reasonably high rate of growth by stimulating domestic investment demand. And Japan does not lack investment opportunities. Can the country sustain a 4-5 per cent annual growth for the next 5 to 10 years as many forecasts suggest? Could it reorient its growth strategy from one that is traditionally export-led to one internally demand-led? Policy authorities are confident about engineering such an adjustment and point to the change in the pattern of growth that has taken place in recent years.

Under pressure and also for its own welfare, Japan has allow its dollar exchange rate to appreciate by almost 100 per cent since 1984. Japanese policymakers have also pursued rather expansionary fiscal and monetary policies since the Plaza Accord. The Japanese government has been carrying out some of the structural reforms recommended by the Maekawa Report including: one, a major improvement in foreigners' access to the Japanese market; two, investment expansion in housing and social infrastructure; and three, restructuring of Japanese enterprises to promote intra-industry division of labour with foreign firms and foreign direct investment.

To what extent, then, does the change in the pattern of growth for the last two years reflect efficient implementation of the structural reforms? Or is it the result of the market mechanism at work? On this question, Yoshitomi (1989b) argues that the working of the market mechanism has, more than anything, pushed forward the restructuring. In particular, the huge yen appreciation has been the driving force for internal adjustment and structural reforms as well, even if it has not been effective in chipping off the trade imbalance. Much of the reorientation of the Japanese economy has been dominated and led by a very speedy adjustment in manufacturing, as evidenced by its strong investment for the last two years. Japanese enterprises in manufacturing have diversified their products, moved into other lines of business and expanded their foreign operations to cope with the high yen. In fact, the Japanese manufacturing sector has adjusted to the high yen so well through technological adaptation supported by flexible attitude of management and labour that it could not only survive but also gain competitiveness at the current real exchange rate in international markets.

Japanese enterprises have also developed and innovated new technologies. In fact, technological innovation—in particular, the rapid spread of microelectronics-based information technology—has been the key to domestic demand expansion. Household consumption is not likely to increase, but will include more high quality goods. For example, the demand for high quality consumer durables and electronics products has risen steeply. As a result, electronics and machinery industries that have relied traditionally on foreign demand are now retooling to meet growing domestic demand.

However, the sharp appreciation of the yen has not affected, as much as it could have, investment in and output of the Japanese non-manufacturing sector that includes agriculture, distribution, construction, transportation, housing, education, and banking and finance, mostly because these sectors are regulated and protected from outside competition. The non-manufacturing sector remains closed, inefficient, and displays low productivity. These maladies explain why prices for tradeables are so high in Japan (Yoshitomi, 1989b).

Public discontent and market pressures generated by a high yen and growing per capita income will speed up the reforms in the non-manufacturing sector. The lopsided terms of trade and the reforms will induce a shift of resources to the non-tradeable sectors. This reorientation will then improve the efficiency of these sectors and create downward pressures on the prices of non-tradeable goods. As prices of non-durables fall, consumption of these goods will increase. It is therefore expected that the deregulation and liberalisation of the non-manufacturing sector reinforced by the yen appreciation will not only reduce Japan's trade imbalances but also improve its welfare. A nagging question remains, however—why does Japan take so much time to undertake reforms that are universally beneficial? A more serious question would be whether the efficiency improvement in the non-manufacturing sector would necessarily alter the spending structure to reduce the trade surplus. While the efficiency gain could stimulate domestic consumption and investment, it could also lead to a more competitive manufacturing sector as the labour employed by the non-manufacturing sector moves to, and more agricultural land is allocated to, manufacturing. The efficiency improvement may even force Japan to export some of the services in which it has at present no comparative advantage.

Japan is besieged by public demand for political reforms, which in due course would restructure the existing Liberal Democratic Party (LDP) dominated system. A new leadership emerging from a new alliance among different factions within the LDP will have to replace the LDP's old guard. During this political transition, which could take considerable time, the Japanese government will not have the power or consensus to carry out difficult reforms of non-manufacturing sectors, which produce two-thirds of Japan's output. Against this view, one might argue that the power vacuum would facilitate the functioning of the market system since it would loosen up the government bureaucracy's grip on the economy. Market forces would then work to tear down the protection of the non-manufacturing sectors. But only time will tell.

At present, however, Japanese manufactures have weathered the difficult period of adaptation to the high yen and may have regained fully their foreign competitiveness. One magazine article (*Far Eastern Economic Review*, 8 June 1989) claims that even Taiwan and South Korea have failed to penetrate Japan's market for consumer goods despite their competitive edge. Apparently, the marked increase in their exports to Japan petered out early in 1989, because, among other things, 'Japanese companies were quick to come up with simple, one-function products that mimicked the best offerings from Taiwan and South Korea'.[7] Through offshore production, outsourcing and multinationalisation of production processes, Japanese manufacturers have been able to cut down their costs of production. If they were able to block out low price imports of manufactured goods from East Asian NIEs, one can only imagine what it is like for American and European exporters competing against the Japanese for those sophisticated and technology-intensive products.

If the United States is unable to reverse the trend of overspending and continues to support the demand for Japanese products, if Japan limps through with its structural reforms including the market opening, and if the yen/dollar exchange rate remains where it is, future United States–Japan economic relations and those of Japan vis-à-vis the rest of the world can only result in tensions and conflicts.

South Korea and Taiwan

While Japan is optimistic about its future, both Taiwan and South Korea are facing economic prospects that are, by their standards, bordering on recession. Internally, they have been struggling with political and social reforms towards a more democratic society. The economic consequences of the political transition have proved to be costly, and more so in Korea's case. The rate of growth decelerated to about 7 per cent from two years of double-digit growth in Taiwan in 1988, and forecasts showed that Taiwan was unlikely to do any better in 1989 (see Table 7.1). In South Korea, the 5.7 per cent growth during the first quarter of 1989 was about one-third of what it was a year ago. Export growth has slowed down to a crawl in value, reaching a negative number in volume terms (in domestic currency). As a result, the first quarter recorded a current account surplus of US$1.3 billion compared to US$3 billion in 1988. After three years of 12-plus per cent growth, Korea is expected to experience a minor 'recession' with 7 per cent growth shortly.

It was expected that political reforms for democratisation, which were set in motion in June 1987, would impose a heavy economic cost on the Korean economy, but the actual outcome has been much more severe than predicted. During the first quarter of 1989, the pace of price increases has accelerated, speculative transactions in both the stock and real estate estate markets have been mounting, and most important of all, the frequency of labour–management disputes has risen markedly. The drop in export earnings, large wage increases with a declining labour productivity and the continuing political instability have all come together to cloud the prospects for the Korean economy for the next several years.

As one magazine article put it, the current debate in Korea is not over whether it could repeat the performance of 1988 but over 'how much growth will slow and how much inflation will rise' (*Far Eastern Economic Review*, 23 March 1988). All of the available forecasts predict that the GNP growth rate will come down to around 8 per cent for the next two years—close to the potential rate of growth of the economy, with inflation in terms of the GNP deflator ranging from 4 to 7 per cent.

Although export growth is expected to drop to about 16 per cent in 1989 and to 11 per cent in 1990, due in part to a sharp increase in unit labour cost, the current account is forecast to generate a surplus of the order of US$5–6 billion over each of the next two years. Much of this export expansion would come from price increases, according to these forecasts, and, adjusted for price increases, exports will not grow more than 5 per cent a year.

Unlike other periods, economic prospects for the next two years in Korea critically depend on developments in labour–industry relations and political stability. Regardless of Korea's export competitiveness and growth potential, any further radicalisation of union activities directed to advancing political causes of particular interest groups would relegate collective bargaining for work-place interests to secondary importance. If this happens and strikes are used as a political weapon, many fear labour strife could damage Korea's growth to an irreparable degree. The worsening labour–industry relations and an economic slowdown in Korea's major trading partners, which could depress further business investment and outlook, would indeed be a deadly combination.

Some of Taiwan's economic difficulties have been brought about by economic success itself, whereas other problems such as labour unrest and a weaker government may have been unavoidable during a period of political transition. The recent upheaval and confusion in China can only deepen Taiwan's dilemma in dealing with the mainland, with which it has diversified its economic relations, and add more uncertainty to the future of the Taiwan economy.

The most pressing problems facing Taiwan's policymakers at present are reviving investment demand and cooling off the rampant speculation in stock and real asset markets. One cannot help but feel that Taiwan is overwhelmed by the enormity of its accumulated wealth, much of which is in foreign assets and which has been feeding stock, land and housing speculation. Over a three-year period between 1986 and 1988, the stock price index skyrocketed from 153 to 842, indicating how serious the speculation has been.

In an effort to address these problems, the Taiwan government has recently announced its version of Japan's Maekawa Report. It stresses the urgency of further trade liberalisation and expanding domestic demand. The package also includes deregulation of domestic industries, expanding the social security system, building more low income housing units, and supporting research and development efforts by the private sector. It is too early to tell whether these measures will be carried out as planned, and whether they will be able to loosen up the rigid structure built up by the export-oriented development strategy over the last thirty years.

As in Korea, the government sector in Taiwan has played a leading role in promoting economic growth and industrialisation. Economic liberalisation and recently the demand for political reforms have reduced considerably the effectiveness and scope of government intervention. The ruling party will have to rely more on consensus, but has yet to develop a system that could bring into the decisionmaking process all the parties vying for a larger slice of economic and political power.

In the next few years, few in Taiwan believe that political reforms, even if their pace is accelerated, could lead to an eruption of social and political discontent on the scale of that which has transpired in Korea. While Taiwan's trade with China will suffer and it could lose much of its extensive foreign direct investment in the mainland, it could also gain as more foreign importers come to Taiwan as China languishes.

Recent export and import figures also suggest that Taiwanese exporters may have overcome the appreciation of the NT dollar and recovered their competitiveness. During the first four months of 1989, exports grew 11 per cent whereas imports did not move very much, registering a hefty surplus of US$3.7 billion. Over the next five years, policymakers plan to steer the economy gradually to a more domestic market oriented structure, and in so doing are prepared to suffer a setback in economic growth of up to 6–7 per cent. Prices are expected to remain stable, and, most important of all, trade surpluses relative to GNP would come down to below 5 per cent. Taiwan is fortunate in that it will not suffer from any serious resource constraint as it is likely to maintain a high rate of saving in coming years and hence could experiment with an internal demand oriented growth strategy, though the potential for success of such a policy is uncertain at this stage.

ADJUSTING TRADE IMBALANCES: THE TRILATERAL TRADE RELATIONSHIP IN EAST ASIA

To East Asian NIEs and Japan, the United States has provided by far the

Figure 7.6 United States imports from East Asia

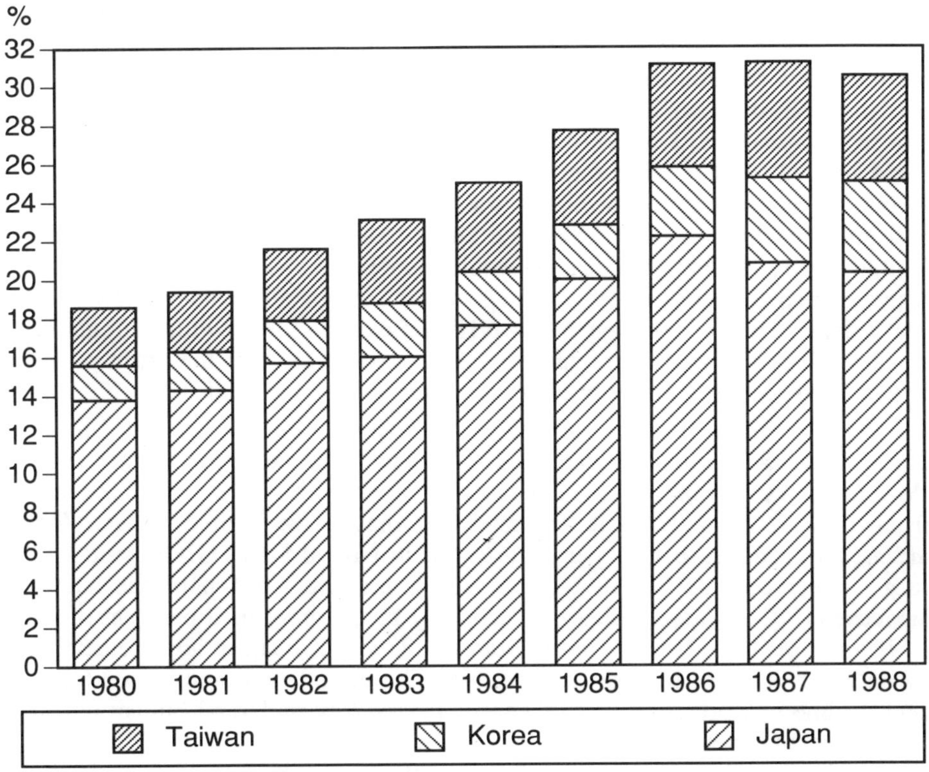

Sources: Bank of Japan, *Economic Statistics Annual 1987*, March 1988; Japan Statistics Bureau, *Monthly Statistics of Japan*, March 1989; Korea Foreign Trade Association, *The Trend of Foreign Trade*, various issues; Taiwan Ministry of Finance, *Monthly Statistics of Exports and Imports*, December 1988.

largest market for their exports. In recent years, Japan, Taiwan and Korea as a group accounted for more than 30 per cent of United States imports (Figure 7.6). Notwithstanding their market diversification efforts, there is little doubt that the United States will continue to be their number one trading partner.

In both academic and policy circles, there is agreement that trade liberalisation and currency appreciation of the East Asian economies must be accompanied by a United States fiscal correction to bring down the United States deficit vis-à-vis East Asia. With a new administration in Washington, the prospects for a substantial budgetary adjustment in the United States have become more realistic than before. To many Pacific Asian countries, in particular the East Asian NIEs, the United States budgetary adjustment could also mean a major loss of their export market. The difficult question of what could and will happen when the United States market stops growing, begins to shrink, or is closed, has occupied the minds of many trade officials and policymakers throughout Pacific Asia. One of the major consequences of the United States budgetary cutback would be slow economic growth in the region, which could in turn affect the growth of the global economy. Given the heavy dependence of the East Asian NIEs on exports for growth, the bulk of which is absorbed by the United States, it is easy to see that the brunt of the impact of the United States budget cut would fall on the East Asian NIEs.

Several empirical studies show that the income elasticity of the United States demand for imports from the East Asian NIEs and Japan is very high, close to 4, whereas the income elasticity of Japan with respect to its imports from the East Asian NIEs is less than half that of the United States. This means, for example, that a 2 per cent decline in United States GNP could lead to a 4.6 per cent decline in Korean GNP[8] and about a 1 per cent fall in Japanese GNP. If Japan deflates its economy in the order of 2 per cent of its GNP to offset the effect of United States deflation, Korea can hope to benefit by only a 1 per cent increase in its GNP. The net effect would be a 3.6 per cent decline in Korean GNP (Takenaka, 1988). Any unilateral budget cut in the United States will unleash serious deflationary effects, triggering a recession in the East Asian NIEs, and choking off the economic vitality of Pacific Asia.

The price elasticity of United States imports from the East Asian NIEs is twice as high as the elasticity of imports from Japan. One possible reason for this high elasticity is that the products which the East Asian NIEs export to the United States consist mostly of labour-intensive consumer goods with many substitutes from other countries, whereas Japanese products are more sophisticated and technology-intensive with a limited number of substitutes. Largely due to this high price elasticity, a recent simulation study by Cline (1989) shows that a real appreciation by 12 to 14 per cent in 1989 shifts the 1992 baseline current account balances for Taiwan and the group that includes Korea, Hong Kong and Singapore from deficits of 2 and 3 per cent of exports of goods and services to deficits of 10 and 11 per cent. In contrast, a real appreciation of the yen by 28 per cent, with a one percentage point growth increment above the baseline during the 1989–92 period, reduces Japan's surplus to 16 per cent from 34 per cent of exports of goods and services on the baseline. Although Japan appreciates its currency by more than the East Asian NIEs do theirs, its surplus with Taiwan remains unchanged at its 1988 level (simulation) of US$6.4 billion, while its surplus with the Korea group rises above the 1988 level of US$21 billion.

What then could these East Asian countries do collectively or individually to offset at least some of the deflationary effect of the United States budget cut and the real appreciation forced on them? One idea that has captured the imagination of many in Pacific Asia is regional economic integration. There is a growing expectation that Pacific Asia based cooperation could expand intra-regional trade and through this expansion the region could compensate for, at least in part, the shrinking United States market. Because of its super-economic power status, Japan will naturally be pushed into playing a central role in any regional cooperation in Asia. It is not clear whether any regional integration or cooperation dominated by Japan would be politically acceptable to many countries in Asia. Even when political issues are set aside, given some of the economic characteristics of the region, it is not clear whether setting up a regional cooperation network would work and if it works whether it would provide an alternative to the United States market.

Despite its super-power status, Japan's market is not large enough to absorb the region's exports and make any integration efforts credible and worthwhile. Ironically, Japan's trade expansion with and foreign direct investment in other Pacific Asian countries could complicate the region's trade problems with the rest of the world and create obstacles to the formation of a regional cooperation network. It is true that there are strong economic forces and shifts in regional economic power that may justify a Pacific Asia based integration, but they must be put in perspective against those forces and regional characteristics that could interfere with or at least slow down the integration process. When this is done, the idea of regional integration loses much of its appeal.

Countries in the Pacific region differ from one another not only in terms of their resource endowment but also, of course, in terms of their cultural backgrounds and economic and political systems. This diversity could serve as a source of complementarity that helps bind the countries in the region together, but it also makes it difficult to define common economic and political objectives. In recent years, rapid growth and increased flows of goods and services and factors of production have contributed to a narrowing down of the differences in trade and industrial policy. Yet, Pacific Asian countries have a long way to go before agreement on any plan for the proposed integration is reached. There is, however, a more serious economic problem than the structural constraints that stand in the way of regional cooperation. For successful integration to occur, the Pacific Asian countries must find ways to liberalise further their trade regimes. Japan must also be prepared to increase its capacity to import manufactured goods from its Pacific Asian partners. The prospects for these changes are not promising.

Because of the striking similarity of their industrial and trade structures, which limits inter-industry trade, the volume of trade among the East Asian NIEs has been insignificant as a proportion of total Asian trade. Although the intra-East Asian NIEs trade has been growing recently, it is too early to tell whether this trend will continue. They could of course specialise along lines of comparative advantage within industry, which will help expand intra-industry trade. This would require a mutual openness of markets and, more importantly, a close coordination in industrial policy. Since they are not competing with one another in their own markets, but in third markets such as the United States and the European Community, policy coordination has been more difficult than otherwise. Partly because of severe competition among themselves in the third markets, they have been more protective of their domestic markets with respect to each other than they have to other trade partners.

Although Japan is the second largest economy in the world, it is highly doubtful whether it could become a major absorber for other Pacific Asian economies. Only two years after Japan undertook market opening measures, it is claimed that East Asian NIEs have already saturated Japan's market for labour-intensive manufactures including electronics and machinery. In 1987 the total value of Pacific Asian exports to the United States was almost as large as the total value of the intra-regional trade in Pacific Asia. Japan purchased less than 10 per cent of total manufactured exports of the East Asian NIEs, ASEAN and China, while the United States absorbed more than 30 per cent. The United States imports from all of the East Asian NIEs, ASEAN and China in 1987 were six times as large as the Japanese imports from these countries.

The value of manufactured imports per capita for Japan was US$540 as compared to US$1,333 for the United States in 1987. It is simply unrealistic to expect Japan to grow into an export market for other Pacific Asian economies large enough to supplant the United States market in the event that the United States brings down its deficits with East Asia, no matter what it does to transform its economic policies and lifestyle. Over the next five years, Japan's earnings on its holdings of foreign assets will begin to pile up and, in fact, the interest income will be growing so fast that Japan's invisible trade will record a surplus of almost US$60 billion by 1995, and US$80 billion by the year 2000. This means that Japan could run a huge current account surplus even if it succeeds in balancing the trade account. This development also means that Japan will have plenty of room to run a deficit on its manufactures trade, although whether Japan could actually do so is a totally different matter.

In order to run a deficit on manufactures trade, Japan should be able to induce a shift of labour from declining industries to competitive and expanding ones. According to one estimate (Okumura, 1988), foreign direct investment will cause a loss of half a million manufacturing jobs by 1995, and the steel industry will reduce its work-force by one-third, and shipbuilding by almost half by the year 2000. It is predicted that growth in service sector employment will make up for the decline in manufacturing employment. As a result, the share of the service sector will rise to 20 per cent of total employment, from 24 per cent in 1987.

It is not clear whether by 1995 Japan will be able to generate such a large number of job opportunities in the service sector, and, if indeed it does, whether it will adjust to such an abrupt structural change in employment in a country known for its lifetime employment system. There is also another macroeconomic characteristic which may interfere with Japan's structural adjustment efforts. Japan has maintained one of the highest savings rates in the world and in all likelihood will continue to do so for some time in the future. Only after the mid-1990s when the percentage of the population over 59 years of age starts to increase rapidly is Japan's saving rate projected to decline. For the next seven years, therefore, Japanese households are not likely to increase their spending on luxuries and vacations despite the expected reduction in working hours. Unless investment demand rises enough to exhaust domestic savings, the saving–investment imbalance will persist, hold back its import demand, and hence complicate Japan's current account management.

Aside from these structural problems, one might ask whether regional cooperation would be a viable solution to the region's trade problems with the rest of the world. Contrary to the general expectation, any integration centring on Japan could expand its trade imbalances and hence worsen trade conflicts with North America and Europe for a number of reasons. One is the poor resource endowments which the East Asian NIEs share in common and which require them to rely heavily on imported oil and other raw materials. This is also true for Japan. In order to pay for these imports of primary commodities, while maintaining their overall trade in balance, they must obtain a surplus on their trade in manufactures with other countries. The ASEAN countries with a rich resource base have traditionally maintained a deficit on their manufactures trade with Japan and the East Asian NIEs. Through the promotion of labour-intensive products, however, the ASEAN economies and China are trying to balance their manufactures trade. This means that as a whole the Pacific Asian region will have to obtain a surplus from outside the region, a proposition that is hardly acceptable to the rest of the world.

Another reason is the process of development underway in Pacific Asia in which the East Asian NIEs are trying to catch up with Japan while being hotly pursued by other countries in Asia, in particular, the ASEAN economies and China. In this process, all of these countries rely heavily on Japan as the major source of capital and technology needed for their development. As a result, all of them, except for the two resource-rich countries (Indonesia and Malaysia), have been running chronic trade deficits with Japan. This dependence means that these countries will have to run a surplus in trade with the rest of the world if they are going to balance their trade account.

A third reason is related to Japan's expansion of foreign direct investment[9] in its transfer of technology to other Asian countries. Japan's foreign direct investment in Pacific Asia has been concentrated on manufacturing. Since all the Pacific Asian economies are promoting exports of labour-intensive manufactures, it is not difficult to see that the ultimate destination of most of the products made by firms in which Japan has an interest will be the United States and Europe, and that other Pacific Asian countries will depend even more on Japan than in the past for the supplies of parts, components and industrial materials. This dependence will deepen the trade imbalances between Japan and the rest of Pacific Asia. This imbalance will then build more pressure for the East Asian NIEs, the ASEAN economies, and China to obtain larger surpluses in their trade with the United States and Europe.

This chapter has argued that Pacific based economic integration centring on Japan will not be a viable alternative to a shrinking United States market. What then would be a more realistic and effective policy response on the part of the East Asian NIEs? The trade imbalance problem cannot be resolved by any unilateral policy adjustments by either side. Unless both the United States and East Asia put absorption policies in place and coordinate them, exchange rate changes alone will not lead to a substantial correction of the existing imbalances between the two sides. However, if a United States fiscal correction is matched by more internal demand oriented policies and trade liberalisation of Japan and the East Asian NIEs, then there is the possibility that the existing trade imbalance will gradually decline in an adjustment process that manages to avoid a worldwide recession.

8 Macroeconomic management in the ASEAN countries

MARI PANGESTU

Various external shocks occurred in the 1980s that affected the small open economies of the ASEAN countries. First came the economic recession in the early 1980s, ending only in 1983, followed by falling oil prices after 1982, with commodity prices remaining depressed. Since 1985 there has also been a realignment of the currencies of the major industrial economies accompanied by restructuring, especially in Japan and the NIEs. These external shocks have adversely affected the balance of payments and budget deficits of the ASEAN countries, leading to various policy adjustments.

Most analyses indicate that, in general, the ASEAN countries[1]—Indonesia, Malaysia, the Philippines, Singapore and Thailand—performed better in the 1980s than other developing countries in the wake of these external shocks. Table 8.1 provides a picture of the experience of the ASEAN economies compared with that of other developing countries with respect to inflation, GDP growth, current account and fiscal imbalances. GDP serves as a measure of economic growth while the others measure the degree of macroeconomic instability.[2]

During the oil shocks and recession of the 1970s, the non-oil ASEAN countries on average experienced lower inflation rates (except for the Philippines), current account and budget deficits (except for Malaysia), and higher GDP growth than the non-oil developing countries of Africa, Europe, the Middle East and the Western hemisphere (Latin American and the Caribbean).

Inflation rates in the only major oil exporting ASEAN country, Indonesia, were higher than the average for oil exporting countries, but comparable with other non-oil developing countries. The high inflation rates were a reflection of the ineffectiveness of sterilisation policies to offset increases in reserve money due to monetisation of oil revenues. During the 1970s, while oil prices were rising, Indonesia had current account deficits lower than non-oil developing countries.

The relatively better performance of the ASEAN countries compared with that of other developing countries continued into the 1980s. The decade began with the world recession and was marked by falling oil and commodity prices as well as currency realignments (Figure 8.1). Inflation was lower, current

Table 8.1 Comparative inflation rates, current account balances, real GDP growth and central government deficit/surplus by region, 1971–88 (annual unweighted averages)

	Inflation rate[a]		Current account balance[b]	
	1971–80	1981–88	1971–80	1981–88
Non-oil developing countries:				
Africa	13.1	16.0	-11.4	-13.8
Europe	16.7	32.4	-13.4	-5.4
Middle East	13.7	15.2	21.0	-3.3
Western hemisphere	36.5	117.4	-20.5	-14.4
Asia	10.4	7.5	-4.8	-2.6
Hong Kong	8.5	7.9	na	na
Korea	16.4	6.2	-20.0	1.3
ASEAN	9.1	6.7	-10.3	-9.5
Malaysia	6.0	3.4	-1.6	-7.2
Philippines	13.9	15.0	-13.6	-14.3
Singapore	6.7	4.3	-9.9	-1.3
Thailand	9.8	4.1	-15.9	-15.0
Oil exporting countries	12.5	9.9	13.0	-4.2
Indonesia	17.6	9.0	-7.2	-16.1

Notes: na—not available.
Some 1988 figures are still provisional.
a Percentage change in Consumer Price Index.
b Includes official transfer and is expressed as a percentage of total exports of goods and services.
c Compound annual rates of change.
d Calculated as the difference between revenue and if applicable grant received and expenditures and lending minus repayment. It is expressed as percentage of GNP. For 1971–80 government deficit, Africa (1972–80), Europe (1975–80), Middle East (1972- 80), Asia (1972–80) and oil exporting countries (1972–80).

Sources: IMF, *International Financial Statistics* for inflation rates (all, non-ASEAN, Korea and Hong Kong), current account balance (ASEAN and Korea), GDP growth rates (ASEAN and Korea 1971–80), government deficit (all, non-ASEAN, Korea and Hong Kong 1971–80); *World Economic Outlook*, April 1989 for current account balance and real GDP growth (all, non-ASEAN, Korea and Hong Kong), government deficit (all, non-ASEAN, Korea and Hong Kong 1981–88); ADB, *Asian Development Outlook*, 1989 for inflation rates (ASEAN, Korea and Hong Kong), real GDP growth (ASEAN, Korea and Hong Kong, 1981–88) and government deficit (ASEAN, Korea and Hong Kong).

account deficits of the non-oil ASEAN countries improved enormously and were much lower than in other non-oil developing countries. The other developing countries, especially in the Western hemisphere, faced a mounting external debt burden, due to massive borrowing of recycled petrodollars and rising interest rates. In the ASEAN region, only the Philippines, and perhaps Indonesia, experienced external debt problems. Both Indonesia and Malaysia were adversely affected by the oil price declines, which began in 1982 and worsened in 1986, and the realignment in exchange rates in 1985 on debt repayments.

The ASEAN countries on average experienced higher GDP growth than other developing countries in the 1980s, but in common with other developing countries, the non-oil ASEAN countries experienced a slower growth of GDP in the 1980s than in the 1970s. Growth in the Philippines became negative, mainly owing to adverse political developments and the external debt problem. Indonesia also experienced a slowdown of growth.

On balance it seems that the ASEAN countries have been more successful

(Table 8.1 cont'd)

Real GDP growth[c]		Central government deficit/surplus[d]	
1971–80	1981–88	1971–80	1981–88
3.8	1.5	-4.4	-6.5
5.0	2.8	-3.1	-2.7
7.2	0.7	-0.9	-9.7
5.9	1.6	-2.2	-4.7
5.3	7.3	-3.6	-3.5
na	7.3	1.8	0.8
8.2	9.4	-2.2	-1.4
7.6	4.5	-2.9	-3.8
8.1	4.7	-8.3	-11.3
6.3	0.8	-1.3	-3.1
8.8	6.1	0.8	1.9
7.2	6.5	-2.7	-2.7
6.6	0.6	0.5	-7.4
8.1	3.9	-3.6	-8.2

than other developing countries, at least as measured by the macroeconomic indicators, in coping with major external shocks. Furthermore, all the ASEAN countries experienced an upturn in their economic growth in the last two years of the decade (Figures 8.2a and 8.2b). While more favourable initial conditions and external developments provide part of the explanation, the domestic policies that were followed obviously played an important role. The aim of this chapter is to analyse and compare the experience of the ASEAN countries with regard to policy adjustments that were made in response to the various external or internal shocks that occurred in the 1980s.[3]

MACROECONOMIC MANAGEMENT

Macroeconomic adjustment policies are undertaken when there are changes in the composition and/or levels of aggregate demand or aggregate supply, which are in turn reflected in higher inflation rates, growing external and budget deficits, and a slowdown of economic growth. The appropriate policy response is a policy mix that will allow the supply–demand imbalance to be eliminated in an orderly way before the economy becomes too distorted and external finance is exhausted.

Several types of adjustment policies can be undertaken.[4] In the short run, there are demand management policies in the form of monetary and fiscal policies which are aimed at changing absorption levels. Policies of exchange rate adjustment are aimed at changing the composition of absorption and production between tradeable and non-tradeable goods.

In the medium and longer term, structural policies aimed at increasing the current and potential output through those that improve efficiency and resource allocation and policies to expand the productive capacity of the economy should be implemented. Improvement of efficiency and resource

Figure 8.1 ASEAN countries, term of trade

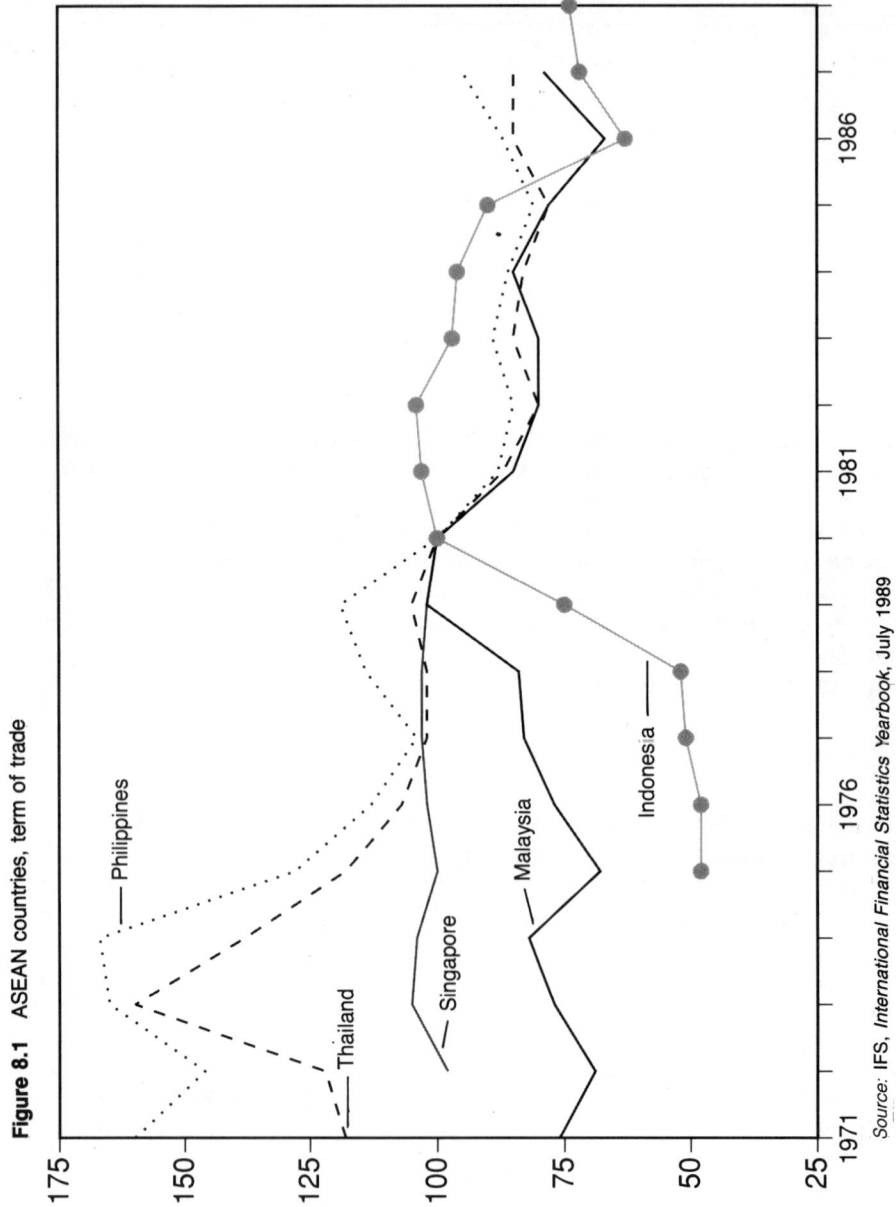

Source: IFS, *International Financial Statistics Yearbook*, July 1989

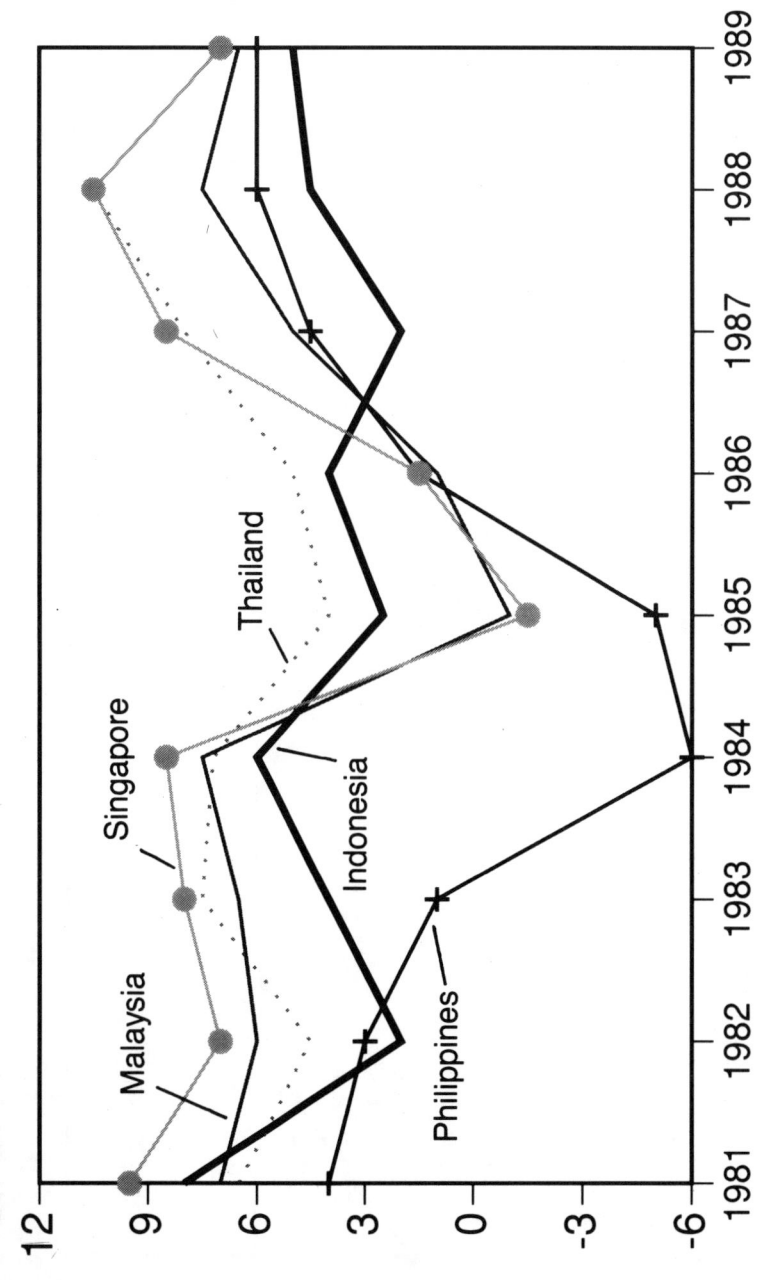

MACROECONOMIC MANAGEMENT IN THE ASEAN COUNTRIES 125

Figure 8.2a ASEAN countries, GDP growth rates

Source: ADB, *Asian Development Outlook*, 1989.

Figure 8.2b ASEAN countries, inflation rates

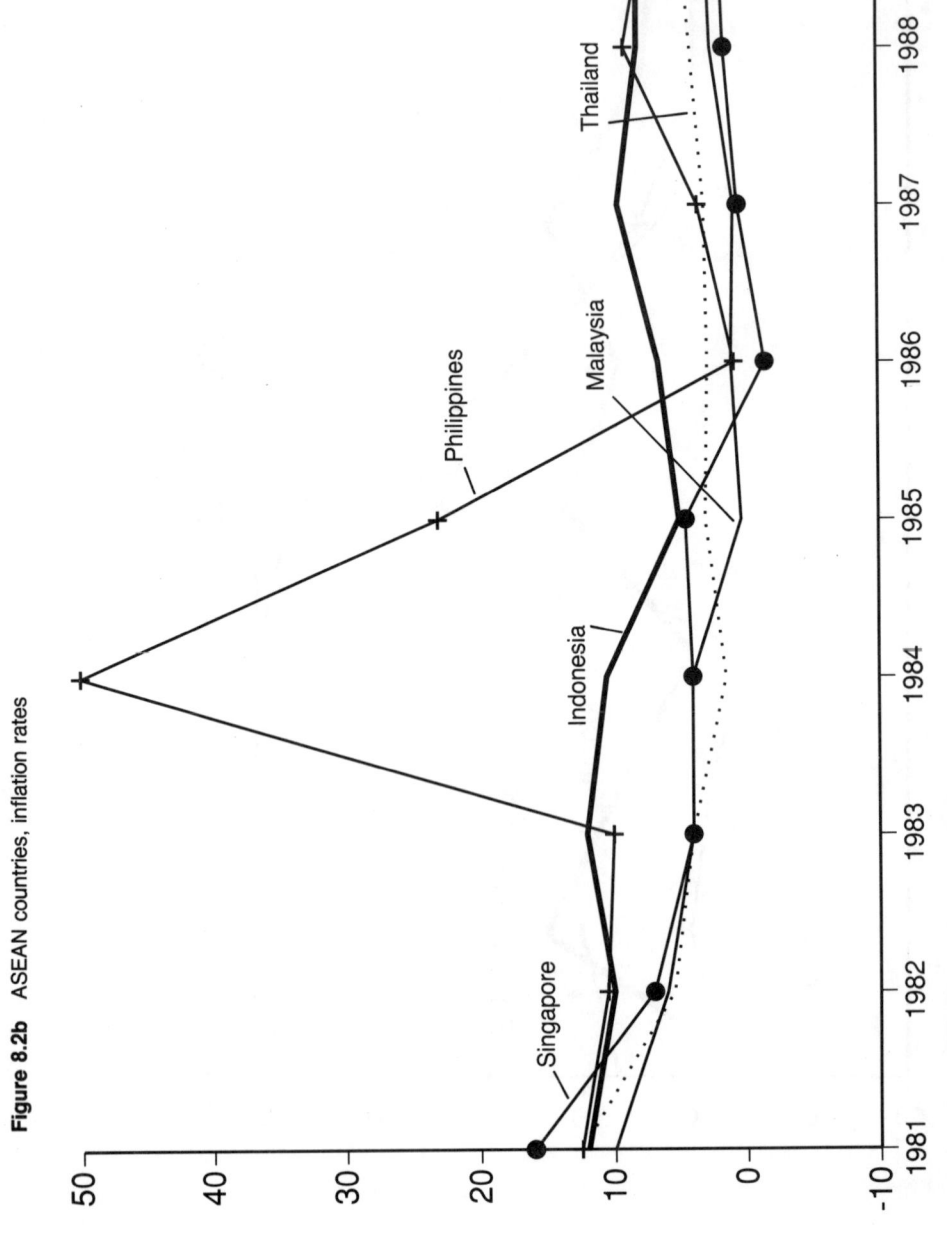

Source: ADB, Asian Development Outlook, 1989.

allocation requires policies to reduce distortions between prices and marginal costs such as those which arise from price controls, imperfect competition, discriminatory taxes and subsidies and trade restrictions.

Expansion of capacity can be achieved by policies that favour investment and saving. Such policies include improvement of government saving through fiscal reforms, and private saving and investment through interest rate policies and financial sector reforms.

Structural policies encounter many practical difficulties. In developing countries, the goal of achieving a more efficient allocation of resources and faster growth may conflict in the short run with that of reducing current account deficits since investment requires imports of capital goods. Structural policies also take longer to yield results. During the lag, unemployment may arise because of sectoral immobility of factors in response to changes in price incentives. Distortionary policies which serve equity objectives, such as job creation, consumer subsidies, price controls on basic necessities and regional development, are politically difficult to remove. Finally, removal of one distortion may not raise efficiency if other distortions remain.

A country can avoid adjustment by borrowing abroad or restricting trade and payments. However, the costs of this type of strategy in terms of overvaluation of the exchange rate, loss of international competitiveness, reduced economic growth, increased foreign debt and inefficient allocation or resources are so high that the strategy in fact only delays the need for adjustment (Khan, 1987: 23).

While the literature is clear on the types of measures to be included in an adjustment program, it provides little guidance on the appropriate mix or sequencing of adjustment policies. Both will differ according to initial conditions, the link between policies and objectives, the relevant time frame and the specifics of the country in question. It is the aim of this chapter to attempt such an analysis given the conditions of the ASEAN countries and to attempt to draw some lessons from their experience.

POLICIES AND PERFORMANCE OF THE ASEAN COUNTRIES

Each ASEAN country will be examined separately in the following, beginning with an overview of the macroeconomic indicators. Relevant comparisons to ASEAN neighbours are made and performance measures given to evaluate the relative success of the adjustment policies.

Comparative macroeconomic indicators of GDP growth, inflation, current account and budget deficits are given in Table 8.2. Money supply growth and comparative interest rates can be found in Table 8.3, while trends in nominal and real effective exchange rates are provided in Figures 8.3a and 8.3b. External debt and debt service ratios are given in Table 8.4. Finally, Table 8.5 shows gross investment and savings comparisons.

Table 8.2 ASEAN countries, macroeconomic performance, 1971–88

	Inflation rates (percentage change of CPI)		Growth rate of GDP[a]	
	1971–80	1981–88	1971–80	1981–88
Non-oil ASEAN countries (unweighted averages):	9.1	6.7	7.6	4.5
Malaysia	6.0	3.4	8.1	4.7
Philippines	13.9	15.0	6.3	0.8
Singapore	6.7	4.3	8.8	6.1
Thailand	9.8	4.1	7.2	6.5
Indonesia	17.6	9.0	8.1	3.9

	Current account balance as percentage of merchandise export		Central government deficit/surplus as percentage of GDP	
	1971–80	1981–88	1971–80	1981–88
Non-oil ASEAN countries (unweighted averages):	–14.0	–13.1	–2.9	–3.8
Malaysia	–1.8	–9.0	–8.3	–11.3
Phillippines	–18.8	–21.7	–1.3	–3.1
Singapore	–14.4	–1.5	0.8	1.9
Thailand	–20.9	–20.0	–2.7	–2.7
Indonesia	–26.0	–16.5	–3.6	–4.6

Note: a Compound growth rate.

Sources: IMF, *International Financial Statistics* for growth rate of GDP (1971–80), current account balance (1971–80); ADB, *Asian Development Outlook* 1989 for inflation rates (1971–88), growth rate of GDP (1981–88), current account balance (1981–88), government deficit (1971–88).

Indonesia

The decade prior to the 1980s was the oil boom period for Indonesia. As Indonesia entered the 1980s it was more than ever dependent on oil as a source of government revenues (60 per cent in 1982) and as source of foreign exchange (85 per cent of exports in 1982). The oil boom years were also characterised by more protectionist and interventionist policies. Foreign investment regulations had become more restrictive, and trade and industrial policies were directed at influencing the pattern of industrialisation through protection of domestic industries.

The trade and industrial regime was characterised by escalating protection

Table 8.3 ASEAN countries, growth rate of broad money, 1971–88 (per cent per annum)

	1971–80	1981–88
Non-oil ASEAN countries (averages):	19.0	14.2
Malaysia	21.1	10.2
Philippines	20.5	17.0
Singapore	15.7	13.0
Thailand	18.6	16.7
Indonesia	36.1	23.9

Source: ADB, *Asian Development Outlook*, 1989.

MACROECONOMIC MANAGEMENT IN THE ASEAN COUNTRIES

Table 8.4 ASEAN countries, deposit rate, external debt outstanding, debt-service ratio

Deposit rate	1981	1982	1983	1984	1985	1986	1987	1988
Indonesia	6.0	6.0	6.0	16.0	18.0	-	16.8	-
Malaysia	9.7	9.8	8.0	9.5	8.8	7.2	3.0	-
Philippines	13.7	13.7	13.6	21.2	18.9	11.3	8.2	11.3
Singapore	10.7	7.2	6.3	7.0	5.0	3.9	2.9	2.7
Thailand	12.5	13.0	13.0	13.0	13.0	9.8	9.5	-
United States	15.9	12.4	9.1	10.4	8.1	6.5	6.9	7.7
Japan	4.4	3.8	3.8	3.5	3.5	2.3	1.8	1.8
West Germany	9.7	7.5	4.6	4.9	4.4	3.7	3.2	3.3

External debt outstanding	1981	1982	1983	1984	1985	1986	1987	1988	1989
Non-oil ASEAN countries (averages):	10342	12686	13923	14720	16348	17819	19210	18140	19260
Malaysia	7544	11617	14896	16249	18268	19999	21675	18400	17740
Philippines	20750	24299	24124	24358	26190	28853	29962	29900	32300
Singapore	2263	2629	2803	3290	3406	3875	4491	2260	2000
Thailand	10809	12198	13868	14981	17528	18549	20710	22000	25000
Indonesia	22723	26500	30138	31952	35999	43039	52581	55600	57600

Note: Total net flow of resources; million US dollars.

Debt-service ratio (per cent of exports)	1981	1982	1983	1984	1985	1986	1987	1988	1989
Non-oil ASEAN countries (averages):	10.0	12.4	13.2	13.4	32.7	18.5	17.1	15.7	13.9
Malaysia	6.8	9.2	10.2	12.8	82.9	19.7	20.0	20.4	16.6
Philippines	17.4	22.7	21.3	17.5	19.0	26.0	25.2	23.4	21.9
Singapore	1.4	1.5	2.2	1.9	3.5	2.6	2.4	1.9	1.3
Thailand	14.4	16.0	19.1	21.5	25.3	25.5	20.6	17.0	15.7
Indonesia	12.9	16.5	18.4	18.9	24.9	32.6	33.3	40.0	38.0

Sources: IMF, *International Financial Statistics*; ADB, *Asian Development Outlook*, 1989.

through tariff and non-tariff barriers, high and variable effective rates of protection which were biased against export production, proliferation of administrative procedures and excessive government intervention. Because of high costs of operations and the adverse relative price movements resulting from the familiar 'Dutch Disease' effect, non-oil exports stagnated.

Macroeconomic indicators

Indonesia averaged growth rates of 4.4 per cent in the 1981–88 period compared with 7.9 per cent for the previous decade, but never experienced negative growth. The world recession in the early 1980s and the fall in oil prices which was accompanied by fiscal restraint contributed to the lower growth in the early 1980s, especially in 1982. Growth picked up again and reached 6 per cent in 1984, but fell again with the recession in 1985. Since 1986 growth seems to have stabilised at around 4–5 per cent and is expected to sustain or even surpass that level.[5]

Table 8.5 ASEAN countries, gross domestic saving and gross investment, 1971–89 (per cent of GDP)

	Gross domestic saving									
	1971–80	1981–88	1981	1982	1983	1984	1985	1986	1987	1988	1989
Non-oil ASEAN countries (averages):	26.5	29.3	29.2	28.7	30.1	30.4	27.7	27.2	29.8	31.3	30.2
Malaysia	30.2	33.1	28.8	28.6	30.8	35.5	32.7	31.5	37.7	38.8	37.2
Philippines	23.4	19.4	24.1	22.6	22.5	18.8	16.2	16.2	17.1	17.4	17.2
Singapore	30.0	41.8	41.7	42.3	45.0	45.3	40.8	38.9	39.8	40.7	40.8
Thailand	22.2	23.0	22.2	21.3	21.9	21.8	21.2	22.2	24.7	28.3	25.7
Indonesia	21.6	26.1	23.5	18.7	28.3	30.5	28.5	24.9	29.1	25.1	26.7

	Gross investment									
	1971–80	1981–88	1981	1982	1983	1984	1985	1986	1987	1988	1989
Non-oil ASEAN countries (averages):	28.4	29.9	34.6	34.2	34.2	31.0	27.0	24.6	26.1	27.7	28.8
Malaysia	20.5	31.0	35.0	37.3	36.1	33.6	27.6	25.3	24.0	28.7	29.1
Philippines	26.7	20.4	30.6	28.3	26.7	17.0	13.9	12.9	15.3	18.1	19.7
Singapore	41.1	43.4	46.3	47.9	47.9	48.5	42.5	38.2	39.1	36.6	36.6
Thailand	25.3	24.9	26.3	23.1	25.9	24.9	24.0	22.0	25.8	27.5	27.2
Indonesia	19.3	23.3	21.4	22.6	25.7	2.5	26.5	20.6	24.6	22.7	24.0

Source: ADB, *Asian Development Outlook*, 1989.

After experiencing high rates of inflation in the 1970s as a result of monetisation of oil revenues, inflation rates in Indonesia began to come down as growth also slowed, especially after 1985. The slightly higher inflation in 1987 can be explained by the devaluation in September 1986 and the relatively higher rate in 1988 by the push against capacity limits in some industries.

Indonesia's current account deficit jumped during the years of falling oil prices, 1982–83 and 1986, but has gradually declined since then. Because of dependence on oil revenues, the same applied to the government budget deficit.

Demand management policies, exchange rate and external financing

The Soeharto government's macroeconomic policy has throughout been characterised by concern for controlling inflation and prudent fiscal policy. During the oil boom years, unlike many other oil exporting countries such as Mexico, Indonesia did not increase external borrowing. The rule of thumb of a debt service ratio of 22 per cent, the balanced budget principle and the debt crisis of the state oil enterprise Pertamina contributed to a relatively conservative external borrowing strategy.

The government responded to the recession and the fall in oil prices by adopting drastic fiscal austerity measures. Among these were the postponement of several capital and import intensive projects in 1983 and a gradual phasing out of subsidies on domestic fuel, fertiliser and state enterprises. More attention was given to disbursement of foreign borrowing. A restrictive monetary policy was also employed to keep control of prices.

MACROECONOMIC MANAGEMENT IN THE ASEAN COUNTRIES 131

Figure 8.3a ASEAN countries, quarterly nominal exchange rates

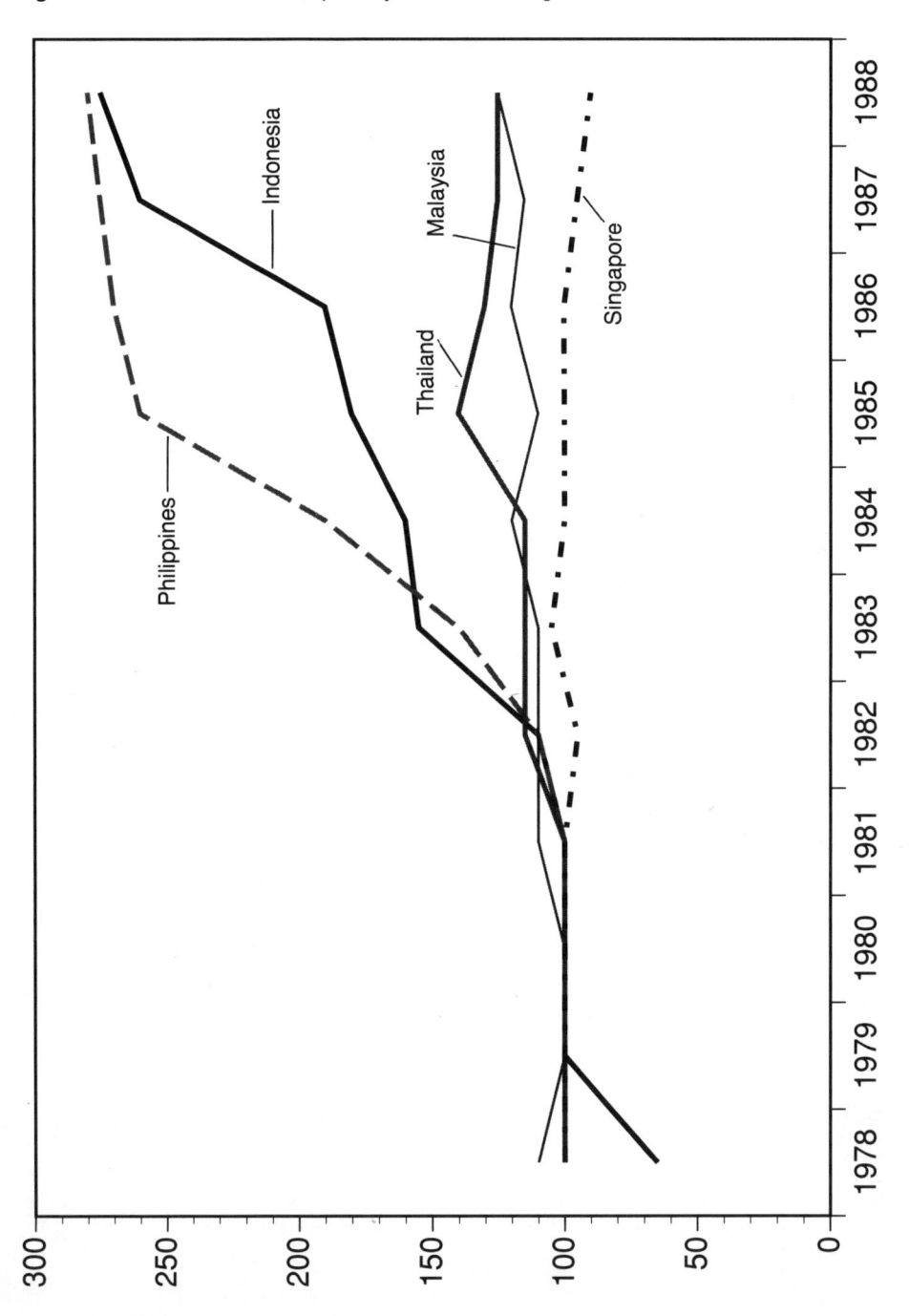

Note: 1980 = 100.

Sources: For trade weights: IMF, *Direction of Trade*, various issues; for exchange rates and inflation rates: IMF, *International Financial Statistics*, various issues.

Figure 8.3b ASEAN countries, quarterly real effective exchange rates

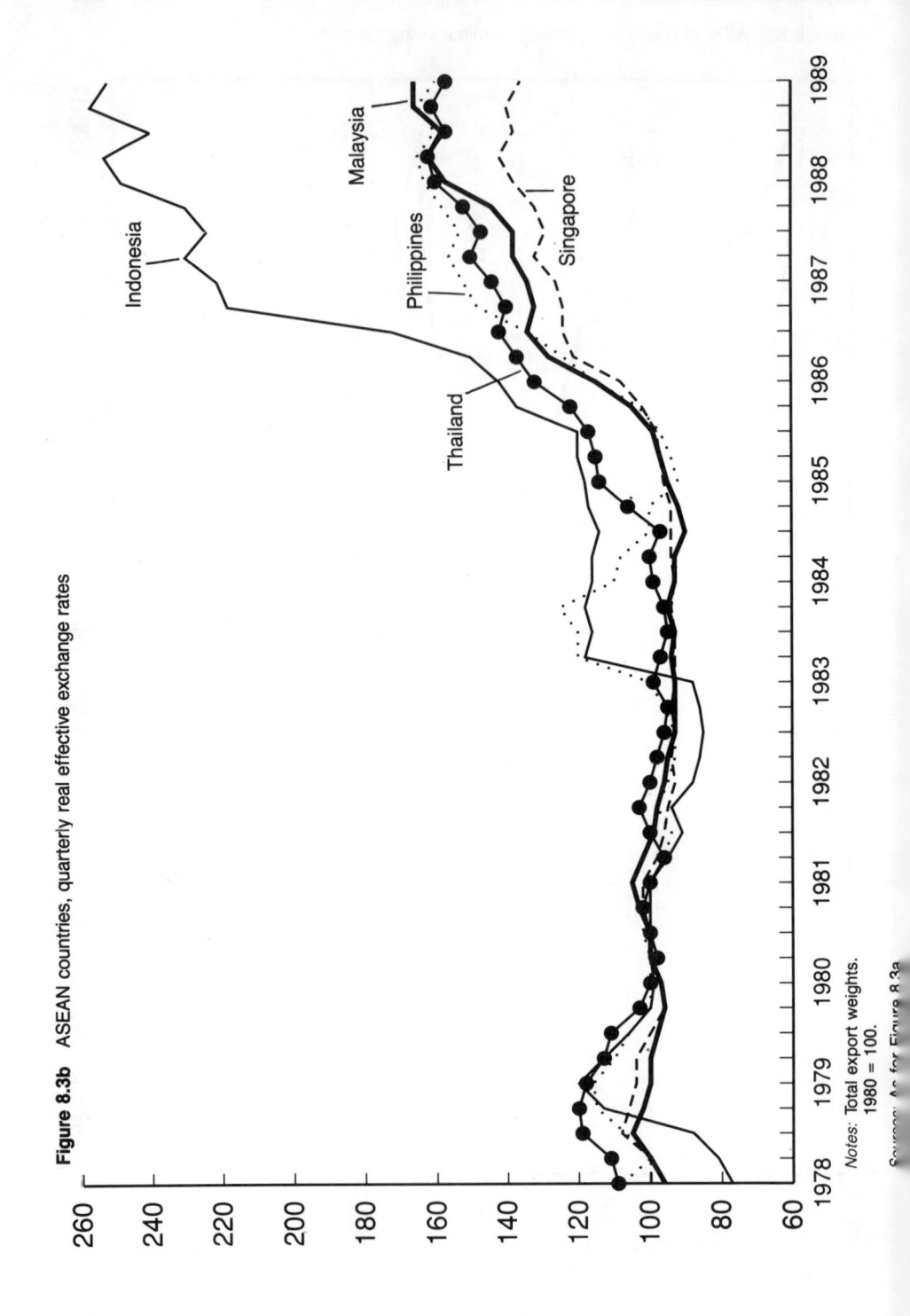

Notes: Total export weights.
1980 = 100.

Since 1969 Indonesia has maintained an open capital account system with no exchange control and until 1978 the rupiah was tied to the US dollar. Indonesia has shown willingness to react quickly to changes in economic conditions with appropriate exchange rate management, but this has often failed to achieve its aim of increasing non-oil exports since it is not accompanied by other necessary policies.

In 1978 the rupiah was devalued by 50 per cent to compensate for the adverse effects on the non-oil tradeables sector due to the 'Dutch Disease' effect. There was some boost to exports, but because inflation was not controlled, the real effective exchange rate was back at its pre-devaluation level. Furthermore, the devaluation was not accompanied by real sector reforms to reduce the high cost economy factors that affected the competitiveness of exports so that there was no long-term growth in exports. The fall in oil prices and the worsening deficit situation which began in 1981 led to the second 50 per cent devaluation in 1983, amidst much speculation that resulted in a significant anticipatory capital outflow. Once again devaluation did not achieve the sustained growth in non-oil exports because of inflation and lack of accompanying reforms.

It was only in 1986 that another 50 per cent devaluation was preceded and accompanied by substantive deregulation which reduced costs to exporters. The result has been substantial growth in non-oil exports, especially manufactured exports. Control of inflation helped to keep real effective exchange rates competitive. Since 1988 exchange rate policy has allowed the rupiah to depreciate gradually to maintain the competitiveness of the real effective exchange rates. After barely moving, except for the big devaluations, the rupiah depreciated 4.5 per cent in 1988 and close to 4 per cent in 1989. The gradual depreciation has helped stem speculation on another big devaluation. To counter speculation on the exchange rate under the open capital account system, interest rates have had to be kept high. As devaluation expectations have subsided the banking system has become very liquid in the aftermath of the 1988 banking deregulations, and lending rates have begun to fall.

Structural policies

The initial response of the government to the balance of payments crisis of the early 1980s was ambivalent. The government was quick to respond with financial and fiscal reforms, but the initial response with regard to trade and industrial policy was increased protection.

Major fiscal reforms were introduced in 1984, aimed at improving the collection of tax revenues from non-oil sources. The reform was undertaken in stages beginning in 1984 with the abolition of the withholding tax, tax holiday for investments approved by the Board of Investment and the introduction of a value added tax. Subsequently, income and sales taxes were rationalised. An important component of the reform was improvement of tax administration and collection. Recently, new and additional sales taxes on luxury goods and services have been introduced.

Banking reforms in the form of abolition of credit ceilings, reduction of liquidity credits from the central bank, and removal of control on the interest rate on deposits of state banks were introduced in June 1983. The aim of the reform was to increase the efficiency of the state bank dominated banking sector, whose main function in the oil boom years was to channel oil revenues through various credit schemes, and to mobilise funds. Additional money market instruments were introduced in 1984, and improved upon since then, to enhance control of money supply.

In trade policy, the period 1983–86 at first witnessed increased protection in the form of non-tariff barriers. Quantitative restrictions under the approved importers system were introduced ostensibly for balance of payments reasons, but also to promote import substitution industrialisation aimed at intermediate and upstream products such as iron, steel, cement, fertilisers and motor vehicle engines.

The turning point came with a major crisis in 1985–86. The appreciation of the yen in 1985 and rapid decline in oil prices in 1986 increased current account deficits substantially and led to a debt service ratio of 33 per cent. Ironically, the decline in petroleum revenues and deteriorating balance of payments situation provided the political will for substantive structural reforms to take place. In accordance with the usual stages of trade deregulation, the first stage aimed at tariff reforms and rationalisation, shifting the emphasis from non-tariff barriers to tariffs, and removing the bias against exports.

The major deregulation steps were: the tariff reforms in March 1985; the steps which essentially amounted to abolition of the customs service in 1985 and its replacement by a private Swiss surveying company, Societe General de Surveillance (SGS); improvements in the duty drawback scheme in May 1986; and replacement of non-tariff barriers by tariffs in several stages during 1986–88, so that the percentage of imports covered by non-tariff barriers dropped from 43 per cent in mid-1986 to 21 per cent in 1988.

There was also substantial deregulation on the investment side, with the relaxation of licensing and capacity requirements of domestic firms, liberalisation of equity ownership by export-oriented foreign investors, relaxation of distribution activities by foreign firms and the replacement of the complicated priority list of investment by a simpler negative list that excluded areas of investments.

Since December 1987 there has been extensive deregulation of the financial sector encompassing banks, non-bank financial institutions, insurance and other financial services and the stock market. The essence of deregulation is open entry and minimal government intervention. Although there has been a considerable upsurge of activity in the financial sector with increased competition and mobilisation of funds, it is not without problems of supervision for safety and soundness.

Performance

Despite the cuts in expenditure and recession, GDP growth remained positive, although it was lower than in the other ASEAN countries (except for the

Philippines) which actually followed expansionary policies, as discussed later. While GDP growth fell in 1985 it did not reach negative rates as in other ASEAN countries (except for Thailand). Growth has since improved and remained stable, without the rapid turnaround of the other economies. This may be a reflection of the size of the Indonesian economy and the size of the slow growing agriculture sector, as well as initial conditions. Current account deficits have substantially improved and while government deficits have improved little, collection of non-oil and non-tax revenues have increased substantially, especially in the last two years.

Other positive indicators of the outcome of the adjustment policies are the impressive performance of non-oil exports and growth in investment approvals. Non-oil exports rose by 31 per cent in 1987 and 35 per cent in 1988, with manufactured exports growing at much higher rates. The share of non-oil exports has also shifted considerably, from 15:85 in 1982 to 55:45 in 1988. A more diversified export base will cushion any future oil and other primary commodity price shocks. Foreign investment approvals have increased from under US$1 billion in 1986 to over US$4 billion in 1988, with similar trends in domestic investment growth. Particularly noteworthy is the increase of export-oriented projects, from an average of 45 per cent in 1986 to almost three-quarters of total investment approved in 1988. There is also a clear trend of investments motivated by relocation from Korea, Taiwan, Hong Kong and even Singapore.

Malaysia

The orientation of policy in the 1970s focused on state intervention in development and deliberate ethnic and equity restructuring. The policies include promotion of manufactured exports through investment incentives and free trade zones, regulations to reduce foreign ownership in the domestic sector with the object of increasing indigenous (*bumiputera*) ownership of corporate wealth from 1 per cent in 1970 to 20 per cent in 1990 and reducing the foreign share from about 70 per cent to 30 per cent (the rest being held by non-*bumiputera*); and increased government participation in productive activities through the establishment of public enterprises.

Industrialisation was oriented towards heavy industries such as the national car project, cement plants, iron and steel mills, pulp and paper industries. These projects were financed by foreign borrowing.

By the end of the 1970s the record of success was mixed. Most of the state-owned enterprises suffered heavy losses. However, foreign investment in the free trade zones succeeded in creating jobs and exports, mainly in electronics and textiles. Nearly 70 per cent of manufactured exports in the early 1980s were in these two industries. The Malaysian industrial base remained narrow with few linkages.

Macroeconomic indicators

The growth rate of GDP for the Malaysian economy was positive and relatively high at an average of 6.7 per cent in the early years of the recession,

1981–84. However, growth plummeted to a negative 1 per cent in 1985. It has recovered since 1987. Inflation rates were rather high in the first two years of the 1980s but declined subsequently, especially after the 1985 recession.

The current account deficit as a percentage of exports was very high in the early 1980s at around 20–30 per cent but has come down quite rapidly since 1984, even reaching a surplus since 1987. Budget deficits as a percentage of GDP were also high in the early 1980s and although lower since 1983 remained at 6 per cent of GDP in 1988.

In the case of Malaysia, one needs to explain the cushioning of the effects of recession in the early 1980s, the severity of the recession when it did hit in 1985, and the policies taken to regain recovery by 1987. Since then growth has been strong and was expected to be 8.7 per cent in 1988.

Fiscal and monetary policies

In the face of recession in the early 1980s, countercyclical fiscal measures mitigated the slowdown in growth. In the 1981–84 period, growth was still positive. Public investments increased by 41.5 per cent in 1981 and by 20.7 per cent in 1982, at the price of high budget deficits of 19 per cent and 17.9 per cent of GDP in those years (compared with 1980 of 13.6 per cent).

Monetary policy was restrictive to offset the deterioration in the current account and to reduce the inflationary pressure on the economy. As pointed out by Gan (1989), this policy mix placed great pressure on the domestic interest rate and the exchange rate and must be held partly responsible for the recession in 1985.

Slowdown in monetary growth has been due to the decline in net foreign exchange reserves resulting from the current account deficit, but also due to the decline in net lending to the public and private sectors (as part of the deflationary and balance of payments objective). Excess demand for loans caused the base lending rate to rise from 8.5 per cent in 1982 to 12 per cent in 1984.

By 1982 the Malaysian economy was beset with a large fiscal deficit, a current account deficit due to the effects on exports of worsening terms of trade, high real interest rates and appreciation of the real effective exchange rate, and an increasing debt service burden. These conditions, which were partly a result of the countercyclical policy that was followed and of adverse external shocks, especially declining commodity prices, led to the severe recession experienced by the Malaysian economy in 1985. GDP growth was negative one per cent in that year.

Since 1986 a program of fiscal austerity and appropriate monetary policies has helped to lead the economy back to recovery. Favourable external conditions undoubtedly helped also. In October 1986 the reserve requirements and the liquidity ratio were reduced. These measures further accelerated the depreciation of the ringgit and eased the interest rate situation at the end of 1986.

Several steps were taken to affect public spending: substantial cuts in Fifth Development Plan development expenditure from M$74 to M$47.7 billion, postponement of projects not yet committed to contract, introduction of screening criteria for project selection based on high value added, greater use of local inputs, shorter gestation period, and foreign exchange earnings, and cuts in operating expenditures of the government.

The reduction in public spending and private investments helped the current account deficit by reducing import demand, but the debt service burden remained high. After 1986, as commodity prices began to go up, additional public sector allocations for anti-recession programs such as employment creation and rural development projects were stepped up. Monetary policy was now geared towards facilitating growth and providing liquidity for private investment. Interest rates were reduced.

Growth is expected to slow down slightly in 1989-90, but there is increased concern about inflation due to full utilisation of industrial capacity, monetary growth, depreciation of the ringgit and foreign inflation. Monetary restraint will be needed to avoid erosion of price competitiveness of manufactured exports. Semudram (1989) points out that, since recent empirical evidence has revealed the importance of inflationary expectations, it will be important to pursue an ongoing price stabilisation policy.

Exchange rates and external borrowing

In the early 1980s external borrowing to finance the expansionary fiscal policy led to appreciation of the real exchange rate of the ringgit (Figure 8.3b). Higher inflation partly reflected the extent to which government spending was on non-traded goods. Gan's (1989) analysis indicates that relative prices of non-tradeables rose relative to tradeables, with adverse effects on the supply and price competitiveness of manufactured exports.

Appreciation of the ringgit also led to increasing expectation of a depreciation, and consequent increase in real interest rates in 1985-86 in order to stem speculative outflows. Gan (1989) classifies this as 'the classic illustration of the effect of an inconsistency between monetary and exchange rate policy objectives in an open economy'.

Since 1985 the ringgit has been effectively depreciated against the currencies of its major partners and has helped to make Malaysia's exports more competitive. The rebound of exports in the recent recovery has contributed to the surplus on the overall balance of payments. In 1989 the ringgit appreciated against the currencies of Malaysia's trading partners. The appreciation helped dampen inflationary expectations, but is in conflict with the long-term need to have a more competitive exchange rate to facilitate the export drive.

The shortfall in the public saving–investment gap which increased in 1982 as a result of the increase in public spending was met by increased foreign borrowing. Following new initiatives in 1986 and 1987 Malaysia was able to reduce its external debt in 1988. The new official policy was to use domestic financial resources to finance development programs and to repay costly external loans, while restraining external borrowing. There is in fact a stated target of a debt service ratio of 20 per cent.

Rationalising and restructuring the long-term debt through refinancing and prepayment exercises by both the public and private sector have been undertaken in 1987 and 1988 by utilising the accumulated foreign exchange reserves from the commodity export boom in 1986. This approach was made possible in 1988 by the strong growth of the economy and a significant improvement in the financial position of the government. Thus for the second consecutive year there was a net repayment of external debt amounting to M$5.8 billion in 1988.

Structural policies

After the 1985 recession there was a significant shift in policy direction which emphasised increased private sector participation by improving the investment climate.

Important changes in the direction of industrial policy were undertaken. First, rationalisation of government participation in industry through changes in management and privatisation, and an embargo on setting up of new state enterprises. Second, promotion of small and medium-sized enterprises to take advantage of the relocation policies of the NIEs and Japan. Resource-based industries were also to be encouraged.

In the area of foreign investment, equity participation requirements were relaxed in September 1986, freeing up locational restrictions and increasing investment promotion missions. For domestic investment the equity limits for compliance with the employment restructuring rules was substantially raised from M$0.5 to M$2.5 million. Export-oriented foreign and domestic investors were also given more liberal treatment. In the 1988 budget further liberalisation was introduced: 100 per cent foreign equity allowed for export of a minimum of 20 per cent production. A new package to promote small-scale industries was also introduced.

Confidence in the financial system suffered a major setback following the financial scandals and bank failures in the early 1980s, with a high liquidity position and low deposit rates as visible symptoms. Despite the fall in deposit rates, average lending rates have not followed suit. To overcome rigidities, the 1988 budget liberalisation and deregulation of the banking system introduced a number of measures aiming at improving competition and efficiency.

Fiscal reforms have taken the form of a reduction in corporate tax rates to bring the tax burden into line with neighbouring countries, to remove bias against foreign investment, and to stimulate private investment.

Privatisation to reduce the financial and administrative burden of government began in 1985. Since then twenty major projects have been privatised. An additional nine projects are to be finalised, among them proposals to privatise the National Electricity Board, Postal Services Department, airports and major ports.

Performance

The turnaround in GDP is evidence of the success of the policies, with the manufacturing sector contributing most to growth. The current account turning into surplus was also a measure of success. The remarkable performance of the external sector can be traced partly to the fall in imports related to cuts in public expenditure, but also to high growth in exports which rose by 26.4 per cent in 1987 and 22.9 per cent in 1988. An improved external environment, including improved terms of trade, contributed, but policy factors such as the more export-oriented strategies and the weakening of the Malaysia ringgit also played a part. Manufactured exports accounted for 50 per cent of total exports in 1988, with the electrical and electronic machinery sub-sector accounting for half of the exports. The other major contributor is textiles and footwear.

Philippines

The Philippine economy has undergone traumatic and substantive adjustments in the decade of the 1980s. Prior to 1983, the economy still had the distorted incentive structure typical of import substitution policies, which has led to an inefficient pattern of investment and heavy dependence on foreign resources. Since 1983, and especially since 1986, various adjustments have been made.

Demand management, exchange rate and external financing policies

The Philippines did not adjust to the second oil shock and the recession of the early 1980s by the orthodox absorption reduction approach. Instead, it adopted an expenditure increasing set of policies through expansionary fiscal and monetary policies and allowed the real exchange rates (relative price of tradeables to non-tradeables) to appreciate (see Daquila, 1989). Fiscal expansion, largely financed by external borrowing, led to larger budget deficits; the budget deficit reached 4.6 per cent of GDP in 1982 compared with 3 per cent in 1976. The current account deficit also increased to 64 per cent of merchandise exports compared with an average deficit of 18 per cent of exports in the 1970s. Money supply also rose very rapidly. There was substantial credit creation by the central bank in order to help finance the budget deficits.

As a result, external debt rose from US$21 billion in 1980 to US$24 billion in 1981 and to almost US$30 billion in 1988. About 30 per cent of the external debt was due to borrowing of the banking sector, the rest mostly from the public sector. Most of the loans were medium and long-term concessional loans. Daquila (1989) has estimated that two-thirds of the increase in external debt was used to finance current account deficits and the rest used to finance capital outflows (capital flight, net portfolio and direct investment flows).

The next question to ask is whether the increased debt was used to finance domestic investment and the economic effectiveness of the investments. Daquila found that while external debt was matched by the accumulation of capital (namely physical investments), there is some evidence that the investments undertaken were not very productive—rising ICOR and the observation that expenditures on highways, waterworks, large public buildings, and participation in hotels yielded little or no cash returns to the government.

Even had investment efficiency been higher, the debt problem would have still affected the Philippines because of the failure of domestic saving to respond to rising real interest rates in the late 1970s and early 1980s. The widening investment–saving gap continued to be financed by expensive foreign borrowing.

Increased government spending on non-tradeables (especially utilities and infrastructure) also caused an appreciation of the relative price of tradeables to non-tradeables (appreciation of the real exchange rate), which in turn led to resource movement away from tradeables and a worsening current account. Real effective exchange rates as shown in Figure 8.2 indicate appreciation during the expansionary period, in the early 1980s.

The recovery since 1985 and in the first three years of the Aquino government, has relaxed the restraints on fiscal spending imposed by debt restructuring in the 1985–87 period. This allowed some increase in government spending in 1987 without raising the deficit. In 1988 the deficit continued despite a fall in expenditure because below-target value added tax (VAT) collections caused a shortfall in revenue.

The new restructuring agreement in March 1987, which did not involve any new funds, but amounted to rescheduling, turned out to have been deficient. The result was a US$1.5 billion capital outflow and a negative overall balance of payments effect. To overcome this problem, the Aquino government recently obtained a 3-year extended fund facility from the IMF and it seems that other countries such as Japan will be willing to provide additional funds.

But the funds have come tied to a stabilisation package of tight fiscal and monetary targets which will lead to a slowdown in growth. The stringent fiscal and monetary targets mean that the Philippines will not be able to finance the investments required to achieve its growth targets. The budget deficit must be financed by domestic finance, particularly through the flotation of government bonds, and this will affect interest rates and money supply.

The interest rate had been used to slow down inflation and bolster the depreciation of the peso. The increase in the interest rate was undertaken to encourage more bond purchases and thus reduce money supply growth in order to meet the IMF targets. An increase of reserve requirements was also imposed to control liquidity.

Structural policies

Reforms since 1983 have been extensive. They cover most sectors and include the dismantling of monopolistic marketing arrangements for agricultural commodities, the removal of interest rate ceilings and subsidised credit programs, a streamlining of the public investment program and a simplification of the tax system. This means that the central bank no longer serves to allocate credit but can concentrate on its stabilisation role. More recently the VAT was introduced.

Import liberalisation has taken the form of removing import quota restrictions and replacing them with tariffs in the range of 10–50 per cent. By 1988 only about 10 per cent of the items are said to be still subject to restrictions. Despite liberalisation and restructuring, some industries remain heavily protected and inefficient.

However, the IMF sponsored package of stabilisation measures alone, without further structural reforms, may not lead to sustained growth in the Philippines. As Yap (1989) points out, this will not be easy to achieve since it will 'require a great deal of resolve and political will ... to reform basic institutions and structures ... and reforms, which also aim at the widening of domestic markets'.

Further restructuring would need to go beyond simple removal of controls and policies that distort factor and commodity prices. Reforms of basic institutions and dismantling of the monopolistic-oligopolistic structure of the Philippine economy are the problematic and difficult areas.

Performance

The Philippine economy has experienced low and negative growth and high inflation in the 1980s, with recovery only beginning to be felt as late as 1987. Adverse political developments which began with the assassination of Benigno Aquino in 1983 and led to the fall of the Marcos regime were the main explanation for the negative growth and much higher inflation in 1984 and 1985. Since 1987 the economy has started to recover and growth is expected to continue in 1988 and 1989 although at lower than targeted rates. Inflation has since fallen although there has been some increase in 1988. The political troubles of late 1989 in Manila will of course affect the 1989–90 growth and inflation predictions.

The Philippines also experienced higher current account and budget deficits in the 1980s than in the 1970s, with high deficits occurring in the early years of the recession, 1981–84. The current account improved after 1986, even reaching a surplus in that year. On the other hand, budget deficits, which had improved up to 1985, worsened in 1986, but have also fallen since then.

An indication of the return of confidence is the increase in foreign investment of US$17 million in 1985 to US$140 million in 1986 and US$618 million in 1988. The Philippines is also increasingly receiving relocation-motivated investments, especially from Taiwan.

Singapore

Singapore must specialise and rely on exports. The Singapore economy is a small city state with limited domestic markets, exceptionally open, with heavy reliance on external markets, foreign investment and foreign technology, and increasingly also foreign labour.[6]

Singapore made the transition to export-oriented industrialisation much earlier than the other ASEAN countries, in the 1966–72 period. The 1970s brought considerable export diversification, into electronic components and capital-intensive industries such as petroleum refining and chemical products.

The two oil shocks on balance benefitted the Singaporean economy because it had already become an important oil refining and exporting centre. Some slowdown in growth did occur subsequently due to world and regional economic recession, though the construction boom in 1983–84 offset some of the effects from the downturn.

While entrepot trade is still important, its role is declining in the economy, and diversification into services such as storage, banking, insurance, transportation and communications has become important. Singapore's location and infrastructures have also contributed to the development of shipbuilding and repairing activities, tourism and financial services.

Labour shortage led to a restructuring strategy in 1979 away from labour-intensive manufacturing and service activities towards higher value added activities which are more skill, capital and technology intensive. Policies included increasing wages, reducing the foreign labour inflow, encouraging automation and computerisation, an active promotion of new investments in industries and services with higher value added.

Other features of the Singapore economy are that the rate of private saving is very high[7] because of large compulsory contributions to the Central Provident Fund (CPF) and that the government budget is unusually decentralised, comprising autonomous budgets of various statutory boards.

Macroeconomic indicators

Singapore growth rates were not significantly affected by the recession in the early 1980s, but a severe downturn in 1985 brought negative growth and only slightly positive growth in 1986. Since 1987 the growth rate has again picked up considerably.

Inflation rates in 1980 and 1981 were slightly higher than the average of the previous decade, but slowed down in the following years, especially since 1985. In 1986 Singapore experienced a negative inflation rate.

Singapore's balance of payments has become increasingly favourable, going from relatively high current account deficits in the early 1980s to surpluses since 1986. For most of the period the government budget was in surplus.

The 1985 recession had a strong and unexpected impact on the Singaporean economy, leading to a negative GDP growth in 1985 of 1.6 per cent. The main external cause of the downturn was a fall in oil refining and petrochemical activities related to the decline in oil prices. The lower volume of crude oil being shipped also caused a fall in demand for repair facilities.

The fall in the growth rate in the United States also hurt Singapore as the United States is its largest market. Slowdown in the electronics business in the United States led to a sharp reduction in demand for Singaporean parts and components. The concurrent fall in commodity prices also reduced export earnings of the ASEAN countries and thus Singapore's trade with ASEAN countries, especially entrepot trade.

The sharp downturn, however, also had internal causes, some of which are related to earlier adjustment policies to offset the effects of the recession in the early 1980s and labour shortages. What were these policies and what were the policy adjustment responses taken to lead to the rebound in economic growth?

Demand management policies

In general, the Singapore government has adopted a conservative budget policy with little reliance on foreign borrowing. Public sector development expenditures have mostly been financed by domestic savings (compulsory in the form of CPF contributions) and borrowing. The overall surplus of the budget balance also reflects the savings philosophy of the government.

Public sector construction activities had been used as a macroeconomic stabilisation tool as well as for provision of housing and infrastructure. In the 1970s such investments were used to offset downturn in economic activity in other sectors and this countercyclical fiscal policy continued in the early 1980s. The growth rate of the construction sector was 11 per cent in 1980, peaking at 36 per cent in 1982 and falling to 14 per cent in 1984. Construction contributed around 50 per cent of gross fixed investment in 1983-84. By 1985 there was an over-supply of building space for residential, business and tourism purposes.

Given the openness of Singapore's financial system, which has not had exchange controls since 1978, and Singapore's role as an international financial centre with a high degree of capital mobility, monetary policy could not target domestic interest rates. The inadequately developed domestic secondary market for securities has ruled out the use of domestic open market operations to influence liquidity. Nor are reserve requirements and the discount rate available as effective instruments.

The official position is that liquidity is controlled by foreign exchange intervention. That is, the exchange rate is used as the target for monetary policy and the main instruments used are purchases and sales of US dollars and foreign currency swaps. The money stock, therefore, emerges as a result of exchange rate targeting.

Since the recession in 1985 there has been concern over such policy. It is suggested that monetary policy led Singapore into an unintended liquidity squeeze which had a negative effect on the economy. That is, the nominal money supply affects the real economy through changes in the real money supply, real exports and changes in real fixed capital formation. Reduction of liquidity will also affect property values and real consumption could then be affected.

The evidence does indicate that there was a marked reduction in liquidity prior to the recession. Growth in narrow and broad money began to decline in 1983 and continued to decline sharply in 1985, the growth becoming negative for narrow money, and nominal interest rates rose in 1984 before falling in 1985 (real rates rose since the fall was less than fall in prices). The growth rate of bank loans also began to fall in 1982. The only industries which received significant increases in loans were building and construction and financial institutions.

Others have argued, however, that the fall in money supply and bank loan growth rates followed the slowdown in economic activity and slack demand for loans. Low interest rates do not seem to have stimulated more borrowing and low rates themselves cast doubt on the proposition that there was a liquidity squeeze. No significant monetary variables have been found to explain real net investment (Lim and Associates, 1988, ch.16).

Exchange rates and external financing

The Singapore dollar has been on a managed float since 1973, linked to a trade-weighted basket of currencies. In the 1980s the Singapore dollar has on average maintained its value against the US dollar, depreciating by an average of 0.6 per cent a year. However, this implies appreciation against other currencies and loss of competitiveness compared with competitors, such as the NIEs. The Singapore dollar is thought to be overvalued, and this has worsened the competitive position of Singapore goods already adversely affected by high operations costs. Figure 8.3b shows that the real effective exchange rate of Singapore remained below its 1980 level until towards the end of 1985.

The policy to maintain a strong Singapore dollar can be explained by the shift in monetary policy by the Monetary Authority of Singapore (MAS) from interest rates and monetary policy growth targets to an exchange rate target. The exchange rate target was used primarily to stabilise prices, but it also had the additional objective of supporting the restructuring strategy. In 1983 the second objective was modified to become one of safeguarding export competitiveness. To achieve its first objective of controlling liquidity there is pressure to reinject Singapore dollars into the system to offset the drain from the CPF and budget surplus.

The utilisation of one instrument to achieve two objectives can be problematic. It also appears that there has been a failure to account for the effects of other policy instruments such as the CPF contributions on export competitiveness. The policy changes in the early 1980s appear to reflect insufficient coordination and consultation among the different government agencies.

Only since 1985 has managed depreciation occurred and this was a prompt response to the oncoming recession. Since 1985 real effective exchange rates appear to have been maintained, subject only to gradual depreciation with the depreciation of the US dollar in this period.

Structural policies

The utilisation of wages policy to restructure the economy towards higher value added activity also contributed to the recession. In the early 1980s there was a sharp rise in business costs from rentals, interest costs and wage costs. The rise in wage costs occurred as part of the restructuring strategy to higher value added industries by increasing CPF contributions, levies, payroll tax and annual wage increments. Thus the 'restructuring effort itself becomes a supply induced cause of the recession' (Lim and Associates, 1988: 35).

One of the problems in using the wages policy was timing: while wages were rising, the supporting infrastructure and manpower for high technology industries were not yet ready. Productivity increase was higher in 1979–84 compared with 1973–79, but wages rose even more than productivity.

To restore business confidence, the Economic Committee[8] realised that there was an urgent need to act promptly to overcome domestic factors contributing to the recession, the main one being high business operating costs. As a result, even during 1985 (signs of recession could already be detected at the beginning of the last quarter of 1984) and before the announcement of the

Committee's recommendations, various cost cutting measures were implemented. These measures included wage restraint by trade unions, a property tax rebate, removal of various levies and minor taxes and reduction of statutory board fees. Since wage costs were viewed as the most important component in increased costs, further measures were introduced such as reducing the rate of employer contribution to the CPF to 10 per cent compared with 25 per cent (equivalent to a 12 per cent reduction in wage costs), severe wage restraint to preclude wage increases for at least two years, and reform of wage structures by employers in cooperation with the trade unions.

The success of these measures required the full support of all sides, especially the trade unions. Since Singapore's trade unions are heavily influenced by the government, cooperation was successful. As a result of quick responses in structural policies, though the negative growth of 1985 could not be avoided, the recovery to positive and increasing growth came about very quickly.

While Singapore has enjoyed a prudent fiscal policy and high savings rate, the emphasis on construction and infrastructure sectors rather than on more productive investments in manufacturing and related sectors has led to an imbalance in the composition of investment. The high growth achieved in the construction sector could not be maintained, and when the boom ended there was unemployment, over-supply of buildings, and this in turn affected the financial sector, with bad loans from developers and mortgages from buyers. Confidence was further affected by the stock exchange malaise, the outcome being more regulations and safeguards by the MAS.

The recession has once again underlined the vulnerability of the Singaporean economy and the need to maintain competitiveness. Besides a more flexible wage policy, this requires closer monitoring of indicators of Singapore's international competitiveness—the unit labour cost index relative to the other three Asian NIEs (Hong Kong, Taiwan and South Korea), the unit business cost index of the manufacturing sector and the share of net operating surplus in value added for the manufacturing sector. It is hoped that close monitoring will impose discipline on coordination of policies affecting competitiveness and prevent independent policies which raise business costs.

Singapore continues to be highly dependent on the international economy for trade as well as investments. To reduce vulnerability to external markets it needs to diversify not only economic activities but also markets in the face of overcoming protectionism. Singapore has lost some of its attraction as a low cost base; other factors such as infrastructure and human resources therefore need to be promoted as 'pull' factors.

Several policies have been initiated to achieve this aim: promoting foreign investment in higher value added industries and service based industries, and emphasis on developing Singapore as a 'total business centre', no longer just a financial services centre. Fiscal incentives for services similar to those already available to manufacturing industries have been introduced such as pioneer service, investment allowance, international consultancy service and operational headquarters incentives.

Dependence on foreign labour is believed to impede economic restructuring away from labour-intensive industries. The levy on foreign workers was therefore raised in January and June 1989, supplemented by amendments in the immigration law and deportation of illegal workers.

Performance

GDP growth has recovered spectacularly, from a negative 1.6 per cent in 1985 to a positive 8.8 per cent in 1987 and an expected 11 per cent in 1988. The main factors behind the recovery are the cost cutting measures and aggressive investment promotion, which has resulted in a resurgence of foreign investment, but also favourable external developments, including the recovery of regional ASEAN economies.

The growth in the world economy has led to substantial increases in exports, especially of electronics and electrical products in 1986-87. As a result, external trade increased by 23 per cent in 1987 compared with 3-4 per cent in 1985-86. The usual deficit in the trade balance was more than offset by the surplus in the services account, and the current account reached a surplus in 1986 which continued to rise until 1988. In line with the increase in foreign investment, the capital account has been in surplus, causing a surplus in the overall balance of payments.

High growth has not upset price stability—inflation has remained low thanks to lower oil prices and prudent fiscal policy. Real effective exchange rates have depreciated slightly compared with 1986, but the cost cutting and wage restraint measures were probably more important in restoring competitiveness.

Thailand

At the beginning of 1980 the Thai economy was faced with unmanageable fiscal and current account deficits which resulted from lack of adjustment to the oil shocks in the 1970s. Monetary and fiscal policies had not been sufficiently restrictive in response to the oil price increases in the 1970s, especially the second oil shock. The reason is partly that the first shock was cushioned by the commodity price boom in 1972-73, the inflow of United States military assistance in relation to the Vietnam War, increased remittances from Thai workers overseas, and external debt was still small. Another reason was demand-driven growth just prior to the second oil shock.

The result was that at the beginning of 1980s the macroeconomic problem faced by the Thai government manifested itself in persistent fiscal deficits, rising current account deficits, rapid accumulation of external debt, some overvaluation of the baht, and artificially low (subsidised) energy prices. The second oil shock in 1978-80, the global increase in real interest rates in 1980-82, and the severe recession in most industrial countries worsened the situation facing the Thai economy.

Macroeconomic indicators

The Thai economy appears to have performed best of all the ASEAN countries. The recession of the early 1980s did lower growth but not to the same extent as in the other countries. In Thailand, too, the low points in growth were 1982 and 1985. The pickup in growth since 1986 has been impressive: the growth rate of real GDP recovered from a low of 3.5 per cent in 1985 to 4.5 per cent in 1986 and accelerated to 8.4 per cent. At the time of writing (early 1989), the expected growth for 1988 was 11 per cent, while a fall was predicted for 1989.

Thailand once again appears to have been able to keep inflation at low levels, with some pickup evident in 1988. A higher inflation rate is expected in the following years with approaching saturation of capacity unless appropriate anti-inflationary policies are adopted.

There has also been a turnaround in the current account from high deficits in the first few years of the 1980s to a surplus in 1986 and smaller deficits in subsequent years. Meanwhile, government deficits have remained fairly low, and in fact began to decline in 1987, finally reaching a surplus in 1988.

The year 1980 proved to be the turning point for the Thai economy. Until 1982 economic growth was maintained through macroeconomic policies, while the tariff structure and investment incentives protected the industrial sector. In response to the evident imbalances, the Thai government adopted policies to reduce demand to slow down growth, by reducing public sector expenditures and monetary restraint. It also undertook structural policies to remove distortions in many areas such as energy consumption, trade, taxation, and promotion of exports.

Demand management policies

Faced with the mounting external and budget deficits, after a high spending year in 1980, the Thai government began to introduce fiscal restraint by reducing public expenditures beginning in 1980-82. The public expenditure program was reviewed, a priority list drawn up and strict requirements for project justification introduced to reduce public spending in a systematic way. For instance, investment in the Eastern Seaboard Project, the Petrochemical Complex and in basic infrastructure were slowed down. Strict controls on government salaries and on the level of government borrowing were also introduced. The subsidy on fuel was removed, reducing expenditure as well as correcting one of the price distortions. Restraint on public expenditure continued through the 1980s. Only in 1988 was there some relaxation with an increase in public expenditure to meet demand for badly needed investments in public infrastructure to service the economic boom.

Because of the relative openness of the Thai economy, monetary policy has had a limited influence on controlling inflation. The main stabilising function of monetary policy up to the early 1980s has therefore been to maintain external balance by ensuring adequate foreign exchange reserves. With the onset of fiscal austerity, however, monetary policy also had to be used to induce economic expansion. The additional objective gave rise to an inherent conflict in monetary policy between the aims of expansion and exchange rate stability.

The operational targets of monetary policy in Thailand are changes in reserve money and domestic credit from the central bank. The main tools are access to central bank credit by commercial banks, setting interest rate ceilings on deposits and loans, and open market operations. Initially, monetary restraint was introduced in the early 1980s along with fiscal policy restraint by increasing the central bank discount rate and short-term deposit rates. The combination of restrictive fiscal and monetary policy meant that by the end of 1982 inflation rates had been brought down, current account deficits had fallen, but real GDP growth had also fallen to 4.1 per cent.

In response to these deflationary effects, monetary policy was relaxed until mid-1983, but increases in domestic credit and demand, as well as anticipation with respect to devaluation of the baht, led to a worsening of the current account deficit. As a result, in early 1984 a less expansionary monetary policy was adopted. Reduced demand was expected to reduce imports and delay the need for a devaluation.

The squeeze on credit adversely affected a large number of firms and several financial institutions. Nevertheless, money supply growth did fall and the trade balance did improve slightly, aided by the fall in oil prices. Sluggish growth in 1985 induced another phase of expansionary policy, with low rates until recently.

Exchange rates and external financing

The second oil shock led to a huge import bill for oil and meant that the government had to borrow heavily from abroad. This occurred at a time when the US dollar was high, and with the baht tied to the US dollar, the baht became overvalued, making imports cheaper and exports more expensive. Thus by 1983 the current account deficit and debt service ratio were rising at alarming rates. The response was devaluation and control over external borrowing.

Relative price adjustment was intended to influence the composition of demand as well as increase the supply of tradeables. In 1981 the baht was devalued twice, by 1.07 per cent in April and a further 8.7 per cent in July. The initial small devaluation showed the hesitancy of the government in devaluing, but it led in fact to speculation of a further devaluation, which forced the government to undertake the second devaluation. There was the predictable public outcry. Since the baht was then tied to the US dollar, the subsequent appreciation of the US dollar eroded the competitiveness of Thai exports.

Despite large increases in imports and a sharp deterioration of the external deficit by the end of 1983, it took over a year until November 1984 before the baht was again devalued by 14.7 per cent. The delay was related to fear of rising debt service payments and opposition from the military and import substitution interests.

The Thai government has since followed a policy to keep the real effective exchange rate of the baht competitive, deliberately favouring exports. Since December 1985 the baht has no longer been tied to the US dollar; it is linked instead to a trade-weighted basket of currencies. The depreciation of the dollar which followed the second devaluation has led to a depreciation of the real effective exchange rate by 30 per cent and improved the competitive position of Thai exports.

External borrowing was curbed by imposing a ceiling on external borrowing, which also helped keep down capital expenditure by state enterprises. As a result, actual borrowing did fall to US$1.2 billion compared with the planned average of US$2.6 billion for the 1981–86 period. It has proved to be a powerful device to counter political pressures to increase investments to public enterprises. As a result, there has been a fall in the use of net external borrowing to finance the public sector deficit. But the debt GDP ratio has risen because of the depreciation of the US dollar since 1985.

Structural policies

Substantive structural reforms introduced in the 1980s explain a large part of the relative success of the Thai economy. Besides the above mentioned devaluation, the reforms undertaken included fiscal reforms, changes in tariffs and improvements in the export promotion policy, and a new credit policy.

Fiscal reforms were aimed at increased tax collection and streamlining of revenue administration. The estimated low income elasticity of Thailand's tax system has been attributed to heavy reliance on indirect taxes, inefficient administration and low levels of compliance, especially income tax.

In February 1986 Thailand revised the structure of most major taxes as well as tax administration. The aim was to increase revenues and to reduce the cost to private sector businesses. The top marginal tax rate on personal income was reduced from 65 per cent to 55 per cent and the corporate income tax for non-public companies from 40 per cent to 35 per cent. Some of the reforms could also be seen as moves towards a more economically neutral tax regime. The reduction in the corporate tax rate mitigated the bias against small and unlisted firms compared with listed firms, which are taxed at 30 per cent. The taxation of interest income on government bonds and other types of deposits has reduced the differences in the effective tax rates on different forms of savings.

With growth in 1988 there has been a significant increase in revenues collected from the private sector in the form of import duties, corporate taxes and taxes on real estate transactions. Government revenue rose by 40 per cent between 1986 and 1988, and in 1988 the government deficit turned into a surplus, the first time since the commodity price boom of 1974. The increase in tax revenues made possible some reduction in income tax rates at the end of 1988.

Private investment has moved cyclically in response to developments in the Thai economy. Private fixed capital formation slowed down until 1986 but rebounded with the higher economic growth in 1987 as government investment declined in line with the longer term strategy to limit public expenditures. Thus the rebound in gross investment in 1988 has mostly been due to the private sector, with an increase in the share of investment of the private sector to as much as 3 per cent of GDP. The latest investment surge is therefore more market oriented.

A rise in gross savings has been due mainly to government savings, chiefly savings by state enterprises resulting from adjustments in the prices of key services including electricity, water, and bus and train services.

Like many other developing countries, Thailand initially adopted import substitution policies with protective tariffs and local content regulations. Taxes on trade in addition comprised an important source of revenue. But export-oriented industrialisation policies were introduced in the early 1970s in the form of investment promotional incentives, credit subsidy, electricity cost reductions and tax rebates. The system of effective rates of protection, however, still had an anti-export bias. Industrial restructuring policies have not gone very far as yet, and the tariff and tax structure which favours import substitution industries has prevailed because of the importance of trade taxes as a source of revenue and the presence of vested interests. It required the recession of the early 1980s to lead to significant changes in policy direction (see Phongpaichit, 1989: 14).

With the fall in commodity prices in the early 1980s, Thailand could no longer rely on agricultural exports to earn foreign exchange. At the same time, the import bill was growing due to the rise in oil prices. The initial reaction to the deficit was to raise tariffs. During the oil crisis in 1982 the government levied an extra 10 per cent surcharge on a broad range of imports and made further upward revisions in 1983 when the deficit was still a problem. Thus government policy, as well as vested interests, still leaned towards import-substitution policies.

The worsening deficit, however, forced the government to assess its strategy. There was also an increasing number of manufacturers who had turned to the export market in the face of weak domestic demand. These exporters exerted pressure for policy changes to facilitate exports.

The turning point came with the devaluation of the baht in November 1984. After the commitment to maintaining competitive exchange rates, it became necessary to follow through with trade reforms to facilitate exports. In 1985 and 1986 some adjustments in existing export promotion policies were undertaken. Reforms in trade policy took the form of additional investment promotion schemes and activities to encourage exports, streamlining of tax rebates and refund schemes for import duties and other taxes on materials used for the production of exports, and changes in tariff structure. The tax rebate system had not been efficiently administered in the past and exporters usually had to wait for many months to obtain the refund or get the bank guarantee.

These reforms were reinforced by trade promotional and assistance measures in the form of the establishment of an Export Development Committee chaired by the Ministry of Commerce and marketing assistance by the Export Service Center and Department of Commercial Relations. Export taxes were also gradually removed.

These policies still belong to the first phase of trade liberalisation, that is, offsetting the export bias and tariff rationalisation. A substantial part of the protection system remains.

Price adjustments

In order to strengthen public enterprises, the prices of public transportation and electricity were raised in 1980–81. The rice premium was also removed in 1986. Finally, the price of domestic fuel was adjusted by removal of the subsidy component. Over the 1978–81 period, domestic fuel prices were raised by 250 per cent by tying them to international prices, and the fall in oil prices in 1986 was not fully passed on to the consumer. It is hoped that the removal of the distorted fuel price will encourage fuel conservation.

Performance

The Thai economy has experienced surging exports and booming direct investment, which is mainly export-oriented and from Japan and the NIEs. The share of manufacturing in exports has increased so that textile exports have exceeded rice exports since 1985. Merchandise exports have grown at an average of 25 per cent a year since 1986, and the share of manufactured exports in total merchandise exports has risen from about 30 per cent to 60 per cent in the last five years. As a result, the ratio of exports to GDP has risen from 19 per cent to 28 per cent in the 1980–88 period.

CONCLUSIONS: LESSONS TO BE LEARNED

All the ASEAN economies experienced fluctuating or declining growth in the early 1980s, with the low points being 1982 and 1985. However, all of the ASEAN countries have experienced a turnaround in GDP growth since 1986 as well as improvement in other performance indicators: improvements in current account and fiscal deficits, lower inflation rates, realistic exchange rates, falling debt service ratios, diversification and growth of exports and improved investment climate.

The above analysis has shown that economic performance of small open economies such as the ASEAN economies is affected by external changes. Since external conditions faced by ASEAN countries and other developing countries are similar, differences in economic performance must be explained by differences in domestic policies pursued and initial conditions. Several important policy lessons can be learned from the experience of macroeconomic management and policies of the ASEAN countries.

First, unfortunately it takes a crisis before needed policy reforms and adjustments are undertaken. The reasons are twofold: economic myopia and political will. While the economic conditions are positive it is often difficult to predict adverse effects from present policies. Unpopular reforms or changes that have untested results are easier to justify in crisis conditions. The ASEAN economies have shown different propensities to respond to adverse developments, but what is clear is that prompt pragmatic and flexible responses tend to work better.

The case of Singapore and its quick rebound in growth is a case in point. Delaying real sector reforms in the case of Indonesia and Thailand slowed down the recovery. As for Malaysia, Salih and Yusof (1989: 16) conclude that 'without the shock of the recession in the early eighties and without the political commitment of the government in introducing the policy changes in response to the effects of the recession, the package of policy reforms would not have seen the light of day'.

Second, countercyclical policy of financing an externally generated government deficit with external borrowing will only boost growth in the short term. If the source of imbalance is long term and the investment financed by borrowing is not undertaken with a longer term view of whether the investment will yield returns to pay back the debt, then the countercyclical policy becomes untenable. Furthermore, conservative demand management policies are not sufficient. To sustain growth, medium and long-term structural policies that improve efficiency, resource allocation and productive capacity of the economy will necessarily have to follow.

Out of the four ASEAN countries only Indonesia did not pursue a countercyclical policy in the face of recession in the early 1980s. However, though appropriate demand management policies such as reducing spending and devaluation were undertaken in 1983, turnaround in growth was not achieved because it was not accompanied by structural change policies. These policies only came about after the rapid decline in oil prices in 1986.

The other ASEAN countries pursued a countercyclical policy to boost growth. This was financed by increased foreign borrowing (except Singapore), which led to increased debt burden by mid-1980s, the current account deficits, budget deficits and inflation. In the case of Singapore, increased spending in public sector construction was financed by domestic savings. Only when growth declined did all of these countries respond by conservative demand management policies followed by structural change policies. In the case of Malaysia, additional government revenues from the commodity boom in 1986 were used to repay debt rather than being absorbed.

Third, the experience of macroeconomic management policies of the ASEAN countries also points to two features of small open economies: the ineffectiveness of monetary policy and the importance of maintaining the 'right' level of exchange rates. The two are related. Having an open capital account means that the interest rates are needed to maintain exchange rates such that the interest rate target cannot be used to maintain monetary policy. Monetary policy can function to a certain degree to stabilise prices, but depending on the monetary instruments available, monetary policy is often inadequate to sterilise capital inflows. Furthermore, the objective of stabilisation of prices of monetary policy will also conflict with exchange rate stability.

Increased government spending on non-traded goods financed by external borrowing (Malaysia and the Philippines) or inadequate devaluation policies (Indonesia and Thailand) or using the exchange rate for price stabilisation and restructuring objectives (Singapore) have meant that the real effective exchange rates of the ASEAN countries did not remain competitive. The cost was on deteriorating exports at the time of current account deficits and recession; subsequently, all countries have switched to a policy of keeping real effective exchange rates competitive.

Fourth, medium and long-term structural adjustments encompass fiscal, financial and real sector reforms. Tax reform is an essential component because there is a greater need to finance public expenditure from domestic sources including taxation, rather than borrowing abroad. Fiscal reform should also be directed towards a neutral taxation system for businesses to operate in. Since the trend in industrial countries during the 1980s has been to lower nominal rates of income and corporate tax, the ASEAN countries can no longer raise tax rates to increase revenues. Instead, the fiscal reforms undertaken by all the ASEAN countries reflect trends to reduce nominal rates on corporate and income tax, broaden the tax base, lessen variation among various types of property income and improve administration of the taxes (see Asher, 1989).

It is too early to tell what lessons can be drawn from financial reforms. Some progress has been made with financial reforms, although some have been more conservative than others. Only Indonesia has undertaken the full range of financial deregulation measures. The result has been increased competition between banks, but the crucial issue is of course whether safety and soundness regulation will be implemented. Maintaining confidence in the financial system is a crucial component in a highly deregulated market. In addition, the experience of the ASEAN countries also demonstrates that interest rate controls are not particularly useful. All the ASEAN countries have removed government control over interest rates.

Real sector reforms include trade and investment deregulation, often with the purpose of promoting exports and diversifying the export base. All of the ASEAN countries now show a clear tendency towards a more open and outward-oriented economy. In the case of Singapore, in fact, restructuring has also occurred towards export of services. Restructuring of exports is crucial to facilitate flexibility in overcoming external changes and restructuring has been due to changes in policy as discussed below.

There also appears to be a change in perception over the role of the government in general, notably in the last two to three years. In the 1960s and 1970s there was much confidence in the ability of government to guide the economy. From taxation to industrial policy, there is now a move from the role of government in influencing resource allocation to one of creating the right and neutral investment climate to do business in. Private sector investment, domestic and foreign, and increased efficiency and competitiveness are increasingly emphasised.

Fifth, it is difficult to draw a conclusion on the proper sequencing of policy adjustments. However, some generalisations can be made that macroeconomic adjustments by means of appropriate demand management policies should precede the structural micro changes, but both are necessary. Macroeconomic stabilisation measures will bring inflation rates down and fix exchange rates at a realistic level, such that structural policies can work.

This is clearly illustrated by the experience of the ASEAN countries. In the case of Indonesia up to 1986, the policy package was unsuccessful in overcoming the adverse impact of the oil price decline on the balance of payments because macroeconomic adjustments were undertaken without structural policy changes. By contrast, in the Philippines, structural policies were undertaken before stabilisation policies were in place and they were also not successful in obtaining the right kind of adjustment.

Lessons on the sequencing of structural reforms are less clear. Conventional wisdom on policy reforms indicates that real sector reforms should precede financial sector reforms and liberalisation of the capital account should be the last step. The ASEAN experience clearly does not fall into this mode. Indonesia initially started with an open capital account and proceeded with financial sector reforms before real sector reforms.

Sixth, there are bound to be conflicts in objectives and transition problems experienced in implementing structural reforms. Consideration must be given to the potential of such problems. For instance, the conflict between maintaining balance of payments, that could be affected by rising imports, and efficient resource allocation, caused by trade reforms, can be overcome by ensuring that export growth is realised early in the reform process. Furthermore, as the cases of Indonesia and Thailand indicate, achieving initially strong export growth can remove much of the resistance for further deregulation from the bureaucracy and increase support by exporters for reforms, especially export promotion policies.

Finally, it is important that the process of reform be seen as an ongoing one. A clear indication of policy direction is needed for businesses to undertake planning.

9 Exchange rate regimes and practices: Malaysian perspectives

LIN SEE YAN

The breakdown of the Bretton Woods system and, later, the Smithsonian Agreement in the early 1970s marked the end of the fixed exchange rate regime. The generalised floating rate system that emerged, and that has been in practice since 1973, has allowed different countries to adopt different exchange rate arrangements best suited to the structure and objectives of their economies.

As of March 1989, for example, the 1989 IMF *Annual Report* had classified 19 countries as being on the independent floating arrangement, 24 on managed floating, 13 countries on a regime with limited flexibility, 51 on single-currency pegging and 39 on basket pegging. Details are presented in Table 9A.3.

In general, the developed countries have tended to float their currencies, while most LDCs have relied on a more controlled system, either in the form of pegging or managed floating.

The IMF's *World Economic and Financial Surveys* (September 1989) noted that the exchange rate policies of member countries have shown a distinct tendency to move towards more flexible arrangements and away from single-currency pegs, continuing a trend that began in the mid-1970s. A major development has been that, by the end of March 1989, 19 countries maintained independent floats for their currencies (compared with 10 in early 1982) and the number of currencies in the managed floating category also increased during the period.

As for the LDCs, in particular, the majority of the classification changes during the period 1982–86 reflected greater flexibility, and the bulk of these changes represented clear shifts in policy: 23 were shifts from currency pegs to either managed or independent floating, whereas only 8 were changes from more flexible arrangements to pegging.

Relatively flexible exchange rate arrangements are also practised by most countries in the ASEAN region. Following the IMF classification, as of 31 March 1989 the Philippines stood out as the only ASEAN member which appeared in the independent floating category. Indonesia and Singapore were classified under managed floating, and Thailand and Malaysia were considered to be pegging to composite baskets of currencies. For Brunei, its currency is pegged one-for-one to the Singapore dollar. In the case of the Philippines, the peso has been allowed to float freely since December 1984 as a result of highly destabilising balance of payments deficits in the early 1980s. Prior to that, the peso was under a managed floating system where the exchange rate was allowed to fluctuate within a certain band around the guiding rate determined in terms of the US dollar.

In the early period of generalised floating, Indonesia pegged its exchange rate to the US dollar. The practice continued until November 1978 when the country switched to a regime of managed floating. As for Thailand, the shifts in exchange rate policy and practice were more frequent.

In March 1978 the exchange rate regime was changed from one that was pegged to the US dollar to a system of pegging to a basket of currencies of its major trading partners. However, the basket pegging arrangement did not last long as the country reverted to a policy of pegging to the US dollar under the Daily Fixing System. The latter was discontinued in July 1981 when the daily fixing practice was abandoned and the currency was again fixed against the US dollar, at 23 baht to the dollar. After a period of three years, the exchange rate regime of the Thai baht was switched again, this time to the current practice whereby the value of the currency is determined in terms of a basket of currencies of its major trading partners.

Singapore and Malaysia largely shared a similar exchange rate regime during the generalised floating period. Following the breakdown of the Bretton Woods system, the currencies of the countries were allowed to float in June 1973. Subsequently, in September 1975 the two countries chose to determine the values of their currencies in terms of separate but distinct composite baskets of currencies.

As the exchange rate of the Singapore dollar became more flexible over time, the IMF changed the classification of Singapore's exchange rate system from basket pegging to managed floating in March 1988. In this regard, the current IMF classification of the Malaysian exchange rate system where the value of the ringgit is pegged to a composite basket of currencies is just as inappropriate. As is discussed further below, this classification for Malaysia is not quite correct in practice.

Although the value of the ringgit is being determined, in principle, in terms of a composite basket of currencies, it is operationally not pegged strictly to the basket. Instead, the value of the ringgit is allowed to be determined by the forces of supply and demand and, in practice, fluctuates on the basis of market conditions in terms of the 'basket' rather than a single currency.

Over the years, the drastic shift in the exchange rate policy from fixed to floating has created the need for countries to continuously monitor and, in some cases, manage their exchange rates. The problems and issues associated with fluctuating exchange rates have confronted virtually all trading nations of the world.

While the experience of the developed countries in terms of exchange rate management is well discussed and documented in the literature, the experience of the LDCs, on the other hand, has virtually been ignored.

The main purpose of this chapter is to discuss the issues surrounding exchange rates from the perspective of a rapidly developing commodity-based economy, with particular reference to the Malaysian experience, which perhaps is not very different fom the experiences of many other developing countries at about the same stage of development. In this regard, the chapter addresses specifically the subject of exchange rate regimes and practices from a developing country's viewpoint. In the process, policy issues and implications relevant to Malaysia in particular, and developing countries in general, will be highlighted and analysed.

The rest of the discussion is organised in five sections. The first section presents, as background, a brief history of exchange rate regimes and practices in Malaysia. This is followed by a brief rundown on the performance of the floating system in the second section, which highlights issues of global significance as well as those directly relevant to Malaysia. The third section discusses recent developments in the management of exchange rates, while the fourth section outlines the likely future trends in exchange rate policies and practices. This is followed by some concluding remarks in the fifth section. As background material, a number of statistical tables have been included in Appendix 9A for those interested in more details, especially with respect to the Malaysian economy.

BACKGROUND ON EXCHANGE RATE REGIMES AND PRACTICES IN MALAYSIA

Malaysia is essentially an open developing economy, with exports and imports representing 65 per cent and 51 per cent of GNP respectively. Petroleum, tropical hardwoods, natural rubber, palm oil, cocoa and liquefied natural gas constitute the major export commodities of the country. Although Malaysia is primarily an agricultural economy, industrial development has been rapid over the past decade.

Consequently, the share of the manufacturing sector in the economy, at 24 per cent of GDP in 1988, has surpassed that of agriculture (21 per cent of GDP). Agriculture used to account for as much as 40 per cent of the economy in the mid-1950s. Increasing industrialisation of the economy has resulted in the structure of imports being characterised by the dominance of intermediate goods (40 per cent of total imports in 1988), followed by investment goods (29 per cent) and consumption goods (24 per cent). The major trading partners of Malaysia comprise Japan, Singapore and the United States, which together accounted for about 54 per cent of both total exports and total imports of the country in 1988.

Since independence in 1957, Malaysia consistently achieved a high rate of growth, at least until about the mid-1980s. The pace of growth slowed down considerably in 1983–86. This was brought about initially by the global recession (associated with the second oil shock), and later by the second collapse of commodity prices across the board in 1985–86. Growth in real GDP accelerated from an average annual real rate of 5 per cent in 1960s (with the accompanying inflation rate of less than 1 per cent annually), to 8 per cent in 1970s (with significantly higher inflation averaging 6 per cent), but slackened to 5.2 per cent during the 1981–85 period (average inflation of 4 per cent). However, the economy has since recovered with real GDP growth of 5.3 per cent in 1987 and 8.7 per cent in 1988. At the same time, inflation was contained at 0.8 per cent and 2.5 per cent during 1987 and 1988 respectively.

Prior to independence, the exchange rate of the ringgit, which was then known as the Malayan dollar, was fixed at 2s. 4d. sterling. The Currency Board, which was the sole currency issuing authority in Malaysia, assumed the role of converting sterling into Malayan dollars and vice versa at a small administrative charge of 1/8d. During this period, sterling was the premier currency not only for foreign exchange settlements in Malaya but also for holding as reserves.

Moreover, most of the country's imports and exports were conducted by the British trading agencies and settled in sterling, with the bulk of the international trade financing being channelled through the British banks. For all practical purposes, the rate for sterling was virtually the only exchange rate that mattered.

Upon the assumption by the central bank of the sole power to issue currency in 1967, after the formation of Malaysia in 1963, the par value of the Malayan dollar (established at 0.29099 grammes of fine gold) was maintained for the new Malaysian dollar.

Consequently, the old Malayan dollar was redeemed in exchange for the Malaysian dollar at par. Following the devaluation of sterling by 14.3 per cent in November 1967, however, the Malayan dollar was automatically devalued to the same extent, resulting in the exchange rate for the Malaysian dollar being equal to 2s. 8.67d. instead of 2s. 4d. previously, so that the Malayan dollar was equal to only 85.71 cents of the Malaysian dollar. The central bank's new support rates for the Malaysian dollar were fixed at 32.7761d. and 32.5573d. = M\$1, representing a margin of 0.3348 per cent on either side of par.

The outbreak of a series of international gold and exchange crises between 1968 and 1973 saw some changes in the exchange rate of the ringgit (the new legal name for the Malaysian dollar as of August 1975).

For example, in March 1968 the central bank increased the margin of its support rates from 0.3348 per cent to 0.5 per cent on either side of par. In November 1968 the margin was widened further to approximately 0.77 per cent on either side of the parity. Following the suspension of convertibility of the US dollar to gold in August 1971, the central bank again increased the margin to the full one per cent on either side of parity, coinciding with the maximum exchange rate limit allowed by the IMF.

As the Smithsonian Agreement took effect in December 1971, the parity of the ringgit remained unchanged in terms of the pound sterling at M\$7.3469 = £1, but the parity in terms of the US dollar was changed from M\$3.06122 = US\$1 to M\$2.81955 = US\$1, in response to the devaluation of the US dollar by 7.89 per cent. The central bank, however, maintained the previous margin of one per cent and did not increase it to 2.25 per cent on either side of par, as allowed by the new exchange rate regime of the IMF.

With the floating of sterling and the dismantling of the sterling area, Malaysia adopted the US dollar as the intervention currency in place of the sterling in June 1972. This historic event marked the severance of the close link with the sterling which had existed since 1899. Later in the month of June, the central bank adopted for the first time the wider margin of 2.25 per cent, while maintaining the parity of the ringgit at M$2.81955 = US$1. Finally, the parity was changed to 2.5376 and the support rates were established at 2.4805 and 2.5947, following the 10 per cent devaluation of the US dollar in February 1973 (the official price of gold was raised from US$38 = one troy ounce to US$42.22).

In the face of continuing uncertainty in the international foreign exchange markets, the ringgit was allowed to float upwards in June 1973. This new arrangement implied that the central bank was no longer obliged to buy US dollars with ringgit at the floor rate of M$2.4805 to the US dollar. Moreover, the Association of Banks ceased to issue best-agreed merchant rates, and each bank was free to determine its own exchange rates in respect of all foreign currencies, including the Singapore dollar, for any amount.

In its desire to maintain orderly exchange rates, the Malaysian government in September 1975 adopted a new exchange rate regime whereby it was no longer desirable for the central bank to determine the exchange rate of the ringgit in terms of the US dollar alone, and to buy and sell the US dollar in order to maintain an exchange rate so determined. Instead, the value of the ringgit was to be determined in terms of a basket of representative major currencies, weighted on the basis of the major currencies of settlement as well as those of countries which were the major trading partners of Malaysia. This exchange rate arrangement has since continued to form the basis of the existing exchange rate policy of the country.

Although the value of the ringgit has been determined in terms of a representative composite basket of currencies, it was never pegged in a strictly stable way to the basket. Indeed, the value of the ringgit has been fluctuating relative to the basket, in line with prevailing conditions in the foreign exchange market. During 1981–84, for example, the composite index ranged between 103.5 and 109.5, with September 1975 assuming the base value of 100.

As a matter of policy, interventions by the central bank were undertaken only in the event of fluctuations in exchange rates being so excessive as to destabilise the exchange market. More specifically, the central bank operates to ensure that conditions in the market are conducive to orderly trading of the ringgit, including the availability of continuous quotations, intervening whenever desirable to avoid expectations of excessive changes in the exchange rate and to provide the necessary counterparts for the continuous operations of a two-way market. Perhaps, it is for this reason and the fact that the composite basket has never been revealed by the authorities that writers, such as Aghevli (1979), considered it more appropriate to classify the exchange rate policy of Malaysia as one of managed floating rather than basket-pegging. Such characterisation may not be inaccurate since in most cases, particularly since 1985, the ringgit exchange rate is determined largely by the free play of supply and demand conditions.

PERFORMANCE OF THE FLOATING EXCHANGE RATE REGIME

The move to the generalised floating exchange rate regime was the direct consequence of the balance of payments crises of several industrial countries in the late 1960s and early 1970s. The move was further influenced, at least conceptually, by the consideration of efficiency in economic adjustment, not to mention the economic gains to be derived by countries which choose to adopt flexible exchange rates. Philosophically, these gains stem from the following: a greater degree of independence of action by the monetary authorities in the conduct of monetary policy; the ability to insulate the domestic economy from external shocks, particularly financial disturbances; the increased effectiveness of stabilisation policies in the pursuit of domestic objectives; and the likelihood of improved economic efficiency, as the allocation of resources would no longer be guided by arbitrarily fixed and out-of-equilibrium exchange rates.

However, the experience with floating exchange rates in a period spanning over a decade has not been all that good. The advantages as described above did not materialise, at least not to the extent expected. External imbalances, which were supposed to be corrected more readily by floating exchange rates, not only persisted but in some cases were aggravated. This is evident in the case of the United States on the one hand, and Japan, West Germany and the NIEs on the other.

Furthermore, the globalisation of financial markets (made possible by rapid advancements in computerised telecommunication technology) contributed not only to the presence of a high degree of capital mobility across countries, but also to the interplay of massive amounts of capital with no allegiance to any single nation, which in practice had tended to obscure and even reduce the advantages of floating over the fixed regimes. In practice, the world's foreign exchange markets are effectively a single large market, with a daily trading volume in the order of US$400 billion.

The integration of capital markets worldwide and the ensuing high degree of capital mobility across international boundaries no doubt have contributed to sharp fluctuations of exchange rates during the floating period. This volatility has been reinforced by the divergence in economic policy and performance among the major industrial countries, particularly with respect to economic growth, government spending, inflation and savings. The persistence of volatility in exchange rates has given rise to concern among policymakers and traders alike with regard to increasing uncertainty of the international trading environment and the high costs involved in the management of exchange risks.

In Malaysia, the performance of the ringgit during the period of floating exchange rates has seen mixed results. The ringgit was relatively stable during the period 1976–80, with the index of the composite basket fluctuating between 100 (the base in September 1975) and 102.8 in 1979. This stability was achieved in the face of strong improvements in the merchandise and current account balances of the balance of payments; the surpluses in both these accounts during the period 1976–80 averaged M$4.7 billion and M$842 million a year, respectively. With the ensured stability of the exchange rate, the central bank was able to accumulate international reserves to the tune of M$6 billion during the period. However, weaknesses in the balance of payments began to surface from the end of the 1970s. The onset of the global recession (arising in part from restrictive monetary policies in the major industrial countries which were undertaken to control inflation in the aftermath of the second oil shock) resulted in lower demand for Malaysia's exports and, consequently, a significantly weaker merchandise balance position. As a result, the balance on the current account turned from a surplus of over M$2 billion in 1979 to a deficit of $620 million in 1980. Reflecting the emerging weakness in the balance of payments, the ringgit weakened by 4 per cent against the composite, from 102.8 in 1979 to 98.6 in the final quarter of 1980.

The deterioration in the balance of payments position worsened further in the period 1981–84. The current deficit peaked in 1982–83, at the height of the most prolonged and severe recession for Malaysia since the Great Depression, to the tune of over M$8 billion annually. The merchandise balance, which had always been in surplus, registered deficits in 1981 and 1982. Despite the poor performance in the current account, the ringgit regained strength in terms of the composite basket although it weakened moderately against the US dollar. During the period 1981–84, the official composite index moved within the range of between 103.5 and 109.5, which in some instances represented an appreciation of the ringgit by up to 5 per cent a year. This seemingly contradictory development in the balance of payments and exchange rates movement reflected several important considerations.

The large deficits in the balance of payments could be traced to the countercyclical fiscal policy of the government in the early 1980s to ride out the global recession, which was thought would be short-lived. Increased government expenditure resulted in large overall budgetary deficits, which as a proportion of GNP averaged about 19 per cent annually during 1981–82, compared with a more sustainable ratio of 7–8 per cent in the 1970s.

Much of the government expenditure involved spending on large projects, including several heavy-industry projects, with high import content. The 'big push' fiscal policy contributed directly to the sharp increase in imports which, in the face of slackening exports, caused the balance of payments to deteriorate. The large fiscal deficit was financed through significant foreign borrowing, which raised the federal government's foreign debt from M$4.8 billion in 1980 to M$20.9 billion by the end of 1984. For the country as a whole, the increase in external debt was more pronounced, reaching M$37.6 billion at the end of 1984.

The rapid increase in foreign borrowing was reflected in the sharp increase in the inflows of official long-term capital of the balance of payments during the period, which averaged M$4.8 billion a year compared with less than M$1 billion annually in the earlier years. The inflows of loan proceeds created the demand for the ringgit, which restrained the currency from depreciating despite the poor current account position prevailing during the period.

It is interesting to note here (as emphasised again in the latter part of this chapter) that the Malaysian experience reflected the gradual shift, globally, from conditions in the current account to movements in the capital account in the determination of exchange rates over the short run. While this has been increasingly true in the case of many developed countries, it does appear that the role of capital movements has become increasingly influential in the determination of exchange rates in the developing countries as well, particularly those with a relatively developed capital market.

Another factor that contributed to the appreciation in the ringgit during the recession period of 1980–84 was the periodic intervention operations of the central bank, which acted to prevent the ringgit from depreciating excessively against the US dollar (which during the period strengthened considerably vis-à-vis other major currencies). The policy at that time was to keep the ringgit relatively stable against the Singapore dollar. But, since the US dollar was the intervention currency, intervention through this currency resulted in keeping the ringgit relatively strong vis-à-vis the US dollar.

The stability of the ringgit against the Singapore dollar was considered desirable not only on political grounds but also to maintain public confidence in the ringgit (the relative stability in the exchange value of these two currencies being perceived by the public as an indicator of strength). Consequently, during the period 1981–83, the premium of the Singapore dollar over the ringgit was maintained at about 9 per cent and the depreciation of the ringgit against the US dollar was kept at a minimal 4.3 per cent. At the same time, from February 1981 to August 1984 the index in the value of the ringgit peaked at 110.7 against the basket (September 1975 = 100), and appreciated by 67 per cent against the sterling, 34 per cent against the Deutschmark, and 14 per cent against the Japanese yen.

Looking back, this policy stance clearly generated definite costs to the economy. However, some benefits did emanate from the strong currency during the period 1980–84. First, it helped to contain the impact of imported inflation in Malaysia in the face of strong inflationary pressures in the major industrial countries, associated with the second oil shock. Indeed, inflation in Malaysia during the period 1980–84 averaged 5.9 per cent annually, compared with an average of 8.3 per cent in the OECD areas. Second, the policy had succeeded, to some extent, in sustaining confidence in a fundamentally weak economy. Private investment remained relatively strong, growing at an average rate of 10.9 per cent a year, and real GDP growth averaged 6.9 per cent annually during the period.

The appreciation in the ringgit exchange rate later proved to be unsustainable. During the time when the ringgit strengthened to keep pace with the appreciating US dollar, the currencies of other ASEAN countries weakened. The subsequent devaluations of the Thai baht, the Philippine peso and the Indonesia rupiah in 1983–84, together with the nervous foreign exchange markets abroad associated with the strong US dollar, caused bouts of speculation on the ringgit. The growing twin deficits in the external and fiscal accounts of Malaysia increased the frequency and intensity of the attacks.

In October 1984 the speculative bubble burst. The central bank promptly diffused the pressure on the exchange rate through heavy interventions in the market. In addition, the policy of sterilisation, which had rarely been undertaken previously, was quickly implemented through the recycling of a substantial amount of government balances with the central bank to the banking system. The measure managed to ease considerably the tight money market conditions and reduce the high interest rates which had prevailed at the beginning of 1984.

Moreover, in the period after the speculative attack in October 1984, the thrust of exchange rate policy was redirected from trying to maintain the relative stability of the ringgit vis-à-vis the US and Singapore dollars to an increasing reliance on market forces to determine the principal exchange rates. Indeed, since 1985, the ringgit has been on the depreciating trend against the composite, the Singapore dollar and all major currencies except for the US dollar. The long period of progressive depreciation ended in March 1989, after which the ringgit appreciated across the board and against the composite in line with the continued strong performance of the Malaysian economy.

It has often been argued that the problem of twin deficits which confronted the country in the early 1980s could have been handled more effectively if the government had undertaken a significant adjustment in the exchange rate early in the process of adjustment. Instead, the adjustment policies which began in mid-1982 were spearheaded by massive cutbacks in public sector spending, particularly in high import content development expenditure. The massive withdrawal of government spending from the economy, together with the second collapse in commodity prices in 1985 and 1986, in turn produced significant adverse effects on growth and employment.

Indeed, real GDP growth plunged to negative 1 per cent in 1985 and continued to be sluggish at 1.2 per cent in 1986 (but negative in per capita terms) before recovering to 5.3 per cent in 1987. The rate of unemployment was on the rise, reaching 8.3 per cent in 1986. It was felt that drastic cutbacks in government expenditure were absolutely necessary as the government had become too big and too involved in almost all important spheres of economic activity in the country, which threatened to dampen and crowd out private sector initiatives. To address the structural weaknesses of the economy through adjustments in exchange rates would not be sufficient as the gradual impact of such policy might not be able to contain the rising twin deficits within sustainable limits, at least in the short run. Moreover, it could be argued that the adjustment process was right on course and would not have been as painful were it not for the second collapse of commodity prices in 1985.

Like most developing countries, the economic slowdown in Malaysia in the early 1980s resulted mainly from the decline in the country's terms of international trade as a result of the global recession. The terms of international trade declined by 9 per cent in 1981 and by another 2 per cent in 1982. Subsequently, they picked up in 1984 to record a 10.6 per cent improvement, before falling again sharply in the following two years. In 1986 the terms of trade declined by a large 19.1 per cent.

It is interesting to draw a parallel here between the Malaysian experience and the case of Kenya as analysed by Branson and quoted in Leiderman (1989). Kenya too experienced a negative external shock in the form of a sharp deterioration of terms of trade during 1979–80. In his study, Branson concluded that under Kenya's conditions in 1979–80, the best adjustment program may well have been a reduction in government spending and not a devaluation of the domestic currency. Granted that both measures would reduce the balance of payments deficit, the costs associated with devaluation appeared to be far greater as it would increase both inflation and unemployment. The latter could be brought about by the contractionary impact of devaluation on domestic aggregate supply, which could well lead to economic stagflation. For example, devaluation may result in an increase in variable costs faced by firms, which could subsequently cause a reduction in the level of production. The findings by Branson appear to have been consistent with the choice of adjustment policy in Malaysia in the early 1980s.

Admittedly, active exchange rate management has been pursued effectively by several countries in this region (including Malaysia) as part of their adjustment programs in response to pressing balance of payments conditions in the late 1970s and early 1980s. Specifically, several countries depreciated their currencies to correct distortions in order to achieve the two major objectives of improving the international competitiveness of their exports as well as speeding up the adjustment process in their balance of payments. When Indonesia changed its exchange rate arrangement from pegging to the US dollar to that of managed floating in November 1978 for example, the rupiah was at the same time devalued by 26 per cent against the US dollar. Later, in the first quarter of 1979, another devaluation vis-à-vis the US dollar occurred (by 17.4 per cent). On 30 March 1983 the rupiah was devalued further by 27.6 per cent against the US dollar, which was followed by another large devaluation of 31 per cent against the US dollar in September 1986 as the country attempted to cushion the adverse impact of a sharp fall in oil prices. In the case of Thailand, severe imbalances in the balance of payments led to two occurrences of devaluation against the US dollar in the early 1980s; one in July 1981 and the other in November 1984, by 8.7 per cent and 11.1 per cent respectively. Korea too adjusted its exchange rate downward by 18 per cent vis-à-vis the US dollar when the country switched its exchange rate practice from pegging to the US dollar to managed floating in 1980.

In addition to significant exchange rate adjustments in the form of devaluation, which were transparent, countries in the region also allowed their exchange rates to depreciate discreetly against most major currencies in the late 1970s and early 1980s. For the period 1978–85, for example, depreciations against the US dollar were 63.1 per cent for the Indonesian rupiah, 60 per cent for the Philippine peso, 23.5 per cent for the Thai baht, 45.7 per cent for the

Korean won and 9.5 per cent for the Taiwanese dollar. In comparison, the depreciation of the Malaysian ringgit against the US dollar during the same period was a marginal 2.4 per cent. Depreciations against the Japanese yen of the above currencies during the same period were equally large: 69 per cent for the rupiah, 67.2 per cent for the peso, 35 per cent for the baht, 54.3 per cent for the won and 12.4 per cent for the Taiwanese dollar. In the case of the ringgit, it was 18 per cent.

Significant adjustments in the nominal exchange rates of the countries in the region have helped improve considerably these countries' competitiveness in the international market as evident by substantial reductions in their real effective exchange rates, which were significantly lower in 1985 compared with the positions in 1980. This represented a significant achievement, particularly in the face of high inflation experienced by these countries in the period following the second oil shock. During the period 1978–85, for example, the average annual inflation rate was 18 per cent for Indonesia, 16 per cent for Korea and 10 per cent for Thailand. Equally significant was the contribution of the exchange rate adjustment towards recovery in the balance of payments situation and overall growth performance of the countries in the region in the second half of 1980s. Thailand's success in posting high growth rates in recent years on account of sharp expansions in manufacturing activity and exports has been well recognised. In the same vein, the ability of Indonesia to sustain creditable growth despite the drop in oil prices was commendable. Similarly, the success story of Korea needs no further elaboration. In all these experiences, adjustments in exchange rates would have been a major contributing factor.

It is interesting to note that, like Malaysia, Singapore did not resort to exchange rate measures to spearhead its adjustment programs in the first half of 1980s. Instead, it appears that exchange rate policy was used largely to control inflation since some 40 per cent of consumer goods are imported from abroad and over 70 per cent of the content of exports of goods and services of Singapore are sourced from overseas markets. Indeed, as Lee (1988) argued, the only powerful policy instrument available to the Monetary Authority of Singapore (MAS) is its ability to alter the size of its portfolio, which at once represents both the monetary and exchange rate policy instrument. That is to say, in the context of the Singapore economy, there is no scope for the independent conduct of monetary and exchange rate policies. Due to the importance attached to price stability, the exchange rate cum monetary policy has been targeted towards controlling inflation, while adjustments in wages and other domestic costs were used to achieve other structural and macroeconomic objectives. In the Singapore experience, therefore, the assignment of policies to achieve different economic objectives is clearly established, with the exchange rate (and necessarily monetary) policy being reserved primarily for the purpose of maintaining price stability.

It would appear that the Singapore experience is rather unique in the region, as perhaps befits the special structure of this services-oriented city state economy, with extensive financial and commercial linkages with the rest of the world. For the other ASEAN economies of the region, on the other hand, the scope for the conduct of monetary policy separately from the exchange rate policy is much greater (although the degree of independence may be reduced under certain circumstances). As a result, while monetary policy is used primarily to preserve price stability, there is a greater leeway in these countries for the use of the exchange rate policy to promote international competitiveness of their exports, which, at the same time, would have positive effects on their balance of payments positions. The experiences of Thailand, Indonesia and Korea in the early 1980s, for example, can very well be classified in this category. Finally, while it is easy in theory to assign a particular policy to a particular objective, such a clear-cut assignment is much more difficult in practice, considering that objectives do overlap, and sometimes it may not make good practical sense to dichotomise them. Moreover, it is clearly rather difficult to distinguish, in practice, the effects of one policy from those of the others, as such effects permeate across objectives to the entire economy. Therefore, it is often the case that in practice, policymakers do assign more than one instrument at one time to achieve one or more objectives simultaneously. In the final analysis, the bottom line is what works and makes the most practical sense. This may not be theoretically neat, but so long as it works in meeting the desired objectives, the policy measures are implemented.

RECENT DEVELOPMENTS IN EXCHANGE RATE MANAGEMENT

Dissatisfaction with the performance of the floating exchange rate system caused the major countries to move away from a regime of independent floating towards a coordinated floating arrangement, particularly after the Plaza Accord on 22 September 1985. The Accord by the G-5 countries was motivated by the sharp fluctuations in the US dollar, which rose to record levels against the Japanese yen and the major European currencies in February 1985 and subsequently weakened to reflect slower growth in the United States economy, lower United States interest rates, and the increasing current account deficit in the United States of close to 3 per cent of GNP in 1985.

The Plaza Accord enabled the G-5 countries to undertake concerted intervention to bring about further depreciations in the US dollar vis-à-vis the Japanese yen and the Deutschmark to reflect better the economic fundamentals of the respective economies.

Aside from the efforts to coordinate exchange rates, coordination of broad economic policies has also been attempted, to some extent, through the measures to encourage the United States to reduce (or at least, contain) its fiscal deficit, while Japan and West Germany would increase domestic demand to help sustain the expansion in the world economy. Other measures included coordinated cuts in central bank discount rates to prevent any major shift in capital flows, and a reduction of interest rate differentials, consistent with the external payments positions of the relevant countries. As a package, the coordination measures were aimed at reducing the internal and external imbalances in the United States and promoting policy convergence among the major industrial countries, which is critical to the creation of a stable exchange rate environment in the world.

Another significant development in the management of exchange rates by the major industrial countries was the adoption of the Louvre Accord in February 1987, whereby the central banks were committed to intervene in the market to attain an exchange value at levels prevailing during the time at around ¥153 and DM1.84 to the US dollar. The measure signalled the increasing importance of 'target zoning' in the management of exchange rates by the major countries.

A period of relative stability was maintained in the foreign exchange market up until the October 1987 stock market crash, when the dollar again fell sharply to reach a record low at US$1 = ¥120.20 and US$1 = DM1.56 on 4 January 1988. Another concerted central bank intervention on a massive scale was required before the dollar stabilised in the remaining course of 1988.

Continued fluctuations in the exchange rates of the major industrial countries, even after the Plaza Accord, underscored the difficulty of targeting exchange rates in a huge and enormously globalised market. Coordinated interventions could perhaps maintain exchange rates within a certain zone, but seldom at a certain targeted level. In fact, Obstfeld (1988) went so far as to argue that 'sterilised intervention' has little or no effect on exchange rates, and that any such effect is likely to last for only a few days or at most a few weeks. Some research has suggested that even the modest impact of sterilised intervention exists only because financial markets interpret exchange market intervention as a signal that the government is prepared to shift monetary or fiscal policy to achieve the desired currency shift.

The important point to make here is that the adjustment in exchange rates alone would not be effective without the use of complementary shifts in other macroeconomic policies. To have some chance of success, the coordinated measures must be packaged to include appropriate monetary and fiscal policies both in the United States and other major industrial countries. Feldstein (1989), for example, argued that:

> The pursuit of good policies in the United States and abroad in the future should reduce the likelihood of such substantial exchange rate swings in the years ahead. But elevating exchange rate stability to a separate goal of economic policy would have serious adverse consequences. Trying to achieve that goal [primarily] would mean diverting monetary and fiscal policies from their proper roles and thereby risking excessive inflation and unemployment and inadequate capital formation. And succeeding in the effort to achieve dollar stability [as an overriding objective] would mean harmful distortions in the balance of trade and in the international flow of capital.

Notwithstanding the various reservations expressed by the authors cited above, it is evident that policy coordination since the Plaza Accord has achieved a considerable measure of success in the realignment of the exchange rates of major countries. The ringgit exchange rate has also benefitted from this realignment exercise as it helped to speed up the depreciation of the ringgit from its unrealistic high level during 1981–84. From the time of the Plaza Accord to the end of 1985, the ringgit depreciated by 8.6 per cent against the composite. In 1986 another large 13.7 per cent depreciation of the ringgit against the composite was recorded.

Indeed, the downtrend in the value of the ringgit against virtually all major currencies continued unabated until March 1989. By that time, the ringgit had depreciated since the Plaza Accord by 27.8 per cent against the composite, 19.3 per cent against the Singapore dollar, 50.3 per cent against the Japanese yen, 27.5 per cent against the sterling and 40.6 per cent against the Deutschmark. However, a lower depreciation of 9.2 per cent against the US dollar was recorded.

The gradual depreciation of the ringgit since the Plaza Accord has contributed positively to the strong recovery in the economy after the recession in 1985 and 1986. Manufacturing output and exports have since soared at annual growth rates of 18 per cent and 32.1 per cent respectively in 1988, partly on account of improved international competitiveness arising from the competitive exchange rate of the ringgit. In real effective terms, the ringgit depreciated by 27.9 per cent during the period 1985–88. This compared well with the estimated depreciations of 12.5 per cent for the Thai baht, 5.9 per cent for the Singapore dollar, and an appreciation of 16.6 per cent for the Korean won. Only Indonesia, in this region, depreciated its currency by a more significant 40.8 per cent.

The strong performance in the manufacturing sector together with favourable developments in commodities contributed to the robust growth in real GDP of 8.7 per cent in 1988 and an estimated 7.6 per cent in 1989. At the same time, the policy of fiscal restrain undertaken since mid-1982, coupled with the maintenance of a competitive exchange rate, turned around the peak current account deficit of M$8.4 billion (14 per cent of GNP) in 1982 to a balanced position in 1986, generating large surpluses as well in 1987 and 1988. It is meaningful to note that all these benefits were achieved in an environment of price stability as inflation was less than one per cent in 1986 and 1987 due to the prevailing excess capacity in the economy. While inflation rose to 2.5 per cent in 1988, it is expected to remain below 3.5 per cent in 1989 as a whole.

The management of exchange rate policy in Malaysia since the Plaza Accord has its share of difficulties and challenges. As I have shown elsewhere (Lin, 1988), the impact of the appreciation of the Japanese yen on the external debt of Malaysia, for example, has indeed been very telling. Against Malaysia's entire external debt (both public and private), the Japanese yen component is one of the largest, accounting for 35 per cent of the total (20 per cent in 1986) or M$17.5 billion at the end of 1987. Yen-denominated loans outstanding from Japan's Overseas Economic Co-operation Fund (OECF) and the Exim Bank amounted to M$6.6 billion, or 38 per cent of total yen loans outstanding. This level of official assistance was somewhat smaller than yen-denominated market loans, amounting to M$8.4 billion or 48 per cent of the total. Other sources of yen debt, including the loans of private enterprises, totalled M$2.5 billion, or the remaining 14 per cent.

Official assistance (through the OECF and the Exim Bank) is on concessional terms: the rate of interest ranged from 3.25 to 5.57 per cent a year for 15 to 25 years, with a grace period of 4 to 7 years. The interest rates are below market rates. For 1987, for example, the interest cost for the government of its yen market loans was 6.6 per cent, and the OECF and the Exim Bank project loans, 5.2 per cent. Though attractive, their cost to Malaysia remains higher than that for Thailand, Indonesia and the Philippines. The real problem, of course, is the exchange risk. As a result of the sharp appreciation of the yen against most international currencies, including the ringgit, the impact of servicing the nation's yen debt was significant. The ringgit had weakened against the yen by 20 per cent in 1985, 26 per cent in 1986, 20 per cent in 1987 and another 5.6 per cent in 1988. As a result, this factor alone cost the nation about another M$8.5 billion over two years (1985-87) in terms of more outstanding yen debt, of which the 'loss' on official assistance was about M$3.5 billion. With another exchange loss of M$1.1 billion in 1988, the share of yen-denominated loans in the total external debt of the nation reached 35 per cent in 1988, compared with 17 per cent in 1984. In addition, the effective interest cost of the total yen debt, in ringgit terms, was raised to 8.8 per cent in 1986 and 6.9 per cent in 1987. It is quite clear that the real cost of servicing the yen debt, regardless of whether the debt was in the form of official assistance or market loans, was very high—certainly no longer concessional.

A major challenge to exchange rate management in Malaysia in the post-Plaza Accord period came in 1986 in the wake of significant capital outflows following speculative pressures stemming from expectations of a sharp depreciation in the ringgit, which turned out to be unfounded. To diffuse these pressures, the central bank further tightened bank liquidity, which drove interest rates to record levels, particularly during the months of April-May and August-September. For example, during the first week of May, the interbank interest rates for overnight and 7-day money rose as high as 55 per cent and 38 per cent respectively. The management of financial policy during 1986 was difficult as the central bank was confronted with conflicting objectives of maintaining stability in the foreign exchange market (which required high interest rates to prevent capital outflows) and reducing interest rates in the money market to promote greater private investment in the face of recession in 1985 and 1986. Priority in the short run was given to maintaining stability in the value of the ringgit against mounting speculative pressures, so that high interest rates had to be tolerated as a short-run phenomenon. Indeed, under these circumstances, there was not much that could be done to bring down interest rates since further injections of liquidity into the system would only leak abroad so long as speculative pressures remained. Nevertheless, during the period January to October 1986, central bank operations injected M$4.4 billion of liquidity into the financial system. While interest rates would have been significantly higher in the absence of these operations, these rates did not come down considerably until towards the end of the year when exports and commodity prices began to strengthen. Therein lies the necessary trade-off between exchange rate and monetary policies which the authorities must occasionally face under the present exchange rate regime. That is to say, the management of exchange rates often entails sacrifices in the conduct of monetary policy. The policy of targeting exchange rates, for example, may often require the abandonment of interest rate targets. One cannot have one's cake and eat it too!

Finally, the sharp correction in the current account position in Malaysia's balance of payments after 1986 did not seem to have the expected positive effect on the exchange rate of the ringgit. Instead of strengthening, the ringgit depreciated further in 1987 and 1988. There were two main reasons for this development. First, the large prepayment and repayment of foreign loans amounting to M$8.7 billion and M$10.7 billion in 1987 and 1988 respectively, undertaken deliberately by the government (given the comfortable international reserves level during the period), meant that net inflows of official long-term capital were significantly negative. Second, the interest rate differentials which prevailed during the period in favour of foreign markets resulted in funds flowing abroad to seek higher returns. These explanations indicate the increasing importance of conditions in the capital account in influencing movements in the exchange rate of the ringgit, at least in the short run. The traditional dominance of developments in the trade and current accounts is likely to diminish gradually as the economy progresses into a more advanced stage, bringing with it a greater degree of maturity and depth in the financial system.

LIKELY FUTURE TRENDS IN EXCHANGE RATE PRACTICES

Despite its weaknesses, the system of generalised floating is likely to continue well into the future. The realistic option is not to go back to the fixed system but rather to make the floating system work better in the face of changing international environment and policy imperatives. This would call for a more active and coordinated management of exchange rates by the major industrial countries in order to reduce exchange rate volatility and promote a more stable and less risky world trading environment. The recent measure by the United Kingdom to prop up its currency through a high interest rate policy, and another round of concerted intervention to bring down the US dollar in September 1989, lends credence to the expectation that major currencies will continue to be actively managed in the future.

While some progress has already been made in reducing the external imbalance of the United States vis-á-vis Japan and Western Europe, trade balance improvements vis-á-vis the newly industrialised countries are more modest. There is even a danger that the external imbalance of the major industrial countries will widen in nominal terms in the near future. According to the

IMF's October 1989 *World Economic Outlook*, the United States current account deficit will widen to US$139 billion in 1990 from about US$125 billion in 1989. On the other hand, the Japanese surplus will increase again, from US$72 billion in 1989 to US$90 billion in 1990. In the case of West Germany, the surplus will rise to US$57 billion in 1990 from US$53 billion in 1989.

On another front, despite the Gramm–Rudman–Hollings Act to control United States government spending and hence contain its budgetary deficit, it is expected that the deficit for the fiscal year 1989 will remain high at US$148 billion or 2 per cent of GNP, compared with US$155 billion in fiscal year 1988. This represents US$12 billion more than the amount envisaged by the Act. For 1990, a deficit of US$145 billion is expected to materialise, compared with the target of US$100 billion. Indeed, it is doubtful that the United States internal imbalance could be narrowed significantly in the future, or even if it was, it is not likely to result in substantial improvements in its current account position. Therefore, if the brunt of the adjustment in its external imbalance is to be undertaken mainly through exchange rate policy, one would expect that the exchange rates of major currencies would have to shift even more sharply in the future. The prospective uncertainty of exchange rate movements in the future would further ensure that a policy of coordination and target-zoning of exchange rates among the major countries will continue to be relevant, at least over the medium term.

It is also interesting to speculate how the current efforts towards monetary unification in Europe might influence the future exchange rate arrangement of major industrial countries. The ultimate objective of such monetary unification is to achieve irrevocably fixed parities among all the main currencies of the European Community, which will subsequently evolve towards the establishment of a single currency. The underlying objective is to remove within Europe uncertainty about future exchange rate changes and the costs involved in the transaction of currencies of member countries, in line with the move towards a single European market in 1992. While the United Kingdom has expressed its reservations in joining the various stages of the move towards monetary unification, there appears to be considerable enthusiasm among the other European members to move along the unification path with or without the United Kingdom. The success of the move will depend on the direction to be taken by West Germany, and to some extent France and Italy, as these are the key players in Europe. If they are successful in establishing a more certain and stable exchange rate environment in Western Europe, then it is possible that greater coordination of exchange rates will prevail among the industrial countries, as the key countries of Europe are also the members of the G-5 and G-7 groupings.

Recent developments in trade relations between Japan and the Asian NIEs have increased the feasibility of internationalisation of the Japanese yen, which would provide another dimension to the need for greater exchange rate policy coordination among the major industrial countries in the future. Tanaka (1989) outlined three important factors which would promote an increasing use of the yen as a common standard of value for the purpose of trade settlements.

First, the opening of the Japanese market to foreign manufactured products and increased domestic demand in Japan have resulted in the gradual shifting of the centre of the whirlpool of trade from the United States to Japan. From mid-1987 to mid-1988, for example, manufactured imports from the Asian NIEs to Japan increased by 50 per cent measured in terms of the US dollar and 30 per cent in terms of the yen. The more the Japanese market becomes a major outlet to the exports of the NIEs, the more these countries will be attracted to the yen.

Second, as the manufacturing network spreads throughout East Asia, partly motivated by the relocation of production bases from Japan, Taiwan and Korea on account of currency realignments, the yen will be more widely accepted by the East Asian manufacturers because the machinery and equipment supplied by Japan would form the nucleus of this manufacturing network.

Third, the growth in the manufacturing network will be accompanied by a growing demand for capital funds, which could be satisfied mainly by the abundant yen funds carrying low interest rates, provided the higher exchange risk could be managed effectively. The internationalisation of the yen would require a corresponding increase in the role and responsibility of Japan to the international community in the design and conduct of its macroeconomic policy. Such a role and responsibility would be best served through greater policy coordination vis-à-vis other major countries in the promotion of greater stability in the world markets.

For the developing countries, exchange rates are likely to be shaped by the problems and challenges that lie ahead. First, there will be much keener competition in the world market for products from the developing countries as many of these countries have moved towards greater economic liberalisation and the adoption of outward-looking strategies. The competition will be enhanced further by the formation of solid trading blocs in North America recently and in Western Europe in 1992. Hence, the maintenance of international competitiveness (which is sustained by the adoption of appropriate exchange rate policies) will be vital to the success of industrialisation and export-oriented development strategies of the developing countries. Second, while some progress has been made to facilitate the resolution of the international debt problem, particularly in Latin America, no immediate comprehensive solution is in sight to relieve the heavily affected developing countries of the substantial amount of external debt over the medium term. Effective management of the debt problem will not only require greater sacrifices by the creditors and renewed commitment by multilateral institutions, it will also need to be complemented with appropriate domestic macroeconomic policies, including realistic and appropriate exchange rates. Third, the globalisation of financial markets will gain greater momentum in the future, which in turn will increasingly be extended to the relatively more advanced developing countries. The gradual integration of these young financial markets into the world network will give exchange rates a greater role in the determination of economic performance of such countries. In view of the above, proper management of exchange rates will be more important than ever before. Under certain circumstance, it may even be that exchange rate targeting in a broad sense will prove an attractive practice, not only among the developed countries but also for the developing economies.

In the case of Malaysia, the practice of non-intervention will continue to form the basis for future exchange rate policy. Such policy has to be designed within an overall macroeconomic framework that promotes economic growth with price stability and international competitiveness. At the same time, institutional developments will continue to be pursued with vigour to broaden and deepen financial markets in the country in the desire to render greater efficiency and stability to these markets. In this regard, the government has adopted important measures to reform the capital market in the country to make it more efficient and responsive to the needs of the private sector, as the latter increasingly assumes its place as the permanent engine of growth in the economy. While the equity market is already quite developed and would be further strengthened by the recent separation of the Kuala Lumpur Stock Exchange from the Singapore Stock Exchange, the main focus has largely been on the development of the Malaysian Government Securities (MGS) market to make it more comparable in practice with the equity market. Among the measures introduced have been the continued liberalisation of the financial system, the introduction of a principal dealership system for MGS, and the adoption of the auction system for the shorter end of MGS primary issues. The next phase of the reform will naturally be the extension of the auction system to the MGS of all maturities. The phased introduction of auctions for Treasury bills and MGS will go a long way towards meeting demands for both a greater reliance on market forces in setting rates and for a wider variety of instruments.

While the principal thrust of strategy during the late 1980s was to develop a viable market in MGS, the approach in the 1990s will be to further build on this solidifying foundation and step by step develop a viable private debt securities market. The development of such a market would require several key measures to be implemented: the extension of the system of principal dealers (market makers), which have now been established for MGS and Cagamas bonds, to the private debt securities market; the removal of regulatory constraints that inhibit the development of a secondary market in private debt securities; and the expansion of the investor base by attracting corporate and institutional investors as well as the 'man-on-the-street' to participate in the corporate bond market. With the development of the corporate bond market, new hybrid instruments are also expected to come on-stream in Malaysia during the 1990s such as RUFs, SNIFS, flip-flops and many sorts of other exotic instruments. Some of these instruments may not succeed, but those which meet investors' needs should survive. Also, the sustainability of property trusts will be put to the test. In addition, the feasibility of establishing financial futures and options markets will be studied to provide for the hedging requirements of the investing public. In the final analysis, much depends on whether the demand for such new instruments is there. If the demand exists, the initiative to meet this demand effectively will not be found wanting.

Positive developments in the efforts to widen and deepen the overall capital market in the country will not only make the market more efficient, but will make available a wide array of new instruments which should satisfy investors' preference for a more varied range of papers (from short to long term) to invest their cash surpluses. This should prevent domestic capital from being driven out of the country in search of suitable instruments abroad, as much as it would serve to attract larger inflows of foreign capital, particularly in the form of portfolio investment. All these exciting possibilities underscore further the increasing role of the capital account of the balance of payments in the determination of the exchange rate (the ringgit), reinforcing the shift away from the earlier dominance of current account transactions in influencing exchange rates, as witnessed in the 1960s and 1970s. In this context, the future role of exchange rates will assume increasing importance, and the effective management of exchange rates in the years ahead will have a special place in the design of an integrated, coherent and balanced macroeconomic policy for the country.

CONCLUSION

This chapter has traced briefly the developments in international exchange rate regimes and practices since the Bretton Woods system, as a background to understanding the evolution of exchange rate policy in Malaysia. Indeed, the experience of exchange rate management and performance in Malaysia has very much been influenced by the changes in the international monetary system and the increased uncertainty in the international trading environment associated with the large and often random fluctuations in the exchange rates of major currencies.

The management of exchange rates in Malaysia during the period of generalised floating has not been always easy. Many issues and problems were encountered, partly due to the prolonged global recession in the early 1980s and the second collapse in commodity prices across the board in 1985 and the early part of 1986. The resulting weaknesses in the country's balance of payments during the period gave rise to occasional speculative bouts on the Malaysian currency, which necessitated an active and effective management of exchange rates to ensure the return of relative stability to the market. Such measures often entailed costs to the economy in terms of the 'loss' in international reserves as well as sacrifices in the conduct of monetary policy when other monetary objectives had to be relegated to secondary importance over the short run.

Recent efforts by the major industrial countries towards greater coordination of exchange rate and other macroeconomic policies is a useful step in the direction of creating a more stable exchange rate and trading environment in the world. The greater reliance on 'target zoning' of exchange rates has produced some of the desired effects, and its implementation is likely to continue well into the future. Obviously, this policy alone has its limitations and should be reinforced by a more vigorous attempt to eliminate the external imbalances prevailing among the major industrial countries, especially the United States. The prospective worsening of the external imbalance in the United States and the inability of the Gramm–Rudman–Hollings Act to contain fiscal deficits within the targeted limit may undermine whatever progress has been made in the past. On the other hand, the current move towards monetary unification in Europe and the possibility of the yen becoming increasingly internationalised might have a stabilising effect on the overall performance of the international monetary system in the future.

As in the case of most developing countries, Malaysia will continue to place special emphasis on the proper management of exchange rates in the future. It is quite clear that exchange rate policy must form an integral part of a coherent and carefully thought out macroeconomic strategy to sustain the economy on a high growth path, maintain price stability and preserve the competitive edge in the international market. This should not be surprising since the exchange rate has taken on new significance in terms of promoting rapid and efficient industrialisation. Moreover, recent and prospective developments in the capital market and the increasing sensitivity of capital flows to price signals in the market can be expected to impact significantly on future changes in the exchange rate.

10 Resource gaps and external financing in the Asia–Pacific countries

MANUEL F. MONTES

INTRODUCTION

With the exception of the Philippines, the developing countries of Asia managed to escape the international debt crisis of the 1980s (Naya, 1983; Rana, 1985). In the early part of the decade, South Korea and Indonesia were thought to be skirting perilously close to crisis but, in the end, only the Philippines was forced to undergo an overall rescheduling of its payments.

The Asian record contrasts markedly with that of Latin America.[1] In the 1980s, with the exception of Colombia, the countries of Latin America have participated in extensive rescheduling of their international debt, executed abrupt reductions in their current account deficits, and experienced severe reductions in their rates of growth. At the start, it was thought that countries that appeared to have retained the ability to service both principal and interest, such as Venezuela, would be spared the rigors of the crisis. This has not turned out to be the case; at the time of writing (early 1990), there is a positive probability that even Colombia may find it expedient to reschedule payments on its debt.

Table 10.1 summarises the debt/GNP ratio and the debt service/exports ratio for selected Asian and Latin American countries. Comparison of debt/GNP ratios would have made it difficult in 1983 to foresee a significant difference of experience between the Asian and the Latin American countries in the lead up to the latest international financial crisis. (The immediately preceding crisis occurred in the 1930s, during the Great Depression.) Malaysia, the Philippines and Korea had debt/GNP ratios comparable to those of Brazil, Mexico and Peru. Chile, which with its subsequent return to international acceptability proved to be the least difficult of the Latin countries, had the highest ratio of all at 100 per cent.

Judged by their debt service/exports ratios, the Asian countries were already better placed in 1983; in the case of Korea, this ratio was 16.3 per cent, while Brazil's was 46.2 per cent. Even the Philippines had a better ratio than any of the Latin countries. The statistic reflected the greater outward orientation of the Asian countries and their greater ability to service foreign debt with hard currency, as long as world economic conditions continued to

Table 10.1 Debt indicators

	Foreign debt outstanding as per cent of GNP		Debt service as per cent of exports of goods and services	
	1983	1987	1983	1987
Developing countries				
NIEs				
Hong Kong	22.1	21.5	3.5	2.5
Korea	53.2	34.3	16.3	27.5
Singapore	16.2	21.9	2.2	2.4
Taiwan	23.0	17.1	7.1	4.1
ASEAN-4				
Indonesia	39.0	79.7	18.4	33.3
Malaysia	62.9	89.8	11.7	22.2
Philippines	70.8	86.5	21.3	25.2
Thailand	35.3	44.2	19.1	20.6
South Asia				
Bangladesh	45.5	54.4	9.0	16.5
Burma	38.2	47.2	33.6	59.1
India	14.4	18.8	11.9	21.6
Nepal	18.1	34.2	3.0	9.7
Pakistan	42.6	47.1	17.3	17.8
Sri Lanka	57.3	72.4	9.9	16.8
Latin America				
Brazil	50.1	39.4	46.2	33.2
Mexico	66.4	77.5	45.4	38.4
Chile	100.2	124.1	47.4	26.4
Colombia	30.1	50.2	29.7	33.4
Peru	63.7	40.5	29.0	12.9

Notes: 1987 debt service: for Hong Kong and Taiwan, 1986.
1987 debt outstanding: for Hong Kong, 1986.

Sources: Asian Development Bank, *Key Indicators of Developing Member Countries of ADB*, July 1989; Hong Kong, Census and Statistics Department, *Estimate of Gross Domestic Product*, 1966–87, 1988; OECD, *Financing and External Debt of Developing Countries*, 1987 survey; World Bank, *World Debt Tables* 1986–87 and 1988–89.

improve. In 1983, as the industrial economies were just coming out of a long recession but then faced the prospect of turbulent financial markets, it was not obvious that greater openness was necessarily an advantage.

In fact, the recovery in the industrial economies proved sturdy, permitting both Asian and Latin countries to export more. Brazil and Mexico actually reduced their debt service/export ratios, while the ratio actually worsened for some key Asian countries; in Korea, which was retiring the debt it built up from the mid-1970s and that was coming due in the 1980s, the ratio actually increased from 16.3 per cent to 27.5 per cent.

The explanation for this surprising development was that external credit virtually ceased to be available to the Latin American countries, while the Asian countries managed to finance their resource gaps. The Asian economies (except for Korea, which was retiring debt) actually increased their debt/GNP ratios faster than their Latin counterparts (Table 10.1) in the midst of the crisis. Indonesia increased its debt/GNP ratio from 39.0 to 79.7 per cent.

These developments from 1983 cast light on significant differences between the Asian debtors (except possibly the Philippines) and other debt distressed countries that can be found only beneath the macroeconomic debt statistics. This chapter discusses the nature of these differences.

DOMESTIC ORIGINS OF THE RESOURCE GAP

Standard economic accounting conventions state that the resource gap is identical to the excess of domestic investment over domestic savings, which is also identical to the excess of imports (including net transfers abroad) over exports of goods and services. Table 10.2 presents the resource gap identity by country of interest for the periods 1960–69, 1970–79 and 1980–87.

Where the resource gap actually originates is not a straightforward matter, since it results from the interplay of the forces of demand and supply, government intervention and private activities, short-term effects and long-term trends, and, quite critically, access to external funds.

Demand-side origins of the resource gap

From a demand-side point of view, the maintenance of a high investment ratio is vital to the achievement of a steady rate of economic progress. Developing country governments have regularly worried about the investment ratio and have often sought to exercise greater control over the investment ratio through various forms of intervention: investment by its own parastatals, and the provision of guarantees for private, including foreign, borrowing.

A high investment ratio does not automatically translate into a sustainably robust rate of growth. From a demand-side point of view, in the tradition of the two-gap model of Chenery and Bruno (1962), the intervening factor is the efficiency of investment: the rate of growth equals the reciprocal of the incremental capital–output ratio times the investment rate.

On an *ex post* basis (and cognisant of its limitations when applied over short periods of time) the incremental capital–output ratio itself can be a measure of the efficiency of investment. Table 10.3 provides a measure of average incremental capital–output ratios of the countries of interest. Based on this statistic, it is difficult to identify significant differences between the Asian and Latin countries in terms of overall efficiency of investment.

Table 10.2 shows that the ASEAN-4 countries have managed to sustain a higher investment rate (the middle three numerical columns) than the Latin American countries, while the NIEs, in turn, exhibit higher investment rates than the ASEAN-4. The achievement of the Asian countries that have sustained growth is all the more remarkable because it means that they have managed to sustain a higher investment ratio over a longer period of time. The investment ratio columns of Table 10.2, over twenty-seven years, bear this out very well. This achievement is possible only if the supply-side provides the wherewithal to maintain a higher investment ratio.

Domestic supply-side origins of the resource gap

The insight to be derived from Table 10.2 is that the supply-side is the most

Table 10.2 Savings, investment and resource gap (per cent of GDP)

	Gross domestic savings			Gross domestic investment			Resource gap		
	1960–69	1970–79	1980–87	1960–69	1970–79	1980–87	1960–69	1970–79	1980–87
Developing countries									
NIEs									
Hong Kong	20.8	28.6	29.0	20.7	28.0	27.2	0.2	0.6	1.7
Korea	11.2	24.6	30.4	22.1	29.9	29.3	(10.9)	(5.3)	1.1
Singapore	11.0	29.7	41.8	20.9	40.2	44.4	(9.9)	(10.5)	(2.6)
Taiwan	19.9	32.6	34.1	22.2	30.6	22.4	(2.3)	2.0	11.7
ASEAN-4									
Indonesia	3.9	23.7	28.6	9.8	19.8	26.6	(5.9)	3.9	2.0
Malaysia	20.2	30.1	32.4	15.4	25.3	31.0	4.8	4.8	1.4
Philippines	16.1	23.8	19.6	19.9	27.7	19.4	(3.8)	(3.9)	0.2
Thailand	20.1	23.6	21.9	22.0	26.8	23.0	(1.9)	(3.2)	(1.1)
China		na	35.4	40.5	na	34.2	na	1.2	(1.0)
South Asia									
Bangladesh	na	1.7	2.7	na	8.8	10.9	na	(7.1)	(8.2)
India	13.1	19.2	21.2	17.7	21.4	23.9	(4.6)	(2.2)	(2.7)
Nepal	na	12.0	10.9	na	15.9	20.1	na	(3.9)	(9.2)
Pakistan	12.4	9.8	7.9	16.5	16.9	17.2	(4.1)	(7.1)	(9.3)
Sri Lanka	12.5	13.8	13.4	15.2	18.4	26.2	(2.7)	(4.6)	(12.8)
Latin America									
Brazil	na	23.3	24.2	na	22.2	21.0	na	1.2	3.2
Guatemala	10.0	15.1	10.8	11.7	18.2	12.8	(1.7)	(3.1)	(2.0)
Mexico	18.4	22.3	24.2	19.1	23.5	19.6	(0.7)	(1.1)	5.5
Panama	18.3	23.4	20.4	20.3	29.4	21.2	(2.0)	(6.0)	(0.8)
Chile	na	14.5	14.9	na	16.8	14.8	na	(2.2)	0.1
Colombia	18.6	20.3	21.6	19.5	18.4	19.1	(0.9)	1.9	2.5
Nicaragua	15.2	16.0	15.5	19.0	17.3	12.7	(3.9)	(1.2)	2.9
Peru	18.0	18.7	20.3	18.1	15.4	15.5	(0.1)	3.4	4.7
Developed countries									
Japan	36.6	34.4	31.5	35.5	33.6	29.4	1.1	0.7	2.1
United States	19.5	19.2	16.2	19.2	19.6	18.4	0.3	(0.5)	(2.2)
Australia	21.0	15.9	12.2	27.1	24.8	25.0	(6.1)	(9.1)	(12.6)
Canada	19.2	17.2	15.1	23.6	24.1	21.1	(4.4)	(6.9)	(6.0)
New Zealand	24.2	24.1	21.8	24.5	26.7	24.9	(0.3)	(2.6)	(3.1)

Notes: na—not available.
1960–69: for Korea, based on 1961–69; for Indonesia, 1965–69; for Hong Kong, 1966–69.
1970–79: for China, 1977–79; for Bangladesh and Chile, 1973–79; for Nepal, 1975–79.
1980–87: for Burma, Chile, 1980–86; for Peru, 1980–85.
For China: percentages of net material product.

Sources: Asian Development Bank, *Key Indicators of Developing Member Countries of ADB*, July 1986, 1987, 1988, and 1989; IMF, *International Financial Statistics Yearbook*, 1988 and 1989 and June 1989; Hong Kong, Census and Statistics Department, *Estimates of Gross Domestic Product, 1966–1983*; *Hong Kong Monthly Digest of Statistics*, August 1988; Republic of China, Council for Economic Planning and Development, *Taiwan Statistical Yearbook*, 1988 and 1989, and June 1989.

critical influence in maintaining a sturdy rate of growth over the long term.

One can distinguish between the domestic and the foreign supply-side elements of the resource gap identity. The domestic elements provide the basis for gross domestic saving (the first three numerical columns of Table 10.2), while the foreign elements generate the values of the measured resource gap.

Table 10.3 Average incremental capital-output ratios

	1961–69	1970–79	1980–86
Developing countries			
NIEs			
Hong Kong	4.3	3.5	4.8
Korea	2.1	3.3	4.8
Singapore	2.9	5.1	8.8
Taiwan	2.3	3.4	3.9
ASEAN-4			
Indonesia	2.6	3.0	8.7
Malaysia	3.1	3.5	7.1
Philippines	4.5	4.6	61.2
Thailand	3.4	4.0	5.0
South Asia			
Bangladesh	3.7	3.6	4.8
India	6.6	7.3	4.4
Pakistan	3.9	4.2	2.7
Sri Lanka	2.5	4.3	5.7
Latin America			
Brazil	3.1	3.2	4.8
Guatemala	3.0	3.4	ng
Mexico	2.9	3.8	13.7
Panama	3.5	7.4	5.5
Chile	4.2	8.0	9.9
Columbia	3.8	3.4	6.9
Nicaragua	2.5	na	13.1
Peru	7.3	7.1	16.9
Developed countries			
Japan	3.3	7.1	8.7
United States	5.3	7.6	7.7
Australia	5.4	8.0	8.5
Canada	4.5	4.9	9.1
New Zealand	9.5	9.3	10.8

Notes: ng—negative because of negative growth rates of output, ill-defined.
na—not available.
1961–69: for Brazil, 1962–69.
1980–86: for Guatemala and Nicaragua, 1980–85.
Source: World Bank computer data tapes.

In relation to developing countries, the public sector's contribution to domestic saving is the typical focus of the discussion. It has been the particular focus of IMF stabilisation programs that have sought to rapidly reduce government consumption, based on the identity that, all other things remaining the same, a government deficit translates into a current account deficit.

A rethinking of the 1980s experience of a continuing search for stabilisation in debt-troubled Latin America and the United States (and the relatively easy transition to stability in Asia), has suggested that it is the private sector's ability or willingness to restrain its consumption that is no less important. In Latin America, a government's responsibilities in the provision of goods and services (in the form of parastatals) is not matched by its access to domestic private sector resources. All other things had not remained the same in the course of the adjustment effort; for example, devaluations provoked inflation and cost increases for the state enterprises, whose operations, in turn, could only be sustained by further increases in the fiscal deficit financed by money creation.

The fiscal adjustment required in Latin America, a drastic improvement in the fiscal effort and the dismantling of the state enterprise sector, has amounted to a complete reassessment of development strategy and the private-public sector delineation of responsibilities in the economy.

No such drastic readjustment was required in the Asian economies. Table 10.2 provides evidence that the domestic saving rate, particularly for the NIEs, had dramatically increased in the course of the growth. In the period 1970-79, saving rates for the NIEs already exceeded 25 per cent, and this rose even further in the 1980s.

The role of the financial sector and of positive real interest rates have already been extensively stressed in the literature.[2] The presence of positive real interest over extended periods designates the formal financial sector as a locus of financial resource mobilisation instead of a mechanism of public taxation.

It has been more difficult to provide evidence that saving rates are positively related to the level of interest rates. In an extensive analysis of LDC data, Giovannini (1985) found that the relationship between saving and the real interest rate in LDCs to be at best weak and at worst perverse. Fry (1984), in a study of six Asian developing countries (Bangladesh, Korea, Nepal, Pakistan, Sri Lanka and Thailand), found only a 'modest' effect of the real deposit rate on saving; the real deposit rate regressions were significant only in Bangladesh, Pakistan and Thailand.

More critical are likely to be the long-term factors in the economy. Because financial markets are not extensive in the developing economies of Asia, the decision to save and the decision to invest are often one and the same.[3] This would apply both to the case of the tenant farmer and the most modern private corporation in an Asian economy.

But this non-market allocation process can go awry if the prices on which the internal decision is based are non-sustainable (as in the case of a foreign exchange bonanza, whether due to commodity price booms or an external financing binge) or differ from the scarcity value of resources in the economy. An inappropriate trade and industrial policy regime generates a vector of prices that does not reflect the social cost of using resources. Merely to provide the 'market infrastructure', such as formal rural savings banks and urban stock markets, will not be sufficient as long as the underlying prices are socially inappropriate.

Other long-term influences on domestic savings supply are relevant. In the rural sector, property relations, such as tenurial arrangements, are important; property relations determine in part who does the saving and investing. The stability and the logical consistency of the policy regime and the length of the planning horizon affect the saving-investment decisions of the modern private sector. All these factors have generally been favourable to the Asian economies, with the exception, again, of the Philippines.

Table 10.4 Average annual capital inflows (million US dollars)

	1970–78						
	Total inflow	Unrequited transfers	Long-term capital	Short-term capital	Reserves, errors	Total inflow	Unrequited transfers
Developing countries							
NIEs							
Korea	1 068	244	1 048	303	-513	4 664	472
Singapore	555	-26	287	280	-123	1 141	-125
Taiwan	-260	6	265	-341	-196	-645	-136
Column sums:	1 363	224	1 600	242	-823	5 160	211
ASEAN-4							
Indonesia	525	39	921	-231	-375	629	117
Malaysia	-28	-46	466	-39	-475	1 337	-24
Philippines	641	235	449	271	-330	2 614	434
Thailand	519	83	305	250	-138	2 089	157
Column sums:	1 657	311	2 141	251	-1 318	6 669	684
South Asia							
Bangladesh	753	375	360	-9	10	1 721	1 094
India	468	873	452	-17	-977	4 564	2 825
Pakistan	1 362	650	437	62	19	3 412	2 475
Sri Lanka	80	43	69	3	-23	668	312
Column sums:	2 663	1 941	1 318	39	-971	10 365	6 706
Developed countries							
Japan	-4 830	-371	-3 752	-2 643	-3 448	555	-1 413
United States	-4 456	-4 850	-10 251	-6 967	1 319	-7 298	-7 523
Australia	1 400	-194	1 439	30	38	5 869	-114
Canada	2 310	538	2 388	671	-1 900	2 893	897
New Zealand	578	4	149	-21	50	1 171	51
Column sums:	-4 998	-4 873	-10 027	-8 930	-3 941	3 190	-8 102

Table 10.2 provides evidence that in the 1980s many countries have apparently moved into the net resource surplus column. In the case of the debt-distressed countries, the positive resource figures reflect the disappearance of international financing for their countries in the period. In the case of the NIEs, the figures probably reflect a shift as significant as the demographic transition in the study of populations. Taiwan's resource surplus of 11.7 per cent of GDP is particularly astounding. These countries must now seek to identify where, beyond their geographical boundaries, their financial surpluses are to be utilised.

SOURCES OF FUNDS FOR THE RESOURCE GAP

In the 1980s, in the midst of the debt crisis, the Asian NIEs (as a group) changed into net international creditors, while the Asian developing countries, instead of experiencing a decline, actually achieved an increase in capital inflows. Table 10.4 provides a breakdown of the sources of the totals and the sources of capital inflows for these countries for the periods 1978–78, 1978–82 and 1983–87.

RESOURCE GAPS AND EXTERNAL FINANCING

1979–82			1983–87				
Long-term capital	Short-term capital	Reserves, errors	Total inflow	Unrequited transfers	Long-term capital	Short-term capital	Reserves, errors
2 623	2 379	-863	1 328	794	-789	-376	-1 005
1 456	308	-476	-225	-208	728	25	-1 007
1 212	460	-2 233	-11 263	-291	-1 045	3 201	-14 153
5 291	3 147	-3 572	-10 160	295	-1 106	2 850	-16 165
2 681	-260	-1 839	3 312	171	3 128	609	-668
2 031	-32	-557	723	25	1 906	-162	-997
1 215	1 063	-401	947	446	1 254	-1 030	117
1 635	272	-48	1 779	210	988	278	-11
7 562	1 043	-2 845	6 761	852	7 276	-305	-1 559
431	7	98	1 688	1 269	553	-34	-78
728	-161	1 100	6 066	2 787	3 035	58	40
533	72	45	3 843	3 153	493	-44	-12
316	32	68	627	367	290	6	-40
2 008	-50	1 311	12 224	7 576	4 371	-14	-90
-8 233	6 808	3 368	-57 644	-2 092	-79 538	33 636	-9 694
-10 053	-15 938	23 648	99 380	-13 138	42 422	34 466	15 728
6 373	96	-473	8 832	488	7 614	-434	786
1 526	2 920	2 571	3 431	939	4 435	1 051	-4 288
-285	-47	-247	1 441	112	-1 613	119	387
-10 672	-6 161	28 867	55 440	-13 691	-26 680	68 838	2 919

Notes: Total capital inflows – current account deficit + unrequited transfers.
Long-term capital – direct investment + portfolio investment + other long-term capital.
Reserves, errors – net errors and omissions + reduction in reserves.
Due to rounding errors and statistical discrepancies, sum of components does not numerically equal total inflows.
Source: East-West Center, *Asia Pacific Report*, 1989, Appendix Table 10: 122.

In the case of the NIEs, the 1983–87 resource surplus is practically all accounted for by Taiwan. During this period, Taiwan's surpluses have principally reappeared as reserves. But there has also been an important shift in the NIEs' role in relation to long-term capital flows. A comparison of the relevant columns in Table 10.4 between 1979–82 and 1983–87 shows a dramatic change from net recipients of long-term investment of about US$5 billion per year to net senders of investment overseas of about US$1 billion per year.

In the 1983–87 period, Japan's capital outflow increased dramatically to an average of US$58 billion per year; the United States changed from a net supplier to a user in the order of US$99 billion per year. The other developed countries—Canada, Australia and New Zealand—are net users of capital (Tables 10.2 and 10.4); in the case of Australia in the order of 5 per cent of GDP in 1980–87.

Table 10.5 Average annual financial disbursements from OECD and OPEC economies (million US dollars)

	1970–78				
	Total inflow	Official bilateral	Official multilateral	Private bilateral	Total inflow
Developing countries					
NIEs					
Hong Kong	251	47	2	202	1 229
Korea	923	371	206	346	1 360
Singapore	180	35	21	124	895
Taiwan	189	70	25	94	495
Column sums:	1 543	523	254	766	3 979
ASEAN-4					
Indonesia	1 381	581	161	639	2 407
Malaysia	241	65	55	94	808
Philippines	510	177	93	241	1 079
Thailand	220	89	75	56	1 215
Column sums:	2 352	912	384	1 030	5 509
South Asia					
Bangladesh	724	505	214	5	1 252
India	1 154	754	395	2	2 045
Pakistan	752	611	151	-10	992
Sri Lanka	127	99	37	-9	413
Column sums:	2 757	1 969	797	-12	4 702

Figures from Japan's Ministry of Finance indicate that 42 per cent of Japanese foreign investment in the period 1983–87 went to the United States, 17 per cent to Europe, 8 per cent to the NIEs, 4 per cent to the ASEAN-4, and 3 per cent to Australia. It has proved difficult to construct a comprehensive account of capital flows in the region. These figures, however, indicate that part of the Asian–Pacific dynamism is that the sources of funds to finance the gap are the dynamic economies in the region itself. This permits a greater reliance on private flows, which, as shown later, is a major explanation of the better resource gap experience of the Asian economies.

Table 10.5 gives a breakdown of financial flows between official bilateral, official multilateral and private bilateral flows among the countries in the Asian regions. These figures indicate that as early as the 1970s the NIEs relied heavily on private bilateral flows. As they have continued to progress, this reliance has heightened: in the period 1970–78, 50 per cent of financial flows to the NIEs were provided by private bilateral sources, rising to 71 per cent in 1982, and to 88 per cent by 1986. The ASEAN-4 countries exhibit a more varied pattern. Malaysia is the country pulling up the average in the group. Since 1979 it has relied on private flows for more than 50 per cent of the average annual financial inflows. The Philippines received only 4 per cent of its total inflows during the period of the debt crisis from private bilateral flows.

Private international lending is, of course, part of the stuff the international debt crisis was made of. An understanding of the role of private flows is critical to understanding why the Asian countries fared better than others in resource gap management.

	1979–82			1983–86		
Official bilateral	Official multilateral	Private bilateral	Total inflow	Official bilateral	Official multilateral	Private bilateral
16	15	1 198	-1	-2	1	-106
417	431	513	1 330	121	253	956
42	1	852	304	-35	-12	351
239	-20	275	-281	-168	-18	-94
714	427	2 838	1 246	-84	224	1 107
768	493	1 146	2 479	711	820	949
115	123	570	863	295	55	513
260	395	424	1 061	636	384	40
373	371	472	1 045	422	401	222
1 516	1 382	2 612	5 448	2 064	1 660	1 724
871	374	6	1 226	715	504	7
663	1 254	129	2 655	748	1 351	557
504	376	112	799	343	493	-37
284	96	33	576	369	151	56
2 322	2 100	280	5 256	2 175	2 499	583

Source: East-West Center, *Asia Pacific Report*, 1989, Appendix Table 11: 123.

Except for the most advanced countries, credit rationing is the context in which most countries must fill their resource gaps.[4] Credit rationing is, in turn, the midwife of the debt crisis. There are no regularly functioning international markets where a developing country project with a positive net present value can be submitted for financing. A panoply of institutions operate to carry out the rationing process; the most important of these are the international bureaucracies in the World Bank and IMF, and also to some extent the US Agency for International Development, and the provision of government guarantees on foreign borrowings.[5]

In the nature of these institutions, the ultimate borrower is the government of the borrowing country, and its ultimate ability to service the debt depends on its ability to extract resources from the private sector. When limits on the ability of the government to tax are not sufficiently taken into account, a case of foreign over-borrowing results. In the Asian countries, stronger domestic saving rates provide greater leeway.

Because of credit rationing, the decision to finance the resource gap is often the same decision as the choice of projects to be externally financed; that is, the supply and demand decisions are intimately related. As pointed out in the previous section, when these decisions are based on prices that deviate considerably from sustainability and scarcity, the projects that receive financing will prove to be a future burden. The government appears to be expertly filling a resource gap when it is actually building up unserviceable debt.

A rationing mechanism such as the above does not have to be as damaging. The use of an appropriate shadow foreign exchange rate and cautious com-

Table 10.6 Direct investment flows (million US dollars)

	Direct investment				
	1985	1986	1987	1988	Total
Developing countries					
NIEs (not incl. HK)	1 269	1 064	1 465	(1 375)	2 423
Korea	200	325	418	720	1 663
Singapore	809	479	1 036	1 066	3 390
Taiwan	260	260	11	(3 161)	(2 630)
ASEAN-4	1 179	1 135	1 332	3 181	6 827
Indonesia	310	285	446	542	1 556
Malaysia	695	489	397	611	2 192
Philippines	12	127	307	936	1 382
Thailand	162	261	182	1 092	1 697
South Asia	164	137	189	225	715
Bangladesh	0	2	3	2	7
Burma	0	0	0	0	0
India	0	0	0	0	0
Nepal	0	0	0	0	0
Pakistan	139	106	110	179	534
Sri Lanka	25	29	76	44	174
China	1 031	1 425	1 669	2 344	6 469
Sum: Developing	3 643	3 761	4 655	4 375	16 434
Developed countries					
Japan	(5 810)	(14 250)	(18 330)	(34 710)	(73 100)
Australia	331	464	(2 005)	(303)	(1 513)
New Zealand	94	101	104	119	418
Sum: East	(5 810)	(13 685)	(20 231)	(34 894)	(74 195)
Canada	(5 449)	(1 731)	(643)	(3 320)	(11 143)
United States	960	6 280	2 690	40 920	50 850
Sum: West	(4 489)	4 549	2 047	37 600	39 707
Sum: Developed	(9 874)	(9 136)	(18 184)	2 706	(34 488)

modity price projections will identify which projects must be eliminated from further consideration. The incentive structure for international lending in the 1970s did not encourage such prudence. Governments, as always, worried about maintaining a high investment ratio; private creditors were reassured by the government guarantees. In the event, the debtor countries have actually borne the cost of failed loan projects.

The setting of the exchange rate is the key variable in this regard. As enterprises in the debt-troubled countries found out in the 1980s, the project studies on which many of their activities were based became obsolete moments after a currency devaluation. Given the volatility (and unpredictability) of commodity prices, a commodity exporter might be better served in maintaining a domestic currency value which is consistently undervalued in relation to the 'market' rate. Exchange rate management in the Asian NIEs allowed them to reduce the incentives problems created by the rationing of international credit.

RESOURCE GAPS AND EXTERNAL FINANCING 187

		Portfolio investment		
1985	1986	1987	1988	Total
1 111	302	(260)	(2 057)	(904)
982	301	(113)	(482)	688
175	(68)	224	135	466
(46)	69	(371)	(1 710)	(2 058)
1 200	851	(671)	(520)	860
(35)	268	(88)	(134)	11
355	599	(948)	(966)	(980)
5	13	19	50	87
895	(29)	346	530	1 742
103	83	132	117	435
(7)	0	0	0	(7)
0	0	0	0	0
0	0	0	0	0
110	83	132	117	442
0	0	0	0	0
764	1 607	1 191	1 216	4 778
3 178	2 843	392	(1 244)	5 169
(41 750)	(102 040)	(91 330)	(52 770)	(287 890)
1 825	1 152	4 607	5 240	12 824
0	0	0	0	0
(39 925)	(100 888)	(86 723)	(47 530)	(275 066)
6 503	14 112	8 174	10 328	39 117
64 430	71 590	31 030	40 160	207 210
70 933	85 702	39 204	50 488	246 327
31 008	(15 186)	(47 519)	(2 958)	(28 739)

Sources: IMF, *International Financial Statistics Yearbook 1989*; Central Bank of China, *Financial Statistics, Taiwan District*, July 1989.

The other source of strength in the Asian economies has been the flow of direct foreign investments from within the region. Vigorous direct investment flows, including portfolio flows, from the year 1985 are documented in Table 10.6. Total Japanese (net) direct investment flows from 1985 to 1988 exceeded US$70 billion, and (net) portfolio flows exceeded US$280 billion. Canada and Australia were also net outward investors during this period. The United States was an important direct investment and portfolio recipient, absorbing US$50 billion in direct investment in the four-year period, and US$207 billion in portfolio investment.

Over the same four-year period, the ASEAN-4 countries received a total of US$6.8 billion in (net) direct investment. China received US$6.5 billion in (net) direct foreign investment. The South Asian countries have been absorbing noticeably less.

Table 10.6 calculates sums of investment flows among developing countries. The developing countries were net recipients of a total of US$16.4 billion in (net) direct foreign investment between 1985 and 1988; the developed countries were net senders of US$34.5 billion. Japan and Canada were the largest sending countries. These sums are graphed in Figure 10.1. A worrying pattern in Figure 10.1 and the figures in Table 10.6 is the strong pull of investment flows being exerted by the United States economy, so that by 1988, developed economies as a total are being reflected as net recipients of foreign investment flows. Figure 10.2 shows that United States absorption had grown so strongly in 1988 that it exceeded Japan's total foreign investment contributions.

What is hidden within the sums of Table 10.6 is the fact that Korea became an important investing country during the period, even though it provides some indication that Korea has become a net portfolio investor during the years 1987–88. Koo and Bark (1989) provide evidence that for the years 1986 to 1988, Korean enterprises invested US$782.1 million overseas; in the previous eighteen-year period, 1968–85, Korean overseas investment totalled only US$626.3 million. Table 10.7 gives a breakdown by region of the direction of Korea's flows. In 1987 there was a leap of investments by Korean firms to Southeast Asia, so that at the present time, the region is second only to North America in terms of 'remaining investment' (the last column of Table 10.7).

Foreign direct investment flows, when these are directed into non-industrialised countries, are a particularly forceful case where supply creates its own demand. In the initial years when the flow occurs, a significant portion of the foreign investment reappears as the imports of capital equipment and new demands for imports of intermediate goods. This is particularly the case where the direct investment represents a diversification of the structure of production of the receiving economy.

In effect, direct foreign investment tends to create and finance its own resource gap. It permits a receiving country to maintain a higher investment ratio and a higher resource gap. This provides part of the answer to the puzzle of how the NIEs have shown higher resource gaps in Table 10.2 but have not walked into the debt crisis.

Table 10.7 Korea's overseas investment by region (million US dollars)

	1968–85	1986	1987	1988	1989:3	Total	Withdrawn	Remaining
Southeast Asia	146.0	7.2	131.1	41.5	27.7	354.4	39.7	314.7
Middle East	50.4	76.1	71.4	41.6	7.3	246.7	63.6	183.1
North America	185.1	79.2	177.2	96.3	30.4	568.2	125.5	442.8
Oceania	99.0	1.6	5.7	3.4	0.6	110.2	21.3	88.9
Central and South America	102.8	2.4	4.5	9.9	14.9	134.4	93.5	40.8
Europe	13.8	5.6	6.8	18.8	6.0	50.9	3.3	47.6
Africa	62.5	0.0	0.6	1.5	5.2	35.9	17.9	18.0
Total	660.5	172.1	397.2	212.9	92.2	1 500.8	364.9	1 135.9

Note: Rounding discrepancies exist in the totals.
Source: Koo and Bark (1989, Table 23: 43).

RESOURCE GAPS AND EXTERNAL FINANCING 189

Figure 10.1 Asia–Pacific direct investment flows

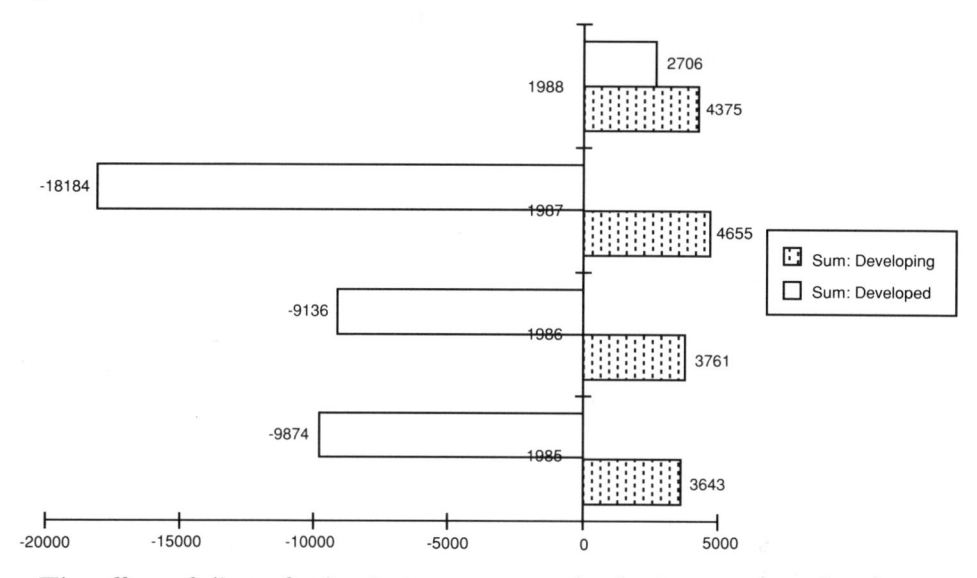

	Developed	Developing
1988	2706	4375
1987	-18184	4655
1986	-9136	3761
1985	-9874	3643

The effect of direct foreign investment on a developing economy therefore depends more critically on the efficiency of the investment, and less on the size of the flow itself. Diaz–Alejandro and Brecher (1978) have demonstrated how foreign investment flow can be immiserising if it is drawn in by a protectionist industrial regime.

The positive aspect of the most recent flows to the developing countries of Asia is that much of these are being impelled by the needs of the sending

Figure 10.2 Japan and United States direct investment flows

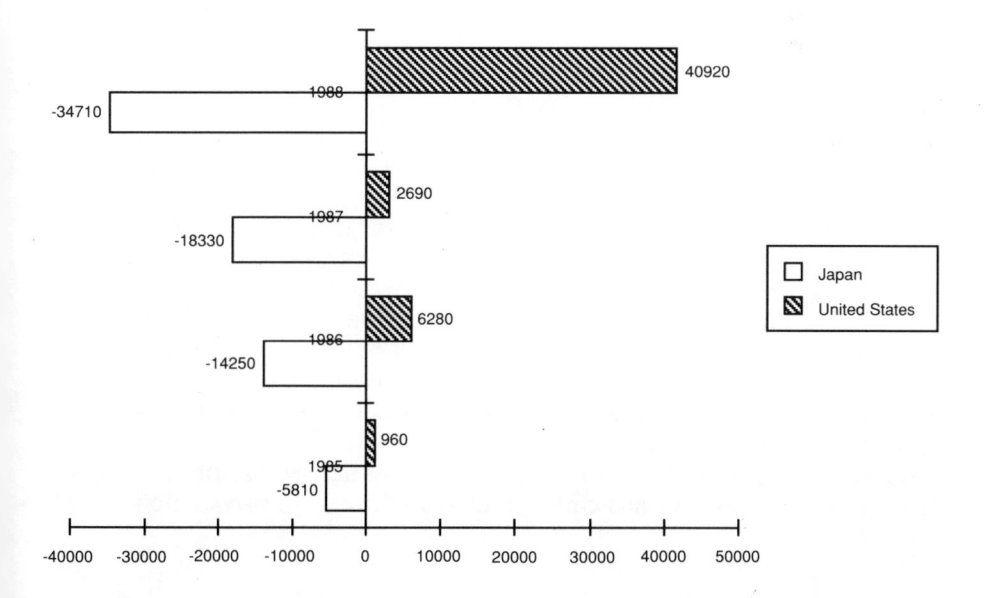

	Japan	United States
1988	-34710	40920
1987	-18330	2690
1986	-14250	6280
1985	-5810	960

countries to carry out their own structural adjustment. The movements in production operations, particularly to the ASEAN countries, are being motivated by efficiency-seeking, instead of market-protecting, considerations.[6]

Table 10.8 attempts to provide an indication of changing comparative advantage in manufacturing, based on the pattern of Japanese direct investment abroad. The 'manufacturing advantage index' is computed by means of a ratio whose numerator is the ratio of the manufacturing investment to total investment for a particular country and whose denominator is the ratio of total Japanese manufacturing overseas investment to total Japanese overseas investment. Table 10.8 shows indexes for each country versus all developing regions, versus developing Asia, and versus the world, based on data from Urata (1989, Table 1). A value less than 1 indicates that the country is less advantageous as a manufacturing location than the overall average, while a value greater than 1 reveals the country to be more advantageous than others.

Against other developing regions and all of Japanese investment, the NIEs continue to appear to have increasing advantage as manufacturing locations: Korea's index has increased from 1.7 in 1983 to 1.8 in 1988, while Taiwan's increased from 2.5 to 3.1. Against developing Asia, however, the NIEs are losing their advantage: between 1983 and 1988 Korea's index has fallen from 1.6 to 1.3, Singapore's from 1.8 to 1.4, and Taiwan's from 2.3 to 2.1. The ASEAN countries are beginning to exhibit increasing advantage as manufacturing locations in developing Asia: between 1983 and 1988 Malaysia's index increased from 1.8 to 1.9. Compared to all developing countries and the whole world, the improvement of the ASEAN countries as manufacturing locations is more marked. Against all developing regions, between 1983 and 1988 Indonesia's index increased from 0.7 to 1.1, Malaysia's from 1.9 to 2.7, and Thailand's from 2.0 to 2.7.

CONCLUSIONS

This chapter started with the puzzle of how most Asian countries have avoided participating in the debt crisis, when their level of indebtedness did not appear to be clearly different from that of the Latin countries. Asian countries had a better export base and were helped by the strong growth in the OECD countries in the latter half of the 1980s.

It was pointed out that there were deeper reasons behind the relative success of the Asian debtors. The Asian debtors actually exhibited higher investment ratios over a longer period of time than other debtors. The suggestion is that the domestic supply-side of the gap relationship was the critical factor, since, where financial markets are not extensive, the saving and investment decisions are often made jointly. That these decisions were based on prices that reflected sustainability and scarcity more closely in the Asian countries is a key factor in the better overall performance.

Foreign saving flows were examined in the second section of the chapter. The Asian countries have had consistently better access to private flows. With

RESOURCE GAPS AND EXTERNAL FINANCING

Table 10.8 Japanese investment and manufacturing advantage, cumulative approvals (million US dollars, per cent)

Region	Year	Direct investment			Manufacturing advantage index		
		Total	Manu-facturing	Manu-facturing	vs. dev regions	vs. dev. Asia	vs. world
World	1978	26 809	9 174	34.2			1.000
	1983	53 131	16 952	31.9			1.000
	1988	186 356	49 843	26.7			1.000
Developing regions	1978	15 150	6 619	43.7	1.000		1.277
	1983	28 390	10 536	37.1	1.000		1.163
	1988	71 786	19 307	26.9	1.000		1.006
Developing Asia	1978	7 668	3 410	44.5	1.018	1.000	1.300
	1983	14 552	5 800	39.9	1.074	1.000	1.249
	1988	32 227	12 371	38.4	1.427	1.000	1.435
Hong Kong	1978	715	145	20.3	0.464	0.456	0.593
	1983	1 825	215	11.8	0.317	0.296	0.369
	1988	6 167	492	8.0	0.297	0.208	0.298
Korea	1978	1 007	697	69.2	1.584	1.556	2.023
	1983	1 312	839	63.9	1.723	1.604	2.004
	1988	3 248	1 589	48.9	1.819	1.274	1.829
Singapore	1978	541	395	73.0	1.671	1.642	2.134
	1983	1 383	1 009	73.0	1.966	1.830	2.287
	1988	3 812	1 990	52.2	1.941	1.360	1.952
Taiwan	1978	284	266	93.7	2.144	2.106	2.737
	1983	479	439	91.6	2.470	2.299	2.872
	1988	1 791	1 473	82.2	3.058	2.143	3.075
Indonesia	1978	3 745	1 166	31.1	0.713	0.700	0.910
	1983	7 268	2 001	27.5	0.742	0.691	0.863
	1988	9 804	2 955	30.1	1.121	0.785	1.127
Malaysia	1978	471	302	64.1	1.468	1.442	1.874
	1983	764	533	69.8	1.880	1.750	2.187
	1988	1 833	1 350	73.6	2.738	1.919	2.754
Philippines	1978	434	152	35.0	0.802	0.788	1.023
	1983	721	290	40.2	1.084	1.009	1.261
	1988	1 120	510	45.5	1.693	1.186	1.703
Thailand	1978	309	233	75.4	1.726	1.696	2.204
	1983	521	390	74.9	2.017	1.878	2.346
	1988	1 992	1 456	73.1	2.718	1.904	2.733

Source: Urata (1989, Table 1).

the exception for a brief period of the Philippines, they continued to have access to external financing in the 1980s. The NIEs have emerged as net suppliers of finance following Japan's quantum leap in external financing activity.

11 Commodity trends and policy responses with reference to the Pacific

RONALD C. DUNCAN

This chapter deals with two areas insofar as they will affect the Pacific region: trends in commodity markets and future directions in policies affecting commodity markets. In order to discuss these topics comprehensively, a global setting is needed which defines the likely role of primary commodities. The chapter is structured as follows. It first discusses the role of primary commodities in terms of global production, trade and development and, in particular, their changing role in the developing countries and in the Pacific region. Next, it examines the recent and likely trends in commodity markets of importance to the Pacific region. Finally, it focuses on the likely and desirable policy responses in reaction to macroeconomic or commodity market developments.

DEVELOPMENTS IN AGRICULTURAL PRODUCTION, TRADE AND PRICES

Changing structure of production

While primary commodity production is still an important component of GDP in developing countries, it has become much less important in the past twenty years. For example, the share of agriculture in GDP of the low-income countries has fallen from 42 per cent to 32 per cent in the 1965–86 period (World Bank, 1988b). For the middle-income countries, agriculture's share has declined from 22 per cent to 15 per cent within this period.

In many developing countries, this change in sectoral composition has been achieved by strong growth in the industrial sector, accompanied by strong but slower growth in agriculture. Brazil, China, India, Indonesia, Malaysia, Mexico, Pakistan, Thailand and Turkey are examples of this kind of healthy economic performance. However, less healthy performance is reflected in low GDP growth and agricultural growth of less than 2 per cent in many of the low-income countries (including most sub-Saharan countries).

The fast agricultural production growth experienced in developing countries in the 1965–86 period relied heavily on the yield growth in cereals, the so-called Green Revolution. Rapid yield growth was also achieved in the beverages (coffee, cocoa and tea) and in some of the vegetable oilseeds. The

Table 11.1 Growth trends in agricultural production (per cent)

	1965–86	1965–73	1963–80	1980–86
Developing countries	3.0	3.1	2.9	3.8
Asia	3.2	3.3	3.0	4.8
South America	2.9	2.6	3.3	1.9
Africa	1.8	2.5	1.9	0.4

Source: Food and Agriculture Organization, *Production Yearbook*, various issues.

growth rate was highest for Asia and lowest for Africa (Table 11.1). The available evidence suggests that the observed differentials in productivity resulted from differences in levels of investment in research, differential returns from research, and importantly for Africa, poor agricultural policies such as high export taxes and overvalued exchange rates which adversely affected the incentives to invest and innovate.

The slow growth in total agricultural production in many developing countries—often together with fast growth in production—has been reflected in declining per capita agricultural production. Even those countries performing as well as Kenya in its agricultural sector have been unable to maintain agricultural production growth ahead of population growth.

While the share of agriculture in the GDP of most developing countries has fallen sharply, the decline in the share of employment in agriculture has not been so dramatic. In fact, the decline in the share of the labour force in agriculture in the low-income countries over the 1965–80 period (the latest available data) has been quite modest. By comparison, in the middle-income countries there has been a substantial decline. Therefore, the labour intensity of agriculture in many low-income countries remains very high and may have even increased. The corollary of the slow growth in agriculture and the very high (and increasing) labour intensity of this sector in the low-income countries is that the low-income earners are (increasingly) concentrated in this sector. There are no cross-country data to allow measurement of the sectoral composition of incomes. However, the widespread decline in food production per capita may be an approximate indicator that (at least for those at the subsistence level in agriculture in these countries) there has been a decline in living standards.

The sharply differing rates of economic growth among the developing countries have given rise to much concern within the World Bank. This 'two-track' growth pattern is characterised on the one hand by countries with: one, fast growth in production of both industrial and primary commodities; two, fast growth in manufactures exports in some primary exports; three, fast growth in imports of some primaries (foodstuffs and raw materials); and four, a rapid slowdown in population growth. On the other hand, the poor growth countries are experiencing slow or no growth in industrial goods and primaries, slow export growth and loss of export market shares for primary commodities, fast growth in food imports because of inability to increase food production and high population growth. Those countries caught in the debt crisis face the

Table 11.2 Shares of non-fuel primary commodities in developing country merchandise exports, 1971–86 (per cent)

	1971	1976	1981	1986
Africa	53.6	32.7	22.8	33.2
America	63.0	50.6	36.1	48.0
Asia	25.9	13.0	10.3	14.0
West Asia	8.4	2.9	2.6	7.6
South and Southeast Asia	41.9	29.7	21.3	16.3
Oceania	65.8	62.8	73.6	60.7
Total developing countries	42.3	24.5	18.1	23.9

Source: UNCTAD, *UNCTAD Commodity Yearbook 1988*; United Nations, New York, 1989.

added problem of diminishing capital inflows and hence difficulty in financing investments to stimulate growth.

Primary commodity trade

In general, the importance of non-fuel primary commodities in the trade of developing countries changed considerably with the sharp increases in petroleum prices in the 1970s. For many developing countries, the growth of manufactures exports and/or the discovery of petroleum resources considerably reduced their reliance on non-fuel primary exports (see Table 11.2). However, most of the low-income countries (and certainly many of the small countries of the Pacific, whether low-income or not) still rely heavily on non-fuel primaries for foreign exchange. Coffee, cocoa, copper, cotton, rubber, sugar and timber are the most important agricultural commodity exports for these low-income countries—with coffee and sugar being the most important (World Bank, 1988a).

World agricultural food exports (SITC 0+1+22+4) and agricultural raw material exports (SITC 2–22–27–28) have increased in nominal value terms at annual rates of 10.3 per cent and 8.5 per cent respectively during the period 1970–85. These are significantly lower rates than those for fuels (18.2 per cent per year) and manufactured goods (13.2 per cent per year). However, growth rates of food and agricultural raw materials exports vary widely from one region to another. As shown in Table 11.3, growth rates of agricultural commodity exports of African countries were considerably lower than those of developing countries in America and South and Southeast Asia. In fact, in real terms—that is, deflated by the unit value of manufactured goods exports from industrial countries—Africa's food and agricultural raw material exports have had negative growth rates of -2.5 per cent per year and -4 per cent per year respectively during this period. Growth rates of agricultural commodity exports from South and Southeast Asian developing countries, measured in nominal terms, were more than twice as high as those of African countries.

As a result of this poor export performance, Africa's shares of world exports of all food items declined by one-half during the period 1970 to 1985 (see Table 11.4). Almost all the loss in their share was taken by developing coun-

Table 11.3 Growth rates of agricultural commodity exports of developing countries by region, 1970–85 (per cent per year)

	World	Africa	America	South and Southeast Asia
All food items				
In nominal terms	10.3	5.3	10.2	13.1
In real terms[a]	2.5	-2.5	2.4	5.3
Agricultural raw materials				
In nominal terms	8.5	3.8	7.1	8.4
In real terms [a]	0.7	-4.0	-0.7	0.6

Note: a Deflated by World Bank's index of the unit value of manufactured goods exports (MUV).
Sources: UNCTAD, *Commodity Yearbook*, 1987; United Nations, New York.

tries in South and Southeast Asia. Data for agricultural raw materials show the same trends for Africa and Asia.

There has been an important difference in the destination of agricultural exports from African and Asian developing countries. In 1985 only about 20 per cent of Africa's agricultural commodity exports went to other developing countries, while about 40 per cent of Asian agricultural commodity exports went to other developing countries. This difference is important, because developing countries' imports of agricultural commodities increased by about sixfold during this period while those of developed countries increased by only one-half as much.

Primary commodity price trends and variability

Much has been made of two aspects of primary commodity prices: their volatility and their trend relative to prices of industrial goods (the net barter terms of trade). The hypothesis put forward by Prebisch (1950) and Singer (1950) that the net barter terms of trade of primary commodities would inevitably decline has had a very influential, but unwarranted, impact on developing country policies since the 1950s. Several studies (Prebisch, 1950; Lewis, 1952; Sapsford, 1985, and Grilli and Yang, 1988) have purported to show through statistical analysis that this hypothesis has been borne out by history. This conclusion is in doubt for two reasons. First, there has been much greater improvement in industrial goods that in primary commodities (for

Table 11.4 World shares of agricultural commodity exports by developing country regions (percentage)

	Agricultural raw materials				All food items			
	Total	Africa	America	South and Southeast Asia	Total	Africa	America	South and Southeast Asia
1970	30.9	7.2	5.6	15.1	32.4	7.6	15.6	6.6
1975	25.2	5.4	4.6	12.8	29.2	5.1	14.6	7.7
1985	25.5	3.7	4.5	14.9	31.5	3.8	15.6	9.6

Sources: UNCTAD, *Commodity Yearbook*, 1987; United Nations, New York.

example, cars and computers versus wheat). This quality change has not been and cannot easily be allowed for in measuring price changes in industrial gods, while such changes are usually allowed for in primary commodity price series (which are quoted in terms of specific qualities). Second, primary commodity prices are usually quoted in f.o.b. terms while industrial goods are usually quoted in terms of c.i.f. prices. Changes in freight costs have reflected the highly improved efficiency of transport. As this factor has not been allowed for, there is an upward bias in the price index for industrial goods (Dorrance and Woldekidan, 1989).

But more to the point, the net barter terms of trade should not be a very critical factor in policymaking—except for short-run purposes. A much more relevant measure is the 'income terms of trade'; that is, the total receipts from exports divided by import prices—a concept which generally takes into account the productivity gains made by a country. A commodity-exporting country can increase its 'welfare' even in the face of declining net barter terms of trade if its productivity is increasing and a larger volume of commodities is exported. To illustrate this, income terms of trade for non-fuel commodity exports have been calculated for five developing country regions for the period 1965–85 and the results are shown in Figure 11.1 (without any allowance for the quality and freight biases mentioned above). The non-fuel primary commodity income terms of trade for the East Asia and Pacific region grew at nearly 5 per cent per year during this period. By contrast, those of East and West Africa and South Asia were essentially stagnant.[1] The income terms of trade for the Middle East and North Africa regions declined by 1.5 per cent per year. The difference between the regions with fast and slow growing income terms of trade was primarily due to the very slow growth rates in the export volumes of the regions with the poorly-performing income terms of trade (about 2 per cent per year for East Africa and South Asia and 1 per cent for West Africa).

The export pessimism that was generated by the Prebisch–Singer hypothesis led to policies which, in fact, ensured the very effect they were trying to avoid. By promoting import-substituting policies and the accompanying policies of trade restrictions and overvalued exchange rates, exports (of both primary and secondary goods) were penalised and export growth was stunted. By contrast, those countries which did not pursue such policies saw their exports, particularly of manufactures, grow rapidly.

The high variability of primary commodities is a well-documented phenomenon and arguably represents one of the major policy problems faced by the highly primary commodity-dependent developing countries because it leads to fluctuations in their ability to import or service their external debts, and because it can adversely affect fiscal and monetary management.

Developing countries may be divided into two broad groups: fuel-exporting countries and non-fuel exporting countries (the latter are mainly fuel importers). As can be seen from Table 11.5, the export earnings of the fuel exporters have been more variable in the 1979–88 period than the export earnings of the non-fuel exporters. Among the non-fuel exporters, the mineral exporters have

Figure 11.1 Income terms of trade of non-fuel primary commodities by developing country regions, 1965–85 (1965 = 100)

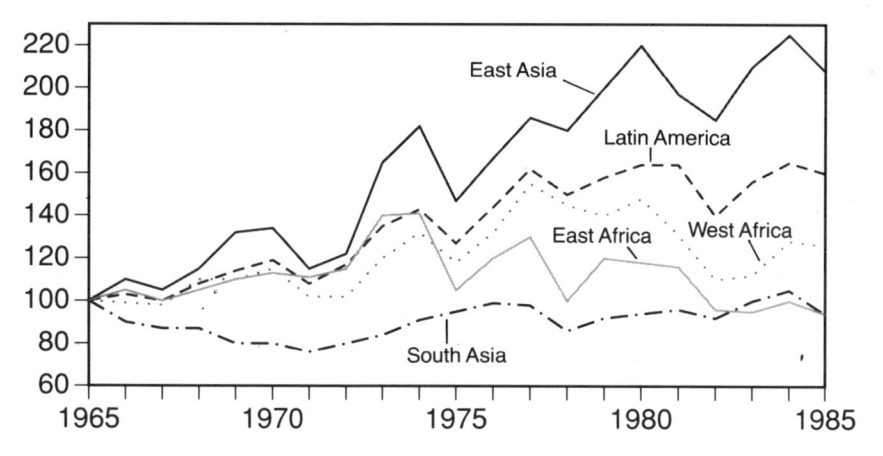

Note: Deflated by import unit value of manufactures

experienced more variability than the agricultural exporters or the manufactures exporters. The movements in primary commodity exporters' export earnings have been dominated by fluctuations in international primary commodity prices. The period 1979–80 was a boom period for commodity prices. From 1980 through 1986 there was an extended decline in commodity prices, particularly in the raw materials markets (both fuel and minerals). The upturn in agricultural prices in 1984 and 1988 and in minerals prices in 1987 and 1988 can also be seen in the data in Table 11.5.

The instability of commodity prices and exchange rates will remain important sources of external disturbance for developing countries. International and domestic price stabilisation programs have largely proven ineffective in stabilising commodity prices. However, recent developments in financial markets appear to offer attractive opportunities for developing countries to hedge their commodity price risks (imports as well as exports), as well as their exchange rate and interest rate risks. All institutions and organisations within the country exposed to such risks, such as the central bank, the government itself,

Table 11.5 Annual changes in export earnings, developing countries, 1979–88

Country groups	1979	1980	1981	1982	1983	1984	1985	1986	1987	1988
Fuel exporters	47.1	41.2	-5.5	-17.9	-15.5	-1.2	-10.2	-33.7	21.9	-5.0
Non-fuel exporters	24.7	22.7	2.6	-4.6	3.3	11.5	-0.7	8.2	22.6	18.3
Primary product exporters	27.7	22.9	-4.3	-8.3	3.0	10.4	-3.0	0.3	3.8	13.5
Agricultural	23.3	18.1	2.9	-7.0	3.4	16.0	-2.9	-1.4	-0.4	12.2
Mineral	37.4	32.6	-17.3	-11.4	2.1	-2.9	-3.4	5.0	13.4	17.3
Manufactures exporters	21.1	22.4	8.2	-1.5	4.8	13.4	1.4	15.6	25.6	19.6

Note: Annual percentage change in US dollars.

Source: IMF, *World Economic Outlook*, various issues.

as well as commodity marketing boards and producers, should be concerned to hedge themselves against these risks. Such hedging will also serve to improve the creditworthiness of countries whose main revenue-earning assets are natural resources. The World Bank is developing risk management programs in which it will identify the various sources of commodity risk facing a developing country, including those associated with the World Bank-financed projects, and determine: one, the impact of the various risks on the performance of the different organisational units within a country; two, the optimal hedging requirements of the different organisational units; three, the risk management instruments that best suit the country's needs; and four, the institutional, regulatory and human resource (training) needs for the country to be able to implement such risk management strategies.

PROSPECTS FOR PRIMARY COMMODITIES

As shown above, many developing countries—particularly small and/or low-income developing countries—depend heavily on a few export commodities. The prospects for these will determine to a large extent, at least in the short run, their import capability, investment levels and per capita income growth. As argued above, over the long run the most important determinant of their export performance will be the growth in productivity of these export industries and an enabling environment for the development of new export industries—which will be positively influenced by market-related producer incentives and investment in infrastructure, research, and human capital. In the short run, export revenue performance will depend on world price movements and on producer responses to output and input price incentives. Therefore, the commodity market outlook given below should have little relevance to an individual country's export performance over the long run, but only give an indication of the environment in which they will be operating. Year-to-year price movements will continue to be highly variable and a country's ability to manage effectively the risks associated with such instability will be an important factor in its performance.

Important factors affecting commodity prices recently include variations in industrial production growth, changes in agricultural price-support measures in industrial countries, major interest rate changes, and lags in supply response to earlier price changes. Other, less important, factors include policy reforms in the raw materials' intensity of production in the industrial countries. I believe that these latter two factors are nowhere near as important contributors to the 1980s decline in prices as argued by many observers. While some developing countries have adopted policies which have improved their commodity export performance, others have moved in the opposite direction. Research in the World Bank (Choe, 1989; Duncan, 1988) has shown that the so-called structural change in demand for raw materials in the industrial countries (see Drucker, 1986) has been more likely a cyclical phenomenon rather that a permanent new downtrend in the raw materials' consumption.

The slow investment and GDP growth and the high crude oil prices in the 1970s and early 1980s were the main factors behind the changed demand for raw materials and these are not likely to be permanent.

Macroeconomic forecasts

Future market developments in primary commodities will depend on: economic activity (particularly in industrial countries), interest rate and exchange rate movements, domestic policies in the major producing and consuming countries, and technological developments as well as random weather effects. The World Bank is presently forecasting slow GNP growth in the OECD countries in 1990 and 1991 (near 2.2 per cent per year on average) as a consequence of adjustment of the major imbalances between the main trading nations; with recovery to about 3 per cent per year by the mid-1990s; and a declining trend in the rate of growth thereafter (about 2.7 per cent per year by the year 2000). Inflation in the OECD countries is expected to average around 4 per cent per year during this period. Real interest rates are expected to decline from their present level of 4.8 per cent (six-month US$ LIBOR) to about 3 per cent by the year 2000. Other scenarios which could be played out, and which have a reasonably high probability at this point, include: one, a sharper economic downturn triggered by a financial crisis, leading to a faster macroeconomic adjustment; two, a much slower adjustment resulting in low growth over an extended period; and three, an extended period of fast economic growth in the 1990s as a result of the recent upturn in investment and technological change. Case two is a pessimistic scenario which could incorporate an increase in protectionism as policymakers become frustrated with the poor growth. Case three is an optimistic scenario which could include a sustained period of high raw material prices which would be necessary to trigger increased investment in these commodities to meet the higher levels of demand.

Likely commodity market developments

Foodstuffs—grains, oilseeds, meats, fruits and vegetables

The postwar period has seen world food production growing at the annual rate of about 2.5 per cent, with the developing countries doing better than the average by achieving a growth rate of about 3 per cent per year. Given their rapid population growth, it seems remarkable that per capita food output has grown in the developing world by about 0.5 per cent. Developing country performance would have been even better were it not for the fact that per capita output in Africa declined by nearly 0.5 per cent over this period. The recipe for the success of Asian agriculture has been appropriate pricing policies, investment in infrastructure and successful research, while the lack of success in Africa has generally been accompanied by the absence of these ingredients. During this period there have been times of high international prices in food commodities, usually associated with adverse weather conditions; but overall, prices have tended downwards in real terms (deflated by per capita incomes).

Factors giving reason for concern to some about the future food situation are, first, that the increases in production from increases in area planted have been shrinking and the potential for increased production from planted area expansion appears limited. This means greater reliance on increased yields. In this respect, the growth in output from the use of hybrid varieties of rice and wheat has been slowing as the area planted to these varieties nears saturation point in those countries where they have been most rewarding. Adding to this concern is the current assessment that new sources of yield growth in grains from the field of genetic engineering are not yet highly promising, at least not for the next ten years or so.

Although I largely agree with these assessments of the potential for growth in grains output, I see offsetting factors to these concerns. First, within the developing countries there can be substantially increased production from improved policies towards the rural sector which would result in better management and hence increased yields. Second, because per capita consumption of grains has been rising over most of the developing world and in the centrally planned economies, the future rate of growth of per capita demand for these commodities will slow down as people improve and diversify their diets by increasing the absolute quantities and proportions of meats and vegetables and fruits. This can be seen from Table 11.6, which shows how consumption of meat of various kinds is growing in major developing countries—in most cases much faster than population growth. In Brazil's case, as has happened in most of the industrial countries, there has been a swing from beef to poultry and pork as these latter meats have become relatively less expensive. Brazil has become a major producer and exporter of poultry. In other cases where per capita incomes have grown from very low levels—rapidly as in the Republic of Korea's case or less rapidly and more recently as in the case of China and India—consumption of all meats has grown rapidly.

Greater demand for meats in developing countries, particularly of pork and poultry, will put emphasis on production of grains and oilseeds for feedstuffs rather than for basic calories. This is borne out by recent World Bank experience in China where there is now much less concern about rice production and increased emphasis on production of grains and oilseeds for feedstuffs.

Over the longer term, it is expected that grains prices will continue to decline in terms of purchasing power and greater emphasis in production and trade will be given to grains and oilseeds for livestock feeding. This conclusion does not apply generally in sub-Saharan Africa where it is hoped that there will be the needed policy emphasis on increasing grains production for basic foodstuffs. A factor which could bring about an increase in grains prices in the medium term would be a period of per capita income growth in those countries which have had poor economic growth during the 1980s. As a result, food consumption suffered. An alternative scenario would be a depreciation of the

Table 11.6 Growth in meat consumption, selected countries, 1975–88 (per cent per year)

	Beef and veal[a]	Pork[a]	Poultry[b]
Industrial			
France	0.4	1.1	2.8
Germany, Federal Republic	0.1	1.5	1.2
Japan	6.8	4.4	6.3
United Kingdom	-1.3	1.0	4.2
United States	-0.3	2.5	5.1
Developing			
Brazil	-0.03	3.0	11.2
China	7.5	7.5	na
India	4.5	na	11.5[c]
Korea, Republic of	8.5	12.6	7.9
Philippines	1.1[d]	3.8	3.4[e]
Centrally planned			
Soviet Union	1.9	1.4	6.0

Notes: na—not available.
    a Carcass-weight equivalent.
    b Ready-to-cook equivalent.
    c For period 1985–88.
    d For period 1980–87.
    e For period 1980–88.

Source: United States Department of Agriculture, *World Livestock Situation and Outlook*, various issues.

US dollar to bring the United States current account into balance, which would lower prices.

The emergence of the European Community as a significant producer of oilseed products and protein meals, the rapid increase of productive capacity for palm oil in Indonesia and Malaysia, and expanded soybean plantings in South America have brought an increased competitiveness to world markets which will be reflected in a downtrend in real prices over the long term.

However, the world market for vegetable oils will remain viable and dynamic. Investments in low-cost areas offer high rates of return despite the expectation of falling real prices. World demand, spurred by falling real prices and expanding supplies, is expected to grow significantly—especially among developing countries. Per capita consumption in Indonesia grew from 3.08 kg in 1970 to 8.7 kg in 1980; in China it grew from 2.65 kg to 7.5 kg over the same period; and in India from 5.48 kg to 7.2 kg. The average annual per capita consumption in the United States and the European Community is more than 38 kg.

Potentially, the largest sources of vegetable oil demand growth are India and China. Incomes and caloric intake have increased greatly in both countries in recent years. However, imports of vegetable oils are controlled in both countries. At very low levels of income, when per capita calorie intake is around 2,000 calories per day, vegetable oils are a luxury good. As per capita incomes increase, the demand for vegetable oils grows rapidly from levels below 100 calories per day to in excess of 200 calories per day. At per capita calorie levels in excess of 3,000 per day, the demand growth for vegetable oils tends to taper off. The data in Table 11.7 illustrate this pattern. If per capita incomes in

Table 11.7 Calories per capita per day from vegetable fats and oils and from all sources, average for 1979–81

	Vegetable	Percentage share of total	Total
Argentina	320	(10.1)	3 164
Bangladesh	40	(2.2)	1 837
Brazil	152	(6.0)	2 533
China	65	(2.7)	2 402
Cote d'Ivoire	231	(9.0)	2 567
France	350	(10.7)	3 260
Ghana	117	(6.7)	1 746
India	130	(6.3)	2 056
Indonesia	143	(6.0)	2 367
Italy	499	(14.5)	3 259
Malaysia	220	(9.1)	2 422
Nigeria	269	(11.6)	2 327
Pakistan	168	(7.7)	2 180
Philippines	85	(3.6)	2 377
Soviet Union	202	(6.3)	3 207
Senegal	293	(12.5)	2 339
Switzerland	331	(10.2)	3 259
United States	491	(14.2)	3 455
Zaire	159	(7.6)	2 097

Source: Food and Agriculture Organization, *Food Balance Sheets 1979–81 Average*, 1984.

China and India grow as anticipated, their vegetable oil consumption should grow rapidly—if the controls on consumption are removed. As can be seen from the data in Table 11.8, retail prices for vegetable oils in India are substantially above world market levels. The same is true of China. Indonesia also represents an important source of demand growth.

Table 11.8 Wholesale Indian vegetable oil prices, 1981–82 to 1986–87 (Bombay and New Delhi)

	Groundnut oil	Soybean oil	Cottonseed oil	Rapeseed oil
Rupees/100 kilos				
1981–82	1 364	1 259	1 242	1 165
1982–83	1 536	1 306	1 285	1 256
1983–84	1 626	1 394	1 352	1 470
1984–85	1 524	1 233	1 228	1 217
1985–86	1 821	1 405	1 506	1 272
1986–87	2 164	1 957	1 987	1 901
Percentage of world market price				
1981–82	216	288	226	281
1982–83	259	279	208	285
1983–84	138	170	140	186
1984–85	135	159	130	168
1985–86	224	296	233	298
1986–87	314	479	319	493

Source: World Bank, *Commodity Price Data File*; *Oil World*, various issues.

Beverage crops—cocoa, coffee and tea

The beverage crop markets have been or are going through a period of very low prices—both in nominal and real terms. Several factors explain this. Demand for these products, especially cocoa and coffee, is concentrated in the industrial countries where price and income elasticities of demand are very low and population growth is slow or even negative. On the supply side, output has been growing quickly because of the plantings of new, higher-yielding varieties since the boom in prices for these crops in the 1976-79 period. Moreover, the currency depreciations in recent years by the three largest coffee producers (Brazil, Columbia and Indonesia—by about 35 per cent in real terms over the past five years) have meant that they have been able to maintain or increase their production even as world coffee prices have been declining in real terms. The world cocoa market is entering its fifth consecutive year of excess supply. The largest cocoa producer Cote d'Ivoire's average annual rate of growth in output over the past four years was 6.5 per cent; while for Indonesia and Malaysia it was 22 per cent and 27 per cent per year, respectively. In Ghana, recent policy changes (exchange rate devaluations and producer price increases) have encouraged a sharp turnaround in cocoa output.

The recent collapse of the International Coffee Agreement led to a fall in coffee prices of over 30 per cent as producers increased their sales from stocks accumulated under the Agreement. The disagreements among members over export quota re-allocations in favour of *arabica* producers and the sales of non-quota coffee at much lower prices to non-members are unlikely to be resolved soon. The trend away from *robusta* coffees towards the higher quality, milder *arabicas* is widespread among consuming countries and should persist, so that we expect the increase in the price differential between *arabicas* and *robustas* from about 10-15 per cent to 20-30 per cent to be maintained. This is bad news for the producers of *robustas*, especially those in East and West Africa and Indonesia, the Philippines and Thailand in the Southeast Asia region.

We expect the low cocoa and coffee prices to last for several more years, in the absence of a major weather-induced output decline. However, the period of low prices will induce lower levels of new plantings and less use of inputs, which will eventually reduce the growth of output. According to simulations of our global models, the imbalance between demand and supply will close and prices will increase in real terms by the mid-1990s.

Rubber

Over the period to the year 2000, we expect rubber consumption to grow on average at about 2.4 per cent per year. The main growth will be in the developing countries, especially in Asia, with developing country consumption surpassing that in the industrial countries by 1990. Recent events in China raise some doubts about China's future absorptive capacity. For the centrally planned economies, much lower (1.6 per cent per year) consumption growth is expected because of their greater dependence on synthetic rubber.

Consumption in Japan is expected to grow more slowly than in the past

(1.4 per cent per year compared to 3.8 per cent per year for the 1970–86 period) because of the auto industry transplants to the United States and Europe and tyre industry transplants to North America, the Republic of Korea and Taiwan (China).

The increased demand for high-performance radial tyres and high-value rubber goods in the industrial countries and the move to automated tyre making will increase the demand for higher-quality natural rubber (sheet and crumb rubber and latex concentrate). The lower-quality rubber will go more to the developing countries where the poorer road conditions favour the use of traditional cross-ply tyres. (Such tyres are less stringent in the raw material quality requirements.)

The projected increase in natural rubber will come mainly from Indonesia, Malaysia and Thailand. Growth rates over the period to the year 2000 should be much faster in Indonesia (3.2 per cent per year) and Thailand (2.9 per cent per year) than in Malaysia where an annual output growth of 1 per cent is expected. However, the recent run-up in prices of natural rubber seems to have slowed the diversification from rubber to oil palm in the estate sector in Malaysia.

Natural rubber markets will be under sustained threat from developments in synthetic rubber where, for example, molecular engineering techniques are leading to improved properties. Natural rubber producers will have to fight back by improving the consistency and quality of their product to make it more attractive to manufacturers who are demanding raw materials of consistent quality for their automated processes.

Tropical timber

Growth of tropical hardwood log production is expected to slow down, mainly due to concern about increasing deforestation and its adverse impact on soils and air quality. Production of sawnwood and plywood is shifting from industrial countries and the centrally planned economies to developing countries. This shift is the result of restrictions on log exports and the direct encouragement of timber processing in developing countries, as well as the fact that the processing costs are lower in developing countries. While timber products will continue to face competition from alternatives such as plastics, the strong growth in demand for timber products and the restraints being imposed on their supplies should ensure that timber prices increase in real terms.

Metals and minerals

Since the recession of 1981–82 there has been a running-down of the surplus capacity which had been built up in the metals industries as a result of the high prices of the 1970s. This reduction in surplus capacity was an important factor behind the upswing in metals prices when industrial production rose sharply in major industrial countries as well as in the Asian–Pacific industrialising ones. There has been a complication in the 1987–89 period of high metals prices that we did not foresee. As prices increased and producers attempted to increase output, those countries which had not been able to maintain their plants during the low-price period of 1982–86 suffered major breakdowns, which served to fuel the price increase.

As noted earlier, there has been a declining trend in the raw materials intensity of output in the industrial countries since the mid-1970s. While this is partly the result of the continuing improvement in the efficiency of use of raw materials and of competition from substitutes, it has been much more a result of the high crude oil prices, the high real interest rates and the slowdown in the growth in economic activity in this period. These factors are reversible. We have seen crude oil prices come down. Real interest rates may well fall. Hence, we could have a period of much faster industrial growth in the 1990s. The industrial countries are reducing the materials intensity of output as they shed their heavy industries. But this means that we can expect to see the developing countries being the source of fastest growth in raw materials' consumption, including energy.

Petroleum

Given the OECD growth path assumed, we expect an average 1.5 per cent per year growth in global oil consumption over the period to 2000. Other assumptions such as declining petroleum output in the industrial countries (particularly in the United States) and reductions in exports from non-OPEC developing country producers and the centrally planned economies, support our forecast of an uptrend in crude oil prices in real terms over the forecast period. Under this scenario, nearly one-third of the present proven recoverable world oil reserves (around 900 billion barrels) could be consumed by the end of this century. With the bulk of the remaining reserves located in OPEC countries, OPEC should be able to exert greater control over prices for a sustained period. This could lead to another round of high prices, increased investment in exploration for crude oil as well as for substitutes, and another upsurge in research towards conservation and improved efficiency. Therefore, beyond 2000, there may well be another downturn in crude oil prices in real terms.

The increased potential for another upswing in petroleum prices should be of great concern for the countries of the Asia–Pacific region. For the developing countries in this region, oil is of importance either as an export or an import and therefore ranks high as a source of terms-of-trade shocks. Several of these economies experienced difficulties in macroeconomic management following the oil price booms in the 1970s and the oil price crash in 1986. The risk of such events in the future can now be reasonably well hedged and countries would be well advised to adopt such preventative measures.

Concern over the environment is going to be an important factor in the energy market which could push in various directions: more emphasis on cleaner energy sources such as natural gas; higher taxes on 'dirty' fuels such as crude oil and coal; and pressures on developing countries to reduce consumption of manures and wood for household fuel, and of coal for industrial fuel.

The more industrially advanced countries in the Pacific region are undergoing a transformation in energy use. This is taking the form of: rapid growth in energy use in the industrial, transportation and household sectors; rapid urbanisation; spread of electricity grids throughout rural areas; rapid changeover from non-commercial fuels to commercial fuels such as kerosene, gas and electricity; and changeover by households from less efficient fuels (such as kerosene) to more efficient fuels (such as electricity and gas). This transformation is raising questions about domestic fuel policies, particularly pricing.

LIKELY POLICY RESPONSES TO COMMODITY MARKET DEVELOPMENTS

Now let me turn to speculating about the policy changes which we could see taking place and which will impinge on commodity markets. First, I am rather pessimistic about the policy reforms which will come out of the Uruguay Round discussions on agriculture. I would be surprised if United States farm policies were much changed. Subsidisation of United States exports will certainly be reduced in the near future. However, the present levels of subsidies were never intended to be permanent. Rather, they were intended to be used to regain export markets lost under the 1980–85 Farm Bill when the loan rates were increased to compensate farmers for the ban on exports to the Soviet Union (and subsequently the appreciating dollar pushed them much higher in terms of other currencies). But I doubt that the United States will agree not to subsidise exports in the future. Farm lobbies in the United States have almost ignored the US Administration's proposals to GATT—an indication, I believe, of their belief that little will come of them. There will likely be a change in the *form* of the protection given to the United States sugar industry because GATT has found it to be illegal. But again I believe that the level of protection (or the capacity to give protection) to the sugar industry will not be reduced. My pessimism is due to not seeing any change in the political forces which determine the distribution of income between agriculture and the rest of the economy—unlike Japan, where big changes in political power have been under way. I believe developing country exporters can be a strong countervailing force to domestic farm support interest groups in the European Community and the United States. The most effective force is information which the layman can relate to and understand.

The impetus which their own large stocks and the low levels to which the United States was pushing prices were giving to the cause for lowering agricultural protection in the European Community has now largely dissipated because of the fact that, assisted by the 1988 drought, the United States has mostly disposed of its excess stocks. It is likely now that the outcome of any changes in policies in the European Community will be the introduction of production quota arrangements to exert some control over the Community budget with no fundamental reform of policies. Because the weight of pressures for reform of policies in the European Community has mostly been because of the budget constraint, I foresee that policy changes will mainly be directed towards putting the costs of protection off-budget (as, for example, in the sugar industry regulations or the proposed vegetable oils tax) rather than reducing them. However, it may be the case that by paying for agricultural protection directly through price increases there will be increased consumer resistance to protection in the European Community.

If the United States and the European Community do not substantially reform their agricultural policies, I would expect to see business-as-usual with periodic surpluses and low prices as the United States adjusts its policies in an attempt to maximise its revenues from agricultural commodities as an oligopolistic market leader (see Mitchell and Duncan, 1987). With stronger control over production, the European Community may not expand its influence into third markets at as fast a rate as in the past. This may not be true of vegetable oils, if its production of these commodities expand as expected under the present set of policies.

The actions of the European Community in the vegetable oils market are of particular concern for two reasons: one, the pressures within the European Community to discourage production in the cereals industries have led to incentives to increase oilseeds production, which in turn has created a lobby for increasing protection to the oilseeds industry; and two, the inclusion of southern European countries in the European Community, and the likelihood of the inclusion of more such countries, will increase pressures for protection of crops in competition with oilseed industries in the developing countries. The 1988 drought lessened pressures within the European Community for reform of oilseeds policy as well as for other crops. Program expenditures relating to oilseeds grew from 2 billion ECUs in 1979 to more than 6 billion ECUs in 1987. At that time, the European Community began a vigorous debate over the oilseed program which resulted in an attempt to limit production. Penalties for exceeding the quantity ceiling imposed are not severe, however; and furthermore, the rise in international prices since 1988 has eased budget pressures. Radical structural changes in the programs have not occurred, though budgetary pressures should re-emerge in the 1990s as oilseed prices decline once more. This will probably trigger the re-emergence of tensions between the European Community and the United States over oilseeds policy.

Under internal and external pressures, Japan has in recent years consistently reduced its restrictiveness against agricultural imports. Japan's market for fresh and processed agricultural products is growing rapidly. I believe that internal pressures for access to increased supplies will be maintained and that the Japanese market should be of growing importance for agricultural exporters.

Turning now to the likely policy developments in the developing countries, there are a number of trends which I have identified and other forecasts which could have policy implications. I list these as follows:

1 the 'high-track/low-track' development paths which seem to distinguish developing countries;
2 demand for foodstuffs growing at a faster rate than can be supplied domestically in the faster-growing developing countries;

3 the shift in composition of cereals and, more generally, foodstuffs as per capita incomes increase;
4 the shift in the processing of raw materials from the industrial countries to the developing countries and the ensuing shift in trading patterns with the share of raw materials imports by the developing countries increasing;
5 the likelihood of an upswing in the investment cycle in the 1990s and therefore the possibility of a sustained increase in raw materials demand and prices;
6 the increased concern over environmental issues relating to the production and processing of primary commodities;
7 continuing competition from substitutes, with the threat of challenges to many commodities from the new processes such as molecular engineering and new products such as ceramics;
8 the increased emphasis on automated manufacturing and the heavier emphasis on consistency in the quality of raw materials; and
9 the growing intensity of competition between developing countries for export shares in the major primary commodity exports such as coffee and cocoa.

Let me briefly suggest some of the issues that these developments will raise and the policy responses which we may see. Points 1 and 9 above are in many ways related. The lowest-income, most heavily commodity-dependent countries have done least well in terms of growth, export shares, and so on. This poor performance is the result of their low levels of resources, both physical and human, and also the result of bad management in many cases. The first problem can only be changed slowly; the second can be turned around quickly. There is growing concern among these countries for better policies in terms of more appropriate real exchange rates, less oppressive export taxes, more investment in research and infrastructure, less bias in government services in favour of existing industries, more interest in improving marketing of products and more concern for hedging the risks faced by their exposure in the commodity price, exchange rate and interest rate areas. These policies need to be pursued even more vigorously, otherwise the low-income, commodity-dependent countries will continue to lose export shares in existing markets and fail to develop new markets. Such policy reforms should be matters of great concern for the countries depending heavily on coffee and cocoa exports; especially if they accept the forecasts of low prices for these commodities for several more years.

The question is often raised as to the impact of increased efficiency in production and exports leading to declining prices and revenues for all producers. This issue has to be seen in a dynamic context. We cannot ask countries which have a comparative advantage in a commodity to hold back from attempting to increase productivity. If prices fall as a result of increased productivity, this is a signal to the less efficient producers to move out of the market or to increase their own efficiency. For those countries which are becoming less efficient producers because their per capita incomes are rising, the rational decision is to move out of the market. For those which would have a comparative advantage in the product if they had rational economic policies, the decision is obvious—change the policies. Such policy changes are listed above.

The 'high-track' developing countries are those most likely to find that food consumption grows at a faster rate than can be met by increases in domestic production—even though domestic production is increasing quickly. The gap can be most efficiently closed by increasing imports. It is to be hoped that the policy response is *not* to restrict imports and increase self-sufficiency by raising domestic prices. It should be recognised that this fast growth in food consumption is a function of the stage of economic growth and that as per capita incomes grow further the marginal dollar of income will be spent on other goods such as clothing, housing and transportation rather than on food. This will increase the demand for raw materials. For the large low-income countries where per capita incomes are growing steadily, such as China, India, Indonesia and Pakistan, the most noticeable change should be in terms of improved diets—including more expenditure on vegetable oils, meats and vegetables. Since the numbers of people involved are so large, the demands will mostly be met from domestic production; but there should still be a strong impact on trade.

The shift away from rice, as development takes place, towards other cereals should give additional cause to those countries which subsidise rice production (either directly or through fertiliser subsidies) to remove such subsidies. These subsidies serve only to misallocate resources by encouraging farmers to grow rice when they should be concentrating on other grains for foodstuffs or feedstuffs. Some countries also subsidise rice consumption, which similarly tends to distort consumption patterns. For example, in one province in China it was found that the reduction of the subsidy on rice served to reduce sharply the rice being fed to chickens but not to reduce that for human consumption.

As diets change with per capita income increases, more emphasis will have to be given in terms of research, transport and marketing infrastructure, as well as pricing and production policies, to commodities such as livestock and fruits and vegetables rather than to staple cereals. Or, at least, the policy biases against the production of these foodstuffs should be removed. There are also large biases against the consumption of some of these products—for example, subsidisation of rice consumption and restrictions on consumption of vegetable oils in China and India to which references were made earlier. It would be of tremendous benefit to vegetable oil producers to have these restrictions reduced or abolished. Some support for this will come from consumers within these countries as their incomes increase and their demand grows. Unfortunately, as Anderson and Hayami (1986) have shown in detail, developing countries (as their per capita incomes increase) have a strong tendency to move towards protecting their agricultural sectors, which raises costs to their consumers and lowers the welfare of the countries themselves and their trading partners. Exporting countries should try to resist and reverse such policy trends in other developing countries. Gains from doing so can be as large for some products as similar 'propaganda' in industrial countries.

The increased concern for environmental issues in the industrial countries has played a part in the shift of the processing of primary products towards developing countries. The cost of carrying out these activities in industrial countries has been raised by the imposition of taxes or by regulation. The shift of these 'dirty' activities to developing countries means that they should be focusing on the design of anti-pollution policies to ensure that pollution does not exceed optimal levels. It is likely that there will be additional restraints imposed on commodity production and processing in industrial countries which will further increase the cost of these activities—such as fertiliser taxes to reduce the pollution of water systems and taxes on power generation from fossil fuels to reduce atmospheric pollution. These actions will offer further possibilities from which developing countries can benefit.

Environmental damage is also of great concern in the developing countries, though the concerns are somewhat different from those in the industrial countries. The developing countries are not as much concerned with pollution of air or water as with, for example, the degradation of the soils and forests and the silting up of irrigation systems. These resources need to be restored if they are to support the agricultural growth necessary for continued improvement in living standards. Policies which foster private interest in investment in the improvement of these resources, such as land tenure, will play a critical role. Research into sustainable farming systems is another important ingredient.

Competition from substitutes also places pressure on producing countries to adopt policies which enhance efficiency, as in the case of the threat to natural rubber from synthetic rubbers. Because of this threat and because of the move towards automated tyre production, natural rubber-producing countries should be much more concerned to adopt production, pricing and marketing policies which will ensure that their product is free of contaminants and of consistent quality as in the case of the automated process.

Many developing countries (particularly in Southeast Asia) are experiencing a rapid transformation in energy consumption. Again, these are inevitable consequences of economic growth and the aim of policy should be to ensure their efficient progress. Appropriate pricing policies, meaning policies linked to world prices, are an integral part of a rational approach to these developments. These will allow full scope for substitution between energy sources, from less efficient sources such as wood or kerosene to more efficient sources such as electricity or gas. These latter sources can be less damaging environmentally. Efficient energy investment policies, including pricing for cost recovery, should also be a major concern.

Finally, a note on recent developments in Eastern Europe. Given that the movement towards more liberal economies is successful in some or all of these cases, there could be substantial impacts on commodity markets. With higher incomes, these countries can be expected to increase consumption of many tropical products (for example, coffee, cocoa, vegetable oils and fruits). In the case of some products (coffee, for example) consumption could increase quite sharply and have a significant impact on prices. In the case of other agricultural commodities (such as grains and sugar) or metals (such as nickel), their production could increase substantially with downward pressures on prices.

CONCLUDING REMARKS

First, a caveat. Forecasting of commodity prices is inherently difficult. Because commodity price series are random variables, or at least behave like random variables, in the absence of bias in the forecasting process one can hope to guess correctly the direction of price movement only 50 per cent of the time. But businesses and governments still have to make forecasts for policy and planning purposes; and it is worth expending some resources on that activity, but only up to a point. It is even more important to recognise the uncertainty and variability of commodity prices, as well as production, and to expend some effort on managing or hedging those risks.

One forecast I will make with certainty is that international commodity prices still will remain highly variable—an important source of external shock to developing countries. They can take two approaches to this problem. First, what I call the 'preventative' approach, which is to hedge against the price risks; and I would emphasise here the commodity-linked securities approach which the Commodity Division at the World Bank has been researching. Second, there is the *ex post* approach of using fiscal and monetary measures to manage the terms-of-trade shocks after they occur so that the disruption to the economy is minimised. In recent years, there has been increased research interest in this issue at both the IMF and the World Bank. Developing country governments should give both these approaches much more attention, particularly because domestic and international price stabilising agreements have been broadly unsuccessful.

At an economy-wide level, activity diversification for the purpose of hedging price and production risks has a role in an economy which does not allow free trade in assets and thus cannot take full advantage of the possibilities of risk sharing via financial diversification. At an individual producer level, activity diversification is an important component in an array of hedging measures which also include off-farm work, intra-family income transfers, as well as, in developed countries, market instruments such as futures.

One of the major lessons learned over the past decade or so is that bad macroeconomic policies such as overvalued exchange rates can be more economically costly for primary commodity producers than industry-specific interventions such as export taxes. But industry-specific policies need careful evaluation. Industry policies are often a jumble of policies, adopted at different times to achieve different objectives; and often adopted to try to solve problems created by existing policies so that the controls over industry accumulate over time. There is a need to stand back, specify the objectives which are to be aimed at and derive the most efficient policies to achieve those objectives. (For example, the idea of 'decoupling' of farm policy in the United

States and the European Community is to stop trying to provide minimum incomes to farmers by means of supporting prices—a very costly instrument—but to do it directly via income supplements.) This strategy towards policymaking is very logical but it is very difficult to follow because every form of government control creates a group or groups of special interests which will fight to retain it. But if growth and development are to be maximised it is essential that these vested interests be overcome. And, in the long run, the only sure way to do this is by understanding the costs of the controls and the benefits of better policies and educating the public about these costs and benefits. It should not be believed that this is a simple, quick task. It is a continuing process, one which will always be fought against by those benefitting from existing policies. By its very nature, the 'transparency' of the costs and benefits of policies is not something that governments find it comfortable to live with.

For these reasons, I am not optimistic about the possibility of quick reform in the agricultural policies of the European Community and the United States—nor for that matter in the developing countries (such as China and India, which were mentioned as countries whose agricultural policy reform could benefit other developing country exporters). But I would still strongly encourage other countries to try to change policies in these countries. Information which educates consumers or non-agricultural industries about the adverse effects on them of such policies can be effective. To be effective, such information has to be presented in a format which the layman can easily relate to and which reaches this audience.

12 Evolving patterns of comparative advantage in the Pacific economies

IPPEI YAMAZAWA, AKIRA HIRATA AND
KAZUHIKO YOKOTA

INTRODUCTION

The 1980s witnessed dramatic changes in the world economy, starting with peculiar policy responses by individual governments to the second oil shock, rapid adjustment to triple highs of commodity prices, US dollar and interest rates, followed by dynamic recovery of growth among the Pacific, Western Europe and North America economies. Pacific growth has been the most spectacular and accompanied by great changes in industrial production and trade. Both Korea and Taiwan have quickly returned to their double-digit growth paths since 1986, while the ASEAN countries have resumed their rapid growth since 1987.

The rapid recovery of growth by the Asian NIEs and ASEAN has been accelerated by the restructuring of Japanese industries and foreign trade accompanied by intensified foreign direct investment. New patterns of comparative advantage emerging in the Pacific countries are anticipated through radical adjustments of exchange rates, intensified foreign direct investment and technology transfer, rapid economic growth and restructuring of industrial production.

This study is based on comprehensive statistics of trade flows among the Pacific countries and the export and import structures of individual countries over the 1980s. The importance of trade matrix information is self-evident. Discussion focuses on the dynamic growth and structural changes in the Pacific with ad hoc information on the performance of a few countries.

Although this study is based on extensive statistical research, only five tables and one figure are provided here due to space constraints. The chapter focuses on findings related to structural changes in the Pacific, their underlying forces, and the policy implications that can be derived from these, with supplementary details provided in Appendixes 12A.1–12A.5.

This chapter first sets out our main findings with regard to changes in Pacific trade flows. It then proceeds to identify evolving patterns of comparative advantage of individual Pacific countries, and discusses their underlying forces, focusing on the 'flying geese' hypothesis of the transfer of industry from mature to newly industrialised, and to late-starting economies. We turn

Table 12.1 Trade matrix of the Asia-Pacific countries, 1987, 1980 (million US dollars) and 1987/80 ratio

		Japan	United States	Canada	Australia	New Zealand	India	Malaysia
Japan	1987		84 232	5 611	5 152	1 129	2 990	2 167
	1980		31 649	2 437	3 391	678	3 458	2 059
	1987/80		2.66	2.30	1.52	1.67	0.86	1.05
United States	1987	26 901		56 883	5 330	797	759	1 858
	1980	20 457		32 557	4 054	594	1 392	1 284
	1987/80	1.31		1.75	1.31	1.34	0.55	1.45
Canada	1987	4 811	70 375		529	106	230	84
	1980	3 724	39 821		563	97	183	81
	1987/80	1.29	1.77		0.94	1.10	1.26	1.03
Australia	1987	6 365	2 480	217		1 360	290	322
	1980	5 429	2 200	431		1 081	358	476
	1980/89	1.17	1.13	0.50		1.26	0.81	0.68
New Zealand	1987	1 157	1 090	117	1 128		58	81
	1980	680	696	118	710		78	72
	1987/80	1.70	1.57	1.00	1.59		0.74	1.12
India	1987	7 393	3 349	94	310	35		94
	1980	10 792	4 303	28	339	102		60
	1987/80	0.69	0.78	3.41	0.91	0.34		1.57
Malaysia	1987	3 504	2 972	139	400	30	147	
	1980	2 954	2 114	63	185	52	34	
	1987/80	1.19	1.41	2.22	2.16	0.57	4.29	
Philippines	1987	980	2 060	83	88	11	65	119
	1980	1 540	1 593	64	98	4	107	94
	1987/80	0.94	1.29	1.29	0.90	2.54	0.61	1.26
Singapore	1987	2 594	6 995	230	785	114	1 358	4 074
	1980	1 560	2 464	132	781	351	843	2 906
	1987/80	1.66	2.84	1.74	1.01	0.32	1.61	1.40
Thailand	1987	1 732	2 163	172	216	22	59	388
	1980	982	823	24	70	5	236	293
	1987/80	1.76	2.63	7.12	3.09	4.86	0.25	1.33
Korea	1987	8 420	18 364	1 451	619	130	241	300
	1980	3 030	4 520	343	230	28	364	183
	1987/80	2.78	3.97	4.22	2.69	4.63	0.66	1.64
Taiwan	1987	6 903	23 607	1 554	1 090	171	441	270
	1980	2 175	6 792	459	539	36	478	170
	1987/80	3.17	3.48	3.38	2.20	4.17	0.92	1.59
Hong Kong	1987	2 470	13 513	1 046	848	134	405	308
	1980	908	5 149	394	476	60	617	175
	1987/80	2.72	2.62	2.66	1.78	2.22	0.66	1.75
EC	1987	15 581	82 516	10 335	6 337	1 344	1 814	1 345
	1980	6 617	37 532	4 798	4 247	909	1 734	1 415
	1987/80	2.35	2.20	2.16	1.49	1.48	1.05	0.95
World	1987	31 443	380 000	48 129	24 223	6 530	12 850	12 681
	1980	23 332	240 000	49 032	17 883	4 963	9 751	9 661
	1987/80	1.07	1.58	1.59	1.35	1.32	1.32	1.31

Notes: Values of exports from a country in the left-hand column to a country in the top row. World total includes other countries than the 13 Asia–Pacific countries and the EC. Refer to Appendix 12A.5 for source of data.

then to changing relationships between the Pacific countries to examine whether they become more competitive or complementary before analysing what determines trade flows among the Pacific countries, with some suggestion of factors affecting trade imbalances across the Pacific. The first section of this chapter addresses the policy implications deriving from our analysis.

EVOLVING PATTERNS OF COMPARATIVE ADVANTAGE

(Table 12.1 cont'd)

Philippines	Singapore	Thailand	Korea	Taiwan	Hong Kong	EC	World
1 414	5 947	2 950	13 214	11 274	8 865	37 943	229 055
1 679	3 869	1 917	5 364	5 141	4 743	18 025	129 542
0.84	1.54	1.54	2.46	2.19	1.87	2.11	1.77
1 564	3 860	1 460	7 481	6 456	3 732	56 891	243 610
1 975	2 943	1 084	4 403	4 182	2 557	55 731	212 887
0.79	1.31	1.35	1.70	1.54	1.46	1.02	1.14
92	123	139	823	474	268	6 764	92 886
95	164	122	428	212	144	7 965	63 102
0.97	0.75	1.14	1.92	2.23	1.86	0.85	1.47
191	588	181	1 008	894	955	4 003	26 486
78	566	157	476	462	315	2 851	21 985
1.07	1.04	1.16	2.12	1.94	3.03	1.40	1.20
52	99	34	159	120	103	1 576	7 189
74	84	34	58	53	79	1 288	5 454
0.70	1.18	1.00	2.73	2.26	1.30	1.22	1.32
72	1 449	87	674	507	420	1 545	17 170
181	2 484	35	294	485	152	1 434	21 909
0.40	0.58	2.51	2.30	1.05	2.76	1.08	0.78
323	3 263	511	952	649	506	2 547	17 934
96	2 474	188	262	382	243	2 280	12 939
1.64	1.32	2.72	3.64	1.70	2.08	1.12	1.39
	196	125	98	171	277	1 082	5 696
	113	63	203	105	192	1 012	5 788
	1.74	1.99	0.48	1.63	1.45	1.07	0.98
418		1 215	474	464	1 816	3 500	28 686
274		846	291	199	1 494	2 480	19 375
1.52	1.44	1.63	2.33	1.22	1.41	1.48	
71	1 049		153	180	488	2 561	11 564
23	503		49	81	330	1 691	6 505
3.03	2.09		3.11	2.22	1.48	1.51	1.78
220	927	272		473	2 202	6 598	47 207
151	266	164		187	823	2 717	17 483
1.46	3.48	1.66		2.53	2.67	2.43	2.70
457	1 339	420	632		4 084	7 275	53 190
195	544	176	266		1 542	2 892	19 783
2.34	2.46	2.38	2.37		2.65	2.52	2.69
498	1 331	447	1 270	666		7 792	48 502
328	863	213	227	220		2 566	19 703
1.52	1.54	2.09	5.60	3.03		1.71	2.46
934	3 655	1 883	4 168	3 932	5 420	558 646	951 065
792	2 407	1 005	1 334	1 228	2 948	381 562	688 113
1.18	1.52	1.87	3.12	3.20	1.84	1.46	1.38
6 937	29 302	13 003	36 915	31 132	43 53	855 000	2 471 466
7 465	21 602	8 505	20 005	17 697	19 24	691 495	1 993 312
0.93	1.36	1.53	1.85	1.76	2.20	1.24	1.25

CHANGES IN TRADE FLOWS AMONG THE PACIFIC ECONOMIES

How did the trade relationship change among the Pacific economies in the 1980s? Table 12.1 shows the trade matrix among major countries for the years 1980 and 1987 and the rate of increase over the seven-year period. The European Community (including all twelve current members—EC12) is added as the major trading partner group of the Pacific economies outside the region. China is excluded only because of the unavailability of comparable trade data.

World exports increased 1.25 times (25 per cent) during the 1980–87 period. Trade within the EC12 expanded 1.46 times, nearly twice as much as the world total. However, some elements of intra-Pacific trade expanded much faster. By marking elements with a rate of increase more than 1.5 times in the trade matrix, we notice a peculiar distribution of high growth points, centring on the NIEs, Thailand, Japan and the United States.

Korea, Taiwan, and Hong Kong show high growth points (of the magnitude of a 2–4 times increase) in trade with most partners as well as their overall trade in both exports and imports. Trade performance differs among the ASEAN countries. Thailand recorded a good export–import performance closer to that of the East Asian NIEs, followed by Singapore and Malaysia with less impressive showings. On the other hand, Indonesia and Philippines recorded only a small increase, especially in imports. ASEAN economies were slow to recover from the setback of the mid-1980s and achieved a turnaround only in 1987. The 1988 figures will show better growth. However, it is to be noted that intra-ASEAN trade expanded more than ASEAN's trade with the rest of the world.

Among developed countries, Japan and the United States recorded contrasting growth rates, with Japan registering high growth only in exports and the United States only in imports. Japan's exports more than doubled with all trading partners except for three of the ASEAN countries. Its imports increased greatly over the NIEs, Thailand and the EC, while its total imports increased by only 7 per cent during the period. This poor import performance reflected complex factors such as drastic declines in petroleum prices, appreciation of the yen, and stagnant domestic demand until 1986. Japan's total imports declined between 1980 and 1985, before a rapid increase, especially in the case of manufactures, by 25 per cent in 1988 and 35 per cent in 1989, contributing to a 20 per cent reduction in its trade surplus over the last two years.

United States imports expanded more than exports during the period, with an accumulation of huge trade deficits. Its imports from the NIEs, Thailand, Japan and the EC increased far more rapidly than its total imports, while its exports were more diversified than its imports in terms of market destination in the Pacific region. However, United States imports increased at a faster rate between 1987 and 1989, expanding by almost 50 per cent, compared with a 24 per cent increase in exports in the period, which reduced its trade deficit by approximately 33 per cent. Canada, Australia and New Zealand recorded more balanced but less spectacular trade performance than the United States, though in the case of Canada and Australia, imports grew faster than exports.

The EC's exports increased by 50 per cent more than its imports, while intra-EC trade doubled. Its Pacific trade expanded even faster, with exports to all Pacific countries except Indonesia, Malaysia and the Philippines, exceeding intra-EC trade. This contradicts the gloomy picture painted by European economists of stagnant growth of EC exports to its traditional ASEAN market. Indeed, the EC expanded its share in such new markets as Japan and the NIEs during the 1980s. Its exports to the East Asian NIEs amounted to only three-quarters of its exports to ASEAN in 1980; however, the former exceeded the latter by 40 per cent in 1987.

Trade flow figures among individual countries are affected by the size of both exporting and importing countries. The index of trade intensity is calculated by dividing an importing country's share in an exporting country's total exports by the importing country's share in world imports and measures trade intensity independently of the size variables. Since the average of the index is unity, above-unity indexes imply intensive trade (see Appendix 12A.1).

Table 12.2 shows a trade intensity matrix for thirteen Pacific countries and the EC in 1980 and 1987. At first glance, one finds above-unity intensity in many elements of the matrix, which reflects intensified trade among the Pacific countries. A stable intensity pattern is apparent in both years also. Very high trade intensity indexes (5, 6–19, 27) are recorded for such country pairs as Australia–New Zealand, United States–Canada, Singapore with other ASEAN members, Malaysia–Thailand, Malaysia–Philippines, Singapore–Hong Kong, Hong Kong–Taiwan, and Hong Kong–Philippines. These are easily explained by traditional trade ties, geographical proximity and entrepot trade relations.

High trade intensity (2–5) is observed between Japan, Korea and Taiwan on the one hand and ASEAN and Australia–New Zealand on the other, which is explained by complementary trade between manufacturers and primary commodity suppliers. Trade intensity of above 2 is often observed between other pairs of Pacific countries except Canada, which has a peculiar pattern of Pacific trade intensity. It has a very high trade intensity with the United States but below-unity trade intensity with all other countries. Its very high concentration reflects a high degree of economic, social and cultural integration with the United States as well as geographical proximity, but underscores the need for diversification. On the other hand, very low trade intensity (0.1–0.6) is recorded between the EC and the Pacific countries, while the EC's intraregional trade intensity is as high as 1.6- 1.7. This low trade intensity suggests a possible further increase in trade between the EC and the Pacific as indicated above.

These intensity patterns are observed in both 1980 and 1987. Is there any significant change in trade intensity among the Pacific countries during the period? The distinct decline of trade intensity of Thailand's exports to Indonesia (from 7.4 to 0.99) was due to the termination of rice trade between the two after 1986 (which is analysed in a later section). Both Korea and Taiwan increased their import intensity vis-à-vis Australia and New Zealand while, conversely, the intensity of their exports to the United States and Japan increased. Japan decreased its intensity of their exports to the Pacific countries except the United States. The underlying forces for these changes are examined in the following two sections.

Table 12.2 Matrix of trade intensity indexes, 1980 and 1987

From:		Japan	United States	Canada	Australia	New Zealand	India	Malaysia
Japan	1980		2.028	0.764	2.917	2.101	5.456	3.278
	1987		2.411	0.781	2.313	1.88	2.531	1.859
United States	1980	1.552		6.217	2.122	1.12	1.336	1.244
	1987	2.093		7.446	2.25	1.248	0.603	1.498
Canada	1980	0.953	5.24		0.994	0.614	0.591	0.266
	1987	0.981	4.967		0.586	0.434	0.48	0.177
Australia	1980	3.989	0.83	0.796		19.749	3.33	4.47
	1987	4.554	0.614	0.291		19.588	2.123	2.386
New Zealand	1980	2.013	1.059	0.878	14.507		2.937	2.742
	1987	3.05	0.944	1.52	16.135		1.572	2.222
India	1980	7.958	1.631	0.051	1.725	1.868		0.563
	1987	8.161	1.278	0.174	1.857	0.777		1.075
Malaysia	1980	3.688	1.356	0.196	1.593	1.621	0.541	
	1987	3.703	1.086	0.247	2.294	0.638	1.589	
Philippines	1980	4.298	2.286	0.45	1.885	0.3	3.784	3.361
	1987	3.261	2.371	0.464	1.580	0.736	2.212	4.104
Singapore	1980	1.301	1.056	0.277	4.492	0.612	7.269	30.949
	1987	1.713	1.598	0.256	2.815	1.059	9.178	27.905
Thailand	1980	2.437	1.05	0.151	1.197	0.279	7.42	9.279
	1987	2.838	1.226	0.474	1.921	0.725	0.989	6.592
Korea	1980	2.8	2.194	0.798	1.468	0.643	4.253	2.155
	1987	3.381	2.55	0.98	1.349	1.047	0.988	1.247
Taiwan	1980	1.775	2.85	0.944	3.306	0.736	4.941	1.769
	1987	2.459	2.909	0.931	2.107	1.225	1.608	0.995
Hong Kong	1980	0.744	2.17	0.812	2.962	1.232	6.404	1.836
	1987	0.965	1.826	0.687	1.798	1.055	1.619	1.245
EC12	1980	0.155	0.452	0.283	0.688	0.531	0.515	0.423
	1987	0.31	0.568	0.347	0.685	0.539	0.369	0.277

Note: Calculated from Table 12.1. Refer to Appendix 12A.1 for the calculation formula.

EVOLVING PATTERNS OF COMPARATIVE ADVANTAGE

We posit that these changes in trade flows were caused by changes in comparative advantage of individual Pacific economies and by rapid economic growth, both of which resulted from the spread of industrialisation in the developing countries of the region.

The comparative advantage of a country is determined principally by factor

(Table 12.2 cont'd)

			To			
Philippines	Singapore	Thailand	Korea	Taiwan	Hong Kong	EC
3.461	2.755	3.464	4.125	4.47	3.681	0.401
2.217	2.207	2.468	3.893	3.937	2.209	0.482
2.477	1.275	1.193	2.06	2.212	1.207	0.754
2.305	1.347	1.148	2.072	2.121	0.874	0.68
0.401	0.239	0.452	0.675	0.378	0.229	0.363
0.356	0.112	0.286	0.597	0.408	0.164	0.212
2.164	2.376	1.668	2.155	2.365	1.442	0.373
2.583	1.886	1.311	2.567	2.701	2.057	0.44
3.622	1.422	1.462	1.062	1.098	1.459	0.681
2.598	1.175	0.906	1.492	1.335	0.815	0.639
2.208	10.46	0.371	1.335	2.493	0.697	0.188
1.506	7.155	0.97	2.649	2.363	1.396	0.262
4.053	17.641	3.406	2.014	3.325	1.889	0.507
6.486	15.47	5.459	3.582	2.896	1.61	0.413
	1.795	2.547	3.487	2.043	3.329	0.504
	2.925	4.204	1.161	2.402	2.775	0.553
3.775		10.229	1.494	1.157	7.752	0.369
5.228		8.118	1.114	1.293	3.612	0.355
0.963	7.13		0.754	1.402	5.098	0.749
2.205	7.713		0.892	1.245	2.408	0.645
2.298	1.405	2.198		1.204	4.735	0.448
1.675	1.669	1.105		0.801	2.662	0.407
2.631	2.539	2.088	1.341		7.837	0.421
3.082	2.141	1.513	0.802		4.382	0.398
4.44	4.039	2.536	1.145	1.257		0.668
3.685	2.332	1.763	1.767	1.098		0.468
0.307	0.322	0.342	0.193	0.201	0.431	1.598
0.352	0.326	0.379	0.295	0.33	0.325	1.711

endowment (availability of cheap inputs) and the stage of industrialisation (level of technology) it has reached. In the process of industrialisation, the structure of a country's comparative advantage shifts from simple labour-intensive products to sophisticated capital and technology-intensive ones, as was observed in the case of Japan and the Asian NIEs. The ASEAN-4 countries and China will be no exception to this if they promote industrialisation.

Comparative advantage is analysed here through a comparison of costs between trading partners, but reliable cost data are hard to come by. We therefore assume that a country's comparative advantage is reflected or revealed in its exports to the world market. This leads to the index of revealed comparative advantage of exports (RCAX), defined by Balassa (1965) as a country's commodity composition of exports vis-à-vis that of total world trade. Similarly, we can also define the index of comparative disadvantage as the country's import composition vis-à-vis the world total. This is the revealed comparative advantage of imports (RCAM) (see Appendix 12A.2 for details).

These are often referred to simply as indexes of trade specialisation, but we prefer the term RCA since our purpose is to identify the structure of comparative advantage behind actual trade specialisation. Obviously, RCA indexes, especially RCAMs, are affected by such protective measures as tariffs, quantitative restrictions and import bans. RCAXs are also affected by export restrictions such as Multi-Fibre Arrangements (MFA) and voluntary export restraints (VERs). Thus, RCAX and RCAM give a distorted pattern of comparative advantage. But, since there are no other practical measures of comparative advantage available, we have to rely on the index while exercising caution in our interpretation.

We have calculated both RCAX and RCAM for 178 commodities (all product groups at the 3-digit level of the UN's Standard International Trade Classification (SITC) for individual countries). RCA indexes are often calculated for several broad commodity groups, which are far from homogeneous in the trade specialisation of individual commodities within a group. The SITC classification of 7 digits provides more detailed information of trade specialisation of individual commodities. However, it is not detailed enough to differentiate between an assembled product and its parts; besides, it requires a formidable amount of calculation. Our sample of about 180 commodities serves best for the purpose of making international comparisons.

It is difficult to read RCAXs and RCAMs for 180 commodities for individual countries, but a 'skyline map' can be used to illustrate RCA structures. All commodities are plotted in the order of code numbers discretely set along the horizontal axis, with the vertical axis measuring values of RCAXs (RCAMs) in a natural logarithm to illustrate the divergence of individual RCAXs from unity symmetrically. In this framework, 0 depicts the RCAX of unity, +1 depicts the RCAX of 2.32, while -1 depicts the RCAX of 0.43. Skyline maps are not presented, as they are somewhat unwieldy, but major findings are as follows.

Skyline maps for RCAMs show that they are in general symmetric to the corresponding RCAXs around the unity line but are more diversified than the RCAXs. Furthermore, intra-industry specialisation is observed in some commodities under the 3-digit SITC classification with high RCA and RCAMs. We will identify the comparative advantage structure mainly by the RCAX, referring to the RCAM structure when necessary.

Japan has a clear structure of specialisation, with above-unity RCAXs in a limited range of industrial products, SITC 65 (textiles), 67 (iron and steel), 69 (metal products), 7 (machinery), and selected items of 8 (miscellaneous), and almost all below-unity RCAXs in SITC 0–4 (all primary products), and 5 (chemicals). The RCAXs of many 0–4 groups are very low (-4 or below). Through the 1980s RCAXs of above-unity tended to decline in such industrial product groups as SITC 65, 67, 69 and 8 and increased only in the machinery group (especially industrial machinery).

Japan's RCAM structure is largely symmetrical to its RCAX structure. Many primary commodities (SITC 0–4) had above-unity RCAMs. Many industrial products with above-unity RCAXs had below-unity RCAMs, but such products as cement, pearls, clothing, handbags, and steel ingot increased their RCAMs above unity. Such agricultural products as fish, maize, other cereals, and fruits also increased their RCAMs rapidly. But, a few foodstuffs maintained very low RCAMs (as well as very low RCAXs): rice (0.025), wheat flour (0.001), and butter (0.015), all under strict import quota. However, semi-processed products are free from import restrictions, and imports of these products have started to increase recently owing to large price differentials between home and abroad, thanks mainly to yen appreciation.

The specialisation of the United States is more diversified, with above-unity RCAXs in many primary product groups (such as cereals, tobacco, cotton and coal) and substantially lower RCAXs in industrial product groups. Here, too, a clear decline of RCAX is observed in many SITC 5–8 groups (textiles, non-ferrous metals, toys and office supplies), leaving only several products with above-unity RCAXs (such as inorganic chemicals, industrial machinery, electric machinery and aircraft).

The RCAX structure of Canada, Australia and New Zealand is more concentrated in fewer product groups, mainly foodstuffs and resource products with very high RCAXs: for Canada, crude minerals, cereal meal, wood and pulp, coal and gas; for Australia, wool, iron ore, coal, inorganic chemicals, cereals and fresh meat; and for New Zealand, wood, dairy products, meat, hides and skins, and animal oil. Conversely, their RCAXs are below unity for many industrial products, although they increased recently in Canada for processed resource products such as steel structures, wire products, wood fuel and crude rubber; in Australia for aluminium and nickel, non-alcoholic beverages, and margarine; and in New Zealand for fruit and canned fish, cereals, and sugar preparations.

ASEAN countries have RCAX structures similar to those of resource-rich developed countries, with a much higher concentration in a few products such as tin, LNG, and crude rubber, vegetable oil, wood, sugar and rice. On the other hand, their RCAXs were far below unity in many industrial products, which started to rise in the 1980s, however, some of them emerging above unity as promising new exports. These include veneers, vegetable and animal oils for Indonesia; veneers and furnitures, animal and vegetable oils, pig iron, electrical equipment, and clothing for the Philippines; and pig iron, telecommunications equipment, ships and clothing for Malaysia. The emergence of new industrial exports is more evident in Thailand—for example, leather products, textiles and clothing, jewellery and footwear.

Korea and Taiwan have RCAX structures similar to Japan's, with high above unity (2–5) in industrial product groups and low below unity (less than 0.2) in primary product groups. They have larger RCAXs in SITC 6 and 8 than Japan (for textiles, clothing, footwear), reflecting their comparative advantage in labour-intensive production, although their RCAXs have tended to decrease in these areas but to increase in such new areas as electric machinery, watches and some steel products, resembling Japan's structure to some extent.

Hong Kong's structure is similar to that of Korea's and Taiwan's, while Singapore's is closer to that of other ASEAN countries. But both Hong Kong and Singapore have RCAM structures similar to their RCAXs, reflecting their engagement in entrepot trade. It is necessary to calculate RCAXs and RCAMs based on domestic exports and imports by subtracting entrepot trade from total trade in order to find true comparative advantage for the two.

The EC's RCAX structure shows moderate specialisation (mostly between 1 and -1) over a wide range of industrial products and some primary products (mainly foodstuffs), reflecting the fact that it is an average of the twelve members. However, a decline of RCAXs in SITC 6 to 8 groups took place between 1980 and 1987.

'FLYING GEESE' IN THE PACIFIC

The most striking feature of the evolving pattern of comparative advantage in the 1980s were the contrasting changes in RCAXs in industrial products between developed and developing countries. RCAXs of standardised industrial products (mainly SITC 6 and 8 and some SITC 7) declined below unity in Japan, the United States and the EC, whereas they exceeded unity in the NIEs and tended to increase from very low levels in ASEAN countries. There are two forces underlying this: catching-up industrialisation in the NIEs and ASEAN countries and foreign direct investment (FDI) by American and Japanese firms.

The development of a modern industry in countries that are 'late-comers' typically begins with the import of a new product from advanced countries, followed by import-substitution, leading to export initiatives of sorts. This was first pointed out by Akamatsu (1943) in his statistical study of trade and production of a number of industries in Japan, which was then a newly industrialising country. He gave this pattern of industry development the poetic name 'flying geese', inspired by the shape of growth curves of import, production and export. Kojima (1973) called it the 'catching-up product cycle', associating it with the product cycle model of Vernon (1964).

This 'catch-up' industrialisation is also observed in contemporary developing countries endowed with local enterpreneurial skills and a domestic market of adequate size for modern industries with mature technology. Furthermore, FDIs supplement local enterpreneurs, accelerate technology transfer in starting production and import-substitution (IS), and provide marketing skills in export expansion (EE).[1]

Figure 12.1 illustrates the catch-up development of both synthetic fabric and crude steel production for six Pacific countries (Japan, the United States, two Asian NIEs and two ASEAN countries). Production/consumption (P/C) ratios are indicated on the vertical axis, and their increase above unity shows IS and EE for individual industries. Consumption is calculated as production plus imports minus exports and thus includes inventory changes. Three-year moving averages are taken for all variables in order to show the longer term trend over short-term business cycles and yearly changes in inventory stock.

An upward trend in the P/C ratio is observed in all developing countries, which provides evidence of the catch-up development of IS and EE industries in contemporary developing countries. But there are two kinds of time differentials for the catch-up development. One is an industry's development *within* a country due to less capital requirements, easier technological absorption, and faster growth of domestic demand. The other is observed *between* countries with respect to an industry's catch-up development. Both are illustrated by the transposition of catch-up development curves (P/C curves) and variations of 'flying geese' patterns. The latter type has become popular as an explanation of the transfer of industry among the Pacific countries (see Okita, 1987; Chen, 1989; ESCAP, 1990).

Synthetic fabric weaving has overtaken cotton fabric weaving and forms the core of the textile industry in these Asian countries. Taiwan led this process by exporting before 1970. Korea followed closely on its heels and reached Taiwan's level of export expansion by the mid-1970s. In Thailand, the P/C ratio exceeded unity in the early 1970s and followed in the footsteps of both Taiwan and Korea in export expansion, taking advantage of the earlier development of its cotton textile industry. For Indonesia, only a long-run trend is drawn due to the lack of consistent time series data on production and trade. But based on fragmented information, it appears that the development of Indonesia's synthetic fabric production was lethargic until the mid-1970s and that the P/C ratio exceeded unity only after 1980.

In comparing P/C ratios among the four countries, we must not lose sight of the fact that substantial proportions of domestic consumption comprised inputs into the production of made-up textile products like clothing, bags and other accessories and hence were indirectly exported in the form of made-up textiles. The proportion of indirect export amounted to 70–80 per cent, which tended to raise the overall P/C ratio of the synthetic textile industries (both fabrics and made-up textiles). The indirect export of synthetic fabric started in the 1980s from Thailand and Indonesia, rising to about 15 per cent in recent years. Synthetic fabric production has declined in Japan and the United States after reaching the mature stage. Japan's P/C ratio for synthetic fabrics was still as high as 1.7 by 1982, reflecting its competitive edge in fibre production, while the ratio for cotton had fallen below unity. The United States P/C ratio was below unity (0.98 in 1977 and 0.96 in 1982) for synthetic fabric production.

Steel industry development occurred in the mid-1970s for the Asian NIEs and ASEAN countries, lagging five to ten years behind synthetic fabric production. Here, production figures measure domestic production of crude steel, whereas consumption figures include finished steel products converted to a

Figure 12.1 'Flying geese' in the Pacific: transfer of industries in East and Southeast Asian countries

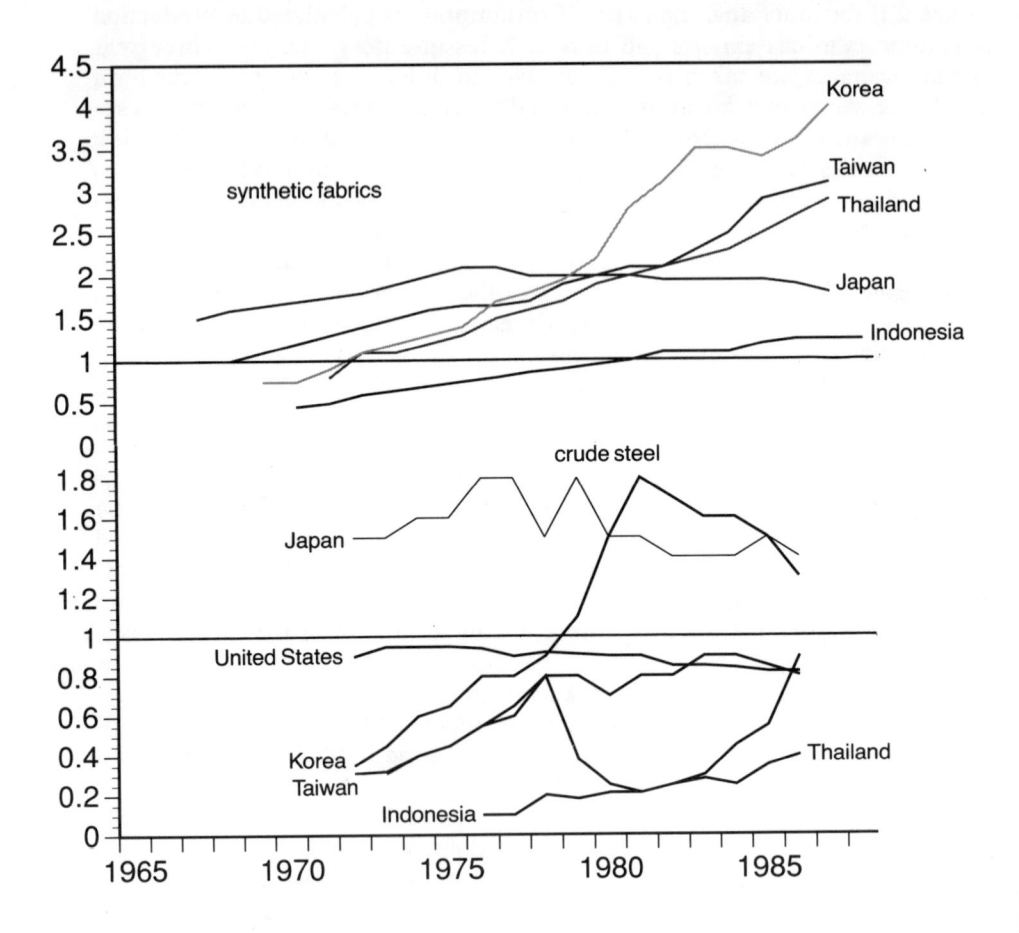

Note: P/C ratios tended to increase, reflecting IS as the ratio approached unity, and EE as the ratio continued to increase above unity. Although the common tendency is depicted, there are observed time lags between the two industries and among the four countries.

Sources: Calculated from statistics obtained from the Japan Chemical Fibre Association and the Japan Iron and Steel Federation. The Indonesian curve for synthetic fabrics depicts only a long-run trend based on ad hoc information of IS and EE stages of industry development because of unavailability of consistent time series data.

crude steel basis. The P/C ratio includes indirect export in the form of steel products. Korea quickly developed this industry and reached the export expansion stage by 1980, whereas Taiwan has lagged way behind with a P/C ratio below unity throughout the 1980s, handicapped partly by the small size of its domestic market. The corresponding P/C ratios of both Thailand and

Indonesia stayed below 0.3 until the mid-1980s, but have recently been rising steadily.

By contrast, the steel industry in both Japan and the United States has already entered the mature or reverse import stage. Japanese steel industry developed rapidly in the 1950s and its exports expanded in the 1960s. Production reached a peak of around 100 million tons in 1972-73, and after stagnating during the two oil shocks, it has recently regained that peak. But its import of standardised steel products has increased in recent times so that its P/C ratio has been declining. United States steel production also reached a peak of 137 million tons in 1973 but declined steadily to 81 million tons by 1987. Its P/C ratio has been below unity and diminishing since the early 1970s. (The EC's combined steel production was 124 million tons and its P/C ratio was on the decline for the past decade but it continues to exceed unity—1.24 in 1987.) It goes without saying that crude steel production by the Asian developing countries is still small in comparison with that of the United States, Japan and the EC (Korea 17 million tons, Taiwan 5.6 million, Indonesia 1.5 million tons, and Thailand 0.38 million tons in 1987).

Table 12.3 shows changes in RCAXs that correspond to those in Figure 12.1, though of course the RCAXs do not correspond exactly to the P/C ratios. For a below-unity P/C ratio implies net import of the product, while a below-unity RCAX implies that export continues, albeit on a lower than average scale. Furthermore, P/C ratios reflect absolute competitiveness of the industry, while RCAXs reflect comparative advantage of the industry vis-à-vis those of other industries.

In fabric production, both the United States and Japan experienced a rapid decline of RCAXs, but Japan's RCAX in synthetic fabrics is still above unity. Both Korea and Taiwan achieved high RCAXs, especially in synthetic fabrics, but their RCAXs have started to decline. In Thailand, RCAXs of fabrics as a whole were above 2; the RCAX of cotton fabrics was on the decline but the RCAX of synthetic fabrics was on the increase. In Indonesia, RCAXs of both fabrics were still small but both were on the increase. In steel production, only Japan and Korea had above-unity RCAXs, but their RCAXs were on the decline, especially Japan's. Taiwan's RCAXs were below unity and have been falling. Both Thailand and Indonesia had RCAXs of well below unity, although they have been increasing steadily. The United States RCAXs of steel were also well below unity. Its RCAMs of steel and fabrics are below unity and have changed little (around 0.4 for many textile products and 0.6 for steel products). The high RCAMs of the United States for clothing (1.64 to 1.85) apparently reflect the restricted nature of trade in this product. Japan's RCAMs of steel ingot increased to 1.2 in 1987, while its RCAMS of other textiles and steel have remained below unity.

FDI in Asia has been most active in the electrical and electronics industries and promoted in a significant manner the transfer of production from the United States and Japan to the Asian NIEs and ASEAN countries. Table 12.3 shows the changing pattern of RCAXs of related product groups, SITC 724 (telecommunications equipment, TV sets, radios and telephones), SITC 725

Table 12.3 Changes in RCAXs of selected products in the Pacific countries, 1980 and 1987

		United States	Japan	Korea	Taiwan	Thailand	Indonesia
Textiles							
652 Cotton	1980	0.75	1	2.28	3.43	2.64	0.03
fabrics	1987	0.26	0.74	1.21	1.6	2.05	1.53
653 Synthetic	1980	0.53	2.6	6.8	3.94	2.13	0.15
fabrics	1987	0.28	1.23	4.93	3.23	2.34	0.65
841 Clothing	1980	0.24	0.31	9.99	7.5	2.5	0.71
	1987	0.11	0.16	4.59	3.4	3.41	1.09
Steel products							
672 Ingots		5.11	0.59	4.24	0.41	0.01	0
673 Bars, rods,	1980	0.23	2.85	2.77	0.61	0	0.04
angles	1987	0.12	1.33	1.65	0.28	0.29	0.26
674 Plates	1980	0.4	3.63	2.77	0.25	0	0
and sheets	1987	0.15	2.48	1.51	0.28	0	0.03

		United States	Japan	Korea	Taiwan	Malaysia	Phillippines
Electrical equipment							
724 TVs,	1980	0.31	4.69	3.23	5.5	0.45	0.2
radios, telephones	1987	0.24	2.98	3.44	2.37	1.18	0.06
724 Refrigerators,	1980	0.22	1.62	0.78	2.05	0.09	0.04
washing machines	1987	0.22	1.07	3.1	2.35	0.38	0.13
729 Lamps, batteries,	1980	0.51	2.54	2.5	2.34	5.25	0.59
auto elect. equip.	1987	0.48	2.47	2.11	1.32	5.9	2.57

Source: Appendix 12A.2.

(domestic electrical equipment, refrigerators, washing machines and so on), and SITC 729 (other electrical machinery and equipment, batteries, lamps, and automotive electrical equipment), which are characterised by large-scale production, standardised technology and production that can be transferred to developing countries relatively easily.

The United States had small and stable RCAXs well below unity for all three product groups and its RCAMs were all above unity. Japan's RCAXs were all above unity but have tended to decrease rapidly. Korea and Taiwan have already achieved high RCAXs in these products, some increasing further while others were decreasing. Malaysia and the Philippines, however, recorded increasing RCAXs and acquired high RCAXs of 2–5 in the SITC 629 group.

Japan's FDI has been active since 1986 and has shifted from the Asian NIEs to ASEAN. It will take some time for its impact on trade and production to be statistically visible, but there is no doubt it will promote further changes in patterns of comparative advantage among the Pacific economies.

COMPLEMENTARITY AMONG THE PACIFIC ECONOMIES

The degree of similarity between an exporting country's RCAX and an importing country's RCAM measures the degree of complementarity and the possibility of trade expansion between them (see Appendix 12A.4 for further details). However, similar RCAX structures between two countries do not necessarily mean a lack of complementarity or absence of trade opportunities between them. As intra-industry specialisation proceeds and two countries trade products from the same industries with each other, the RCAX and RCAM structures of the countries become similar, with a resulting strong complementarity and a large trade volume.

Table 12.4 gives a matrix of complementarity indexes (C_{ij}) among fourteen countries. Here, too, the value unity denotes no correlation between the RCAX structure of an exporting country and the RCAM structure of an importing country, thereby making a demarcation between complementary and competitive trade. The divergence of C_{ij} from unity is much smaller than that of trade intensity shown in Table 12.2. High Cijs (more than 2) are observed between Japan and Canada/Australia/Indonesia/Malaysia, between Korea/Taiwan and Australia/Malaysia, between Malaysia and Singapore, and between Korea/Taiwan and Hong Kong. The first two groups are related through resources trades, the last two through entrepot trade.

On the other hand, very low Cijs are observed among ASEAN countries, between ASEAN countries and Canada/Australia/New Zealand, and between Canada and Australia/New Zealand, all of which are resource-exporting countries. Below-unity Cijs (0.8–0.9) are also recorded among Japan, Korea/Taiwan, and the EC, all specialising in manufacturing production.

Significant changes observed during the 1980s relate to Korea and Taiwan: Cij increased between Canada/Australia/New Zealand and Korea/Taiwan, while Cij decreased between ASEAN and Korea/Taiwan, which is consistent with industrialisation problems in Korea, Taiwan and the ASEAN countries.

A peculiar change of Cij (from 4.6 to 0.7) was observed for Thailand and Indonesia, which is explained by the latter's self-sufficiency in rice and its termination of imports during the 1980s. This change in complementarity between Thailand and Indonesia raises a moot question for Japan: what will happen to Japan's RCAM structure and its complementarity index with agricultural exporting countries if its agricultural imports are liberalised? Japan's RCAM of rice turns out to be 0.2, well below unity, despite an increase between 1980 and 1987. If, say, 3 per cent of its consumption is released for imports, rice imports will expand rapidly from rice-exporting countries. Japan's domestic consumption of rice was 10.58 million tons in 1988, 3 per cent of which amounts to 320,000 tons, which is twenty times greater than its present imports of 16,000 tons. Since world trade in rice was 12.1 million tons in 1988, the increase in rice imports of 320,000 tons does not affect the share of rice in world total commodity trade (the numerator of RCAM indexes). Thus Japan's RCAM of rice will be twenty times as great (4.0) as its present

Table 12.4 Matrix of complementarity indexes, 1980 and 1987

From:		Japan	United States	Canada	Australia	New Zealand	India	Malaysia
Japan	1980		1.034	1.442	1.295	1.254	1.386	1.400
	1987		1.234	1.422	1.152	1.226	1.081	1.280
United States	1980	1.110		1.311	1.166	1.060	1.324	1.441
	1987	1.246		1.184	1.129	1.039	1.289	1.431
Canada	1980	2.1022	1.384		1.252	1.196	1.317	1.734
	1987	1.8444	1.222		0.965	1.450	1.187	
Australia	1980	2.607	0.865	1.014		0.962	1.109	1.144
	1987	2.907	0.630	0.827		0.757	1.531	1.030
New Zealand	1980	1.366	0.659	0.596	0.641		0.512	0.820
	1987	1.967	0.603	0.619	0.623		0.570	0.809
India	1980	2.668	1.339	0.517	0.477	0.592		0.549
	1987	2.515	1.033	0.525	0.543	0.516		0.553
Malaysia	1980	2.126	1.142	0.726	0.752	0.691	0.438	
	1987	2.122	1.014	0.733	0.818	0.774	0.687	
Philippines	1980	1.595	1.065	1.352	0.692	0.564	0.810	0.948
	1987	1.232	0.976	0.911	1.045	0.665	0.457	1.230
Singapore	1980	0.800	0.935	0.807	1.212	1.465	0.996	1.595
	1987	0.872	1.023	0.849	1.141	1.003	0.909	1.559
Thailand	1980	1.360	0.914	0.973	0.800	0.826	4.610	1.538
	1987	1.582	0.914	0.818	0.836	0.806	0.731	1.663
Korea	1980	0.803	1.193	0.960	1.276	1.097	0.912	1.265
	1987	0.486	1.299	0.962	1.075	1.015	0.743	1.197
Taiwan	1980	0.631	1.259	1.062	1.446	0.871	0.746	1.042
	1987	0.833	1.320	0.940	1.212	1.057	0.622	0.959
Hong Kong	1980	0.605	1.224	1.084	1.442	0.830	0.504	0.937
	1987	0.901	1.284	0.863	1.177	1.052	0.584	1.043
EC12	1980	0.714	0.940	1.193	1.215	1.188	1.176	1.310
	1987	0.890	0.976	1.118	1.053	1.104	1.161	1.143

Notes: Calculated for RCAXs and RCAMs indexes of the 14 countries, using the formula given in Appendix 12A.2; the data source is given in Appendix 12A.5. The formula for calculating complementarity is given in Appendix 12A.3.

value (0.2), which will increase its import complementarity with Thailand and the United States.

DETERMINANTS OF THE PACIFIC TRADE FLOWS

Trade flow is determined not only by the complementarity of comparative

EVOLVING PATTERNS OF COMPARATIVE ADVANTAGE

(Table 12.4 cont'd)

			To			
Philippines	Singapore	Thailand	Korea	Taiwan	Hong Kong	EC
1.009	1.139	0.977	0.937	1.158	1.363	0.923
0.667	1.169	0.981	0.918	1.119	1.064	0.951
1.133	0.965	1.135	1.371	1.451	1.016	1.101
1.479	1.001	1.257	1.412	1.456	0.851	1.09
1.323	0.845	1.493	1.284	1.501	0.777	1.506
1.078	0.709	1.263	1.404	1.253	0.588	1.277
1.696	0.581	0.984	1.781	1.444	0.806	1.312
1.660	0.516	0.907	3.666	1.705	0.746	1.165
0.657	0.524	0.541	1.091	1.040	1.178	1.338
0.852	0.556	0.846	1.256	1.251	0.958	1.281
0.879	1.420	0.900	1.681	1.399	0.285	0.954
1.034	1.487	0.802	1.036	0.914	0.551	1.03
0.694	2.720	0.906	2.018	1.664	0.751	0.938
0.988	2.144	0.823	1.647	1.597	0.898	0.996
	0.798	1.206	1.068	0.649	0.884	1.029
	0.954	1.024	0.746	1.220	0.907	0.962
1.265		1.436	0.955	1.133	1.279	0.992
1.048		1.087	0.965	1.171	1.18	0.952
0.847	1.736		1.903	1.150	1.718	1.192
0.640	1.315		0.867	0.909	1.57	1.157
0.808	1.171	0.918		0.969	2.173	1.182
0.585	1.164	0.849		0.812	1.857	1.007
0.522	1.101	0.607	0.642		2.188	1.144
0.461	1.112	0.767	0.685		1.892	1.038
0.553	1.123	0.591	0.635	0.752		1.201
0.597	1.18	0.802	0.77	0.786		1.065
1.026	0.967	1.136	0.864	1.025	1.269	
0.949	0.932	1.065	0.947	1.045	1.05	

advantage patterns and physical proximity between exporting and importing countries but also by macroeconomic factors. Trade flow (Xij) is regressed on economic distance and GDP of both exporting and importing countries as well as on the complementarity indexes. Table 12.5 summarises the results of our regression analysis, which shows a stable relationship with statistically significant coefficients of proper signs for all variables. Economic distance has a negative impact, explaining more intensive trade between neighbouring countries. Coefficients for GDP of exporting and importing countries are both

Table 12.5 Determinants of Asia–Pacific trade flows, 1970, 1980 and 1987

Explanatory variables	1970 Estimate	t-value	1980 Estimate	t-value	1987 Estimate	t-value
Intercept	10.26	(12.8)	11.3	(22.94)	11.74	(27.95)
Distance	-0.591	(5.61)	-0.698	(10.24)	-0.746	(13.06)
Complementarity	0.597	(3.90)	0.811	(5.90)	0.91	(6.59)
Exporter's GDP	0.857	(17.81)	0.767	(22.7)	0.724	(26.73)
Importer's GDP	0.799	(11.94)	0.787	(17.47)	0.783	(21.39)
Dummy for Japanese imports	0.097	(0.26)	-0.095	(0.41)	-0.566	(2.72)
Dummy for United States imports	-0.029	(0.07)	0.209	(0.84)	0.352	(1.68)
Dummy for Singapore's entrepot trade	1.661	(6.3)	1.881	(11.68)	1.49	(11.21)
Dummy for Hong Kong's entrepot trade	1.76	(6.97)	1.171	(7.71)	1.182	(9.20)
R^2	0.759		0.848		0.891	

Notes: The explained variable is the export value from country i to country j, estimated by log-linear least squares (LLS) based on cross-country (14x14 countries/country groups) data. Refer to Appendix 12A.4 for further details.

positive and of almost the same magnitude. That the two coefficients sum up to above unity means that trade flow expanded more proportionately to GDP. If this relationship continues, intra-Pacific trade will expand faster than GDP growth rates in the Pacific. Complementarity has positive coefficients and has tended to increase over time. It is to be noted that absolute values of all coefficients are more or less the same magnitude.

A closer check on the differential between actual and estimated values has suggested the need for additional explanatory variables in the form of dummy variables. First, both Singapore and Hong Kong trade with other countries far more intensively, with no proportionality to their GDPs, because of their heavy dependence on entrepot trade. Thus, an export trade dummy was introduced for all export and import trades of Singapore and Hong Kong, which turned out to yield high positive coefficients that are statistically significant for all three years.

It is often suggested that Japan imports too little while the United States imports too much. An import dummy was introduced for the import trade of both Japan and the United States in order to indicate that the two countries import less or more on average. Estimates of their coefficients turned out to be consistent with our expectations. They are negative for Japan and positive for the United States, although statistically significant results were obtained for the year 1987. However, a similar exercise on Taiwan, another trade surplus country, did not yield statistically significant estimates.

Bilateral trade flows have recently attracted the attention of many economists. Our regression can be employed to test some of the hypotheses relating to such flows. Since our regression equation is symmetrical with respect to distance and our entrepot dummy variables, the bilateral imbalance ($X_{ij}-X_{ji}$) is solely attributed to three differences: asymmetry of complementarity, differences in export and import propensities of the two countries, and insufficient imports of Japan and excessive imports of the United States (Appendix 12A.4).

First, an asymmetry of complementarity (Cij>Cji), implying that country i is less dependent on country j than vice versa, will add to the trade surplus of country i. As we saw in the previous section, complementarity indexes tend to be symmetrical between two countries (Cij = Cji). Generally speaking, two countries with contrasting comparative advantage structures tend to have above-unity Cij and Cji. Table 12.4 shows that above-unity Cijs are observed between resource-abundant countries (Canada, Australia, New Zealand, and ASEAN countries except Singapore) and industrial countries (Japan, Korea, Taiwan and the EC), while below-unity Cijs are observed within the resource-abundant country group and the industrial country group respectively. However, two factors tend to produce asymmetrical complementarity. One of these is a greater specialisation of resource-abundant countries in the export of a few primary product groups (RCAXs of as high as 60 to 90) vis-à-vis that of industrial countries, with a more diversified import structure and lower RCAMs. Thus, resource-abundant countries tend to have higher Cijs vis-à-vis industrial countries as observed in Table 12.4. This asymmetry tends to result in trade surpluses for resource-abundant countries.

The other factor producing asymmetrical complementarity is the protection of domestic industries, which distorts the RCAM structure. Countries often have very small RCAMs for products with small RCAXs, such as rice and dairy products in Japan and textiles and steel in the United States. Trade liberalisation of agricultural trade will increase its Cijs vis-à-vis agricultural exporting countries, thereby reducing its trade surplus.

As regards possible differences in export and import propensities with respect to GDP, our regression estimates turned out to be statistically insignificant. In other words, countries with high export propensity tend to have equally high import propensity, which is consistent with our expectations.

However, some countries may import much less or import more than they export. We have found that Japan had a negative import dummy, while the United States had a positive import dummy, both with statistically significant coefficients. Bilateral trade balances are affected by this abnormal divergence from the average pattern. Thus, Japan, with a negative import dummy, tends to incur bilateral trade surpluses with all other trading partners, while the United States tends to incur bilateral trade deficits with its trading partners.

CONCLUDING REMARKS

The analysis of trade flows among the Pacific economies in 1980s contained in this chapter supplements the country chapters in this volume that focus on macroeconomic analysis and deal with inter-country trade relations only in an ad hoc manner. Our major findings are as follows:

1 Pacific trade flows expanded dynamically as the East Asian NIEs, Japan and the United States played pivotal roles.

2 This dynamic expansion was accompanied by an evolving pattern of comparative advantage, mainly in the Asian NIEs and ASEAN countries, in the manufacturing sector in the wake of structural changes in the advanced countries. Although this evolving pattern of comparative advantage has been discussed elsewhere, we have attempted to measure it systematically by means of revealed comparative advantage and complementarity indexes.
3 The underlying forces of the evolving comparative advantage were the catch-up industrialisation of the NIEs and ASEAN countries and FDI by American and Japanese firms. The 'flying geese' model provides an analytical framework for the harmonious transfer of industries among the Pacific economies. Here, we added production, consumption and FDI to the trade data analysis for textiles and steel—industries which experienced the most dynamic changes in comparative advantage in the region.
4 The 'flying geese' model provides a guiding rule for the coordination of industrial adjustment in this region. Catch-up industrialisation suggests a rational and orderly pattern of industrial development in individual countries, which coexist symbiotically within the framework of the model. However, it is vulnerable to the protectionist moves by individual countries which cause trade conflicts. It is important to reach consensus on the most desirable direction for industrial adjustment and agreement about the dangers of unilateral policy actions that obstruct the process.
5 The determinants of Pacific trade flows are identified and factored into analysis pertaining to bilateral trade balances. Evidently, complementarity of comparative advantage plays a pivotal role in all this. In particular, the empirical evidence for insufficient imports and excessive United States imports provided in this chapter is statistically significant, and lends support to observations made elsewhere in the volume.

The point needs to be made that our analysis is incomplete. For instance, the analysis of ASEAN comparative advantage is based on 1986 figures and fails to capture recent changes in ASEAN industries. There is also a need to incorporate China into our analysis. In addition, the 'domestic' exports of Hong Kong and Singapore need to be separated from the entrepot trade component in order to analyse the real comparative advantage of the two countries. The incorporation of comparable FDI statistics would also render our analysis more useful. Likewise, service industry and trade data need to be incorporated into the analysis, especially since these sectors have started developing more rapidly than the traditional commodity sectors in the Pacific.

13 The Pacific and the world economy: inter-relations

LAWRENCE B. KRAUSE AND
MARK SUNDBERG

INTRODUCTION

The time-tested academic approach to evaluating factors of importance for the next decade is to stare intently into a rear-view mirror. Such a tradition cannot be ignored because serious analysis can only be conducted within a known structure and with variables that have characteristics that are recognisable. Hence we will begin our analysis by identifying some factors and trends that already exist or are scheduled to occur, and then try to analyse them.

The Pacific economies will be impacted by three factors determined outside the region: the rate of real economic growth of the rest of the world, the degree of inflationary pressures being generated, and the global economic environment. Looking at the decade of the 1980s as a whole, the industrial countries had remarkable economic stability despite the severe recession at its start. Real growth on average hardly deviated from 3 per cent per year, and inflation measured by consumer price indexes were on average between 2 and 5 per cent.

A sensible forecast for the 1990s would extrapolate these trends, which would permit the implication to be drawn that annual real growth of international trade will be about 4 per cent (8 per cent in nominal terms). Such a forecast might be near or far from the mark, but it certainly would be uninteresting. Therefore our efforts instead will be directed at evaluating the global economic environment.

Although the numbering system is somewhat arbitrary, we identify five factors for special attention. They are all in the realm of political economy, which is our comparative advantage. It would require other skills, for instance, to evaluate the consequence of global warming on the Pacific or the implications for society of an ageing population in industrial countries, which we will not attempt. Therefore, we do not claim comprehensiveness.

The five factors are: the end of the Cold War, changes in Eastern Europe, closer integration in Western Europe (1992), adoption of export-led growth strategies in Latin America, and structural change in the United States. Certainly, this is a rich enough menu for one chapter.

Evaluating these factors permits a discussion of several scenarios which we distinguish by how the world economy in organised. Three choices are discussed and titled as follows: one-world anarchy, benign bilateral competition, and contentious trilateralism.

One particularly difficult issue for all scenarios of the future, and particularly for the preferred bilateral scenario, is the correction of balance of payments imbalances in the Pacific. This issue is explored empirically in a later section through simulation of a general equilibrium model with special attention to the United States.

FACTORS AND TRENDS FOR THE 1990S

The end of the Cold War

The entire postwar period has been dominated by the division of the world into two camps, a communist and a capitalist one, with supposed irreconcilable differences between them. Three wars have been fought to draw the boundary line; in Korea, Vietnam and Afghanistan.

Quite suddenly, however, the aggressive competition between the United States and the Soviet Union is moderating significantly and may be ending entirely. Whatever the cause for the shift, it cannot be denied that fundamental changes have taken place in the Soviet Union under the leadership of Mikhail Gorbachev, who apparently wants to divert resources to other uses and end the drain of the Cold War. This has created an unprecedented opportunity for arms control agreements and for a fundamental transformation of NATO and the Warsaw Pact. For the two superpowers it means that the 1990s will see sharply declining defence expenditures and a pulling back from forward deployment of military forces. While the United States withdrawal will be disproportionately from Europe, there will also be reductions in Japan, Korea and the Philippines.

Bipolar ideologic competition brought institutional stability in economic relations to both camps. Both the Soviet Union and the United States had to play the role of the hegemon in their respective spheres, providing public goods and operating a series of rewards and penalties to enforce rules of the game that it desired. For the capitalist camp, the United States promoted the freeing of international trade through the GATT, the stabilisation of international monetary arrangements and the liberalisation of international capital movements through the IMF and the OECD, and the development of lesser developed countries through the World Bank (IBRD) and other regional banks, and its own bilateral aid program.

While the United States prospered during this period, it is important to recognise that the United States perceived that other capitalist countries gained much more economically than it did. The United States had to shoulder a huge burden of defence expenditures. It had the most open market in order to let other countries sell exports. It had no controls on outflow of capital, and provided generous amounts of foreign aid. When political necessity required the moderation of import competition, its preferred device was the voluntary export restraint (VER) which permitted other countries to obtain huge economic rents at the expense of American consumers. The United States was prepared to permit free-riders and reduced fare passengers in the system, mainly because all of the gains went to countries within the capitalist camp. Thus United States security prospered even if it was at the expense of the United States economy.

Needless to say, the end of the Cold War means the end of the United States supplying public goods for the global economy at its expense. Some observers believe that in view of the more rapid growth of other countries, the United States is incapable of supplying public goods and attempting to do so would lead to economic disaster.

Other observers believe that the United States is simply unwilling to perform the role of the benevolent hegemon because it no longer considers system stability of overwhelming importance. Hence the end of the Cold War means the end of the way the postwar liberal economic regime among capitalist nations has been organised and sustained.

Diversity in Eastern Europe

A doctrinal and political change of tremendous importance has taken place in Eastern Europe. Events have occurred so quickly as to overwhelm even longtime observers. One after another, the countries of Eastern Europe have opted for economic and political reform. Poland, Hungary, Czechoslovakia, Romania and Bulgaria are now ready to partake in intensive economic interaction with market-oriented economies. The Soviet Union no longer stands in the way of this development.

Of greatest importance is the change in East Germany (GDR). The conversion of East Germany has been so complete, and the opening of its border with West Germany (FRG) so traumatic, that it is only a matter of time until the two German states become one.

Reunification of Germany—whether it be called confederation or whatever—will remake the face of Europe and indirectly impact on the world economy. The FRG is by far the strongest economy in Western Europe. The GDR is the strongest economy in Eastern Europe (helped in part by huge annual subsidies from the FRG). Together they would have a population of 80 million people (about two-thirds that of Japan), considerably larger than any other European country except the Soviet Union, and would be the economic leader.

With this in mind, the other countries of Western Europe are going to give highest priority to solidifying the role of Germany in the European Community so that they will benefit from and not be threatened by a reunified Germany. To accommodate the GDR, close economic relations with all other Eastern European countries will have to be considered. This will present an institutional challenge to Europe. Transition rules will have to be determined to overcome the problems of irrational pricing, market disruption, state trading, joint venturing, financing, trade imbalances, and so forth. This will be complicated by the problem of existing external debts of these countries. Hence one should anticipate a plethora of bilateral agreements, non-market type clearing arrangements, and/or other kinds of special deals. In the process, the postwar rule of non-discrimination will be ignored.

European integration—1992

The culmination of the process of European economic integration which began with the Messina Conference in 1955 is scheduled to occur in 1992. In 1988 the 'Single Europe Act' was approved which set the 1992 target and removed veto power from individual member countries. By that date all of the laws, regulations and policies required to bring about a true economic union are supposed to be in place. In particular, there will be a community-wide right of establishment so that an enterprise, professional or worker who is legally able to do business, practice, or work in any member country will be able to do the same in all other member countries. This will have particular importance, for example, in the provision of financial and other services since they are difficult to export without a presence in the importing country, and it would end discrimination in the awarding of government contracts within the EC. Regulations dealing with the environment, health and safety, labour markets and the like will be unified. Furthermore, the equivalent of a single European currency is to be established which would require a unified monetary policy and coordinated fiscal policy within the Community.

There are numerous obstacles to be overcome to make this a reality, not the least of which is the reluctance of the United Kingdom to accept the basic goal of economic union. Furthermore, the integration of Greece, Spain and Portugal within the customs union is still not complete. Hence some skepticism as to whether the target will be reached by 1992 is quite appropriate. Nevertheless, the effort is real, the forces propelling it are powerful, and the fact that it is making headway is more important than the actual date that it may be completed by.

It is worthwhile to consider the motivation behind the thrust towards economic union in order to give some clues as to its possible consequences. The motivation behind 1992 in certain critical respects is quite different from that in forming the Common Market originally. In 1955 the statesmen of Europe were worried about the threat of Soviet expansionism, and the concern that a group of small and independent countries would be unable to defend themselves. Furthermore, they were intent on creating an institutional maze out of which neither France nor Germany could extricate itself to resume their historic rivalry leading to hostilities. Moreover, they were impressed by the sheer size of the superpowers and were afraid of individually becoming 'mere footnotes to history'. Only in unity could they have importance and be able to influence world events.

Of course, there were perceived economic benefits from forming a customs union; however, the promise of economic gain had never been sufficient to overcome national rivalries in the past. The conclusion that prospective economic benefits were secondary in the creation of the EC is seen from the remarks of Walter Hallstein, the first President of the Commission, who frequently said that the Common Market was not in business but in politics.

To gain the political goals being sought, the EC needed close relations with the United States, and the United States gave strong support to European integration. The EC could not be permitted to divide NATO. Hence all members of the EC also had to be members of NATO, which disqualified Austria, Sweden, Finland and Switzerland from participating.

There were, of course, concerns in 1958 that the EC would become inward-looking and gain economic benefits at the expense of non-member countries. The Europeans were intent on not permitting this to happen, however, because the political goals of the member countries depended so fundamentally on close relations with the United States. The overall orientation of the EC was outward, and it did make efforts to reduce its negative economic impact on some non-member countries, not withstanding the significant economic damage done to Australia and New Zealand. The EC did prosper in the 1960s, but so did its trading partners.

From time to time, efforts were made to directly promote political integration of the EC without result. There were numerous instances where NATO achieved unity on political issues, and the EC achieved unity on economic issues, but very few instances of the EC achieving unity on political issues. In political affairs it was quite clear that the member countries maintained their own national identities. In fact, the EC was in business and not in politics.

The prosperity of the 1960s permitted the members of the EC along with other European countries to develop advanced welfare states. The welfare state is a marvelous institution for sharing benefits, but a terrible system for distributing burdens. The two oil crises of the 1970s exposed the weakness. As a result, European countries experienced rapid inflation in the 1970s, and when that proved unacceptable, inflation was replaced by stagnation in the 1980s. Countries that were used to unemployment rates of less than 2 per cent found that they could not reduce it to below 10 per cent. Overall growth rates were cut in half.

As European economic policymakers peered into the future, it looked decidedly bleak. They found their industries unable to keep up with the technological advances being made in the United States and Japan. Furthermore, they were feeling competitive pressures from below with the rapid growth of the Asian newly industrialising countries—the term NIC was devised and popularised in Europe. They could hardly continue to employ the workforce they had, no less provide jobs for the unemployed. 'Eurosclerosis' was the description of the malady, and it was widely believed to be very serious if not fatal.

The cure for Eurosclerosis as seen by analysts was a fundamental shaking-up of national economies. Governments had to reintroduce incentives to encourage entrepreneurship and generate growth. Flexibility had to be restored to labour and other factor markets, and intra-European competition enhanced in product markets. To accomplish this, the long-delayed plan for economic union was recreated and the program for 1992 devised.

Now the fear is being expressed once again that Europe will become inward-looking, and will seek economic gains at the expense of non-members. The European response is that it did not happen in the 1950s and 1960s, and will not in the 1990s. However, that response is not convincing. No longer is there the overriding motivation on the part of the Europeans to promote closer political relations with the United States. To the contrary, the goal of 1992 can only be achieved if the gains go to European firms and not to American or Japanese ones.

There is good reason to expect that 1992 will indeed lead Europe to become more inward-looking in the sense that the European agenda will be so full that there will be no room for, or interest in, the countries and issues of concern to the Pacific. All of the problems previously noted, plus the need to come to grips with the changes in Eastern Europe, will overload the circuits in the EC. Furthermore, relations between the EC and the Soviet Union will require much attention. This does not mean that Europe will raise new barriers to the trade with non-members. This is unlikely. Rather, it means that the EC will put its economic relations with non-European countries on hold with the end of the current GATT round (regardless of its outcome), and that the special deals and so forth that will be struck to serve European needs will give little thought to or concern about their impact on other countries.

Growth strategies in Latin America

The 1980s has been a lost decade for the countries of Latin America. In most of them per capita income has fallen, and to such an extent as to rival the distress of the Great Depression of the 1930s. Hence it is not too strong a statement to suggest that many countries are in crisis and will be searching for a different economic strategy. Indeed, the cycling of economic policy is one of the characteristics of developing countries in Latin America that differentiates them from those in the Pacific.

Three factors are usually cited in the standard explanation for the poor economic performance of the Latin American countries in the 1980s: heavy external debt, adverse trends in the terms of trade, and fragile political systems. The two economic explanations are not persuasive. Several Pacific countries were heavily indebted at the time of the debt crisis in November 1982—South Korea, Indonesia and the Philippines—yet their economic progress was not unduly inhibited. Furthermore, every member country of ASEAN had adverse terms of trade in the 1980s and still managed impressive growth.

Therefore, much of the explanation must rest on political circumstances which prevented the devising and execution of adequate domestic policy. Some evidence of this is the reliance of many countries on outside pressure—IMF and World Bank conditionality, and foreign commercial bank demands—to give some coherence to their policy. It should come as no surprise that domestic policy fashioned outside a country and perceived as being forced upon it will be less than fully successful. Under these circumstances, implementation of policy will be half-hearted and circumvented by bureaucrats and ministers alike. Furthermore, foreign influence reduces necessary flexibility in domestic policy formation, since foreigners have less than complete knowledge, and many domestic agents have an interest in having the policy fail and therefore will not fight for needed modifications.

Since the existing policy approach appears to be near a dead end, a new direction is likely to be attempted. The model they choose may well be that of the developing countries of the Pacific. Already several countries in Latin America have begun to have greater outward orientation. Chile, which had one of the worst growth records in the 1970s, has improved on its performance in the 1980s by being more market driven and outward-oriented. Mexico under the Solinas Presidency has ended decades of excess protectionism and deadening restrictions on foreign investment. Questions remain about Argentina and Brazil since both have had watershed-type elections; however, the success of outwardly-oriented developing countries will clearly attract their attention for possible emulation.

What would be the implications for the Pacific if most Latin American countries chose export-promotion strategies for development? While emulation may be flattering to the old and new Asian NIEs, the economic reality could be somewhat painful. Some of the Latin American countries would contest for the markets of labour-intensive goods of importance to Thailand and the Philippines, and increasingly to Indonesia and China. Others with the help of foreign direct investors will compete for middle-technology products of importance to the NIEs. For example, Brazil could conceivably become a factor in the world automobile market if it created a proper atmosphere for foreign companies. Ironically, because they are likely to emphasise growth in manufactures, the terms of trade of raw material producers would be aided by their efforts.

Latin American producers might well concentrate their marketing efforts in the United States, Europe and Japan, which are all of great importance to the Asian NIEs. Of course, industrial development creates customers as well as competitors, and Latin American countries will want to strengthen their ties with the countries they are emulating. But since these countries begin the decade having to improve their balance of payments positions, they are likely to be better competitors than customers.

Structural change in the United States

The United States is difficult to understand even by those that live there and spend most of their professional time trying to make sense of what goes on. Hence it is understandable that foreign observers do not understand and indeed are incredulous that the United States would permit the twin structural deficits—the deficit in the budget of the federal government and the deficit in the current account of the balance of payments—to go on for most of the 1980s without taking corrective action. Without trying to present a complete answer, let it suffice to say that United States economic performance from a domestic perspective during the 1980s was seen as reasonably good and there was no groundswell for a change in economic strategy.

Nevertheless, the twin deficits must be ended. Despite the denial of some economists that the budget deficit matters, and the willingness of foreign investors to finance all—and sometimes more than all—of the current account deficit, the simple logic that a country cannot continually live beyond its means is compelling in the long run. The end of the Cold War will create an environment in which the budget deficit can be eliminated, and a political circumstance in which the current account deficit must be ended.

The hegemonic position of the United States in the capitalist camp, especially in the eyes of Americans, was sustained by the preponderance of the United States military contribution to the common defence, and the existence of an external security threat that made a strong defence essential. Now that the threat of the Soviet Union has been attenuated, the United States will no longer view itself as a hegemon. Indeed, polls indicate that as the American public's perception of the Soviet Union as a security threat declines, its perception of Japan as an economic threat rises. The reason for this is that military power is vital. Economic strength is now, and increasingly will be seen as, the basis for national security. The United States won the Cold War (in the sense of preventing a major war in Europe), but it is losing the economic competition with Japan.

Cuts in military expenditure will be the cornerstone of the budget adjustment. Already savings of US$180 billion by FY1994 have been targeted. A great deal of defence savings will be sought from reduced forward deployment. Political pressures will force the United States to ask for complete funding by host countries, that is everything but salaries. Otherwise, American forces will be removed.

United States budget correction has strong implications for other countries, and these are explored in a later section. It is clear, however, that there is not a dollar-for-dollar translation of budget savings to balance of payments improvement; the marginal coefficient is closer to one-third. Hence the current account deficit will not be closed even if the budget is balanced (as currently measured). Something more will be needed.

The United States will find that it has less political security influence on other countries and therefore will have to use economic instruments to correct its balance of payments. Very likely the dollar will depreciate, a natural consequence of declining interest rates as discussed later. However, it will be very important that the balance of payments deficit be seen to be declining in step with the budget deficit, and normal currency correction alone may take too long. One possible approach would be for the United States to become less hospitable to foreign investment to force an undervalued dollar to promote exports and retard imports. Alternatively, the United States might make aggressive use of its '301' approach to opening foreign markets (which would be better than protectionist restrictions on imports). How this is accommodated depends on how the world economy is structured, to which we now turn.

ALTERNATIVE SCENARIOS FOR THE WORLD ECONOMIC STRUCTURE

Following the destruction of the two rival camp construction, the world economy might be structured in three different ways, described below as one-world anarchy, benign bilateral competition, and contentious trilateralism.

One-world anarchy

Neoclassical economic theory suggests that an optimal world economic structure would be one in which there were no government interferences to commerce between nations, and there was a single world currency. There are two reasons why an attempt to have such a system in the circumstances of the 1990s would create anarchy.

The first and most important reason is that Europe will not want to play that game, and there is no hegemon to force them to keep to the rules. Because of the need to create a positive economic environment within Europe while critical political issues are being negotiated, special attention will be given to the economic needs of Eastern Europe as well as the adjustment problems of all European countries to an expanded European Community. Thus it is inconceivable that Europeans will treat Japanese goods the same as those from East Germany and Austria, or Thai exports the same as those from Poland and Turkey.

If Pacific countries were to accept the appearance of one-world, in which, for instance, all trade issues would be handled by GATT, all finance issues by the IMF, and all aid issues by the World Bank (and regional banks), then there would be an endless series of squabbles. One side would be trying to push the international institution into playing the role of a hegemon for which it had no mandate and no enforcement power, and the other side would be undermining the International Trade Organization's credibility. Frustration could easily spill over into unilateral action and reaction and anarchy would result.

The second reason that the one-world concept would flounder is that all non-European countries are not at the same level of development. If the world economy really reflected a model of pure competition, then different levels of development would not be a critical issue. However, the industrial organisation of most industries in most countries is better characterised as oligopolistic competition or even monopolies rather than pure competition. Very few products or services are priced at marginal cost. Most international trade is managed mainly by private firms or parastatal institutions. The managers do not violate cannons of economic efficiency—indeed, they may promote dynamic efficiency. However, there are formidable barriers to entry in most industries.

Few developing countries and many advanced countries will be unwilling to accept the 'judgement of the market' when that judgement is indeed that of a few *keiretsu* in Japan or conglomerates in the United States. Most countries will want to interfere with the market to overcome its imperfections, and will want to be able to bring state power to bear in overcoming barriers to entry.

For a stable economic environment to exist, there must be a mechanism that permits legitimate state interference, but also sets limits to that interference. In the absence of a hegemon, the mechanism must be self-enforcing. Intuition suggests that this could only occur in a repetitive game with all players having a significant interest in each outcome. That circumstance exists among countries where economic interdependence is well advanced, but not on a worldwide basis. Hence regional structures are likely to be more stable and more welfare promoting than an ineffective global structure.

Contentious trilateralism

Skipping over benign bilateral competition (one always leaves the best for last), there is the option of a three-region world centred on Europe, North and South America, and the Western Pacific. Some critics suggest that this is the concept that Prime Minister Hawke had in mind when he first suggested a ministerial meeting in 1989 of only Western Pacific countries excluding North America. The three-region concept might evolve naturally. Europe is already a distinct economic region. North America has its free trade agreement between Canada and the United States to which other countries in the Americas could be induced to join over time. This would leave the Western Pacific without an organisation, but that deficiency would not last long if the other two regions developed in an exclusionary manner.

The major problem with this conception is that relations both within and between regions would be fraught with conflict. The regions could be created because there would be a natural hegemon in each one: Germany in Europe, the United States in the Americas, and Japan in the Pacific. Conflict within a region would be inevitable, however, because from historical experience the hegemon in each region is the country that other countries in that region trust least. Within-region coalitions would be formed to pressure the hegemon, which would prevent the hegemon from taking a benevolent stance even if that was its desire. There would also be much domestic pressure within the hegemon to exploit its position of dominance.

From the perspective of the United States, there would be both gains and losses from a three-region construction. Certainly, correcting its balance of payments deficit would be much easier since most of its deficit is with countries in other regions. For example, the United States could take actions that would eliminate its deficit with Korea and Taiwan, knowing that these countries must turn to Japan to complete their adjustment.

Nevertheless, the losses would be much greater than the gains. The United States would primarily depend for its economic stimulation on a group of countries much weaker than itself, which would be stultifying to its economy. Furthermore, the more dependent each country felt on the United States, the more testy would be its political relations with the United States. The concept could be made to work, but only by absorbing most of the energies of all of the countries in the region.

Relations between the regions would depend on the foresightedness of political leaders in each hegemon, but they might also be contentious. A policy action which in reality was taken without concern about reactions outside the region might well appear as a deliberate assault on other regions if negative results were present. Aggressive reactions are easy to contemplate. Each region will have an armory full of economic weapons to use against the others. It would take the highest level of statesmanship to prevent economic skirmishes from getting out of hand.

A three-region concept is possible, but is likely to be less than satisfying unless one of the regions established clear dominance over the other two. That condition would then approach the one hegemon model, but does not reflect current reality. Hence the most likely outcome of a three-region construction would be contentiousness.

Benign bilateral competition

The third alternative would be a bilateral construction. However, unlike the previous bipolar division of the postwar period, the two regions would be Europe on the one hand and the rest of the world (ROW) on the other. As noted already, Europe as a region already exists, and is on a path to consolidate its character. Hence the question remaining is whether the rest of the world creates some sort or organisation. If not, then one-world anarchy will result as discussed earlier. Region building for ROW must start in the Pacific among countries whose economic interaction is particularly intense, and then spread to other countries as economic links are deepened. Some countries would not have a clear allegiance to one region or the other. This ambiguity does not interfere with the bilateral construction because by definition the unaligned countries are not major players in the world economy.

The bilateral construction holds the promise of being the optimal one for organising the world economy in the 1990s. To establish this presumption, however, the case must be made that two regions will not suffer from the same maladies as the three-region construction. Hence attention must be given to both within region and between region relations.

First, within Europe, even a reunified Germany would not be a disproportionately large hegemon in an area that includes the Soviet Union and other industrial countries of Western Europe. In the absence of overwhelming dominance, the hegemon must act in a more restrained manner and the other countries have less of a benefactor to play against. Furthermore, there would exist sub-regional institutions such as NATO and the Warsaw Pact whose functions could change to negotiate and oversee peaceful relations within the region. Finally, the United States would continue to play some role in Europe, and could be called upon as an impartial arbitrator to help settle difficult internal disputes.

Within the ROW, there might not be clear dominance as between Japan and the United States. The United States and Japan would be forced to work out the modality of their bilateral relations to settle their disputes with the very important proviso that they pay attention to the interests of other countries in the region. Developing countries within the region would have ample scope for intrusive governmental action (following the Japanese model of development), but could easily be reigned in by joint action by the United States and Japan. Clearly, there would be some temptation for developing countries to play off Japan and the United States against each other, but that game can only succeed to the degree that the two larger powers permit. The important point is that this would be a repetitive game in which system stability would become a broadly felt responsibility.

It is particularly difficult to speculate about the relationship between the two regions. At a minimum there would likely be no more conflict than in a three-region conception, and probably less than with a bogus one-world model. In principle, it should be easier to negotiate between two parties than among three. However, a great deal of thought would have to go into planning negotiating structures such that destructive competition could be avoided.

From the point of view of the United States, a bilateral world would be difficult to adjust to, but ultimately would be seen to be beneficial. No longer would the United States be a major player in Europe, nor would its position in ROW be seen as dominant. As already suggested, the United States must recognise the inevitable, that once power shifts from military might to economic prowess, the hegemonic role of the United States is ended. However, within the new construction, the United States defense burden could be lifted without undermining system stability. This is a tremendous societal gain for the United States.

How could the United States correct its balance of payments deficit in a bilateral world? In the next section we simulate the correction of the United States balance of payments deficit to determine what policy measures would be consistent with bringing it about.

CORRECTING INTERNATIONAL PAYMENTS IMBALANCES

Any creditable effort to smoothly correct the United States external deficit will require both reduction in the federal deficit and further depreciation of the dollar. While everyone appears to recognise this, many questions arise over the timing, speed and costs it will incur. Slow correction may lead to greater protectionist pressures and prolonged high world interest rates. Rapid correction threatens a 'hard landing' and contraction in world demand that could harm developing countries in particular. Questions also arise over how the growth of regional trade arrangements may affect the ability of the United States to smoothly correct the deficit.

In this section we assess what progress can be expected towards correcting the United States external deficit through balancing the fiscal budget. We also look at the policy mix that would be required to balance the external deficit within the current global context of relatively open trade relations between the major regions. We make use of a general equilibrium model (the Asia–Pacific MPG model) of the world economy designed to take special account of trade and macroeconomic structure of the Pacific region.

Evidence we present here suggests that much of the corrective process can be managed over a five to ten-year period through United States fiscal and monetary policies. Reducing government outlays to balance the budget in the original spirit of the Gramm–Rudman–Hollings Act (G–R–H) would have a significant impact on reducing the current account deficit and bilateral trade deficits with Germany and Japan. However, G–R–H alone is insufficient to balance the external deficit. Correcting the deficit will require a combination of lower government expenditures, higher taxes and monetary expansion to both depreciate the dollar and offset contractionary effects on the United States economy. Higher private savings in the United States, which demographic models of savings behaviour suggest will occur during the next decade, would assist adjustment and reduce the fall in output and rise in inflation. The impact on Japan and Europe of this policy mix would be largely positive due to lower world interest rates.

Concern over reduced United States demand adversely affecting developing countries is not unfounded. However, the net effect on developing countries depends not only on the policy mix followed by the United States and other industrial nations, but also on the circumstances and policy response of the developing countries themselves. The speed at which they can diversify away from the United States market is one important factor, and this hinges largely on the structure of export production and on entry barriers faced in other markets. An important factor is the openness of the capital account and the extent of sensitivity to international interest rates. Net debtors will gain from lower international interest rates reducing their debt burden, but in general the developing countries fail to capture gains experienced by the industrial countries due to constraints in domestic capital markets.

The model

The model we employ here is an extension of the McKibbon–Sachs model (MSGII), which has been developed to explicitly include developing countries and commodity markets in a global framework. It is a dynamic, forward-looking general equilibrium model of the world economy. The seven regions articulated in the model include the United States, Japan, the rest of the OECD countries, the Asian NIEs (Korea, Hong Kong, Singapore and Taiwan), the ASEAN countries (minus Singapore), and the OPEC bloc, and a rest-of-world developing country region.

The model basically employs a Mundell–Flemming–Dornbusch framework, with Keynesian micro-foundations and forward-looking behaviour on the part of agents. In the industrial countries, agents are assumed to be fully rational, with perfect foresight. However, while agents are assumed to optimise intertemporally, they do not face perfect markets. For example, investment is driven by a Tobin's 'q' specification, but investors also face liquidity constraints and an accelerator effect is also allowed for.

The developing country blocs are built around a four-sector social accounting matrix framework drawing on input–output tables from the region. While agents are 'static optimisers', perfect foresight and rational expectations are not assumed. Behavioural specifications draw on a mixture of econometric estimates and theory. Wherever possible, key parameters have been estimated using time series data from the region. Details of the model's specification are provided in Appendix 13A.

Transmission of fiscal policies

In every year since G-R-H was legislated, Congress has modified the legislation or employed new budget accounting methods in order to escape the across-the-board budget cuts mandated by the bill. In 1989 the United States budget deficit will be around US$135 billion, while under the 1987 legislation, 1989 should have seen the deficit reduced to around US$100 billion.

Experience teaches us not to believe politicians' promises, and it could prove more difficult during the coming five years to achieve the cuts than in the past. However, recent developments in Soviet-United States relations have made the prospects for significant reductions in defence expenditures a serious possibility. In addition, as the United States external liabilities to foreigners rapidly approaches US$1 trillion, there is an increasing appreciation of the costs of failure to act. This is apparent to everyone, including foreign governments, which are pressuring the United States to exercise greater fiscal restraint. High real world interest rates and the growing threat of protectionism are both blamed to a large extent on the United States external deficit.

The impact of changes in fiscal expenditures on the global economy is not obvious. It depends on several parameters affecting external economic relations and the domestic demand response. The simple Mundell-Flemming model offers a useful first step towards predicting the impact. The standard M-F model of the open economy suggests that a fall in government expenditures serves to reduce domestic demand including demand for imports, while at the same time expanding foreign demand for exports through depreciation of the exchange rate. In addition, domestic interest rates fall with the decline in the government deficit, encouraging some expansion of domestic investment, and depreciating the exchange rate as just noted. In this simple story, domestic income falls, but by a fraction of the original expenditure reduction.

In the open economy these effects are transmitted abroad via the terms of trade and the level of demand for their traded goods. A fiscal contraction, by lowering domestic demand and depreciating the real exchange rate, has negative transmission effects. On the other hand, with perfect or high asset substitutability, a fall in domestic interest rates in one country encourages capital to flow abroad, and thereby lowers interest rates elsewhere in the world. One further channel is through the impact of relative prices and interest rates on the present discounted value of wealth. This has an ambiguous impact on consumption behaviour since lower interest rates will decrease the future earnings stream but also increase real wealth through raising Tobin's 'q', the shadow value of capital services. The net impact abroad will depend on the relative magnitude of these three effects.

One additional factor which is not explicitly dealt with in the original Mundell–Flemming model arises over the functioning of foreign labour markets in response to an appreciation of the real exchange rate and a drop in foreign demand. Labour markets in the OECD countries vary in their responsiveness, with Japanese adjustment to shocks historically the most flexible, rapidly returning to full employment, whereas persistent high unemployment has characterised the European Community. By comparison, the Phillips curve in the United States is much flatter than that in Europe, allowing for greater real wage flexibility. This is important to the transmission process since rising real wages in response to a terms of trade shock, for example, will reduce the usual trade balance effect, and in the extreme completely eliminate it.

The impact of United States fiscal policy can be illustrated through simulating the deficit reduction path called for under G–R–H. The fiscal package we examine involves reducing federal outlays through cumulatively cuts in the deficit by 0.5 per cent of GDP annually over five years, with a permanent 2.5 per cent reduction from the fifth year onwards. By 1994 this would bring the United States budget into approximate balance. With a cut in government spending of this magnitude, the government would almost certainly employ monetary policy to offset the contraction in aggregate demand. To account for this, monetary policy is assigned to target domestic employment, and therefore it adjusts endogenously to maintain full employment (that is, employment at the non-accelerating inflation rate of unemployment).

The main impact of fiscal expenditure reduction is to reduce aggregate demand in the economy, depressing domestic output and employment. Three main channels, however, serve to offset the fall in aggregate demand. First, the cut in the government deficit helps to lower interest rates and stimulate domestic investment demand (crowding in). The domestic investment response is stronger than would be the case under static expectations since the future path of interest rates is foreseen by investors. This is reflected in a jump in the marginal value of investment—Tobin's 'q'. Some moderation of the assumption of perfect rationality and foresight would weaken this effect.

A second result of lower interest rates and lower future tax liabilities that accompanies deficit reduction is to raise private wealth in the economy, which serves to help expand private consumption. This wealth effect is more significant than suggested by the initial size of the fiscal cuts, again because of forward-looking behaviour by domestic households. On net, the offset coefficient from government spending is roughly one-half, that is, a one per cent reduction of GNP in government expenditures lowers output by half this amount. Finally, a third channel is through the depressing effect the cut in the deficit has on the exchange rate of the dollar. The fall in demand for United States output depreciates the dollar. The depreciated dollar, along with expanding foreign demand, works to help close the United States trade deficit.

Apart from these effects from the deficit reduction, the response is complicated by using monetary policy to maintain employment. In the absence of any monetary response, output does not decline in the first period since private demand rises by more than the 0.5 per cent fall in government spending. Real wages actually decline, and there is an increase in demand for labour. Only in subsequent periods do aggregate demand and employment fall. Hence assigning monetary policy to maintain employment results in an initial monetary contraction, offsetting the increase in demand for labour, and thereafter monetary expansion. Moderation of the assumption of perfect rationality and foresight would change the first quarter surprise.

Table 13.1 summarises the impact of the deficit reduction on the United States and other economies. Variables reported in values are shown in terms of percentage of GNP for the respective region. In the first year, for example, United States output falls by 0.3 per cent of GNP (approximately US$15 billion). Changes in labour demand are expressed in terms of per cent of workforce in the base year (1987), while interest and exchange rates are reported in terms of absolute deviations (basis points).

Along the path towards balancing the budget there is a small loss in United States output, starting with a fall of -0.4 per cent of GNP (US$20 billion) and ending the period shown with essentially no net effect on growth when the full budget cuts are in effect. This result is at first glance surprising, but it arises for two reasons. The first factor is the policy mix of the government, which involves applying fiscal restraint while also stimulating private demand and employment though monetary expansion.[1] This is close to the deficit reduction path laid out in G-R-H which requires a ceiling on the deficit of US$100 billion in 1990 and calls for full balance by 1993. Contractionary effects of fiscal policy and the expansionary monetary path have offsetting effects on inflation.

It is important to understanding the scope for using monetary policy to reduce the value of the dollar and improve the trade balance. Federal reserve tightening of the money supply to reduce domestic inflationary pressures is often criticised for its adverse impact on the value of the dollar, and hence on retarding trade balance correction. Our results, however, indicate that monetary tightening has a negligible effect on the trade balance since the exchange rate effects are weak and the impact on interest rates offsetting. The main impact of monetary policy is to increase employment and inflation. It is the key instrument determining where, between Scylla and Charybdis, the United States will sail.

Another important factor over which the government has little control is private savings behaviour. A reasonable estimate would be that for a one per cent increase in private savings there is a corresponding improvement in the current account of 0.3 per cent. During the 1980s there has been a decline in household savings in most OECD countries, but it has been particularly pronounced in North America. Net private savings averaged 8.1 per cent of GNP in the United States during the 1980s compared with 10.2 per cent in the 1970s. One factor contributing to this trend is the demographic transition as OECD populations age and the distribution shifts towards cohorts with lower savings propensities. Recent work using demographic models of savings behaviour suggests that demographic factors could raise United States savings by as much as 2 per cent of GNP over the coming decade.

THE PACIFIC AND THE WORLD ECONOMY: INTER-RELATIONS

Table 13.1 Gramm–Rudman–Hollings deficit reduction in the United States with targeting

		1990	1991	1992	1993
United States economy					
Output	%Y	-0.31	-0.27	-0.18	-0.04
Consumption	%Y	-0.32	0.04	0.45	0.93
Investment	%Y	0.25	0.40	0.54	0.67
Government	%Y	-0.50	-1.00	-1.50	-2.00
Trade balance	%Y	0.26	0.30	0.33	0.36
Exports	%Y	0.23	0.28	0.34	0.39
Imports	%Y	-0.03	-0.01	0.01	0.03
Inflation	D	0.46	0.45	0.37	0.20
Japanese economy					
Output	%Y	-0.02	0.23	0.36	0.49
Consumption	%Y	0.18	0.46	0.67	0.80
Investment	%Y	0.29	0.39	0.44	0.47
Government	%Y	0.00	0.00	0.00	0.00
Trade balance	%Y	-0.49	-0.62	-0.75	-0.77
Exports	%Y	-0.40	-0.52	-0.64	-0.66
Imports	%Y	0.09	0.10	0.11	0.11
Inflation	D	-0.28	-0.50	-0.39	-0.30
ROECD economy					
Output	%Y	-0.00	0.22	0.51	0.82
Consumption	%Y	0.17	0.37	0.58	0.80
Investment	%Y	0.25	0.33	0.40	0.47
Government	%Y	0.00	0.00	0.00	0.00
Trade balance	%Y	-0.42	-0.47	-0.47	-0.45
Exports	%Y	-0.47	-0.53	-0.53	-0.50
Imports	%Y	-0.05	-0.05	-0.05	-0.05
Inflation	D	-0.32	-0.43	-0.46	-0.46
Asian NIEs					
Output	%Y	-1.22	-1.22	-0.91	-0.93
Consumption	%Y	-0.66	-0.86	-0.81	-0.93
Investment	%Y	-0.09	-0.27	-0.47	-0.36
Government	%Y	0.00	0.00	0.00	0.00
Trade balance	%Y	-0.48	-0.09	0.37	0.36
Exports	%Y	-1.04	-0.56	-0.11	0.16
Imports	%Y	-0.56	-0.47	-0.25	-0.20
Terms of trade	%	-2.02	-2.41	-2.54	-2.74
ASEAN economies					
Output	%Y	-0.13	0.12	0.49	0.81
Consumption	%Y	-0.12	0.15	0.50	0.81
Investment	%Y	-0.32	-0.36	-0.33	-0.07
Government	%Y	0.00	0.00	0.00	0.00
Trade balance	%Y	0.30	0.33	0.33	0.07
Exports	%Y	0.22	0.23	0.21	0.00
Imports	%Y	-0.09	-0.10	-0.11	-0.07
Terms of trade	%	0.64	1.75	3.04	4.38
Memo items: nominal exchange rates					
$/ECU	%	8.66	11.00	12.97	14.34
$/Yen	%	8.91	11.21	13.22	14.78
$/ACU	%	3.09	3.90	4.60	5.13
$/ASEAN	%	2.20	2.78	3.28	3.65
Interest rates (short-term)					
United States	D	1.93	1.24	0.38	-0.78
Japan	D	-0.37	-0.78	-1.19	-1.44
ROECD	D	-0.41	-0.73	-1.00	-1.24

Notes: D = absolute deviation from base year value (1987).
% = per cent deviation from base year value.
%Y = change as a per cent of GNP from base year value (1987).

Table 13.2 presents the results of a policy mix which would gradually bring the current account into balance over a ten-year period. This is not intended to be prescriptive or predictive, but rather to illustrate the impact that such a corrective path would have for the major industrial and developing countries. The policy package this is based on has four elements: one, a reduction in the federal deficit as described above, phased in over a five-year period; two, a gradual increase in household savings by increments of 0.2 per cent of GNP per year up to a ceiling of an additional 2 per cent of GNP in savings by the year 2000, maintained thereafter; three, a relatively modest and phased increase in federal taxes over a five-year period by 1.5 per cent of GNP (approximately US$80 billion) used to reduce the stock of debt; and four, a monetary policy path assigned to maintaining full employment (non-accelerating inflation rate of unemployment) in the United States. This does not represent a set of policies that would be particularly easy, but it is within the reach of current policymakers to enact over the medium run.

The outcome for the United States economy is more severe than the straight G–R–H cuts, with output falling by 0.7 per cent of GNP, and with private consumption falling by nearly twice this amount. By 1994, however, the effect on consumption is negligible and output has returned to its underlying growth path. The recovery is led by investment, which rises by more than half the level of government expenditure reduction. Stronger export performance also leads to improvement in the trade balance. Despite the depreciation of the dollar by 30 per cent in the first three years, the domestic inflation is only up one per cent and this gradually declines over the period.

For the other industrial countries there are gains similar to those shown in Table 13.1. Output is higher in Japan by one per cent of GNP by the fourth year, and by 1.8 per cent in the rest of the OECD countries. Short-term interest rates decline by around 3 per cent in both regions and remain between 2 and 3 per cent for the decade. The only region to suffer serious losses is the Asian NIE bloc, where output declines by nearly 3 per cent of GNP. Not until 1997 do they regain their potential growth level, led mainly by exports and eventually by investment demand after domestic prices have fallen sufficiently to reverse the real exchange rate shock.

The principal conclusion that we want to make here is that the global saving–investment imbalances that marked the 1980s need not pose a serious threat to economic relations in the 1990s. Correcting the United States external deficit may not be as difficult as many observers believe, but difficult policy steps will need to be taken. It will inevitably result in lower United States performance, a consequence of Americans having 'lived beyond their means' for several years. However, the effects on other regions will be largely positive. For developing countries in the Pacific region the key will be maintaining competitiveness in the United States market vis-à-vis other industrial suppliers and moving rapidly to cultivate new markets. Of course, the events described here would be dramatically different if other industrial countries respond with a new policy mix, aimed for example at protecting their export industries. Moreover, if developing countries continue to liberalise domestic

THE PACIFIC AND THE WORLD ECONOMY: INTER-RELATIONS 251

Table 13.2 Current account balancing act with employment targeting

		1990	1991	1992	1993
United States economy					
Output	%Y	-0.68	-0.59	-0.41	-0.10
Consumption	%Y	-1.28	-1.09	-0.81	-0.35
Investment	%Y	0.52	0.85	1.17	1.46
Government	%Y	-0.50	-1.00	-1.50	-2.00
Trade balance	%Y	0.58	0.65	0.73	0.79
Exports	%Y	0.51	0.62	0.75	0.85
Imports	%Y	-0.07	-0.03	0.02	0.06
Inflation	D	1.01	0.99	0.82	0.47
Japanese economy					
Output	%Y	-0.02	0.50	0.79	1.10
Consumption	%Y	0.40	1.01	1.46	1.76
Investment	%Y	0.65	0.86	0.98	1.05
Trade balance	%Y	-1.08	-1.37	-1.65	-1.71
Exports	%Y	-0.88	-1.14	-1.41	-1.46
Imports	%Y	0.20	0.23	0.24	0.25
Inflation	D	-0.61	-1.08	-0.85	-0.67
ROECD economy					
Output	%	0.01	0.50	1.14	1.82
Consumption	%Y	0.38	0.81	1.28	1.76
Investment	%Y	0.56	0.73	0.90	1.06
Trade balance	%Y	-0.93	-1.03	-1.05	-1.00
Exports	%Y	-1.03	-1.15	-1.16	-1.11
Imports	%Y	-0.10	-0.12	-0.12	-0.11
Inflation	D	-0.69	-0.94	-1.02	-1.02
Asian NIEs					
Output	%Y	-2.68	-2.67	-2.01	-2.05
Consumption	%Y	-1.45	-1.87	-1.78	-2.04
Investment	%Y	-0.18	-0.59	-1.03	-0.78
Trade balance	%Y	-1.05	-0.21	0.79	0.77
Exports	%Y	-2.28	-1.24	0.24	0.32
Imports	%Y	-1.23	-1.03	-0.56	-0.45
Terms of trade	%	-4.42	-5.26	-5.58	-6.02
ASEAN economies					
Output	%Y	-0.30	0.25	1.06	1.74
Consumption	%Y	-0.26	0.29	1.06	1.69
Investment	%Y	-0.71	-0.78	-0.75	-0.16
Trade balance	%Y	0.67	0-.74	0.74	0.21
Exports	%Y	0.48	0.52	0.49	0.04
Imports	%Y	-0.19	-0.22	-0.25	-0.16
Terms of trade	%	1.40	3.78	6.62	9.50
Memo items: nominal exchange rates					
$/ECU	%	18.89	24.00	28.44	31.52
$/Yen	%	19.53	24.55	29.09	32.57
$/ACU	%	6.77	8.54	10.12	11.29
$/ASEAN	%	4.82	6.08	7.21	8.04
Interest rates (short-term)					
United States	D	4.26	2.90	0.94	-1.27
Japan	D	-0.77	-1.65	-2.55	-3.11
ROECD	D	-0.85	-1.54	-2.14	-2.67

Notes: D = absolute deviation from base year value (1987).
% = per cent deviation from base year value.
%Y = change as a per cent of GNP from base year value (1987).

financial markets, adopt freely floating currencies, and open capital markets to unrestricted international transactions, the exchange and interest rate effects would be changed entirely.

CONCLUSIONS

Momentous changes are taking place on the world political scene. They will lead to fundamental changes in the world economy. The countries in the Pacific must decide whether they want to live with a bogus one-world concept in which international organisations are put into the role of a king without clothes, or instead for a region of its own. If regionalism is chosen, then the challenge will be to forge ROW unity, rather than let a split be created by the Pacific Ocean.

Some observers argue that despite the difficulty and the high probability of failure, it is worthwhile to try to obtain a one-world trade regime because it is the optimal system. However, the arguments for the reverse seem more compelling. A regional system that evolves out of the demonstrated failure of a one-world system is likely to see very contentious relations among the regions and even economic warfare. A regional system that is chosen as a matter of preference can evolve peacefully in time into a one-world system, but not the other way round.

The analysis in this chapter suggests that a two-region world dominates the other alternatives. The simulations presented suggests that the most difficult element in the Pacific region—accommodating the adjustment of the United States balance of payments deficit—can be accomplished without undue dislocations. We recognise that there is a difference between what is possible and what may occur. However, the quality of leadership that is required to bring about a Pacific region will also be great enough to solve the less demanding United States adjustment problem.

14 The role of multilateralism and regionalism: a Pacific perspective

H. EDWARD ENGLISH AND
MURRAY G. SMITH

INTRODUCTION

This topic signifies the complexity of modern international relations. The complexity arises out of several major changes since the 1940s. Two of these are especially pervasive in their implications. First, the economic world has ceased to be hegemonic. Now it is multipolar, or perhaps even more important, it has a wide variety of influential actors or groups of actors. The largest actors are less powerful individually or even collectively than they were in the nineteenth and first half of this century. The smaller actors are more numerous and represent significant group interests, exerting from time to time substantial influence; for example, OPEC, UNECLA and ASEAN. Also, of the greatest significance are two or three new economic actors or groups, the Soviet Union, Eastern Europe and China, eager to expand their role in international economic affairs. In the interest of international harmony and security they must be granted an increasing role in the world economy and its governing institutions.

Two, ingredients of international economic relations are more complex than they were in the 1950s and 1960s. Nostalgia for that period is pointless, in the light of the changes above. It seems even more so when one takes into account the shift from tariff to non-tariff barriers. Many of the latter are deeply embedded in national policies that have a rationale unrelated to trade. However, the tendency to subtle or not-so-subtle use of such policies for protective purposes requires new effort to control their trade-distorting efforts. These concerns relate especially to agricultural policies, public procurement practices, subsidies or incentive systems affecting natural resource and high-tech sectors, intellectual property issues and policies governing trade in services.

The challenge to GATT is a formidable one. The Uruguay Round is addressing it, and, as the Secretary-General of GATT has stated, a new GATT is emerging. The most important result of the current round is that it can result in a stronger institution, especially one that has more independent capability to identify and measure the significance of national policies and practices that result in non-tariff barriers.

Nevertheless, it is clear that these challenges require efforts that go beyond the GATT. One reason for this is that some of the policies generating non-tariff barriers are not primarily a GATT responsibility. Examples include intellectual property, governed by WIPO and other copyright conventions, trade in services governed by immigration laws, and financial services regulation jealously guarded by treasuries.

What is the role of bilateralism and regionalism in complementing multilateralism as a means of dealing with the economic challenges associated with the new form and substance of international relationships?

This chapter will focus on multilateralism and regionalism, since it is assumed that bilateral arrangements will continue to play their conventional role in ad hoc dealings between pairs of countries seeking to smooth and sustain traditional relations or to enhance the prospects for expanded contact with countries that are less familiar partners. Sometimes these bilateral relationships adopt more formal long-term or 'framework' agreements—for example, the Canada–United States Free Trade Agreement—but this will be treated as an example of a regional arrangement in what follows.

Probably the most important point to be made on the basis of recent bilateralism is that it has become a means of evading GATT commitments, either in spirit or in letter (or both). The prototype was established many years ago with the antecedents of the Multifibre Arrangement. Even in the 1980s the Europeans and North Americans sought bilateral control of rates of growth of textile product imports and soon made it a pseudo-respectable exemption from GATT based wholly on their unwillingness to face adjustment in a manufacturing sector where low-wage countries had a clear opportunity for export-based development. That occurred in a period of healthy growth rates in most developed countries. The proliferation of bilateralism in more recent years can be attributed to reaction to the combination of slower growth rates of developed countries and the lessened ability of the largest economic powers to achieve their objectives through multilateral organisations.

In general, this form of bilateralism is initiated by what are often termed unilateral demands by major powers. The most often cited are the efforts by the United States to achieve higher intellectual property standards in Korea, China, Thailand and Singapore. Counterfeit trade is one of the main culprits, but as GATT to date has no provisions that directly address the United States concerns, it could also be described as an effort to build pressure towards a stronger and better enforced set of standards under WIPO and copyright conventions. However, clearly a major driving force was to open up markets for various American goods, from tobacco to insurance services. Japanese practices that exploit a similar advantage in bargaining power are often cited as involving the large trading companies affiliated with *keiretsu*, which use access to technology as a lever to their efforts to maximise their advantages in bilateral dealings.

Other pernicious forms of bilateralism involve the proliferation of managed trade regimes in sectors such as steel, automobiles and semiconductors. The European Community and the United States use the threat of application of antidumping or countervailing duties or selective safeguard measures to enforce 'voluntary' export restraints. The prospects for substantial liberalisation of these trade laws during the Uruguay Round appear limited and these issues are likely to remain on the international trade agenda for some time to come.

This experience leads to a preliminary judgement that multilateral and regional institutions must be explored as complementary means of achieving the priority aims of all countries. Two central propositions will be addressed:

1 that *the basic role of multilateral institutions should be to set a framework of principles* that would encompass the new issues as well as traditional ones subjected to multilateral negotiations, and new procedures to strengthen the prospects that those principles will be respected, procedures that promote transparency through fearless monitoring of national practice; and
2 that *regional arrangements* should be committed to the multilateral principles, and *should be addressed to the tasks of applying these principles* and if possible go beyond to set and apply even higher (meaning economically more efficient) standards.

The debate implicit in these propositions is about the mix of means that will best achieve global harmony and prosperity. To argue that only multilateral means should be employed is to claim that alternative means always lead to second-best results, a proposition that multilateral means always have a better chance of succeeding either sooner or later, and that regional means cannot by their nature enhance the rate at which multilateral ends will be achieved or at which multilateral means can be activated. The argument that regional means are essentially contradictory to multilateral means, though frequently used as a rationale for inaction, is without content. The argument that regional means may conflict with multilateral ends is trivial in itself. The whole case can be encompassed in the statement that if multilateral ends are desirable, then both multilateral and other means should be used to achieve them, with full recognition of the dynamic interaction between such means.

The prospects for multilateral institutions in the remainder of the Uruguay Round and beyond will first be explored. The role of regional institutions will then be explored, with special emphasis on Pacific institutions. Ubiquitous bilateral relations will be treated as they impact on multilateral and regional arrangements. Bilateralism is mainly a set of ad hoc arrangements with little or no institutional form or specific time dimension. Where there is a systematic arrangement between two countries as under GATT Article 24, this should and will be treated as 'regionalism'.

WHITHER THE MULTILATERAL ECONOMIC SYSTEM?

The multilateral trading system, or more generally, the multilateral economic relations system, is a relatively recent phenomenon, which emerged from the chaos of the inter-war period and which was implemented in the international vacuum after the Second World War. Indeed, one might explain the origins of the GATT and the Bretton Woods financial institutions as a kind of historic fluke. In the midst of the Second World War, while governments were preoccupied with the war, a few economists, Lord Keynes and Sir James Meade in the United Kingdom, and John White and Clair Wilcox in the United States, developed some proposals for international trade and financial institutions which were implemented in a burst of international idealism after the war.

Diebold (1988) has argued that the shift to unconditional most favoured nation (MFN) treatment in United States trade policy, which underpinned the postwar GATT system, was the result of the recognition that the trade frictions of the preceding practice of reciprocal or conditional MFN embodied in the United States bilateral treaties, and the high trade barriers of Smoot Hawley, had become counterproductive and too costly. Diebold quotes Viner (1988):

> The most-favoured-nation clause in American commercial treaties, as conditionally interpreted and applied by the United States, has probably been the cause in the last century of more diplomatic controversy, more variations in construction, more international ill-feeling, more conflict between international obligations and municipal law and between judicial interpretation and executive practice, more confusion and uncertainty of operation, than have developed under all the unconditional most-favoured-nation pledges of all other countries combined.

In the case of the United States, the shift in policy was embodied in Cordell Hull's Trade Agreements Act of 1933 and the series of bilateral MFN trade agreements that the United States concluded in the 1930s. The United States trade agreements program was intended to achieve lower United States trade barriers and to avoid the corrosive bilateral frictions of reciprocal conditional MFN as well as expanded access to foreign markets. Diebold notes that the United Kingdom came more slowly to this view, clinging to various bilateral managed trade arrangements throughout the 1930s, but the United Kingdom official views came closer to those of the United States during the war and the two countries played a pivotal role in the creation of the GATT and the Bretton Woods institutions. (For its part, Canada played a middle power role in mediating United States and United Kingdom perspectives.)

If the origins of the GATT can be explained as an aberration of 1940s idealism, it was soon to be tested by the realities of trade politics. The intention was to create the International Trade Organization (ITO), which would parallel the IMF and the World Bank, but the US Congress refused to implement the ITO charter. The GATT, which has been intended to be an interim arrangement, continued as a contract among its members, and over time the GATT Secretariat has evolved as a supporting organisation.

Despite its hesitant beginnings, the remarkable success of GATT in achieving significant reductions of industrial country tariffs and a range of non-tariff barriers among the industrial countries through successive rounds of negotiations cannot be questioned.[1] However, the very success of GATT in these areas makes some of the inadequacies of the GATT system more evident.

In a number of areas, GATT rules were modified to accommodate economic or political interests. Clearly, the rules were bent in agricultural trade to accommodate the interests of powerful domestic lobbies. The United States sought and obtained a waiver for its agricultural import measures related to domestic price supports, and in the 1956 review of GATT articles the provisions were modified to permit export subsidies for primary products. Also in the 1956 review, Article XVIII of GATT was amended to make it easier for developing countries to impose import restrictions in order to encourage participation in GATT by newly independent economies emerging in the wave of decolonisation. Again in the 1960s, the reaction of the industrial countries to import competition in cotton textiles resulted in a special multilateral regime sanctioning bilateral restraint arrangements which evolved into the Multifibre Arrangement (MFA).

The first reaction to Japan's membership in GATT reflected a more general fear of competition from a country whose low wages were then the focus of protection. Resort to Article 35 by a large number of European countries, relieving them from the consequences of Japanese competition, was a blatant discrimination analogous in effect to the textile arrangements, but applied across the board. Perhaps it was a portent of the European attitude manifest in the present line that seeks to resort to selective safeguards as well as an ingenious variety of non-tariff barriers against Japan, based only on the crudest and in general unsubstantiated claims of unfair Japanese trading practice. Even where the criticism has some justification, discontinuance of the practices would in most cases have little impact on Japan's general competitive strength. There are many pots and kettles in this kind of verbal competition.

The failure to ratify the ITO created gaps in the fabric of international economic relations. The issues of trade in services, trade-related investment measures (TRIMs), and, most significantly, trade-related intellectual property (TRIPs), loom high on the agenda for the Uruguay Round.

Over succeeding decades, there has been a marked shift in the character of trade barriers in, and trade disputes among, the major industrial countries, which have also influenced trade relations between the developing and industrial economies. As tariffs have been reduced among members of the GATT, industries have sought relief from import competition through application of antidumping and countervailing duties or escape clause measures as permitted under GATT rules, through attempts to introduce selective application of safeguards, and also through negotiation of voluntary restraint arrangements which are outside the GATT framework.

The proliferation of voluntary export restraint and managed trade arrangements stems in part from some ambiguity about their legal status under GATT rules. Yet many voluntary export restrain arrangements are violations of GATT Article XI. For example, there was a GATT complaint on the United States-Japan semiconductor arrangement. The problem is not simply a loophole in the GATT rules regarding export restraints but a more fundamental problem in the trading system. The Leutwiler Report decried the erosion of the trading rules, observing:

> Today, more and more countries are increasingly ignoring the trading rules, and concluding bilateral, discriminatory and restrictive agreements outside the GATT rules. The United States and the European Community maintain restraint programs, for example, with virtually all their steel suppliers, principally through restrictions on export trade imposed after bilateral negotiations ... All these ... attempts to regulate exports or imports have accelerated the trend toward protectionism. Within each country, the force of example prompts constant demands for discriminatory intervention from almost every industry. Internationally, the force of precedent allows national industries to justify their demands by pointing to the protection granted to their competitors abroad. In both cases, managers and workers ask why they should abide by the rules if no one else does. At present, the GATT system is not adequately discharging one of its ultimate functions: to provide help to governments in withstanding such pressures from special interests. In such a disorderly world, each trade dispute has a self-fulfilling effect and undermines confidence in the basic rules of the trading system (Leutwiler et al., 1985: 19-21).

The most important example in the 1980s was the United States imposition of voluntary export restraints on Japanese automotive exports, an action which forced Canada to follow the United States lead for fear of substantial diversion of those exports to its market.

The problems that GATT faced at the outset of the Uruguay Round were partly related to problems which had not been adequately handled in the 1960s and 1970s, and partly to new attitudes and problems of the 1980s.

1. Three main issues left over from earlier failures that haunt those who seek a stronger GATT through current negotiations are: the failure to incorporate agricultural trade in the system, for which the major economic powers all share responsibility;
2. the temptation to which all fell victim to manage textile trade in a way that avoided adjustment in developed countries in the 1960s when it would have been easier; and
3. the response to increasing developing country demands by a system of preferences that was soon eroded by conditionality, especially in ways that limited the exploitation of their comparative advantages, and introduced no incentive to limit the distorting effects of their own often very high levels of protection.

The new issues of the 1980s arose in substantial degree from the failures or contrasts of macroeconomic policy in developed countries and the new perception that GATT did not provide adequate scope for trade in technology-intensive goods and all services. Although they were old issues, new meaning was also attached to the treatment of subsidies and dumping, partly due to the attention attached to export subsidies in agriculture, partly because of the importance of sector-related supports in the tax and expenditure system related to natural resource and technology-intensive sectors, and partly because of the new concern for national regulations affecting trade in services. However, much of the reaction to actual and alleged subsidies was really part of the concern over the declining competitiveness of Europe and North America, a substantial part of which was related to fiscal deficits, especially in the United States, that combined with low savings rates to raise relative interest rates, draw in foreign capital and result in substantially overvalued currencies.

The reaction of both the United States and Europe has been to resort to multilateral and bilateral or unilateral action designed to curb what have typically been called 'unfair trade practices', generally non-tariff barriers associated with national policies. In the multilateral sphere during the Kennedy and Tokyo rounds, the concept of codes governing such practice were introduced.

An essential feature of the codes negotiated during the Tokyo Round is that rights of access to a signatory's domestic market are available only to other signatories. Thus, the codes offer conditional MFN treatment (conditional in this context is quite different than the bilateral reciprocal conditional MFN of nineteenth century United States trade policy). The rights under each code are conditional upon a country's accepting the code's obligations.

As Cooper (1985) has noted, these so-called plurilateral codes reduce the free-rider problem that occurs in MFN tariff negotiations. Plurilateral negotiations do not, however, resolve what is sometimes referred to as the least-common-denominator or 'foot-dragger' problem. Truly, multilateral liberalisation is constrained to the level permitted by the major industrial trading bloc or country least willing to reduce or to eliminate particular trade barriers or non-tariff distortions.

However, if they carry prospects for increasing benefits to those who are initially reluctant to sign them, such codes can have a dynamic effect in trade liberalisation.

Many of the reactions to the new perceptions of the 1980s have been bilateral or unilateral. Those by the United States have had a higher profile. Congressional politics seems to ensure this. The farm bill of 1985 brought export subsidies to agricultural trade. Numerous trade bills culminated in the Omnibus ('Ominous') Trade Bill of 1988. Although cleansed of some of the crudest and most naive proposals that had been made, the Bill still contained 'Super 301', which required the Office of the US Trade Representative to retaliate against those nations named as guilty of practices especially damaging to United States interests.

The naming of Japan as a guilty party has in the eyes of moderate observers of Japan–United States relations raised the emotional level of trade relations and produced threats of retaliation not previously common on the Japanese side. This is undoubtedly because it does focus exclusively on the specific allegations and involves a judgment not governed by independent assessment in the dispute settlement procedures of GATT. In fact, unlike the existing Section 301, the new section is intended as a bargaining weapon hanging over the heads of Uruguay Round negotiators, and poised for use if the Round fails to achieve the main objective of the United States government. Whether United States power in such negotiations is still great enough to produce the desired result and whether the particular 'weapon' can play a significant part can only be judged after the fact. The risks of trade wars are certainly enhanced if the United States has overestimated either its influence in 1990 or the will of trading partners to make the necessary concessions.

The European Community (and also individual members states) is an extensive practitioner of managed trade, but there is less debate there than there is in the United States. The Community has found the antidumping laws a convenient device to enforce the 'voluntary' export restraints, and in effect the antidumping laws can provide the selective safeguard mechanism that the Community was unable to negotiate during the Uruguay Round.[2] It is noteworthy that these and other practices have frequently been directed at imports from Japan. As the 1992 agenda moves forward, there may well be increased use of the Community instrument—the antidumping laws—to substitute for the remaining national import quotas and voluntary export restraints.

The risks inherent in the managed trade approach favoured by many in the United States and the European Community echo the observations of Viner over 60 years ago. Not only will the proliferation of managed trade regimes impose static economic costs, but there will also be dynamic economic costs which will become embedded in industrial structures. Moreover, bilateral frictions will proliferate, corroding inter-governmental economic relations and creating uncertainties for private sector investment.

Many aspects of the external implications of the Europe 1992 agenda remain uncertain. The most contentious issues include agricultural trade, safeguards and antidumping laws, government procurement, and trade in services. These are all issues where existing GATT rules are inadequate, incomplete or non-existent.

Both the United States and the European Community have reason to show restraint in taking action under their own trade rules until they have tested the stronger dispute settlement arrangements and the trade policy review mechanism which were put forward at the GATT Ministerial Review in December 1988 and approved at the Trade Negotiating Committee meeting in April 1989.

If framework agreements can be developed to govern trade in services and intellectual property issues, then it could be possible to achieve further strengthening of the GATT dispute settlement process. Specifically, it could be possible to make acceptance, as well an initiation, of GATT panel reports automatic as is the case with the general dispute settlement mechanism under Chapter 18 of the Canada-United States Free Trade Agreement.[3] If achieved, this could provide a basis for limiting unilateral actions under Section 301 in United States trade legislation.

There is also a case for using more formal bilateral free trade arrangements as a lever in multilateral free trade negotiations.

The rationale for this approach was explained by United States Secretary of State George Schultz:

> From a global perspective, a splintering of the multilateral trading system into a multitude of bilateral arrangements, however, such as we have negotiated with Israel and have offered to discuss with other countries, need not have this result; they can stimulate trade and strengthen the multilateral system. Free trade agreements are sanctioned by the international rules and involve a tighter trade discipline; they can promote freer trade than the multilateral system is currently prepared to accommodate. Our hope, nonetheless, is that the example of greater liberalisation—and the recognition that the United States can pursue another course—will help motivate a larger group of nations to tackle the job of expanding trade on a global basis (Schultz, 1985).

Elaborating on this theme, the report of the United States Council of Economic Advisers says, 'The possibility of FTA ... offers the United States and others the option of using a free-trade instrument, rather than protectionism, as a lever against protectionist countries' (United States, Office of the President. 1985). The Council argues that the preferred access available to members of an FTA provides an incentive for other countries to engage in trade negotiations. This strategy of liberalising trade is preferable to attempts to use threats of trade restrictions to induce other countries to engage in trade negotiations. Threatened protectionist measures would impose costs on the home country, and thus the threats lack credibility. Furthermore, implementing the threats would invite retaliation. However, it is interesting to note how reluctant other nations have been to retaliate against United States protectionist actions; for example, the United States imposition of 100 per cent duties on selected Japanese exports on ground of alleged failure of Japan to observe the semiconductor agreement. The European Community seems more willing to take retaliatory action.

In some respects wider regional arrangements can make similar contributions to the preservation of the multilateral system.

Regionalism options—theory and reality

It serves the purposes of some journalists and politicians to label regional arrangements as essentially incompatible with larger global commitments. This is notably true in Canada where North American continentalism is a favourite 'bogey man'. Ironically, there is in Canada such a general fear of economic and especially cultural absorption by the United States that the case for participation in multilateral or extra-continental regional arrangements is reinforced by the fact and perception that these can save us from perdition by the eagle to the south.

The sweet reason of economics suggests that we should address this issue as a challenge to identify and measure net social benefits of any given regional arrangement or proposal, or, at least, that we should look at the empirical evidence on existing regional arrangements and based on this make judgements on the nature and variety of the reasons for the success and failure of such arrangements. There are no comprehensive comparative studies of the latter kind, though books that encompass description and analysis of many of the better known regional communities generally leave the readers to identify their own criteria for comparison (El Agraa, 1983). Comprehensive quantitative assessments of the static and dynamic effects of regional schemes were not undertaken, even of the widely analysed European Communities (EEC, EFTA and COMECON), until very recently (EC Commission, 1988). It is ironic that one of the earlier comprehensive attempts to evaluate the consequences of a regional group was that on the Central American Common Market (by Cline and Delgado, 1978). It came to a positive conclusion on the merits, especially the dynamic benefits of the group. By the time the study was published, at the end of the 1970s, the Central American common market was well on its way to tragic disintegration.

The numerous efforts to assess in advance the benefits to be expected from a Canada-United States free trade area resulted in very substantial positive numbers, such as those of the Wonnacott brothers in the 1960s (10 per cent of GNP) (Wonnacott and Wonnacott, 1967) and those of Harris and Cox (1983) of the mid-1980s (a range of around 5–7 per cent). Both these estimates were whittled down by updating of assumptions to take account of benefits derived from multilateral liberalisation in the Kennedy Round (in the case of the Wonnocott estimate) and in the Tokyo Round (in those by Harris and Cox). More recently yet, Cecchini, Catinat and Jaquemin (see EC Commission, 1988) have studied the benefits of completing the internal market of the European Community, using a methodology like that of the Canadians. The more searching criticisms pointed out that all these efforts rested heavily on the case for new economies of scale achieved through access to a larger market and through the rationalisation of protected oligopolistic industries.

Although the weight of such criticism indicated a probable over-estimation of unrealised economies of scale, only a few commentators addressed the under-estimation of benefits that should result from the competitive dynamics of the challenge and opportunities made possible in the larger market, in effect the potential for shifting (including new) cost functions as opposed to moving along cost functions. These are obviously very difficult to measure, and in the eyes of the purest constitute a catch-all category like X-inefficiency. One of the useful indications of the substance of these factors is the testimony of members of the Federation of Independent Businesses in Canada. A very substantial fraction of the members of this group in response to a survey by their Executive Director, John Bullock, reported positive expectations from the free trade arrangement in the form of new opportunities for smaller and medium-sized enterprises in the United States market. They see the scope that the United States market provides for such enterprises in the United States and anticipate opportunities both for extending lines of activity from a Canadian base, and the exploration and exploitation of new market niches. It is still too soon to make a judgement on the validity of these expectations. The present higher-than-normal differential in interest rates between the two countries is especially damaging for such aspiring enterprises.

Canada has one other set of characteristics that makes it vulnerable to the trade policies of its partner and others. Its expectations lie in the potential of two groups of industries—one is natural resource-intensive, the other is technology-intensive. Both of these sectors ranks high in factor endowments on which Canada must depend for export earnings. As it happens, both endowments are important to the United States and one or other is significant for many Pacific partners including the larger ASEAN countries, Australia and New Zealand, all heavily dependent on resource-related goods and/or services, and Japan dependent on technology-intensive exports, with the leading NIEs having similar expectations for the future. A recent study on Canadian and United States subsidies and equivalent interventions indicate a greater relative importance of such intervention in these sectors as compared with other industries. If defence spending had been included, the difference would have been more pronounced.

The Canada–United States softwood lumber case and the United States–Japan semiconductor case suggest that such sectors are subject to prescriptions for managed trade or countervail conflict.

The underlying problem is that market failure is seen as characteristic. In the case of 'renewable' resources, the problem is that the cost of sustained development (as well as the benefits) are difficult to assess, and social benefits and costs are not those that private decisionmakers must address under the typical existing national policy environments. In the case of high-tech goods and services, the market failure does not relate to the problem of determining appropriate discount rates for long-term sustained development but rather the extent to which public policy intervention is necessary to optimise private incentive to innovate.

Both situations, and particularly the latter, have already led to a kind of oligopolistic competition among governments as well as among private enterprises, which has tended in general to produce unsustainable development in forestry and fisheries and excess capacity in high-tech sectors. The latter danger seems likely to be heightened by the greater equality of technology-capacity among the great economic powers—the European Community, the United States and Japan. The interests of Pacific countries in both natural resource and high-tech sectors provide an incentive to develop for these sectors the means of dealing with market failure that avoid significant trade distortions. It is a subject worthy of the attention of future PAFTAD conferences.

Moving back to the theoretical model, each regional initiative will answer by the record of its institutional evolution the following questions. What is the equilibrium level of integration for any given time period, and what are the possibilities for change in the defined optimum over time? Presumably the equilibrium is determined where the net benefit of moving away is sufficiently small so as not to warrant the 'transactions cost', in this case the political and administrative costs of moving to a high or lower level of integration. The evidence from integration experiments to date is that very low levels of integration have been achieved in most cases, and failure or stagnation of efforts has characterised many cases, especially among developing countries. A large part of the reason for this would appear to be the high value placed on political independence in new states, especially in those countries that have until very recently been colonies. However, this would not explain the problems of Latin American integration arrangements. Apart from propensities to political instability, one ought to place considerable stress on the relative importance to their economies of trade and other economic relations external to the group. Notwithstanding internal barriers, the level of demand in the markets of developed countries insures that for most members of a free trade arrangement among developing countries internal trade will constitute a minor share of their total trade. In ASEAN, as in Latin America's larger groups, internal trade has not exceeded 20 per cent of total trade. This means that effective arrangement of the external economic relations of such regional groups must be a central concern. It is to the credit of ASEAN leaders that this priority has been more important in practice than for other economic groups in the developing world. The collective bargaining power of the ASEAN has thus characterised the group in its dealings with Pacific and European powers, and in international organisations such as GATT. Substantially greater scope for the exercise of external ASEAN initiative remains available.

When one compares the experience of groups of industrially-developed countries, it is evident that higher levels of integration have been contemplated in the legal instruments establishing these associations—for example, the Rome Treaty, the Canada–United States Free Trade Agreement and the Australia–New Zealand Closer Economic Relations Agreement. In all these instances, the difference in level of development, including basic social infrastructure, is not perceived to be large enough to lead to any general competitive disadvantage for any member of the group. However, the European Community has another unique characteristic. The political motivation, or perception, is that closer economic integration is a 'good thing' politically. This is not part of the thinking of governments in North America or the South Pacific.

The European integration movement, if one accepts the reasoning of the intellectual protagonists, was born during the postwar determination to avoid repetition of conflicts, at least in the western end of the continent. That desire was reinforced by the view that in unity there was a strength necessary to meet the challenge of a Stalin-led Eastern Europe. Hence a new European loyalty was fostered. New economic institutions were expected to establish a climate for the peace through strength. Not only was a substantial bureaucracy established in Brussels, but a European parliament in Strasbourg. Under these circumstances a decision to move to a full common market or economic union need not be driven by the economic benefits of such moves. The political benefits may be greater than such economic benefits, or even sufficient to compensate for economic or administrative costs. For countries in other groups, it appears that significant economic benefits are necessary to offset perceived or actual diminution of sovereignty, however modest in scope.

The drive for monetary union in the European Community illustrates the problem. It is often claimed that a fixed exchange rate helps trade relations, at least in the short run. On the other hand, it is argued that monetary policy as a stabilising force in an open market economy is more effective in a flexible exchange rate environment. The fiscal policy option may be more effective under a fixed exchange rate policy, but as recent experience attests, such a policy is less easily guided by economic considerations. This is especially so in federal states. Why does the European Community seek monetary union? Not only are there the objections cited above, but rigid exchange rates do not allow for the ease of adjustment to changes in competitive positions among member states. Large depressed regions such as Scotland and Southern Italy will have to depend on explicit fiscal transfers or factor migration rather than the automatic benefit of currency depreciation. The Common Agricultural Policy of the European Community, a system of highly controlled prices, heavily depends for its political success upon fixed 'green' exchange rates. As that policy has been highly protectionist, the rationale for fixed rate policy has become rather closely linked to protectionism.

A flexible rate system managed by countries with a commitment to economically meaningful long-term exchange values would seem preferable. If the objective is to reduce exchange rate volatility over relatively short-time frames, this can be achieved by intervention arrangements like the 'snake'. If the concern is about exchange rate overshooting caused by divergent national fiscal and monetary policies, why cannot these be addressed through direct efforts at policy coordination among European Community members? Questions proliferate about the need for much closer economic union. These questions are likely to emerge in considerable force in European consciousness as the possibilities of reintegration of the COMECON countries into 'capitalist' Europe are addressed.

Regionalism in the Pacific: Article XXIV or 'consensus initiatives'

Ever since the more policy-oriented economists began thinking about the Pacific as having some identity in international affairs (that is, since the late 1960s), the two focal points of the discussion have been the free trade areas and a Pacific OECD, early labelled an Organisation for Pacific Trade and Development (OPTAD).[4] The free trade area idea was set aside as impractical for three basic reasons:

1 the prior commitment and preference for GATT-based trade negotiations, especially since GATT parties had just at that time completed their first big post-convertibility reductions in trade barriers, and perceived scope for future multilateral success by the same means;
2 the formidable difficulty of applying the free trade arrangement to United States–Japan relations, given the actual and perceived differences in private and public institutional arrangements in the two countries, including the need to find a basis for trade in agricultural products;

3 the means of accommodating the interest of developing countries which from the time of the second PAFTAD meeting were recognised as essential players in any meaningful Pacific regional initiative; an issue complicated by the already recognised distinction between manufactures-exporting more advanced developing countries and the resource-rich members of ASEAN.

Before setting aside the free trade arrangement concept in the Pacific, it is worth noting that the concept has resurfaced and has been explored by several symposia or research institutions in the past two years. The two initiatives described in these studies have very different origins. The Institute of International Economics sponsored symposium (see Scholt, 1989; Holmes, 1989) brought together a series of suggestions by leading American politicians and officials including, for example, Ambassador Mike Mansfield, William Brock (former USTR), Secretary of State, James Baker, and various congressmen. All had one aim in common, the desire to bias trade negotiations towards liberalisation, both as a stimulus to the success of multilateral negotiations and as provision for fall-back or complementary action at the end of the Uruguay Round, no matter how successful. Some of the motivation, however, rose out of the temptation to achieve more by bilateralism especially in dealing with smaller Asian partners. Jeffrey Schott's evaluation of all this effort is negative, because of his fear that the timing could have adverse effects on the Uruguay Round. But even after that round, he senses that it would generate more heat than light in trade relations. This is partly because of the uneven bargaining power in any dealings between the United States and the smaller states of East Asia—Korea, Taiwan and even the whole ASEAN group. Clearly, an arrangement involving Japan would necessarily lead to a more equal bargain, but the process of achieving such a bargain would encounter the kind of obstacles already identified.

The Holmes book represents an exploratory study for the New Zealand government of the implications of an expansion of the Closer Economic Relations Agreement between Australia and New Zealand (ANZCERTA) to include Canada. Such a study became relevant because of two developments of the 1980s in the coming into force of ANZCERTA on 1 January 1983, and of the Canada–United States Free Trade Agreement (CUSFTA), signed 2 January 1988, and ratified by the Canadian government by legislation passed in December of the same year.

While the concept was given thoughtful consideration in Canada, it was noted at once that it was unlikely that the Canadian government would go much further, since Canada was in the throes of completing the Canada–United States deal, and then fighting the parliamentary battle that would in fact end only after a national election in November 1988. Considering the much greater significance of the North American deal in which Canada was to be more closely linked with a partner having ten times Canada's GNP, the transaction costs of negotiating South Pacific links clearly seemed out of line with the relative expected benefit.

On the New Zealand side, there must also have been qualms about the prospects of access to the Canadian market for at least one category of major importance, dairy products, given the long-term commitment to supply management marketing boards in Canada. Indeed, this latter concern has since been raised in respect to Canada's legitimacy as a member of the Cairns group.

It was also clear that Australian policy specialists consulted were not much interested in the idea of Canada as a new partner for ANZCERTA. Lying behind this initiative was the notion that the three party group would be only a 'stepping stone' to larger deals, first, combining Canada with ANZCERTA, then CUSFTA with 'CANZCERTA', and all of this with Japan, presumably with parallel negotiations of a general set of arrangements linking Pacific NIEs and ASEAN, and the South Pacific Islands in a 'not fully reciprocal' North–South arrangement. The role of other Pacific countries in such an evolving regional system (such as China and Mexico, for example) need not be elaborated, because it is clear that the toughest challenge on which the whole concept would depend for successful application are American–Japanese perceptions of its negotiability and its relative merits among trade strategy priorities that emerge after the Uruguay Round.

Two observations seem safe. First, if the negotiation concerned a Pacific regional arrangement rather than a purely bilateral Japan–United States one, it would likely have more appeal to both of them. At the same time, the complexities of negotiation would be increased, though probably not as much as the added benefits, given the greater importance of a North–South arrangement, especially in the Pacific, as an exemplary force for strengthening the global trade system. For both countries, the multilateral solution is clearly the first choice, so long as productive results can be anticipated.

A very different view of regionalism is one that places less emphasis on institution-building but more on information flows, consensus-forming and policy initiatives or negotiating alliances by a group of countries that wish to take a lead in solving international problems. Institutions might be established to this end, but their role might be much more limited, performing particular functions according to the changing needs of the times.

Various examples of regional or quasi-regional economic consensus-forming groups include the regional commissions of the United Nations, regional groups in particular economic sectors, such as shipping, development banking, OPEC, and the Cairns group in the GATT negotiations. More comprehensive forms of such institutions include the OECD (which is not exclusively regional but mainly trans-Atlantic), SELA (Systema Economico Latino Americano), and LAIA (the Latin American Integration Association), and the Southern African Development Council. These are agencies engaged in one or more of the following:

- gathering of regional information;
- sponsoring studies of aspects of economic development;
- providing a basis for consultation among governments with regional or other parallel interests in macroeconomic or microeconomic policy;

- promoting trade cooperation or other forms of economic cooperation;
- preparing and promoting negotiating positions; and
- establishing new institutional arrangements to perform the above functions or to supply specific services.

Some of the above organisations have affiliated private sector organisations, such as the OECD.

The record of the above institutions is mixed. Many such institutions, like the United Nations generally, are hampered by the bureaucratic constraints imposed by participating governments, and by the variously defined concepts of equitable sharing of the administration and other roles of the organisation.

An overall evaluation of the success of such organisations and activities is very difficult, partly because standards of achievement are not set in the same way as for a free trade area where a relatively clear time commitment for the achievement of free trade or other objectives is usually included. However, it is probably accurate to say that the looser commitment of the above organisations has enabled their survival, while many efforts to develop or sustain Article XXIV agreements have failed.

PECC and APEC

The nature of the Pacific Economic Cooperation Conference (PECC) and the newly emerging inter-governmental forum, Asia Pacific Economic Cooperation (APEC), are considered and compared to some of the other organisations mentioned in this section. Some preliminary judgements are made about the likely strengths and weaknesses of Pacific cooperation in these forms.

The growing role of Pacific regional governmental consultation was major news in 1989. It had roots in the work of PAFTAD and that of the Pacific Basin Economic Council (PBEC), respectively, the groups established by professional economists and business interests over twenty years ago as the first international institutional response to the spectacular growth of Japan.

During the 1970s both groups flourished. The economists group broadened to incorporate participants from all countries that are now part of the established core group, plus periodic representation from the Soviet Union and Latin American countries.[5] PBEC has had a similar evolution, except that the shared costs of its meetings and other obligations have made it more difficult for national business councils from Southeast Asia to participate.

During the 1970s there was also a growing awareness that the lack of regular or systematic consultation among Pacific governments was creating instability in expectations among governments and some unwelcome surprises (see Krause and Sekiguchi, 1980). This was partly the consequence of the increased complexity of commodity market behaviour associated with the food and oil crisis and resulting inflation and problems of coordinating macroeconomic policies.

In 1980, on the initiative of Prime Ministers Fraser of Australia and Ohira of Japan, advised by Sir John Crawford and Saburo Okita (at that time Foreign Minister of Japan), a Pacific Community Seminar was held in Canberra with delegations including government officials as well as business and academic representatives (mainly economists). The business and academic representatives were in many cases active members of PBEC and PAFTAD. After a period of political uncertainty about the desirability of tripartism including government, the series that is known as Pacific Economic Cooperation Conferences emerged, reaching PECC VII in November 1989. In what follows, only its accomplishments and prospects relevant to regional intergovernmental cooperation are summarised.

After the meeting in 1982 in Bangkok, there was more emphasis on interconference preparatory activity, at first mainly to supply more substantive inputs to the plenary meetings, but gradually the task forces switched to the search for an improved base in common information and analysis and consensus-building in policy issues. This characterised the work of the livestock and feedgrains group (now a task force) and the minerals and energy task force (now a forum). In the case of the Fisheries Task Force, the further step of promoting transfer of technology between developing country members has been achieved, notably between ASEAN and Pacific Island nations, and also involving Pacific Coast Latin America states.

The Trade Policy Task Force, beginning before the Fourth (Seoul) Plenary in 1985, focused increasingly on the search for a common negotiating ground and in March 1986 the first forum was held addressing some of the issues considered crucial to the forthcoming Uruguay Round. A statement on Trade Policy by the Standing Committee was drafted and circulated to governments in both PECC members and other major GATT member countries. On several subsequent occasions other statements have been issued, the latest being agreed by the Standing Committee in Auckland in November 1989 (see Appendix 14A.1). (Further comment on this is added later.)

The meeting in Osaka in 1988 witnessed the first output of an important new program—the Pacific Economic Outlook. The product of several meetings each year by macroeconomists of the region, reflecting the information and experience of national research organisations, it reports on the outlook for the year ahead, reconciling data and reporting on the analysis of the international and local factors that explain recent and current aggregate growth and stability indicators. The challenge to integrate data and analysis from fifteen economies is formidable. The result has been very well received.

The most recent additions to PECC working group activity include a Triple-T task force encompassing transport, telecommunications and tourism, a new one on science and technology, and a proposed working group on environmental issues. One new task force was approved on Tropical Forest Cooperation. At least one other topic related to environmental concerns of the region—draft net fishing was noted as an issue to be addressed by the Fisheries Task Force. Attention to more comprehensive environmental concerns such as ozone depletion and the greenhouse effect await further attention to the definition of practical role or the PECC in these areas.

The major problems of the PECC as a foundation for consensus-building in the Pacific arise from its failure to develop effective communications with government. Publication and dissemination of reports on PECC activities, making effective use of its Forum and Task Force outputs, has been limited and not very imaginative. Perhaps more important, the National Committees in most member states have demonstrated only limited success in building bridges with the relevant government officials, and especially with political leaders. Problems exist on both sides, such as the tendency of officials to rely primarily on sources internal to government for their positions on international relations and policies, and the preoccupation of the PECC Standing Committee with institutional development of the PECC, rather than assessment and support of its task force outputs in communications with government. The establishment of the modest new Secretariat for the PECC in Singapore, and especially the appointment of a full-time communications director will help. In addition, 'national' committee members, with the full support of their Standing Committee members, should develop regular contact with relevant government officials. This will serve two purposes—to present and explain PECC positions and to learn from government specific priorities on policy issues on which it would be useful to obtain PECC views and to attempt Pacific consensus-building.

The need for a more concerted role can be illustrated from the output of the Third Pacific Trade Policy Forum. What that forum attempted to achieve was a balanced treatment of issues of importance to PECC members. It was evident from the comments of trade policy specialists at the forum meeting in June 1989 and subsequently at the Auckland PECC VII November 1989 meeting that this objective had been served. It was not clear that strategy existed for carrying this message to governments; for example, that if a regional consensus on Pacific trade policy in the Uruguay Round were to be achieved some countries will have to make specific and substantive commitments on agricultural protection practices, others on textile products quotas, others on adequate intellectual property standards or rewards, some, perhaps all, on subsidy/countervail and antidumping practices, all on transparency and monitoring of national regulations on goods and services trade, and other GATT strengthening measures. No names need be mentioned.

Another problem of PECC has been the uneven role of the business sector in the work of the task forces and forums. Business participants have been most active in the Minerals and Energy Forum and the new Triple-T Task Force. In these cases it is significant that very large multinational enterprises are involved as 'producers'. These are the firms most geared-up for international activity. They have the largest stake in improved information flows and fostering improved investment environment. The same should not be expected in the agricultural or fisheries sectors. In trade policy discussions, the variety of issues is so great that specific business interests are likely to focus on one or two. Also significant, however, was the positive response from some national committees when asked for business representatives to present papers at the Trade Forum in Vancouver. Even in the case of the PECC Investment Conference, held in Bangkok in 1986, while many businessmen present could agree that investment incentives and disincentives should be harmonised, there was no follow-up to achieve this result, not even to foster improvement of Pacific investment data, which is notoriously weak and unreconciled.

In January 1989 Prime Minister Hawke of Australia proposed the initiation of a Pacific forum of economic ministers. After considerable diplomatic activity, the first ministerial meeting was held on 5-7 November 1989, in Canberra. It has acquired the name APEC—Asia Pacific Economic Cooperation—and at its first meeting twelve countries were represented. For political reasons, China, Taiwan and Hong Kong, which most PECC members wanted included, were not present. The meeting was sufficiently 'up beat' so that all participatory delegations agreed to at least two subsequent meetings, one in Singapore in 1990, and one in Seoul in 1991.

The important questions are two: does this governmental consultative group constitute a first step toward OPTAD? And how does its initial set of priorities and procedures relate to PECC?

On the first question, the jury will be out for some time. There is no evidence yet that there will be a Secretariat. Caution is everywhere, even on the extent to which APEC will rely on PECC inputs. However, such caution is characteristic of Asian diplomacy; witness the very slow but steady progress of ASEAN. Even the United States and Japan have shown great restraint but nevertheless fielded very strong representation in the Canberra meeting. MITI and Gaimusho managed to sublimate their conflict, undoubtedly because no very substantial commitments were demanded.

On the second question, it is interesting to note the agenda of initial activities. Clearly the most substantial was the agreement that Pacific Trade Ministers will meet twice in 1990, once in mid-year to consider the 'crunch' agenda of the Uruguay Round, presumably to consider a response to it and especially, if possible, to develop and present, publicly or privately, a consensus view. The second, even more daring, meeting is scheduled for Brussels in early December, just before the scheduled final meeting of the Uruguay Round negotiations. Success in contributing significantly to the final outcome would provide a substantial boost to a Pacific regional consensus-building role. Failure would be more ambiguous.

The relation of this effect to PECC will be tested by the decision of those organising the next PECC trade activity to hold a Trade Forum meeting (one or two months before the APEC trade ministers meeting in mid-1990), hoping to develop consensus views on the issues that appear by early 1990 to be crucial to the success of the GATT negotiations, to be directly relevant to the work of the APEC trade ministers. Close consultation between PECC Trade Forum members and their national government advisors to Trade Ministers is to be attempted. In the context of the rather constrained conditions of the crunch period in a trade negotiation, it is indeed a question of how 'full and frank' communication will be. Perhaps the 'leakiest' governments will determine the scope for a useful APEC–PECC collaboration.

Other activities contemplated by APEC are less sensitive. A few of these are listed in Appendix 14A.2—a section of the final statement emerging from the Canberra meeting.

In a first category, the Ministers declared their interest in improved data on trade and investment in the Pacific. The trade data can always be improved—for example, by adopting more common classification and valuation methods, a trend already underway. Much more is required to improve investment data, which is notoriously incomplete and inconsistent. A Canadian participant (A. E. Safarian of the University of Toronto) in the earlier work of the now defunct investment working group, prepared a brief paper illustrating how very different were the published investment statistics in various sources, and called for joint effort to correct this situation. The resources available were of course much too limited in any case, but the issue was apparently not sufficiently appealing to warrant even a concerted recommendation to governments or international agencies. This priority might need reconsideration now that APEC has endorsed it. Of course, it remains unclear how willing they are to 'pay the piper'.

Without belabouring the potential linkages between PECC and APEC, it can be noted that many elements in the 'work program' attached to the Summary Statement by Senator Gareth Evans, issued on 7 November 1989, after the Canberra APEC meeting, overlap with the current and projected activities of one or more of the PECC task forces or fora listed earlier. Thus, each PECC task force has the opportunity to provide substance to this rapidly sketched agenda. This will happen, however, only if PECC is capable of becoming stronger and more cohesive, and if APEC is willing to admit that governments have no monopoly on wisdom or the ability to exploit and support PECC's existing strengths and potential.

Since PECC is now well established, and APEC is still seen by some as a risky political venture, there is among those who have laboured to develop PECC an understandable hesitation to see PECC's future tied too closely to that of APEC. Will ministers be too preoccupied with the short-term political benefits? Can they resolve the problems of defining participation in APEC meetings so as to accommodate all the NIEs, including those whose political identity is more ambiguous than their economic identity? On the other hand, in some ways APEC can contribute to effectiveness of PECC's output of ideas. Clearly this will depend directly on the extent to which APEC ministers respect and use PECC ideas for enhanced Pacific cooperation. But there are some indirect effects as well. It is clear that in some governments, the commitment to Pacific cooperation will receive a substantially high priority if there is a governmental institution, however informal, involved. It is clear that the presence of three cabinet level participants from Washington at the Canberra meeting will raise the potential demand for the output of PECC activities in the United States government, and possibly also the supply of resources for the support of PECC. The same is true of the Canadian government, and possibly even that of Japan. Others may feel that political images should not be necessary to buttress the PECC process, but such images may indeed be significant in some of the larger countries less single-minded in their devotion to Pacific priorities.

Concluding judgements to date on the 'PECC and APEC' no matter how closely or loosely combined, include the following:

- In order to make PECC more effective, better communication of the useful outputs of the PECC task forces and fora is required, and must be assisted not only by the small new secretariat but also by National Committees; and more substantial networking of the existing research institutions of Pacific countries is necessary. They are already involved in the generation of research-based papers for task forces and fora. The main direct support for these activities is coming from aid agencies, and the Asian Development Bank. On many of the less-directly development-related activities of PECC, such as the Trade Forum and the Pacific Economic Outlook, resources available have been dedicated to financing meetings and some publication, but not to new contributions to the research base.
- To make PECC–APEC links effective, each national or member committee should develop regular links for each specialised (task force) subject between PECC persons with relevant expertise in that area and those in corresponding government agencies, hopefully on a basis that involves some continuity in those personal links.
- Member Committees should be able to devote time to more serious review of the policy issues the PECC and APEC groups are addressing, so that Standing Committee members (who chair Member Committees) as well as other members can more confidentially represent their Committees view in contacts with the national government and in the Standing Committee itself. On some occasions, these relations would benefit by the presence of ministers as well as senior officials for those issue-oriented discussions in National (or Member) Committee meetings.

CONCLUSIONS

The general judgement that leads out of our examination of current trends in the multilateral economic system and in regionalism is that it is counterproductive to try to pass competitive judgement on the relative merits of global and regional institutions or cooperative efforts. Our global institutions are imperfect, and so are our regional systems. Regional systems have had the added disadvantage of enhancing division. But they have the added advantage of demonstrating the leadership in means of harmonising policies and identifying new instruments of cooperation that can be available to all.

In the international monetary system it has been recognised with only limited reservations that the multilateral approach is predominant. Such is the mobility of capital, and the rapid response of short-term money to changes in short-term perceptions.

Trade is for the most part slow moving. Heavy regional concentration reinforces common concerns, especially among high or rising income economies. Those who the system serves well become committed to its strengthening. It may serve them through multilateral or regional systems; the chances are greater that both will be used in the present complex world economy. The only fundamental issue is how to ensure the compatibility or complementarity of these approaches.

Strengthening and broadening the GATT system offers benefits to small and large economies. For the smaller and medium-sized economies, an effective rules-based system moderates the economic power of the United States and the European Community. For large and small economies alike, the trading rules moderate the scope for strategic behaviour by domestic vested interests which are inimical to the public interest.

The Uruguay Round has already made some positive achievements, most notably in the acceptance of proposals for a Trade Policy Review Mechanism. However, much remains to be done to augment this GATT surveillance mechanism through the development of domestic transparency institutions. To be effective in democratic societies, the GATT must be much more than an international or even inter-governmental organisation. The trading system needs to grow stronger roots in national capitals and to develop deeper and broader public understanding of the economic costs of protection.

It appears to be possible to develop the framework for agreements on trade in services and intellectual property issues in the Uruguay Round. These framework agreements could provide a basis for further strengthening of the GATT dispute settlement process and limiting unilateral action under Section 301 type procedures in the United States and the European Community. Developing and giving effect to these multilateral frameworks undoubtedly will require further elaboration in various service sectoral arrangements and in other fora such as WIPO. The Pacific countries could play an important role in contributing to this process and plurilateral approaches involving the Pacific countries should be explored.

Breaking the managed trade nexus, through limiting the application of the antidumping and countervailing duty laws and the resort to safeguard measures, is likely to be much more difficult to achieve in the Uruguay Round. For the European Community, the antidumping laws provide a convenient device to ease internal digestion of the Europe 1992 agenda, while the United States seems preoccupied by an enforcement approach to the trade laws reflecting Congressional concerns about unfair foreign competition, which shaped the Omnibus Trade and Competitiveness Act of 1988. If developing countries are prepared to accept greater obligations in the trading system, that might contribute to genuine liberalisation of the trade laws, but their willingness to do this will depend on the willingness of developed countries to phase out as soon as possible the discriminating treatment of textile products. These issues are going to remain on international trade agenda beyond the Uruguay Round.

In the period beyond 1990, it is essential that both multilateral and regional efforts to maintain the world trading system be sustained. It seems improbable that either can be relied upon to perform the whole task. As suggested above, the multilateral system will continue to play a dominant role in defining the relevant principles, and detailing their relevance to new issues. GATT will also have to face the challenges concerning its interface with other international (and national) institutions, especially those bearing on the new issues (such as WIPO immigration laws, for example). Most importantly, GATT can and should become the major monitor of national practices affecting trade policy.

Regional arrangements of both the Article XXIV type and of the consensus-forming and specific issue alliance variety can apply GATT principles, carrying them further and sooner into practice than may be possible through multilateral negotiations alone.

To achieve a constructive outcome in the Uruguay Round and in subsequent multilateral efforts, the Pacific Trade Ministers and the PECC support system have an opportunity to make an important contribution, predisposed as they are to translating GATT principles into practice that meets the priorities of the variety of economies represented in the region. The PECC and APEC regional system, or PECC acting alone if APEC were not to survive, have the added advantage of an ability to link issues, since they focus not only on trade but on the macroeconomic data systems and policies, on private and infrastructural investment, on transfer of technology, and on the current range of natural resource and environmental issues. They thus contribute to an integrated view of the regional and world economy now acknowledged as essential to the trading system but also to a more coordinated approach among multilateral economic institutions, which is yet another stated aim of the Uruguay Round.

Appendixes

APPENDIX 5A A LONG-TERM ECONOMIC FORECAST FOR THE ASIA-PACIFIC REGION

One can only hesitantly advance an economic forecast for so long a period as a decade. A number of technical difficulties hamper the effort, most importantly the question of how to project changes in the real exchange rate, which is an endogenous variable.

The most straightforward way to go about this is to project each country's current GNP growth rate while holding current exchange rates vis-à-vis the dollar constant. The results of this projection appear in Table 5A.1 and indicate that the Asian countries will have economies roughly one-third the size of Japan's in the year 2000.

Table 5A.1 Relative GNP: case 1 (Japan = 1.00)

	1987	2000
Japan	1.00	1.00
United States	1.87	1.58
West Germany	0.46	0.35
NIEs	0.13	0.19
ASEAN	0.08	0.10

More sophisticated results are produced when an econometric model is used. Table 5A.2 sets out results obtained using a small-scale global econometric model developed by a group which included the author (see Takenaka and Ogawa (1987) for the model used for the simulation.) This model represents an advance on an earlier model developed by Ishii, McKibbin and Sachs (1985) and contains numerous special characteristics designed to facilitate analysis of the mechanism by which domestic macroeconomic policy exerts international effects. Exchange rates are determined endogenously on the assumption that market participants behave consistently with the rational expectations hypothesis.

As Table 5A.2 indicates, continued appreciation of the yen would produce a relative increase in the scale of the Japanese economy. The projection also forecasts an increase in the share of the world market held by the Asian nations. In contrast to the results of the projection shown in Table 5.1, the GNPs of the Asian countries decline in size relative to the scale of the Japanese GNP in Table 5.2. The divergence between cases 1 and 2 depends on how one projects changes in each country's real exchange rate. The projection in Table 5.1 also forecasts a stagnation in economic growth in Asian countries in response to a reduction in the United States current accounts deficit, highlighting the need for a new country to replace the United States as the primary export absorber.

Table 5A.2 Relative GNP: case 2 (Japan = 1.00)

	1987	1999
Japan	1.00	1.00
United States	1.87	1.44
OECD	2.23	1.95
NIEs	0.13	0.11
ASEAN	0.08	0.07

APPENDIX 9A SUPPLEMENTARY DATA

Table 9A.1 Malaysia, macroeconomic indicators

	1986	1987	1988
Population (million persons)	16.1	16.5	16.9
Labour force (million persons)	6.2	6.4	6.6
Employment (million persons)	5.7	5.9	6.1
Unemployment (million persons)	0.5	0.5	0.5
(percentage of labour force)	8.3	8.2	8.1

	1986		1987		1988	
National product	M$ billion	% change	M$ billion	% change	M$ billion	% change
GDP at 1978 prices	57.9	1.2	60.9	5.3	66.3	8.7
Agriculture, forestry and fishing	12.4	4.0	13.3	7.4	14.0	5.2
Mining and quarrying	6.4	7.5	6.4	0.1	6.9	6.6
Manufacturing	12.1	7.5	13.7	13.4	16.2	17.6
Construction	2.4	-14.0	2.1	-11.8	2.1	2.7
Services	24.7	-0.5	25.9	4.8	27.8	7.2
GNP at current prices	67.0	-7.1	74.7	11.7	85.8	14.8
GNP at 1978 prices	54.3	2.6	57.2	5.4	62.6	9.5
Aggregate domestic demand	49.7	-10.2	51.5	3.6	58.3	13.2
Private expenditure	34.3	11.5	35.2	2.4	40.7	15.7
Private consumption	26.4	-10.0	26.9	2.1	31.1	15.7
Private investment	8.0	-16.1	8.2	3.5	9.5	15.6
Public expenditure	16.2	-9.2	15.4	-4.9	16.7	8.6
Public consumption	9.5	1.3	9.7	1.5	10.1	4.9
Public investment	6.6	-20.9	5.7	-13.9	6.6	14.8
Gross national savings/GNP	27.4%		33.5%		33.1%	

(Table 9A.1 cont'd)

Balance of payments	1986 M$ billion	1987 M$ billion	1988 M$ billion
Merchandise balance	8.4	14.7	14.6
Exports	34.9	44.7	54.6
Imports	26.5	30.0	40.0
Services and transfers (net)	-9.0	-8.2	-9.8
Current account balance	-0.3	6.5	4.7
Current account balance (% of GNP)	-0.5	8.6	5.5
Central bank reserves (net)	16.5	19.4	18.3
Reserves as months of retained imports	7.2	7.4	5.1

Prices	1986 % change	1987 % change	1988 % change
Goods and non-factor services			
Export price index	-18.8	13.2	8.1
Import price index	-3.9	0.7	7.5
Change in terms of trade	-15.5	12.4	0.5
CPI (1980 = 100)	0.6	0.8	2.5
PPI (1978 = 100)	-6.2	3.7	7.4

	1986 average	1987 average	1988 average
Commodity prices			
Rubber (RSS 1, sen/kg.)	208	249	310
Palm oil (local delivery, $/tonne)	579	773	1 029
Crude petroleum (weighted average price, US$/barrel)	14.9	18.2	15.3

APPENDIXES

Table 9A.2 Malaysia, financial and monetary indicators

Federal government finance	1986 M$ billion	1987 M$ billion	1988 M$ billion
Revenue	19.5	18.1	22.0
Operating expenditure	20.1	20.2	21.8
Development expenditure	6.9	4.1	4.0
Overall financing		-6.2	-3.9
Overall financing deficit (% of GNP)	11.3	8.2	4.5
Total public sector development expenditure	10.8	6.5	10.6
Overall public sector financing deficit (% of GNP)	10.5	8.0	7.0
External debt	50.4	50.4	47.1
Federal government	28.3	27.6	25.9
NFPEs	14.6	16.8	15.9
Private sector	7.5	6.0	5.2
Debt service ratio (% of exports)	18.9	16.0	13.5

	End 1986		End 1987		End 1988	
Money and banking	M$ billion	% change	M$ billion	% change	M$ billion	% change
Money supply (M1)	14.0	2.8	15.8	13.0	18.1	14.6
Private sector liquidity (M2)	53.8	11.1	56.5	5.0	60.4	6.9
Broad money (M3)	68.2	8.6	70.6	3.5	76.2	7.9

	Change in 1986		Change in 1987		Change in 1988	
	M$ billion	%	M$ billion	%	M$ billion	%
Banking system deposits	5.5	7.5	4.3	5.5	7.4	8.9
Banking system loans	3.9	6.0	0.1	0.2	6.9	9.9
Agriculture	0.2	5.5	-0.2	-3.8	0.2	6.2
Manufacturing	0.4	3.7	0.1	0.8	2.4	23.1
Property sector	2.2	9.4	0.9	3.4	1.4	5.5
Loan–deposit ratio (end of year)	89.1%		84.6%		85.4%	
Commercial bank deposits	4.1	7.7	3.8	6.6	4.8	–
Commercial bank loans	3.3	6.8	-0.1	-0.3	4.3	–
Loan–deposit ratio (end of year)	91.6%		85.7%		85.8%	

(Table 9A.2 cont'd)

	End 1986 % per annum	End 1987 % per annum	End 1988 % per annum
Interest rates			
3-month inter-bank (annual average)	9.18	3.19	3.68
Commercial banks			
Fixed deposits 3 months	6.25	2.25/2.50	3.25
12 months	7.00	4.25	4.25
Savings deposits	6.00	3.50	3.50
Finance companies			
Fixed deposits 3 months	7.50	3.50	3.50/4.00
12 months	7.75	4.50	4.50
Savings deposits	7.00	5.50	4.50
Base lending rate (BLR)			
Commercial banks	10.00	7.50	7.00
Finance companies	11.50	9.25	9.00
Treasury bill rate (91 days)	3.85	3.22	4.26
20-year government securities	8.50	6.82	6.45
Movement of ringgit	1986	1987	1988
Change against composite	-13.7%	-8.9%	-6.2%
Change against SDR	-16.7%	-10.0%	-3.2%
Change against US$	-7.2%	4.4%	-8.1%

Source: Bank Negara Malaysia.

APPENDIXES

Table 9A.3 Balance of payments (million Malaysian dollars)

	1986	1987	1988
Merchandise exports f.o.b	34 970	44 733	54 596
Merchandise imports f.o.b.[a]	26 592	30 030	40 039
Merchandise balance	8 378	14 703	14 557
Services receipts	6 810	8 137	9 156
Services payments[b]	15 600	16 734	19 421
Services balance	-8 790	-8 597	-10 265
Transfers (net)	96	348	428
Goods, services and transfers	-316	6 454	4 720
Official long-term capital (net)	2 124	-2 592	-4 979
Federal government loans	1 611	-2 438	-3 095
NFPEs loans	20	-115	-1 862
Other	493	-39	-22
Corporate investment (net)	1 262	1 065	1 700
Long-term capital (net)	3 386	-1 527	-3 279
Basic balance	3 070	4 927	1 441
Private financial capital (net)	-47	-2 491	-2 893
Commercial banks	-1 050	-2 320	-2 493
Other	1 003	-171	-400
Errors and omissions (net)	1 322	457	348
Overall balance	4 345	2 893	-1 104
Allocation of SDRs	0	0	0
IMF resources	-263	0	0
Central bank reserves[c]	-4 082	-2 893	1 104
SDRs	-73	-55	-30
IMF	-85	-33	-87
Gold and foreign exchange	-3 924	-2 805	1 221

Notes: a Includes imports for offshore installations of the petroleum industry which are not included in trade data.
b Includes the undistributed earnings of foreign direct investment companies. The counterpart of these earnings is shown as an inflow of direct re-investment capital under private long-term corporate investment.
c Accumulation of reserves is indicated as a minus (-) sign.

Source: Bank Negara Malaysia.

Table 9A.4 Exchange rate arrangements as of 31 March 1989

Pegged				
Single currency			Currency composite	
US dollar	French franc	Other	SDR	Other
Afghanistan[c]	Liberia	Benin	Bhutan	Burundi	Algeria
Antigua and	Nicaragua[c]	Burkina Faso	(Indian rupee)	Iran, Islamic	Austria
Barbuda	Oman	Cameroon	Kiribati	Rep. of	Bangladesh[c]
Bahamas[c]	Panama	Central	(Australian	Libya[e]	Botswana
Barbados	Peru[c]	African Rep.	dollar)	Myanmar	Cape Verde
Belise	St. Kitts	Chad	Lesotho[c]	Rwanda	Cyprus
Djibouti	and Nevis	Comoros	(South	Seychelles	Fiji
Dominica	St. Lucia	Congo	African	Zambia	Finland[f]
El Salvador[c]	St. Vincent	Cote d'Ivoire	rand)		Hungary
Ethiopia	Sierra Leone	Equatorial	Swaziland		Iceland[g]
Grenada	Sudan[c]	Guinea	(South		Israel[h]
Guatemala	Suriname	Gabon	African		Jordan
Guyana[c]	Syrian Arab Rep.	Mali	rand)		Kenya
Haiti	Trinidad and	Niger	Tonga		Kuwait
Honduras[c]	Tobago	Senegal	(Australian		Malawi
Iraq	Uganda[c]	Togo	dollar)		Malaysia[g]
	Vietnam[c]				Malta
	Yemen Arab				Mauritius
	Rep.				Nepal
	Yemen, People's				Norway
	Democratic				Papua
	Rep.				New Guinea
				|Poland[c]
				|Romania
				|Sao Tome
				|and Principe
				|Solomon
				|Islands
				|Somalia
				|Sweden[i]
				|Tannzania
				|Thailand
				|Vanuatu
				|Western
				|Samoa
				|Tanzania
				|Thailand
				|Vanuatu
				|Western
				|Samoa
				|Zimbabwe

(Table 9.A4 cont'd)

	Flexibility limited vis-à-vis a single currency or a group of currencies		More flexible		
Single currency[a]	Cooperative arrangements[b]	Adjusted according to a set of indicators	Other managed floating	Independently floating
Bahrain[d]	Belgium[c]	Brazil	Argentina[c]	Australia
Qatar[d]	Denmark	Chile[c]	China,	Bolivia
Saudi Arabia[d]	France	Colombia	People's	Canada
United Arab Emirates[d]	Germany, Fed. Rep. of	Madagascar	Rep. of[c]	Gambia
	Ireland	Portugal	Costa Rica[c]	Ghana[c]
	Italy		Dominican Republic	Japan
	Luxembourg[c]		Ecuador	Lebanon
	Netherlands		Egypt[c]	Maldives
	Spain		Greece	New Zealand
			Guinea	Nigeria
			Guinea-Bissau	Paraguay
			India[i]	Philippines
			Indonesia	South Africa[c]
			Jamaica	Spain
			Korea	United Kingdom
			Lao People's Dem. Rep.	United States
			Mauretania	Uruguay
			Mexico[c]	Venezuela
			Morocco	Zaire
			Mozambique	
			Pakistan	
			Singapore	
			Sri Lanka	
			Tunisia	
			Turkey	
			Yugoslavia	

Notes: Current information relating to Democratic Kampuchea is unavailable.

a In all cases listed in this column, the US dollar was the currency against which exchange rates showed limited flexibility.

b This category consists of countries participating in the exchange rate mechanism of the European Monetary System. In each case, the exchange rate is maintained within a margin on 2.25 per cent around the bilateral central rates against other participating currencies, with the exception of Italy, in whose case the exchange rate is maintained within a margin of 6 per cent.

c Member maintains multiple exchange arrangements involving more than one exchange rate. The arrangement shown is that maintained in the major market.

d Exchange rates are determined on the basis of a fixed relationship to the SDR, within margins of up to +/-7.25 per cent. However, because of the maintenance of a relatively stable relationship with the US dollar, these margins are not always observed.

e The exchange rate is maintained within margins of up to +/- 7.5 per cent.

f The exchange rate is maintained within margins of up to +/- 2.0 per cent.

g The exchange rate is maintained within margins of up to +/- 2.25 per cent.

h The exchange rate is maintained within margins of up to +/- 3.0 per cent.

i The exchange rate is maintained within margins of up to +/- 5.0 per cent on either side of a weighted composite of the currencies of the main trading partners.

Source: IMF, *1989 Annual Report.*

Table 9A.5 US dollar vis-à-vis other currencies (end period)

	yen	DM	sterling	won	S$	M$
1973	280.00	2.7030	2.3232	397.5	2.4861	2.4520
1980	203.00	1.9590	2.3850	659.9	2.0935	2.2224
1981	219.90	2.2548	1.9080	700.5	2.0475	2.2423
1984	251.10	3.1480	1.1565	827.4	2.1780	2.4250
1985	200.50	1.9408	1.4445	890.2	2.1050	2.4265
1988	125.85	1.7803	1.8095	684.11	1.9462.	2.7153

Source: Bank Negara Malaysia.

Table 9A.6 Appreciation(+)/depreciation(-) of US dollar (end period)

	yen	DM	sterling	won	S$	M$
1973–80	-27.5	-27.5	-2.6	66.0	-15.8	9.4
1981–84	14.2	39.6	65.0	18.1	6.4	8.1
1985–88	-37.2	-8.3	-20.2	-23.2	-7.5	11.9

Source: Bank Negara Malaysia.

APPENDIXES

Table 9A.7 Exchange rate of ringgit against selected currencies

	M$ per foreign currency[a]								
	Comp.	US$	S$	sterling	yen	DM	SF	SDR	$A	C$[b]
End 1980	98.64	2.2175	1.0590	5.2988	1.0924	1.1271	1.2455	2.8282	2.6194	1.8618
End 1981	103.49	2.2433	1.0955	4.2903	1.0201	0.9955	1.2466	2.6111	2.5294	1.8925
End 1982	105.20	2.3185	1.0996	3.7595	0.9858	0.9744	1.1581	2.5576	2.2736	1.8813
End 1983	107.53	2.3387	1.0994	3.4016	1.0083	0.8606	1.0745	2.4485	2.1082	1.8750
End 1984	109.50	2.4263	1.1142	2.8254	0.9663	0.7718	0.9377	2.3783	2.0092	1.8384
End 1985	100.04	2.4135	1.1466	3.4755	1.2048	0.9832	1.1649	2.6510	1.6483	1.7302
End 1986	86.38	2.6015	1.1959	3.8242	1.6250	1.3355	1.5980	3.1821	1.7307	1.8815
End 1987	78.65	2.4915	1.2461	4.6679	2.0347	1.5744	1.9472	3.5346	1.7964	1.9085
End 1988	73.81	2.7125	1.3939	4.8683	2.1548	1.5192	1.7931	3.6502	2.3192	2.2755
1988[c]										
Jan	78.54	2.5560	1.2663	4.5523	2.0103	1.5338	1.8864	3.4925	1.8270	2.0011
Feb	77.93	2.5841	1.2853	4.5868	2.0165	1.5327	1.8642	3.5170	1.8617	2.0443
Mar	77.38	2.5638	1.2790	4.8136	2.0499	1.5443	1.8707	3.5567	1.8929	2.0755
Apr	77.01	2.5745	1.2861	4.8272	2.0671	1.5424	1.8589	3.5635	1.9524	2.0922
May	77.25	2.5877	1.2817	4.7813	2.0690	1.5009	1.8002	3.5434	2.0725	2.0894
June	79.09	2.6050	1.2760	4.4884	1.9728	1.4381	1.7361	3.4141	2.0697	2.1447
July	78.56	2.6348	1.2930	4.5424	1.9848	1.4101	1.6935	3.4159	2.1186	2.1791
Aug	78.00	2.6695	1.3095	4.5031	1.9851	1.4269	1.6914	3.4388	2.1394	2.1572
Sept	77.80	2.6795	1.3132	4.5118	1.9916	1.4238	1.6815	3.4576	2.0986	2.1985
Oct	75.30	2.6705	1.3360	4.7348	2.1304	1.5101	1.7929	3.5942	2.2033	2.2174
Nov	73.68	2.6745	1.3769	4.9411	2.1953	1.5420	1.8445	3.6544	2.3494	2.2411
Dec	73.81	2.7125	1.3939	4.8683	2.1548	1.5192	1.7931	3.6502	2.3192	2.2755
1989[d]										
Jan	74.23	2.7294	1.4131	4.8160	2.1135	1.4679	1.7281	3.5802	2.4252	2.3114
Feb	73.70	2.7345	1.4172	4.7602	2.1516	1.4971	1.7552	3.6136	2.1789	2.2727
Mar	74.88	2.7495	1.4037	4.6404	2.0763	1.4548	1.6669	3.5543	2.2547	2.3118
Apr	76.20	2.6959	1.3836	4.5641	2.0354	1.4370	1.6246	3.4930	2.1364	2.2674
May	78.29	2.7173	1.3878	4.2661	1.9032	1.3640	1.5680	3.3792	2.0340	2.2485
June	78.90	2.7034	1.3751	4.1835	1.8780	1.3803	1.6109	3.3695	2.0379	2.2634
July	78.28	2.6630	1.3618	4.4153	1.9234	1.4214	1.6513	3.4285	2.0031	2.2504
Aug	78.78	2.6930	1.3695	4.2751	1.8836	1.3912	1.6160	3.3734	2.0681	2.2953
Sept	77.84	2.6892	1.3720	4.3518	1.9305	1.4381	1.6595	3.4417	2.0864	2.2781
Oct	78.09	2.6964	1.3782	4.2555	1.8935	1.4667	1.6748	3.4455	2.1115	2.2964
Nov	77.73	2.7040	1.3860	4.2331	1.8903	1.5103	1.6969	3.4820	2.1128	2.3198

(Table 9A.7 cont'd)

	\multicolumn{9}{c}{Annual change in percentage[e]}
	Comp.	US$	S$	sterling	yen	DM	SF	SDR	$A	C$
End 1980	-4.0	-1.3	-4.2	-8.2	-16.4	12.5	10.2	1.9	—	—
End 1981	4.9	-1.2	-3.3	23.5	7.1	13.2	-0.1	8.3	3.6	-1.6
End 1982	1.7	-3.2	-0.4	14.1	3.5	2.2	7.6	2.1	11.3	0.6
End 1983	2.2	-0.9	.0	10.5	-2.2	13.2	7.8	4.5	7.8	0.3
End 1984	1.8	-3.6	-1.3	20.4	4.3	11.5	14.6	3.0	4.9	2.0
End 1985	-8.6	0.5	-2.8	-18.7	-19.8	-21.5	-19.5	-10.3	21.9	6.3
End 1986	-13.7	-7.2	-4.1	-9.1	-25.9	-26.4	-27.1	-16.7	-4.8	8.0
End 1987	-8.9	4.4	-4.0	-18.1	-20.1	-15.2	-17.9	-10.0	-3.7	-1.4
End 1988	-6.2	-8.1	-10.6	-4.1	-5.6	3.6	8.6	-3.2	-22.5	-16.1
1988[c]										
Jan	-0.1	-2.5	-1.6	2.5	1.2	2.6	3.2	1.2	-1.7	-4.6
Feb	-0.9	-3.6	-3.0	1.8	0.9	2.7	4.5	0.5	-3.5	-6.6
Mar	-1.6	-2.8	-2.6	-3.0	-0.7	1.9	4.1	-0.6	-5.1	-8.0
Apr	-2.1	-3.2	-3.1	-3.3	-1.6	2.1	4.8	-0.8	-8.8	-8.8
May	-1.8	-3.7	-2.8	-2.4	-1.7	4.9	8.2	-0.2	-13.3	-8.7
June	0.6	-4.4	-2.3	4.0	3.1	9.5	12.2	3.5	-13.2	-11.0
July	-0.1	-5.4	-3.6	2.8	2.5	11.7	15.0	3.5	-15.2	-12.4
Aug	-0.8	-6.7	-4.8	3.7	2.5	10.3	15.1	2.8	-16.0	-11.5
Sept	-1.1	-7.0	-5.1	3.5	2.2	10.6	15.8	2.2	-14.4	-13.2
Oct	-4.3	-6.7	-6.7	-1.4	-4.5	4.3	8.6	-1.7	-18.5	-13.9
Nov	-6.3	-6.8	-9.5	-5.5	-7.3	2.1	5.6	-3.3	-23.5	-14.8
Dec	-6.2	-8.1	-10.6	-4.1	-5.6	3.6	8.6	-3.2	-22.5	-16.1
1989[d]										
Jan	0.6	-0.6	-1.4	1.1	2.0	3.5	3.8	2.0	-4.4	-1.6
Feb	-0.1	-0.8	-1.6	2.3	0.1	1.5	2.2	1.0	6.4	0.1
Mar	1.4	-1.3	-0.7	4.9	3.8	4.4	7.6	2.7	2.9	-1.6
Apr	3.2	0.6	0.7	6.7	5.9	5.7	10.4	4.5	8.6	0.4
May	6.1	-0.2	0.4	14.1	13.2	11.4	14.4	8.0	14.0	1.2
June	6.9	0.3	1.4	16.4	14.7	10.1	11.3	8.3	13.8	0.5
July	6.1	1.9	2.4	10.3	12.0	6.9	8.6	6.5	15.8	1.1
Aug	6.7	0.7	1.8	13.9	14.4	9.2	11.0	8.2	12.1	-0.9
Sept	5.5	0.9	1.6	11.9	11.6	5.6	8.1	6.1	11.2	-0.1
Oct	5.8	0.6	1.1	14.4	13.8	3.6	7.1	5.9	9.8	-0.9
Nov	5.3	0.3	0.6	15.0	14.0	0.6	5.7	4.8	9.8	-1.9

Notes: a With the exception of composite and yen which are expressed in terms of M$ per 100 units of composite and yen.

b The exchange rate for C$ is based on customers' rate.

c Refer to percentage change over end 1987 level.

d Refer to percentage change over end 1988 level.

e Calculated on basis of exchange rates prevailing at end of previous year. Minus (-) sign indicates depreciation; plus(+) sign indicates appreciation.

Source: Bank Negara Malaysia.

APPENDIXES

Table 9A.8 Inter-bank money market rates, 3 monthly (per cent per annum)

	1986	1987	1988	1989 (1 November)
Malaysia	6.1	3.5	4.3	5.2
Industrial countries				
United States	5.9	7.8	9.2	8.4
LIBOR (US$)	6.7	7.9	9.3	8.5
United Kingdom	11.1	8.9	13.0	15.0
Japan	4.4	4.5	4.4	6.6
ASEAN/Pacific countries				
Australia	14.3	11.1	14.6	17.4
New Zealand	22.9	17.4	14.2	13.8
Hong Kong	4.4	1.5	9.1	8.1
Singapore	3.6	3.2	5.3	5.4
Thailand	6.5	6.0	11.5	11.3
Indonesia	15.5	16.5	17.0	17.0

Source: Bank Negara Malaysia.

Table 9A.9 Current account (US dollars)

	United States (billion)	Germany (billion)	Japan (billion)	United Kingdom (million)	Korea (million)	Singapore (million)	Malaysia (million)
1972	-5.78	1.16	6.67	503	-362	-495	-248
1973	7.07	5.08	-0.12	-2 464	-299	-519	105
1974	1.92	10.58	-4.72	-7 755	-2 019	-1 021	-543
1975	18.13	4.41	-0.69	-3 608	-1 889	-584	-496
1976	4.17	3.70	3.74	-1 593	-310	-567	580
1977	-14.49	3.96	10.91	-139	12	-295	436
1978	-15.45	9.14	16.53	1 867	-1 085	-453	108
1979	-0.97	-5.63	-8.74	-1 117	-4 151	-736	929
1980	1.84	-13.99	-10.75	7 309	-5 321	-1 563	-285
1981	6.87	-3.40	4.77	14 114	-4 646	-1 470	-2 486
1982	-8.64	4.98	6.85	8 041	-2 650	-1 296	-3 601
1983	-46.29	5.40	20.80	5 831	-1 606	-610	-3 497
1984	-107.14	9.75	35.00	2 608	-1 372	-385	-1 671
1985	-115.16	16.98	49.17	4 765	-887	-4	-613
1986	-138.50	39.85	85.83	158	4 617	542	52
1987	-143.08	45.63	87.00	-4 913	9 854	553	2 572
1988	-126.19	48.58	79.59	-26 089	14 161	1 660	1 884

Source: IMF, *International Financial Statistics*, various issues.

APPENDIX 12A.1 INDEX OF TRADE INTENSITY

The index of intensity of country i's export trade with country j is defined by:

$$I_{ij} = (X_{ij} / X_i)/(M_j / W)$$

where $X_i [= \Sigma\, iX_{ij}]$, $M_j [= \Sigma_j X_{ij}]$, and $W [=\Sigma\, i\, \Sigma_j X_{ij}]$ represents the total exports of country i, the total imports of country j, and the total volume of world trade, respectively. The weighted average of I_{ij} for all import markets and for all export sources amounts to unity. Thus, above-unity I_{ij} gives a more than average intensive trade relationship between countries i and j, whereas below-unity I_{ij} gives a less than average intensive trade relationship between the two.

APPENDIX 12A.2 INDEX OF REVEALED COMPARATIVE ADVANTAGE

We assume a country's comparative advantage is reflected or revealed in its exports to the world market. The index of revealed comparative advantage (RCA) of exports, RCAX, is defined by Balassa (1965) as the country's commodity composition of exports vis-à-vis that of total world trade. Similarly, we can define the index of comparative disadvantage as the country's import composition vis-à-vis the world total, which may be referred to as the revealed comparative disadvantage of imports (RCAM):

$$RCAX_{ih} = (X_{ih}/X_i)/(W_h/W)$$
$$RCAM_{ih} = (M_{jh}/M_j)/(W_h/W)$$

where

- X_i (X_{ih}) is country i's export of all commodities (commodity h);
- M_j (M_{jh}) is country j's import of all commodities (commodity h); and
- W (W_h) is world trade in all commodities (commodity h).

APPENDIX 12A.3 INDEX OF TRADE COMPLEMENTARITY

The index of trade complementarity of exporting country i with importing country j is defined as the covariance of $RCAX_i$ and $RCAM_j$ minus unity:

$$C_{ij} = \Sigma_h\, W(W_h/W)*(RCAX_{ih}-1)*(RCAM_{jh}-1) - 1$$
$$= \Sigma_h\, W(W_h/W)* RCAX_{ih} * RCAM_{jh}$$

This coincides with the hypothetical trade intensity between two countries when trade is solely determined by comparative advantage and disadvantage. Then country i's export of commodity h to country j is expected to be the product of country j's total import of this commodity multiplied by the share of country i in the world trade of the same commodity, which is expressed as:

Xijh = Σjh*(Xkh/Wh)

where Xijh is the expected value of country i's export of commodity h to country j, which is rewritten as:

Xijh = (Xih*Mjh)/Wh

The expected value of total exports from country i to country j is defined as the sum of expected values of all commodities:

Xij = ΣhXijh

The expected intensity of trade is obtained by replacing the expected value of trade for the actual one in formula (1), which coincides with the weighted product of RCAXi and RCAMj in formula (2) as follows:

Cij = (ΣhXijh/Xi)/(Mj/W)
    = Σh(Xih/Xi)*(Mjh/Mj)/(Wh/W)
    = Σh(Xih/Xi)*(Mjh/Mj)/(Wh/W)
    = Σ(Wh/W)*[(Xih/Xi)/(Wh/W)]*[Mjh/Mj)/(Wh/W)]
    = Σh(Wh/W)*RCAXih*RCAMjh

APPENDIX 12A.4 REGRESSION ANALYSIS OF TRADE FLOWS

The bilateral trade flow (Xij) is regressed on the distance (Dij) and complementarity (Cij) between countries i and j, GDPs of the two countries, and dummy variables which add to or deduct from standardised trade among selected countries:

ln Xij = a_0 + a_1 ln Dij + a_2 ln Cij + a_3 ln GDPi + a_4 ln GDPj, + a_5 DMJ + a_6DMUS + a_7 DSP + a_8 DHK

where

DMJ: dummy variable for Japan's imports, = 1 if j = Japan and 0 otherwise;
DMUS: dummy variable for United States imports, = 1 if j = United States and 0 otherwise:
DSP: dummy variable for Singapore, = 1 if i or j is Singapore and 0 otherwise;
DHK: dummy variable for Hong Kong, = 1 if i or j is Hong Kong and 0 otherwise.

Coefficients are estimated by log-linear least squares (LLS) based on cross-country (14 times 14) data for individual years.

Bilateral trade balance is derived from the regression equation above as:

ln Xij–ln Xji = $_2$ (ln Cij–ln Cji)
  + (a_3–a_4)(ln GDPi–ln GDPj)
  - a_5 if i = Japan and j = United States

- a_6 if i = United States and j = Japan
- $a_5 + a_6$ if i = Japan and j = United States
+ $a_5 - a_6$ if i = United States and j = Japan
+ 0   if i, j = Japan, United States

APPENDIX 12A.5 TRADE STATISTICS

Trade data in this chapter are basically compiled from the AIDXT, the computerised trade data search system of the Institute of Developing Economies (IDE), Tokyo, which in its turn uses two sources — UN, *Commodity Trade Statistics* (Series D), and OECD, *Foreign Trade Statistics* (Series C). As a supplement, Taiwan trade statistics are also included.

The world totals by commodity at 3-digit SITC are necessary for estimating RCAXs and RCAMs. Since they cannot be compiled from the system because of the country coverage, they are collected from Volume 2 of the UN's *International Trade Statistics Yearbook* (various issues), from which world total trade of all commodities is also derived. For 1987, the UN's *The Monthly Bulletin of Statistics* (MBS) May 1989 was used.

Commodity level world totals need some adjustment. The UN's *International Trade Statistics Yearbook*, Volume 2, does not cover centrally planned economies (CPE); when aggregated to the SITC 1-digit level, they are short of UN estimates shown in the same volume and the MBS. An exercise was constructed, therefore, to erase the gap by applying a multiplier to individual 3-digit totals at each 1-digit level. The underlying assumption, of course, is that the CPEs as a group have an identical commodity structure for export at the 1-digit level with the world, which is not very plausible. The exercise was carried out, however, since the multipliers differ from one SITC 1-digit group to the next and it was judged to be a more adequate way of estimating the 3-digit world totals.

For some countries, commodity-wise export and import data for 1987 are not available. For Korea, therefore, Series D was consulted. For Indonesia, Malaysia, the Philippines and Thailand, however, 1986 figures were used as substitutes. Thus the Cij estimates of their exports may contain distortions.

APPENDIX 13A OUTLINE OF THE ASIA–PACIFIC MSG MODEL

This appendix provides a brief description of the principal features of the Asia–Pacific MSG model (APMSG). A full discussion of the specification of the OECD countries is available in McKibbin (1989) and for the developing country blocks in Sundberg (1990). Here we focus on the structure of the developing country blocks and on differences from MSG2. The APMSG model differs significantly from the MSG2 model, particularly with regard to treatment of the developing countries to allow interaction with the industrialised country blocks. In addition, specification of trade relations is quite different, and hence the model's results are not directly comparable with MSG2.

APMSG is a dynamic general equilibrium model of a seven-region world economy. There are three developed country blocs: the United States, Japan and the rest of the OECD countries (ROECD). Developing countries have been divided into three regions comprising the export-led high growth economies of East Asia (the Asian NIES), the middle-income developing countries of ASEAN (Indonesia, Malaysia, the Philippines and Thailand), and the rest of the developing world (ROW). The member countries of OPEC are also treated as a separate bloc (excluding Indonesia).

The behavioural structure of the developed country blocs in the model are characterised by: one, efficient asset markets in which asset prices are determined assuming risk neutrality, intertemporal arbitrage conditions, and rational expectations; two, intertemporally profit maximising firms in which capital stocks adjust according to a Tobin's 'q' model of investment; and three, different wage–price dynamics in the United States (nominal rigidities), Japan (market clearing with a one-period lag), and the ROECD (slow market clearing behaviour, with hysteretic characteristics).

The model solves for a full intertemporal equilibrium in a linearised form. Both the developing and developed regions carefully observe the key stock–flow relationships in the world economy. Government and current account deficits accumulate into public debt or changes in the net foreign asset position, serviced at variable rates of interest, and physical investment accumulates into capital stocks.

The Asian NIEs and ASEAN blocs share similar structures. There are four productive sectors, comprising light manufacturing (X), heavy manufacturing (M), agriculture and mining (R), and services (S). For the purposes of trade classification these may be thought of as: one, consumer manufactures and industrial intermediaries; two, capital goods; three, primary commodities and minerals; and four, non-tradeables. Output from the first three of these sectors is traded. The principal behavioural features of the developing country blocks are presented below.

Production

The basis for aggregate supply in the economy is the representative firm in each sector which maximises revenues. Production is specified using a nested, two-input CES production function of value-added inputs and an intermediate input bundle (see Bruno and Sachs [1985] for a careful discussion of this production specification).

$$Q^i = [\beta_{1i}(V^i)^{\rho_{1i}} + (1-\beta_{1i})(N^i)^{\rho_{1i}}](\frac{1}{1-\rho_{1i}}) \quad (1)$$

$$\beta_{1i} = \frac{1}{1 + \frac{(V^i)}{N^i}^{-\frac{1}{\sigma_i}} \frac{(P_n^i)}{P_v^i}} \quad (2)$$

$$V^i = [\beta_{2i}(K^i)^{\rho 2i} + (1 - \beta_{2i}) \cdot (L^i)^{\rho 2i}] (\tfrac{1}{1-\rho 2i}) \quad (3)$$

$$N^i = [\beta_{3i}(X^i)^{\rho 3i} + \beta_{4i}(M^i)^{\rho 3i} + \beta_{5i}(R^i)^{\rho 3i} + \beta_{6i}(S^i)^{\rho 3i} + \beta_{7i}(IM^i)^{\rho 3} \quad (4)$$
$$+ (1 - \beta_{3i} - \beta_{4i} - \beta_{5i} - \beta_{6i} - \beta_{7i}) \cdot (E^i)^{\rho 3i}] (\tfrac{1}{1-\rho 3i})$$

where V_i = value added in sector i
K_i = capital stock of sector i
X_i = X input to the ith sector, for sectors X, M, R, S
IM_i = imported inputs to sector i
E_i = oil input to sector i

Solution of this yields the familiar derived demand for labour and intermediate inputs equating the marginal product of each input to its marginal cost. Total labour demand is the sum of the sectoral demands. Imported inputs to production are a composite good made up of imports from each trading partner. Imports are treated as imperfect substitutes in production, and hence enter the production function as a separate, non-competing input. This is the familiar Armington (1969) assumption.

Investment

The capital stock in each industry is a function of the current period level of physical investment and the rate of depreciation. A composite 'investment good' is specified with inputs from each sector as well as imported capital goods.

$$K^i_{t+1} = J^i_t + K^i_t \cdot (1 - \delta - \eta) \quad \text{for all i, i = X, M, R, S} \quad (5)$$

$$I_j = (I_{jx})^{\kappa 1} (I_{jm})^{\kappa 2} (I_{js})^{\kappa 3} (I_{jim})^{(1-\kappa 1-\kappa 2-\kappa 3)} \quad (6)$$

$$I_{im} = (I_{us})^{\kappa} \cdot (I_{japan})^{\kappa 5} \cdot (I_{roecd})^{(1-\kappa 4-\kappa 5)} \quad (7)$$

where J_i = net investment in sector i
I_j = gross investment (inclusive of adjustment costs)
I_{ji} = inputs of goods i to gross investment in sector j
δ = rate of capital depreciation (equal in all i)
η = the rate of population growth

Gross fixed capital formation is determined by two terms: a simple static expectations version of Tobin's 'marginal q' and a term representing cash flow constraints on firms. Weights on these terms (α and gamma) need not sum to unity.

$$q_{it} = \frac{MPK_{it} \cdot P_{it}}{P^I_t \cdot r_t}; \quad \text{where } MPK_{it} = \frac{\gamma Q_{it}}{\gamma V_{it}} \cdot \frac{\gamma V_{it}}{\gamma K_{it}} \quad (8)$$

$$I_{it} = \alpha_i \cdot [\frac{(q_{it} - 1)}{\Phi_0}] \cdot K_{it} + \gamma_i \cdot \frac{(Q_{it} - L_{it} \cdot W - Pn_{it} \cdot N_{it})}{P^I_t} \quad (9)$$

$$PI \cdot I^i = [1 + (\frac{\Phi_0}{2}) \cdot (\frac{J^i}{K^i})] \cdot Pj \cdot J^i \quad (10)$$

Gross investment (I_j) includes adjustment costs, and P^I is the log price of the investment good using a simple weighted average of its log input prices. Gross investment differs from net investment by adjustment costs. A rising marginal cost of investment, due to installation costs, is a linear function of the rate of investment.

Savings and consumption

Savings are specified as a positive function of disposable income, the growth rate of GNP, the change in the terms of trade, and the real domestic interest rate. The specification and coefficient estimates are taken from Fry (1989).

$$\frac{S_t}{Yd_t} = \alpha \cdot (\frac{S_{t-1}}{Yd_{t-1}}) + \beta \cdot \frac{(Y_t - Y_{t-1})}{Y_{t-1}} + \lambda \cdot (\psi_t - \psi_{t-1}) + \delta \cdot (r_t - \pi_t) \quad (11)$$

Here Y_d is disposable income, Y is total income, ψ represents the log terms of trade, taken as the (weighted) change in the price of exportables relative to imported goods, Xt is total real exports, and $(r_t - \pi_t)$ is the real (ex post) interest rate.

Consumption is then determined residually. There are no wealth terms affecting consumption, unlike in the industrialised countries. S^P is private real savings, and T is total taxes.

$$C_t - Y_t + T_t + S^P_t \quad (12)$$

Consumption is divided between output in each sector according to the usual consumer's maximisation problem with log utility. Total consumption (C) is expressed as a nested CES function similar to (1) through (4) above, divided between domestic (C^d) and imported (C^{im}) final consumption goods. All goods are normal, and utility functions are continuous and concave. Imported consumption goods originate from every other world region except OPEC.

Prices

Prices are derived from the dual to the CES functions, or in the case of Cobb–Douglas demand they are share weighted indexes of the constituent prices. For example:

$$P_i = \theta_x \cdot P_x + \theta_m \cdot P_m + \theta_r \cdot P_r + \theta_s \cdot P_s + \theta_{im} \cdot Pi_{im} + \theta_e \cdot P_e \,;\, \sum_i^5 \theta_i = 1 \quad (13)$$

Wages adjust according to an augmented Phillips curve. Nominal wages respond to domestic price inflation (P), the terms of trade (Pex/Pim) and the level of domestic employment.

$$w_t = w_{t-1} + \alpha \cdot (p_t - p_{t-1}) + (1-\alpha) \cdot (p_{t-1} - p_{t-2}) + \beta \cdot (Ld_t - Ls_t) + \gamma \cdot (\frac{px_t}{pm_t}) \quad (14)$$

Government and monetary accounts

Only the government undertakes external borrowing, and there is zero private capital mobility. Government revenues derive from lump sum taxes out of labour and capital income of the private sector, and interest earnings on the stock of net foreign assets of the central bank. Government expenditures are for output of the domestic service sector and taxes adjust to balance the government budget. External debt (or foreign assets) are consolidated for the government and central bank. Government spending is set as a share of GNP, and varies only with changes in debt service or investment income.

$$G_t = \alpha^g \cdot (Y_t) + r_t^i \cdot (B_t - R_t) - \alpha^g (Y_t) + r_t^i \cdot (D_t) - T_t \quad (15)$$

where D_t = net national debt (external debt minus reserves)
T_t = tax revenues

The government pegs the exchange rate to a currency basket (0.65 on the US dollar, 0.25 on the yen, and 0.10 on the ECU). Money supply thus adjusts endogenously to changes in foreign assets of the central bank and a standard Goldfeld type money demand specification is used.

Model initialisation and specification of trade flows

Three product categories are exported by developing countries: one, primary goods (agriculture and mining), two, consumer manufactures and manufactured industrial intermediates, and three, capital goods. Demand for imported primary goods and industrial intermediates is derived from the firm's optimisation problem in the importing country, demand for imported consumer goods from utility maximisation, and capital goods are derived from the firm's intertemporal investment decision. Oil exports from the ASEAN countries are handled separately from these categories and are priced according to the OPEC oil price. Disaggregation of goods to match these commodity characteristics was done following the United States Bureau of the Census end-user classification system. A mapping was then made to the SITC classification (at the 2-digit level) as reported by the United Nations.

Import demand of the United States from Pacific exporters has been estimated to obtain price and income elasticities using a modified Almost Ideal Demand System (AIDS) specification, following Deaton and Meullbauer (1980). Demand elasticities for the other OECD blocks are taken from other studies, principally Whalley (1985).

The model has been initialised around 1987. Trade flows reproduce the actual levels and direction of trade between regions in that year. For example, the pattern of trade between Japan, the United States and the Asian NIEs reflects the prevalence of imported capital goods and industrial intermediates by the Asian NIEs and exports of consumer manufactures to the United States market. The ASEAN countries similarly export mainly raw materials to Japan and light manufactured goods to the United States. Table 13A.1 shows the 1987 trade matrix used to initialise the model.

Table 13A.1 Regional trade matrix, 1987 (million US dollars)

Exporter	United States	Japan	ROECD	ASEAN	ANIES	OPEC	ROW
United States	*	22 631	107 017	5 319	18 743	10 877	23 464
Japan	66 684	*	35 356	8 231	31 370	11 253	21 698
ROECD	145 238	21 228	*	7 496	18 347	37 062	113 680
ASEAN	9 230	12 462	8 097	*	8 280	1 100	2 900
ANIEs	49 279	13 530	19 821	8 534	*	4 588	17 600
OPEC	14 610	25 830	23 467	2 300	7 457	*	5 275
ROW	37 861	14 628	106 138	4 000	20 939	9 413	*

These aggregate trade flows are disaggregated into the corresponding sectoral outputs and demand categories mentioned above. The 1986 exports and imports of the Asian NIEs are shown in Table 13A.2.

Table 13A.2 Structure of Asian NIE exports, 1986 (per cent)

Exports	United States	Japan	ROECD
Food and intermediates	2.3	33.6	29.1
Light manufactures	56.7	41.9	42.3
Capital goods	41.0	24.5	28.6

The Asian NIE imports are disaggregated into: fuels 4 per cent (from OPEC), other raw materials 6.8 per cent (from ASEAN and ROW), machinery and transport equipment 30.4 per cent, and other manufactured goods 58.5 per cent. Out of total imports, 6.3 per cent are consumer goods, 9.8 per cent are investment goods (used in production of investment goods), and 84 per cent are intermediate manufactured and raw inputs to production. This last category is very sizeable since it includes, among other things, those imported components into assembly industries.

APPENDIX 14A.1 STATEMENT ON TRADE POLICY BY PECC STANDING COMMITTEE

At the conclusion of the Seventh General Meeting of the Pacific Economic Cooperation Conference in Auckland, New Zealand, 12–15 November, the

Standing Committee of the PECC expressed its strong support of the multilateral trade negotiations and for their successful completion by the end of 1990. The Standing Committee also welcomed the intention of the Asia–Pacific Trade Ministers, announced in Canberra on 7 November 1989, to meet in mid-1990 and again in December 1990 to help achieve a comprehensive and very substantive result from the Uruguay Round of multilateral trade negotiations, and expressed on behalf of PECC its willingness to cooperate in the preparations for this activity.

Commitments made by Ministers representing GATT members during the Uruguay Round and in particular during the Mid-Term Review, covered further general cuts in tariffs, substantial liberalisation of non-tariff barriers, extension of GATT commitments to cover agriculture and the services sector, elimination of trade distortion associated with inadequate protection and enforcement of intellectual property rights and with trade-related investment restrictions, avoiding unilateral and bilateral means of dealing with short-term import surges and balance of payments problems, and the strengthening of GATT monitoring and dispute settlement procedures.

The Standing Committee calls attention, in particular, to the work of the PECC Trade Policy Forum at its 26–28 June meeting in Vancouver, Canada. The papers and discussions at the Forum concentrated on multilateral issues and proposals of greatest relevance to the economies of PECC members, including:

1 *phasing out of export and other subsidies affecting trade* in agricultural products, substantial improvement in access to markets by reduction or elimination of tariff and non-tariff barriers and identifying means of assuring security of supply that are 'transparent' and less trade-distorting;
2 *reduction or elimination of tariff and non-tariff barriers that discriminate against trade in processed forms of natural products*;
3 adoption in 1990 of a plan for *phasing out of the quantitative restriction on trade in textile products associated with the multifibre arrangement* and elimination of related bilateral voluntary export restraints and other practices that are discriminatory and constitute evasion of GATT commitments;
4 generally, recourse to safeguards should be *temporary, non-discriminatory*, based on GATT-determined procedures; this to be accompanied by clearer definition of constraints on the use of subsidy-countervail and antidumping practices;
5 adoption of *adequate standards for the protection of intellectual property* so that they become a more efficient and equitable means of transferring technology, especially between developed and developing countries;
6 *liberalisation of trade in services by adopting a framework agreement and by efforts to harmonise national policies* in sectors as finance and air transport, in which Pacific leadership is regarded as desirable and feasible; and
7 strong support for the improvement of the GATT system, especially through *monitoring of national policies affecting trade, encouragement of independent research and dissemination of results of such surveillance and study*; and a

hope that new progress will be made in negotiations to solve the issue of China's status as a contracting party to GATT.

A notable feature of the Trade Forum was the active and *effective participation of those from newly industrialised and developing economies in the Pacific region*. They especially stressed the need for trade policies that would assure them access to markets, including the importance of liberalising their own trade policies to reduce distortion in economic development and to increase their leverage in trade negotiations.

Ministers responsible for international trade in the Pacific region should confirm their commitment to prosperity and future growth on an restricted global trading system. The maintenance and strengthening of the system is in the common interest of the countries of the region. In this context, Pacific Ministers should also reconfirm their determination to improve market access for all PECC member economies and like-minded countries outside the region.

APPENDIX 14A.2 JOINT STATEMENT MINISTERIAL-LEVEL MEETING, 5–7 NOVEMBER 1989, CANBERRA

Ministers from Australia, Brunei Darussalam, Canada, Indonesia, Japan, the Republic of Korea, Malaysia, New Zealand, the Philippines, Singapore, Thailand and the United States gathered in Canberra, Australia on 6–7 November 1989 to discuss how to advance the process of Asia Pacific Economic Cooperation.

Discussions covered a variety of topics under four agenda items:

- world and regional economic developments;
- global trade liberalisation—the role of the Asia–Pacific region;
- opportunity for regional cooperation in specific areas; and
- future steps for Asia–Pacific economic cooperation.

At the conclusion of this first meeting, Ministers expressed satisfaction with the discussions, which demonstrated the value of closer regional consultation and economic cooperation on matters of mutual interest.

Ministers also expressed their recognition of the important contribution ASEAN and its dialogue relationships have played in the development to date of APEC, and noted the significant role ASEAN institutional mechanisms can continue to play in supporting the present effort to broaden and strengthen regional economies cooperation.

Multilateral trade negotiations

The discussions on world and regional development, and on global trade liberalisation, focused particularly on the need to advance the present round of Multilateral Trade Negotiations. Every economy represented in Canberra relies heavily on a strong and open multilateral trading system, and none believes that Asia Pacific Economic Cooperation should be directed to the formation of a trading bloc.

Ministers agreed that continued close consultation within the region should be used wherever possible to promote a positive conclusion to the Round. In this respect, it was agreed that Ministers concerned with trade policy should meet in early September 1990 to discuss the emerging results and consider how to unblock any obstacles to a comprehensive and ambitious MTN result. Ministers would then meet again in Brussels in early December on the eve of the concluding session. In the meantime, senior officials should consult regularly in Geneva to exchange views on MTN progress.

Ministers expressed strong support for the timely and successful completion of the Uruguay Round. They noted that much remained to be done if the December 1990 conclusion was to be achieved. They called on all contracting parties to work with them more vigorously to that end.

Future steps

Ministers agreed that it was premature at this stage to decide upon any particular structure either for a ministerial-level forum or its necessary support mechanism, but that, while ideas are evolving, it was appropriate for further consultative meetings to take place and for work to be undertaken on matters of common interest and concern.

Accordingly, Ministers welcomed the invitation of Singapore to host a second ministerial-level consultative meeting in mid-1990, and they also welcomed the Republic of Korea's offer to host a third such meeting in Seoul during 1991.

Ministers asked their respective senior officials, together with representation from the ASEAN Secretariat, to meet early in 1990 to begin preparations for the next ministerial-level consultative meeting.

They asked senior officials to undertake or set in train further work on a number of possible topics for regional economic cooperation, on the possible participation of other economies in future meetings, and on other issues related to the future of such cooperation, for consideration by Ministers at their next meeting.

Summary statement

Attached to this joint statement is Chairman Evans' concluding summary statement which records the substance of discussions during this meeting [omitted here].

Visiting participating Ministers and their delegations expressed their deep appreciation to the government and people of Australia for organising the meeting and for the excellent arrangements made for it, as well as for the warm hospitality extended to them.

Notes

CHAPTER 3

* Jorge Quiroz provided able research assistance in the preparation of this study. However, he bears no responsibility for interpretations or conclusions.
1. In fact, distorted price signals can also mislead decisionmakers within the public sector, but that point is not germaine to the topic of this study.
2. The country included in this group which is least similar to the others is probably the Philippines. Prior to the late 1970s, the Philippine growth experience was similar to that of the other Southeast Asian countries. At the present time, however, there is considerably more concern with restoring macroeconomic balance in the context of a heavy external debt and with restructuring the domestic economy away from heavy government intervention than in the other countries of this group.
3. Even this comparison understates the extent to which the four have been super-achievers: several decades ago, Korea and Taiwan would certainly have been classified as low-income countries, and it might be argued that their performance should therefore be contrasted with that of other low-income countries. In the 1950s Korea was one of the poorest countries in Asia.
4. Kuznets' article is also a valuable source of comparative data on many aspects of performance of Korea and Taiwan. Further, it includes comparative data for Japan.
5. In fact, agricultural growth in Korea and Taiwan was more rapid than that of most developing countries, although Korea and Taiwan protect their agricultural producers to an uneconomic degree. See Anderson and Hayami (1986) on Korea, Taiwan and Japan, and Moon and Kang (1987) on Korea for an analysis. Removal of that protection will be one of the challenges for growth in the 1990s. (See the fifth section of this chapter.) It may be noted that any country following a liberalised trading policy could in principle experience rapid industrial growth and import agricultural commodities. In fact, the fact that a large fraction of the population are in agriculture implies that per capita income growth is constrained in part by the rate of growth of agricultural incomes. Moreover, although migration from rural to urban areas, and possibly even rural location of industrial activities, can mitigate increasing income disparities to some degree, from a societal viewpoint it is unacceptable for urban incomes to grow rapidly over long periods of time with stagnation of rural incomes.
6. However, Korea augmented domestic savings by borrowing abroad on the international capital market to increase domestic investment. See Frank, Kim and Westphal (1975) on the importance of foreign borrowing to the Korean economy in the 1960s.
7. Japan, Korea, and Taiwan will certainly lose if they do not reduce their protection of domestic agriculture. However, Thailand, Malaysia, Indonesia and the Philippines

stand out among developing countries as being less discriminatory to agriculture than most.
8 See Krueger, Ruttan and Michalopoulos (1989, ch.2) for a fuller discussion of the analytical underpinnings of these views.
9 See, for example, Bhagwati and Srinivasan (1975), and the references therein on India.
10 Evidence on this point comes from a large number of sources. Balassa (1988) cites the difference in incremental capital-output ratios between countries with outer-oriented trade strategies and those adopting import-substitution. In circumstances in which incentives have altered dramatically towards an outer orientation, evidence of sharp increases in output per unit of input have been reported. See Corbo and de Melo (1987) and the references therein for the Southern Cone experience in this regard. See also Krueger and Tuncer (1982) on Turkey.
11 There are also problems because a single producer of an intermediate good implies great vulnerability of the economy. For example, a strike at the monopolistic producer's factory can then slow or shut down factories using the product throughout the economy, with further losses of efficiency.
12 Even when, as in the Korean case, export subsidies are granted on a uniform basis to all exporters per dollar of exports, there is some variation in incentives depending on the fraction of domestic value added in the international price. Thus, incentives are not completely uniform with respect to exports and most countries following an outer-oriented strategy have in any event failed to eliminate entirely protection to import-competing activities. Moreover, there are built-in pressures to prevent differentials in incentives between production of exportables and of import-competing goods from becoming too large: when export subsidies are used, the budgetary costs limit their size to a greater degree than do the costs of protection limit the extent to which the authorities will restrict imports.
13 For a statement of the view that interventions were far less important in East Asia than in other developing countries, see Balassa (1988). Mason et al. (1980) also appear to downplay the role of government in detailed resource allocational decisions. See, however, Jacobs (1985) and Wade (1985).
14 See Tanzi (1987) and Kuznets (1988) for documentation. See also Mason et al. (1980) for an in-depth analysis of the Korean case.
15 See Yoo (1989) for an excellent analysis of this episode, and an empirical assessment of the Korean government's interventions.
16 It is a terminologically unfortunate fact of life that virtually all countries adopting import-substitution strategies have also put in place policies for 'export promotion'. These policies are ad hoc and discriminatory among activities in much the same way import restrictions are and simultaneously they usually do little more than offset part of the differential incentive in favour of import-competing industries.
17 I assume also that the United States manages to reduce the size of its fiscal deficit and increase its savings rate, and that the success is achieved through a 'soft landing' rather than a major crisis.
18 This will make it all the more crucial for liberalisation of agriculture in Taiwan and Korea to permit more rapid absorption of lower-productivity rural labour into the urban labour force, thereby offsetting some of the pressures for a slower growth rate.

CHAPTER 4

1 It is the cumulative sum of past saving adjusted for general inflation:
   $W_t^* = P_t \cdot (W_t^*-1/P_t-1 + S_t/P_t)$ where P_t is an index of consumer prices in period t.
2 IRAs are tax-deferred retirement plans for employees. Keough plans provide similar coverage for the self-employed.

CHAPTER 5

1 This model extends the Ishii, McKibbin and Sachs (1985) model to cover the Pacific region and includes some improvements. Basic features of the model are that it links regions through both the flow of goods and the flow of money and it incorporates a rational expectations hypothesis for the determination of exchange rates. See Takenaka and Chida (1987) and Takenaka and Ogawa (1987).

CHAPTER 6

1 In practice, the assignment is not so clear cut. The Accord, although assigned to internal balance, has beneficial current account effects. See the decision of the Commission to discount wage increases for exchange rate devaluations.) Similarly, reducing the government deficit may affect business optimism and encourage economic growth. Assignment of the budget deficit to the current account became more clearly articulated after 1985.
2 Of course, these are polar cases. The simple model outlined earlier tends to focus attention on the commodity flows as the determinant of capital flows, but a better, although inevitably more complicated model, would allow for a more explicit modelling of capital flows. Within such a model, relative prices of traded and non-traded goods (affecting and responding to relative production and consumption of the two goods) and interest rates (affecting and responding to the allocation of domestic and foreign asset holdings and decisions to invest and save) would be linked together.
3 A good survey of issues in the relationship between fiscal and current accounts can be found in Genberg (1988). He places emphasis on the way in which the government deficit is reduced. For example, tax increases that discriminate against private savings will have a different effect on the current account than tax increases which discourage investment; the latter tending to improve the current account and the former tending to lead to current account deficits.
4 The statistical discrepancy is the difference between estimates of the sum of gross domestic production plus imports of goods and services and the sum of estimates of components of gross national expenditure and exports of goods and services.
5 These data are taken from *Australian National Accounts* 1987/88 and updated from *Australian National Accounts* June 1989. These data group savings of Public Enterprises with the private sector. If business enterprises are included in the government sector, the reduction in the PSBR is much larger, approximately 8 percentage points.
6 It is also possible that relationships between sectors differ between the short and long run. In the short run, increased government savings in the form of tax increases and expenditure reductions may be financed by reduced private sector savings, but in the long run, consumption may adjust, thus implying a change in the current account. Or demand and supply conditions in traded goods sectors may be slow to respond to changes in relative prices generated by government deficit changes. At a 1989 conference in Canberra, all major Australian model-builders were asked to simulate the effects of a change in government spending. The general result was little short-run effect on the current account but after a period of five years the government sector reduction seemed to spread evenly between private sector offsets and current account adjustments (see Pagan, 1989).

CHAPTER 7

1 For the purposes of this chapter, these include Japan, China, the four East Asian NIEs and the five ASEAN member states.
2 In both Taiwan and Korea, these effects are analysed later in an income-expenditure model where real income is the major adjustment variable. This choice of framework appears to be reasonable in that changes in exchange rates are largely exogenous and the domestic interest rates are not influenced by changes in the foreign interest rates because of the tight control over capital movements in both countries. For Japan, however, it has been suggested that the Mundell-Flemming model is a useful framework for analysing Japan's current account behaviour.
3 For a more detailed discussion of Korea's current account behaviour, from a longer-term perspective, see Dornbusch and Park (1987).
4 According to a recent study (Park, 1989), Korean exporters pass through to the dollar price of their products only 35 per cent of any cost increase due to the won appreciation vis-à-vis the US dollar.
5 Until very recently, changes in the unit value of exports by Japan, Taiwan and Korea have been similar both in direction and magnitude.
6 One might ask where these institutional investors would place their funds in the future and why the 10 per cent level is so important. Once again, many policymakers in Japan seem to subscribe to this view.
7 During the January-July period, exports by East Asian NIEs to Japan increased by 18 per cent compared to 46.4 per cent for 1988 as a whole.
8 Taiwan will also suffer from a similar decline in its GNP.
9 At the end of 1988, the cumulative total of Japan's foreign direct investment was US$186.4 billion, 17.3 per cent of which was allocated to Asia. Japan's overall foreign direct investment in manufacturing stood at US$49.8 billion or 27 per cent of the total, and in Asia US$12.4 billion, or about 25 per cent of the total in manufacturing (these figures are from Japan's Ministry of Finance). The amount of investment per project in Asia was about US$1.3 million, indicating that Japanese investors prefer smaller joint ventures spread around Asia. For North America, investments per project amounted to US$6.1 million.

CHAPTER 8

1 Brunei is not included in this analysis.
2 Following Rana and Alburo (1987), this study uses the current account deficit expressed in relative terms (deflated by total exports of goods and services). Instability or disequilibrium is said to have occurred when any of the indicators remain persistently above the normal or trend rate.
3 For analysis on the 1970s, see, for example, Rana and Alburo (1987).
4 See Khan (1987) for a fuller discussion.
5 New revised figures of the Central Bureau of Statistics indicate a higher growth for 1988 of 5.7 per cent, and this would imply higher estimates for 1989 also.
6 According to the 1980 population census, 10.9 per cent of the Singaporean labour force was recorded as foreign.
7 In 1984 Singapore had the highest savings rate in the world, with 42 per cent of GDP.
8 The Economic Committee was set up to evaluate and formulate economic strategies to overcome recession and to chart out the longer-term direction.

CHAPTER 9

* I wish to acknowledge the invaluable assistance given by Mr Nor Mohamed Yakcop and Dr Awang Adek Hussin of Bank Negara Malaysia (Central Bank of Malaysia) in the drafting of my original paper.

CHAPTER 10

1 Sachs (1985) provides a lively analysis of those contrasts.
2 See, for example, the discussion in Chapter 3 of James, Naya and Meier (1987).
3 An extensive, sophisticated financial system is, by itself, no guarantee of better saving performance; the case of the United States is an example.
4 Sachs (1984) develops a formal model that embodies this fact.
5 In the second half of the 1980s, Japanese development assistance institutions have become more significant in this process.
6 See Urata (1989) for the case of Japan.

CHAPTER 11

* The views expressed in this chapter are those of the author and do not necessarily reflect those of the World Bank, its Board of Directors, its management or its member governments.
1 The non-fuel commodity income terms of trade of both African regions and South Asia also performed considerably worse than the East Asia and Pacific region in the various subgroups—food, non-food agriculture and metals and minerals.

CHAPTER 12

1 For a detailed discussion of the 'flying geese' model, see Yamazawa (1990).

CHAPTER 13

1 See Bruno and Sachs (1985) for a thorough discussion of these points.

CHAPTER 14

1 It is worth recalling that during the early 1950s many of the European economies had exchange controls and maintained import quotas on balance of payments grounds.
2 For a fuller discussion of European Community practices and broader issues with respect to the antidumping laws in the Uruguay Round, see Hindley (1989).
3 See comments by Hudec and Katz (1988) comparing the FTA dispute settlement process and the GATT. See also Davey (1989).
4 Kiyoshi Kojima at the first PAFTAD meeting January 1968; Peter Drysdale and Hugh Patrick before the US Senate Committee on Foreign Relations, July 1979.
5 PAFTAD held ten meetings up to the end of 1970s.

Bibliography

Aghevli, Bijan B. (1979) 'Experience of Asian Countries with Various Exchange Rate Policies' Paper presented at the conference on 'The Crawling Peg: Past Performance and Future Prospects' held in Rio de Janeiro, October

Akamatsu, Kaname (1943) 'Shinko-Kogyokoku no Sangyo-Hatten' [Industrial Development in Newly Industrialising Countries] in *Essays in Honour of Dr Teijiro Ueda* Vol. 4, Tokyo: Kagakushugi Kogyosha; also in English as 'A Theory of Unbalanced Growth in the World Economy' *Weltwirtschaftliches Archive* Vol. 86, No. 2 (1961), pp. 196–217

Anderson, Kym and Yujiro Hayami (1986) *The Political Economy of Agricultural Protection* Sydney: Allen & Unwin

Anstie, R. K., M. R. Gray and A. R. Pagan (1982) 'Inflation and the Consumption Ratio' in A. R. Pagan and P. K. Trivedi (eds) *The Effects of Inflation* Centre for Economic Policy Research, Australian National University

Armington, Paul S. (1969) 'A Theory of Demand for Products Distinguished by Place of Origin' *IMF Staff Papers* XVI (March) pp. 159–76

Asher, Mukul G. (1989) 'Tax Reforms in East Asian Developing Countries: Motivations, Directions and Implications' *Asian Pacific Economic Literature* Vol. 3, No. 1 (March)

Balassa, Bela (1965) 'Trade Liberalisation and Revealed Comparative Advantage' *The Manchester School of Economic and Social Studies* Vol. 33, No. 2 (May)

——(1978) 'Exports and Economic Growth: Further Evidence' *Journal of Development Economics* Vol. 5, No. 2 (June) pp. 181–9

——(1988) 'The Lessons of East Asian Development: An Overview' *Economic Development and Cultural Change* Vol. 36, No. 3 (April) pp. S273–90

Balassa, B. and M. Noland (1988) *Japan in the World Economy* Institute for International Economics, Washington DC

Baldwin, R. (1988) 'Some Empirical Evidence on Hysteresis in Aggregate U.S. Import Prices' *NBER Working Paper* No. 2483 (January)

Barro, R. (1974) 'Are Government Bonds Net Wealth?' *Journal of Political Economy* Vol. 83, No. 6

Bernheim, B. Douglas and John B. Shoven (1985) 'Pensions Funding and

Saving' in Zvi Bodie, John Shoven and David Wise (eds) *Pensions in the U.S. Economy* Chicago: University of Chicago Press

Bhagwati, Jagdish N. (1988) 'Export-Promoting Trade Strategy: Issues and Evidence' *World Bank Research Observer* Vol. 3, No. 1 (January) pp. 27–57

Bhagwati, Jagdish N. and T. N. Srinivasan (1975) *Foreign Trade Regimes and Economic Development: India* Columbia University Press for the National Bureau of Economic Research, New York

Brecher, F. and Carlos F. Diaz-Alejandro (1977) 'Tariffs, Foreign Capital and Immiserizing Growth' *Journal of International Economics* 7, pp. 317–22

Bruno, Michael and Jeffrey Sachs (1985) *Economics of Worldwide Stagflation* Cambridge, Mass.: Harvard University Press

Bryant, Ralph C. et al. (1989) *Macroeconomic Policies in an Interdependent World* The Brookings Institution, Centre for Economic Policy Research and the International Monetary Fund, Washington DC

Chapman, B. J., S. Dowrick and P. N. Junankar (1989) 'Perspectives on Australian Unemployment: The Impact of Wage Setting Institutions in the 1980s' (mimeo) Australian National University

Chapman, B. J. and F. G. Gruen (1990) 'An Analysis of the Australian Consensual Incomes Policy: The Prices and Incomes Accord' *Centre for Economic Research Discussion Paper* No. 221, Australian National University (January)

Chen, E. K. Y. (1989) 'The Changing Role of the ANICs in the Asian-Pacific Region Towards the Year 2000' in M. Shinohara and Fu-chen Lo (eds) *Global Adjustment and Future of Asia-Pacific Economies* Tokyo: Institute of Developing Economies and Asia Pacific Development Centre, pp. 207–31

Chenery, Hollis B. and Michael Bruno (1962) 'Development Alternatives in an Open Economy: The Case of Israel' *Economic Journal* 72, pp. 79–103

Chenery, Hollis B. and Alan M. Strout (1966) 'Foreign Assistance and Economic Development' *American Economic Review* Vol. 56 (September) pp. 679–733

Choe, B. J. (1989) 'Structural Changes in Metals Consumption' *World Bank, Policy Planning and Research Working Paper* WPS 180 (April)

Cline, W. R. (1989) 'External Adjustment by the U.S., Japan and East Asian NICs: Macro- and Micro-Economic Aspects' Unpublished paper, Institute for International Economics (January)

Cline, W. R. and E. Delgado (1978) (eds) *Economic Integration in Central America* Washington DC: Brookings Institution

Cooper, Richard (1985) 'The Future of the International Trading System' in David Conklin and Thomas Courchene (eds) *Canadian Trade at a Crossroads: Options for New International Agreements* Toronto: Ontario Economic Council

Corbo, Vittorio and Jaime de Melo (1987) 'Lessons from the Southern Cone Policy Reform' *World Bank Research Observer* Vol. 2 No. 2 (July) pp. 111–42

Corden, W. Max (1990) 'Macroeconomic Policy and Growth: Some Lessons of Experience' Paper presented at the World Bank Annual Conference on

Development Economics, Washington DC, 26–27 April

Daquila, T. C. (1989) 'Analysis of the External Debt Problem in the Philippines' Paper presented at the Eighth New Zealand Conference on Asian Studies, 17–18 August

Davey, William (1989) 'Reforming GATT: Dispute Settlement and the Functioning of the GATT System' Paper presented at the University of Ottawa, May 5

Dean, Andrew, Martine Durand, John Fallon and Peter Hoeller (1989) 'Savings Trends and Behaviour in OECD Countries' *OECD Department of Economics and Statistics Working Paper* No. 67

Deaton, Angus and John Meullbauer (1980) 'An Almost Ideal System' *American Economic Review* Vol. 70, No. 2, pp. 312–26

Diebold, William (1988) 'The History and the Issues' in William Diebold (ed.) *Bilateralism, Multilateralism and Canada in United States Trade Policy*, Cambridge, Mass.: Ballinger for the Council on Foreign Relations

Dornbusch, R. and Yung Chul Park (1987) 'Korean Growth Policy' *Brookings Papers on Economic Activity* II, Washington DC: The Brookings Institution

Dorrance, G. S. and B. Woldekidan (1989) 'Primary Commodity Prices and Terms of Trade of Developing Countries: A Preliminary Review' *National Centre for Development Studies Working Paper* No. 89/1, Australian National University

Drucker, P. F. (1986) 'The Changed World Economy' *Foreign Affairs* Vol. 64, No. 4, pp. 768–91

Duncan, R. C. (1988) 'The Impact of Technological Change on Primary Commodity Exports from Developing Countries' Paper presented to World Bank Seminar on Technology and Long-Term Economic Growth Prospects, 11 November

——(1989) 'Penetration of Industrial Country Markets by Processed Agricultural Products from Developing Countries' Paper presented to the High Level Policy Seminar on Agroindustrial Development in the Latin American and Caribbean Region, 4–7 April, Brasilia

EC Commission (1988) *Research on the Cost of Non-Europe* Luxembourg (16 vols.), Paolo Cecchini with Michael Catinat and Alexis Jaquemin

Economic Planning Agency (1988) *Economic Survey of Japan: 1988* (in Japanese) Tokyo: Economic Planning Agency

——(1989) *Economic Survey of Japan: 1989* (in Japanese) Tokyo: Economic Planning Agency

El Agraa, Ali (1983) *International Economic Integration* London: Macmillan

ESCAP (1990) *Restructuring the Developing Economies of Asia and the Pacific in the 1990s* Bangkok: ESCAP

Feldstein, Martin (1989) 'The Case Against Trying to Stabilise the Dollar' *American Economic Association Papers and Proceedings* Vol. 79, No. 2 (May)

Forsyth, P. D. (1989) 'Competitiveness, Microeconomic Reform and the Current Account Deficit' (mimeo) (September) Australian National University

Frank, Charles R., Kwang Suk Kim and Larry Westphal (1975) *Foreign Trade*

Regimes and Economic Development: Korea Columbia University Press for the National Bureau of Economic Research

Fry, Maxwell (1984) 'Econometric Analysis of National Savings Rates' *Domestic Resource Mobilization through Financial Development, Volume II, Appendixes* Asian Development Bank Economics Office (February)

——(1989) *Money, Interest, Banking in Economic Development* Baltimore: Johns Hopkins University Press

Fukao, Mitsuhiro and K. Okina (1988) 'Internationalisation of Financial Markets and Balance of Payments Imbalances: A Japanese Perspective' Institute for Monetary and Economic Studies, Bank of Japan (July)

Gan, Wee Beng (1989) 'Macroeconomic Policy, Real Exchange Rate and International Competitiveness—the Malaysian Experience During the 1980s' (draft paper) (June)

Garnaut, Ross and Paul Baxter, with Anne O. Krueger (1983) 'Exchange Rate and Macro-economic Policy in Independent Papua New Guinea' *Pacific Research Monograph* No. 10, Australian National University

Genberg, H. (1988) 'The Fiscal Deficit and the Current Account: Twins or Distant Relatives?' *Research Discussion Paper* 8813, Reserve Bank of Australia

Giovannini, Alberto (1985) 'Saving and the Real Interest Rate in LDCs' *Journal of Development Economics* No. 18, pp. 197–217

Gregory, R. G. (1986) 'Wages Policy and Unemployment in Australia' *Economica Supplement*

——(1989) 'Industry Policy in Australia', Project on Declining Industries, Center on Japanese Economy and Business, Columbia University in the City of New York

Grilli, E. R. and M. C. Yang (1988) 'Primary Commodity Prices, Manufactured Goods Prices, and the Terms of Trade of Developing Countries: What the Long Run Shows', *World Bank Economic Review* Vol. 2, No. 1, pp. 1–48

Gruen, D. and J. Smith (1989) 'A Random Walk around the $A: Expectations, Risk, Interest Rates and Consequences for the External Imbalance' *Research Discussion Paper* 8906, Reserve Bank of Australia

Harper, I. and G. C. Lim (1989) 'Is Monetary Policy Too Tight' *Australian Economic Review* 2nd Quarter

Harris, Richard G. and David Cox (1983) *Trade, Industrial Policy, and Canadian Manufacturing* Toronto: Ontario Economic Council

Heller, P. (1988) 'Ageing, savings, and pensions in the G7 countries: 1980–2025' *IMF Working Paper* WP/89/13 (January)

Hindley, Brian (1989) 'Antidumping Action: The Threat to the GATT' in Murray Smith (ed.) *Canada, the Pacific and Global Trade* Halifax: Institute for Research on Public Policy

Holmes, Frank (1989) (ed.) *Stepping Stones to Freer Trade?* Wellington: Victoria University Press

Hooper, P. and C. Mann (1987) 'The U.S. External Deficit: its Causes and Persistence' *International Finance Discussion Paper* No. 316, The Board of Governors of the Federal Reserve System, Washington DC

Hudec, R. and J. Katz (1988) in Donald McRae and Debra Steger (eds) *Understanding the Free Trade Agreement* Halifax: The Institute for Research on Public Policy

Ishii, N., W. McKibbin and J. Sachs (1987) 'The Economic Policy Mix, Policy Cooperation, and Protectionism: Some Aspects of Macroeconomic Interdependence Among the United States, Japan and OECD Countries' *Journal of Policy Modeling* Vol. 7, No. 4

Jacobs, N. (1985) *The Korean Road to Modernization and Development* Champaign and Chicago: University of Illinois Press, Urbana

James, William E., Seiji Naya and Gerald M. Meier (1987) *Asian Development: Economic Success and Policy Lessons* International Center for Economic Growth: University of Wisconsin Press.

Khan, Moshin S. (1987) 'Macroeconomic Adjustment in Developing Countries: A Policy Perspective' *Research Observer* (World Bank) Vol. 2, No. 1 (January)

Kojima, Kiyoshi (1973) 'Reorganisation of North-South Trade: Japan's Foreign Economic Policy for the 1970s' *Hitotsubashi Journal of Economics* Vol. 13, No. 2, pp. 1–28 (February)

Koo, Bon-Ho and Taeho Bark (1989) 'Recent Macroeconomic Performance and Industrial Structural Adjustment in Korea' Paper presented at a conference sponsored by the Foundation for Advanced Information and Research (FAIR), Japan, Fukuoka City, 28–29 August

Krause, Lawrence and Sueo Sekiguchi (1980) *Economic Interactions in the Pacific* Washington DC: Brookings Institution

Krueger, Anne O. (1978) *Foreign Trade Regimes and Economic Development: Liberalization Attempts and Consequences* Lexington, Mass.: Ballinger Press for the National Bureau of Economic Research

Krueger, Anne O. and Baran Tuncer (1982) 'An Empirical Test of the Infant Industry Argument' *American Economic Review* Vol. 72, No. 5 (December) pp. 1142–52

Krueger, Anne O., Vernon Ruttan and Constantine Michalopoulos (1989) *Aid and Development* Baltimore: Johns Hopkins University Press

Kuznets, Paul (1988) 'An East Asian Model of Economic Development: Japan, Taiwan, and South Korea' *Economic Development and Cultural Change* Vol. 36, No. 3 (April) pp. S11–44

Lahiri, Ashok K. (1989) 'Dynamics of Asian Savings: The Role of Growth and Age Structure' *International Monetary Fund Staff Papers* (March) pp. 228–62

Lee, Eddie (1988) 'Exchange Rate and Monetary Policy in a Small and Open Economy: The Case of Singapore' Paper presented at the Eighth Pacific Basin Central Bank Conference on Economic Modelling, Kuala Lumpur (November)

Lee, Y. S. and T. S. Yu (1988) 'Economic Forecast for Taiwan' The Spring Meeting of Project Link, New York (March)

Leiderman, Leonardo (1989) 'Economic Adjustment and Exchange Rates in LDCs: A Review Essay' *Journal of Monetary Economics* Vol. 24

Leutwiler, F. et al. (1985) *Trade Policies for a Better Future: Proposals for Action* Geneva: GATT Secretariat: 19–21

Liang, K. S. and C. H. Liang (1988) 'Taiwan's New International Role in Light of Changes in Comparative Advantage, Trade Pattern, and Balance of Payments' Conference on Economic Development Experiences of Taiwan and Emerging Asia-Pacific Area, The Institute of Economics, Academia Sinica, Taipei (June)

Lim Chong Yah and Associates (1989) *Policy Options for the Singapore Economy* Singapore: McGraw Hill

Lin See Yan (1988) 'Japan-Malaysia Relations: External Debt With Special Emphasis on Official Assistance' *Opinion* Kuala Lumpur: Institute of Strategic and International Studies

Lewis, W. A. (1952) 'World Production, Prices and Trade, 1870–1960' *Manchester School of Economics and Social Studies* Vol. 20, No. 2, pp. 105–38

McKibbin, Warwick and Jeffrey Sachs (1989a) 'The McKibbin-Sachs Global (MSG2) Model' *Brookings Discussion Papers* No. 78 (August)

——(1989b) 'Implications of Policy Rules for the World Economy' in Ralph C. Bryant et al. (eds) *Macroeconomic Policies in an Interdependent World* The Brookings Institution, Centre for Economic Policy Research and the International Monetary Fund, Washington DC

Mason, Edward S., Mahn Je Kim, Dwight Perkins, Kwang Suk Kim and David Cole (1980) *Economic and Social Modernization of Korea* Cambridge, Mass.: Harvard University Press

Michaely, Michael (1977) 'Exports and Growth: An Empirical Investigation' *Journal of Development Economics* Vol. 4, No. 1 (March) pp. 49–53

Mitchell, D. O. and R. C. Duncan (1987) 'Market Behaviour of Grains Exporters' *Research Observer* Vol. 2, No. 1, pp. 3–21

Munnell, Alicia H. and Nicole Ernsberger (1987) 'Pension Contributions and the Stock Market' *New England Economic Review* (Nov-Dec)

Murphy, C. W. (1989) 'Economic Policy and Foreign Debt' (mimeo) Australian National University

Moon, Pal-Young and Bong-Soon Kang (1987) *A Comparative Study of the Political Economy of Agricultural Pricing Policies—The Case of South Korea* final report (mimeo) World Bank (December)

Nam, S. W. (1988) 'The Determinants of National Saving in Korea—A Sectoral Accounting Approach' *KDI Working Paper* No. 8821, Seoul (December)

Naya, Seiji (1983) 'Effects of External Shocks on the Balance of Payments, Policy Responses, and Debt Problems of Asian Developing Countries' *Economics Office Report Series* No. 22 (December)

Noguchi, Y. (1988) 'Have Budget Increases Really Supported the Expansion of Domestic Demand?' *Toyo Keizai* special issue (August) (in Japanese)

Nurkse, Ragnar (1958) *Some Problems of Capital Formation in Underdeveloped Countries* Oxford: Basil Blackwell

Obstfeld, Maurice (1988) 'The Effectiveness of Foreign-Exchange Intervention: Recent Experience' NBER Conference on International Policy Coordination and Exchange Rate Fluctuations held on Kiawah Island, SC, 27–29 October

Office of EPAC (1989) 'External Debt: Trends and Issues' *Office of EPAC Discussion Paper* 89/06

Okita, S. (1987) 'The Outlook for Pacific Co-operation and the Role of Japan' *The Indonesian Quarterly* Vol. 15, No. 3, Jakarta: Centre for Strategic and International Studies

Okumura, H. (1988) *The Development of Structural Changes in the Japanese Economy* Tokyo: NRI and NCC Co. Ltd (April)

Pagan, A. R. (1989) 'Twin Deficits and the Australian Models: Comments on a Conference' (mimeo) Australian National University

Park, Won Am (1989) 'Empirical Analysis of Korea's Current Account Surpluses' (mimeo) Seoul: Korea Development Institute (May)

Phongpaichit, Pasuk (1989) 'Technocrats, Businessmen and Generals: democracy and economic policymaking in Thailand' Paper presented at the workshop on the Dynamics of Economic Policy Reforms in Southeast Asia and Australia, Centre for the Study of Australia-Asian Relations, Griffith University, Queensland on 7–9 October

Pitchford, J. D. (1989) 'A Sceptical View of Australia's Current Account and Debt Problem' *Australian Economic Review* 2nd Quarter

Prebisch, R. (1950) *The Economic Development of Latin America and its Principal Problems* New York: United Nations

Rana, Pradumna (1985) 'Sources of Balance of Payments Problem in the 1970s: The Asian Experience' *Economics Office Report Series* No. 30 (February)

Rana, Pradumna B. and Florian A. Alburo (1987) 'Economic Stabilization Policies in ASEAN Countries' *Field Report Series* No. 17, Institute of Southeast Asian Studies, Singapore

Reserve Bank of Australia (1989) *Report and Financial Statements* Reserve Bank of Australia

Sachs, Jeffrey D. (1984) 'Theoretical Issues in International Borrowing' *Princeton Studies in International Finance* No. 54 (July)

——(1985) 'External Debt and Macroeconomic Problems in Latin America and East Asia' *Brookings Papers on Economic Activity* No. 2, pp. 523–64

Salih, Kamal and Zainal Aznam Yusof (1989) 'Economic Policy Reform: Lessons from Malaysia' Paper presented at the roundtable on Economic Policy Reform: Lessons from Malaysia and FRG, Kuala Lumpur on 11 September

Salter, W. E. G. (1959) 'Internal and external balance: the role of price and expenditure effects' *The Economic Record* 35

Sapsford, D. (1985) 'The Statistical Debate on the Net Barter Terms of Trade between Primary Commodities and Manufactures: A Comment and Some Additional Evidence' *Economic Journal* Vol. 95, No. 379, pp. 781–88

Scholt, Jeffrey (ed.) (1989) *Free Trade Areas and U.S. Trade Policy* Washington DC: Institute for International Economics

Schultz, George (1985) 'National policies and global prosperity', Address to the Woodrow Wilson School of Public and International Affairs, Princeton University, Princeton, 11 April

Schultz, T. W. (1961) *Transforming Traditional Agriculture* New Haven: Yale University Press

Semudram, M. (1989) 'Economic Outlook for Malaysia', Second Workshop, Asian Economic Outlook, ADB, Manila, 12–16 November

Singer, H. (1950) 'The Distribution of Gains between Investing and Borrowing Countries' *American Economic Review* Vol. 40, No. 2 (May) pp. 473–85

Sundberg, Mark (1990) 'The International Transmission of Macroeconomic Policy Disturbances Among Countries of the Pacific Basin' Ph.D. dissertation, Cambridge, Mass.: Harvard University

Takenaka, H. (1988a) 'Economic Globalisation and the New Cooperation and Role-Sharing between the U.S. and Japan' Unpublished paper, Osaka University (June)

——(1988b) 'Has the Japanese Economy Changed Structurally?' *Ekonomisuto* (July) (in Japanese)

——(1989) 'Re-examining the Sustainability Problem' *NLI Research Institute Review* (July) (in Japanese)

Takenaka, H. and R. Chida (1987) 'Policy Coordination in the Pacific Age' *Economic Eye* (March)

Takenaka, H. and K. Ogawa (1987) 'Macroeconomic Analysis of External Imbalances' *Toyo Keizai* (in Japanese)

Takenaka, H., R. Chida, K. Watanabe and H. Hiraoka (1989) 'Econometric Analysis of Japanese Foreign Direct Investment' *Financial Review* No. 9 (March) (in Japanese)

Tanaka, Naoki (1989) 'Policy Coordination in the ASEAN-Pacific Region' Paper presented in the Tokyo Symposium on 'The Present and Future of the Pacific Basin Economy—A Comparison of Asia and Latin America', Tokyo (July)

Tanzi, Vito (1987) 'The Public Sector in the Market Economies of Developing Asia' *Asian Development Review* Vol. 5, No. 2, pp. 31–57

Ueda, Kazuo (1988) 'Perspectives on the Japanese Current Account Surplus' *Discussion Paper Series* No. 63, Osaka: Osaka University (April)

United States, Office of the President (1985) Economic Report of the President, Transmitted to the Congress with the Annual Report of the Council of Economic Advisers, Washington DC: United States Government Printing Office (February)

Urata, Shujiro (1989) 'The Rapid Increase of Direct Investment Abroad and Structural Change in Japan' Paper written for Direct Foreign Investment Project, Honolulu: East-West Center (September)

Vernon, Richard (1964) 'International Investment and International Trade in the Product Cycle' *Quarterly Journal of Economics* Vol. 80, No. 2, pp. 190–207 (May)

Viner, Jacob (1988) 'The Most-Favoured-Nation Clause in American Commercial Treaties' in William Diebold (ed.) *Bilateralism, Multilateralism and Canada in United States Trade Policy*, Cambridge, Mass.: Ballinger for the Council on Foreign Relations, originally published in the *Journal of Political Economy*, February 1924

Wade, R. (1985) 'The Role of Government in Overcoming Market Failure: Taiwan, South Korea and Japan' in Helen Hughes (ed.) *Explaining the Success of East Asian Industrialization* Cambridge: Cambridge University Press

Watanabe, T. (1988) 'Japan, the US and the NICs in the "Age of Western Asia"' *Toyo Keizai* special issue (May) (in Japanese)

Weil, David (1990) 'Prospects for Saving in the OECD over the Next 35 Years' *Background Paper* No. 22 for the World Bank World Development Report, Washington DC

Whalley, John (1985) *Trade Liberalisation Among Major World Trading Areas* Cambridge, Mass.: MIT Press

Wonnacott, R. J. and Paul Wonnacott (1967) *Free Trade Between the United States and Canada: The Potential Economic Effects* Cambridge, Mass.: Harvard University Press

World Bank (1987) *World Development Report* World Bank

——(1988a) *Commodity Trade and Price Trends* (1987–88 edition) Baltimore: John Hopkins University Press

——(1988b) *World Development Report 1988* Oxford University Press

Yamazawa, Ippei (1972) 'Intensity Analysis of World Trade Flow' *Hitotsubashi Journal of Economics* Vol. 10, No. 2 (February)

——(1990) *Economic Development and International Trade: A Japanese Model* Honolulu: University of Hawaii Press

Yap, Joseph (1989) 'The Philippines: Recent Performance, Prospects for 1990–91, and Policy and Development Issues' Second Workshop, Asian Economic Outlook, ADB, Manila, 12–16 November

Yoo, Jung-Ho (1989) *The Korean Experience with an Industrial Targetting Policy* Seoul: Korea Development Institute (May)

Yoshitomi, M. (1989a) 'Japan's Savings and External Surplus in the World Economy' *Occasional Papers* No. 26, Group of Thirty, New York and London

——(1989b) 'Yen Appreciation, Structural Reforms and External Imbalances—International and Domestic Factors in Japan's Economic Adjustment' Paper presented to a symposium organised by the Harvard Center for International Affairs, Trento, Italy (April)

Yu, T. S. (1988) 'The Economic Outlook for Taiwan, R.O.C.' Paper presented to the Spring Meeting of Project Link, New York (March)

Yu, T. S. and Chin-Sheun Ho (1989) 'The Effect of Changes in the Foreign Exchange Rate on Taiwan's Foreign Trade' Unpublished paper, Institute of Economics, Academia Sinica, Taiwan, ROC (June)

Index

Italicised numbers refer to tables and/or figures.

Afghanistan, 234, 282
Africa, 12, 121, 193, 194–5, 199, 203; see also Cote d'Ivoire, Ghana, Kenya etc
agriculture; and industrialisation, 33, 192; economic importance of, 192–4, 199; Green Revolution in, 192; in China, 192; in Indonesia, 192; in Japan, 111; in Korea, 40; in Malaysia, 157, 192; in Taiwan, 40; in Thailand, 150, 192; in the United States, 206, 257; policy changes for, 206, 253, 257; price protection schemes, 21, 28, 40, 198, 206, 207, 270; productivity improvement, 39–40, 198, 200; subsidies, 209, 257
Aquino, Benigno, 141
Argentina, 202, 239, 283
Ariff, Mohamed, xi, xv, xvi, 1, 20
Ariffin, Dato Raja, 23
arms control agreements, 234
Arndt, Heinz W., xvi, 18
ASEAN countries, 21, 253; and Japan, 63, 119, 213; ASEAN-4, 5, 177, 178, 184, 187; ASEAN-5, 9; debts, 129; markets and trade, 19, 124–6, 264, 266; see also Indonesia, Malaysia, the Philippines, Singapore, Thailand
Asia Pacific Economic Cooperation (APEC), 268, 271–3, 297–8
Asian Development Bank, xvi, 273

assets, appreciation of, 62–3
Australia, 3, 8, 12, 20, 179; and New Zealand, 264; budget surpluses, 15, 17; current account deficit, 12, 15, 17, 18, 23, 24, 71, 75, 77–92; economic issues, 16, 24, 71–92, 183; fiscal policy, 77–8, 85; government expenditure, 71; Labor government, 71, 73, 297
    Accord, 71, 75–7, 301 n 1
    land resources, 29; liberalisation of labour market, 40, 85; overseas debt, 71; Public Sector Borrowing Requirement (PSBR), 71, 85; trade figures, 215–16, 218–19, 221, 228–9
Australian Council of Trade Unions (ACTU), 71
Australian National University, xvi, 6
automation, 142

balance of payments, 72–6, 154, 160; and economic growth, 34; imbalances in, 14
Bangladesh, 177, 202, 282
banks and banking, 111, 133, 142, 166; deregulation, 133, 138; Exim Bank, Japan, 168–9; see also Asian Development Bank, World Bank
beverage crops, 192, 203; see also cocoa, coffee, tea
biotechnology, 42
borrowing, 122, 152, 184; by Malaysia, 161, 279–80; by Thailand,

313

149; by the United States, 45, 49, 52, 192, 244; from private sources, 184–5
Bosworth, Barry P., xi, 8, 13, 14, 19, 44
Brazil, 179, 192, 203, 239; debt load, 15, 176, 177; diet, 200, 202; exchange rate, 283
Bretton Woods, 13, 155, 156, 174, 256
Brunei, 9, 155, 297
budget deficits, 6–7, 152; *see also* under names of countries with such deficits—e.g. Canada, Malaysia, United States
budget surpluses, 6–7; *see also* under names of countries with such surpluses—e.g. Australia, Japan
Burma, 29, 177

Canada, 283, 297; and New Zealand, 267; budget deficits, 4; economic issues, 4, 12, 179, 261, 263; Federation of Independent Businesses, 262; land resources, 29; trade figures, 215–16, 218–19, 221, 228–9
Canada–United States Free Trade Agreement, 4, 29, 254, 260, 262, 264, 266
capital; accumulation of, *see* capital formation; rate of return on, 34
capital exports, *see* foreign investment
capital formation, 167, 292; in developing countries, 33, 162
capital gains, 46–7
capital markets, 48, 52, 64, 79, 134, 143, 162, 173, 182; deregulation, 48, 173; globalisation of, 160, 172, 273; integration of, 11–13, 107, 160; liberalisation, 40, 234; stability of, 13
Central American Common Market, 262
cereals industries, 207, 208, 209; *see also* rice
Chile, 176, 177, 179, 239, 283
China, 114, 187, 253, 283; economic issues, 5, 16, 29, 192; exports, 20, 119; meat consumption in, 200; trade deficit of, 94; vegetable oil consumption in, 201
Closer Economic Relations Trade Agreement, Australia and New Zealand, 264, 266
cocoa, 203, 208, 210
coffee, 203, 208, 210
Cold War, 233, 234–5
Colombia, 176, 177, 179, 203, 283
commodity markets, 192–212, 220; model of, 245–6
commodity prices, 9, 20, 121, 195–8, 211; boom in, 146, 197; fluctuations in, 12, 21, 195–6; slump in, 4, 150, 157, 163
communications, 42, 142
competition, 36, 63, 84; from substitutes, 210; imperfect, 127
computerisation, 142, 160
construction sector, Singapore, 143, 145
consumption, 32; in Japan, 62, 67, 108, 111, 203; in Taiwan, 106; in the United States, 44, 47, 58–9, 180; modelling of, 293; wealth and, 47, 293
copyright, *see* intellectual property issues
costs, 145, 262; competition and, 36, 112; decreasing, 34; of freight, 196; of future retirements, 50
Cote d'Ivoire, 202, 203
Crawford, *Sir* John, 268
credit rationing, 28, 38, 185
currencies, 121, 156, 162; Australian dollar, 75; British sterling, 158; convertibility of, 15; European (proposed), 236; Indonesian rupiah, 5, 133, 164; Japanese yen, 3, 18, 97, 116, 165; Korean won, 4, 97, 164, 165; Malaysian ringgit, 9, 137, 165, 168, 174; New Taiwan dollar, 4, 97, 104, 105, 114, 165; parities, 13, 168, 171; Philippine peso, 164; Thai baht, 148, 156, 164; US dollar, 2, 18, 55, 97, 107, 164, 240; *see*

INDEX

also Bretton Woods, devaluation
current account deficits, 13, 15, 72, 73, 77–9, 151, 152, 176; *see also* under names of countries with such deficits—e.g. Australia
current accounts, 17, *122*

defence spending, *see* military expenditure
deficits, *see* budget deficits, current account deficits, external deficits, payment deficits
demand, 66, 95, 178
demographics, role of, 48
devaluation, 21, 77, 92, 133, 148, 164, 186, 203; of sterling, 158
development assistance, 3; *see also* foreign aid
development, economic, *see* economic growth
distribution, 111
dumping, 258
Duncan, Ronald C., xi, 9, 12, 20, 21, 22, 192

Eastern Europe, 24, 210, 233, 235–6, 241, 253
economic forecast, *276–87*
economic growth, 10, 15–17, 28, 33–5, 93, 213, 233; and increased food consumption, 209; balanced, 34; international comparisons, 30–3, 123, 193–4, 218–22, 308; modelling of, 27, 245, 276, 290–5; of Australia, 28, 86–9; of Canada, 28; of East Asia, 15–17, 23, 93, *94*; of Hong Kong, 27, 28, 30–3; of Indonesia, 123, 129, 135, 165; of Japan, 28, 61, *65*, 66–7, 93, *94*, 106–10; of Korea, 27, 28, 30–3, 93, 103, 165, 213, 308; of Malaysia, 5, 123, 157; of New Zealand, 28; of North Pacific, 19; of Singapore, 27, 28, 30–3, 123, 142; of Taiwan, 27, 28, 30–3, 93, 213, 308; of Thailand, 5, 123, 147; of the United States, 2, 28, 44, 51, 57, 108; outward-oriented, 35–9; *see also* sustainable growth
economic indications, *6–7*
economics, ascendance of, xiii; bilateral world economy, 243–4, 254, 255, 261; communism v capitalism, 234, *see also* Cold War; 'Dutch Disease' effect, 133; groupings, *see* OECD, OPEC, SELA *etc*; Keynes, Meade *et al.* and world trade, 256; McKibbon–Sachs model, 245–6; multilateralism, 254, 255–61; multipolar world economy, 253; one-world economy, 241–2, 252; regionalism, 254, 255, 261–73; resource gap, 178–90; welfare, 13
education, 39, 111
electrical goods, 146, 225–6; Japanese market, 68, 111, 118; United States market, 142
electricity, 151, 206
employment, full, *see* full employment; increases in, 76; lifetime, 118
energy market, 205, 210; *see also* fuel prices
English, H. Edward, xi, 10, 24, 253
enterprise, free, *see* free enterprise
environmental issues, 205, 208, 210
environmental protection, 105
European Common Market, 236–7
European Community, 121, 201, 215–19, 243; and Eastern Europe, 24, 241; antidumping laws, 260; Britain in, 4; Common Agricultural Policy, 42, 265; economic integration, 171, 175, 212, 236, 264–5; inflation in, 199; markets in, 20, 118; political issues, 236–8
Evans, Senator Gareth, 272
exchange rates, 9, 20, 40, *131*, *132*, 151, 153, 155–75, *282*; adjustments to, 13; and the Australian dollar, 77, 84–5, 283; and the Deutschmark, 168; and the Indonesian rupiah, 133, 155; and the Japanese yen, 3,

60-2, 63, 66, 105, 106, 109, 111, 168, 169, 171, 283
  internationalisation of, 171-2, 175 and the Korean won, 99, *100, 101*; and the Malaysian ringgit, 136, 137, 155, 156, 157-65, 169, 170, 173, 282, 285; and the New Taiwan dollar, 105-6; and the Philippine peso, 155, 156; and the Singapore dollar, 144, 155, 156, 165, 168; and sterling, 168, 283; and the Thai baht, 148-9, 150, 155, 282; and the US dollar, 2, 53, 55, 57-9, 105, 156, 159, 166, 168, 170, 247; appreciation of, 96, 105, 116; controls to, 34, 164; effect on markets, 199, 247; fixed, 13, 170, 265; floating, 13, 21, 144, 155, 159-60, 170, 174; foreign currency swaps, 143; overvalued, 28, 144, 148, 193, 196, 211
exports, 6-7, 93, 151, 214; and growth, 36, 40, 93, 251-2, 266; agricultural, 41, 194-5, 207-9, 221, 258; Australian, 86, 221; competitiveness among, 2, 19, 84, 97, 133, 144, 208; diversification of, 22, 245; Indonesian, 129, 133, 134; Japan's share, 67, 108, 214; Malaysian, 157, 278, 281; mining, 196-7, 221; of capital, *see* foreign investment; of manufactured goods, 16, 20, 118; of oil, 205; of primary products, 4, 20, 21, 194-5, 196
  see also exports—agricultural
  revealed comparative advantage of (RCAX), 220-2, 223-32, 288; Taiwan's share, 104; Thai share, 149, 150; United States share, 53-4, 56, 186-7, 206, 228; voluntary export restraints (VERs), 220, 235, 255, 257
external deficits, Australia, 4
external financing, *see* foreign investment
externalities, xv
extractive industries, *see* mining

farm produce price protection, *see* agriculture—price protection schemes
financial markets, *see* capital markets
fiscal deficits, 151, 166
fiscal policies, 9, 16, 17, 27, 77, 123, 153, 167, 211, 265, 310; of restraint, 58
food exports, *see* exports—agricultural
food imports, 193, 207-8, 209
food markets, 20, 21, 199-202
Ford Foundation, xvi
foreign aid, 234
foreign exchange rates, *see* exchange rates
foreign investment, 1, 4, 9, 32, 185-90, 213; by Canada, 188; by Japan, 61, 62, 117, 119, 188, 190, *191*, 222, 225, 226, 302 n9; by Korea, *188*; by the United States, 222, 225; controls, 23, 128; in Indonesia, 128, 135, 191; in Japan, 110; in Korea, 191; in Malaysia, 135, 138, 169, 191; in Singapore, 145, 191; in Thailand, 5, 191; in the Philippines, 141, 191; in the United States 56, 240
foreign securities, 107
Foundation of International Education, xvi
France, 202, 283
Fraser, Prime Minister Malcolm, 268
free enterprise, 35, 39, 270
Free Trade Agreements (FTA), 260, 261, 264
fruits, 209, 210
fuel prices, 151, 196-7, 210
fuels, 205-6, 210
full employment, 73, 247, *251*

Garnaut, Ross, xi, 8, 11, 15
GATT, 234, 241, 253-4, 256-60, 274; Cairns group, 267; Kennedy Round, 262; Tokyo Round, 259, 262; Trade Negotiating Committee, 260; Uruguay Round, 42, 206, 253, 257, 266, 269, 270, 274

Germany, 166, 171, 235, 242, 243, 283
Ghana, 202, 203, 283
Gorbachev, Mikhail, 234
government; economic role of, 28, 32, 34, 37-9, 50, 69, 79, 153, 212, 272; and the allocation of capital, 33; and resource use, 33, 38, 186; intervention, 35, 37, 114, 134, 178
government expenditure; and balance of payments, 50; Australia, *see* Australia—government expenditure; Japan, *see* Japan—government expenditure; national income and, 37; on interest payments, 50, 137, 152; practices, 253; reductions in, 71, 143
government guarantees, 186
government ownership, 35, 135, 138
grains prices, 200, 211
Gregory, R. G., xi, 8, 13, 71
Guatemala, 179

Hawke, Prime Minister R.J., 271
Henry Luce Foundation, xvi
high technology industries, *see* industries
Hirata, Akira, xi, 9, 213
holidays, *see* vacations
Hong Kong, 8, 191; economy, 37, 116; growth of, 30-3; foreign debt, 177; industrialisation, 11, 32; trade deficit, 94; trade figures, 215-16, 218-19, 222, 228-9; trade practices, 4
housing, 111; investments in, 62, 93, 108
hysteresis, 66-7, 109

imbalances, 1, 18-20, 63, 107; and recession, 56; external, 70, 167
IMF, 234, 241
immigration, 32-3, 146, 254
imports, 3, 4, 6-7; duty on, 149; Japan's share, 67, 172, 214; liberalisation of, 25; licensing of, 28, 36; Malaysia, 157, 161; of manufactured goods, 62; Philippines, liberalisation, 140; price elasticities, 97, 106, 108; restriction of, 34, 134; revealed comparative advantage of (RCAM), 220-2
incentives, 37, 253; for saving, 48-9; price, 127
income; and diet, 200, 209; distribution, *see* income distribution; elasticity, 116; per capita, 28, 200; comparisons of, 29, 30; saving and, 48
income distribution, 23-4; equality of, 32
India, 283; economy of, 192; trade figures, 215-16, 218-19, 228- 9; foreign debt, 177; government expenditure, 37; meat consumption in, 200; vegetable oil consumption, 201, *202*
Indonesia, 4, 20, 127-130, 133-5, 154, 283; banking in, 134; coffee production, 203; economy, 4-5, 16, 20, 21, 29, 127-30, 165, 177, 191; fiscal policy, 130, 133; government deficits, 23, 130, 133, 134; industrialisation, 128, 192; investment in, 12, 134, 191; monetary policy, 130; non-tariff barriers, 128, 134; rubber production, 204; tariffs, 134; taxation in, 133; textile industry in, 223; vegetable oil consumption in, 202
industrialisation, 8, 11, 33, 172, 218-19, 222, 232
industries; and metals prices, 204; competitiveness of, 67, 172, 258; equipment for, 34, 142, 172; 'flying geese' hypothesis, 213, 222-26; high value added, 142, 144, 145, 259, 263; improvement in products of, 196; protection of infant industries, 34; restructuring of, 1, 3, 118, 138, 144, 150
inflation, 6-7, 28, 121, *122-3*, 151, 152, 162, 233; in Australia, 4, 84, 85; in Europe, 199, 237; in Indonesia, 21, 121, 130, 133, 165;

in Japan, 62; in Korea, 38–9, 113, 165; in Malaysia, 136, 158, 162, 168; in New Zealand, 4; in Singapore, 142; in Thailand, 5, 147, 165; in the Philippines, 141; in the United States, 51, 52, 57, 109; measures of, 57; of assets, 62
information technology, 42, 111
infrastructure, 35, 39, 142, 145, 147
Institute of Strategic and International Studies (ISIS), Kuala Lumpur, xiii, xv
insurance, 142
intellectual property issues, 253, 254, 270
interest rates, 18, 153, 166, 181; effect on commodity prices, 198, 199; effect on investments, 2, 44, 170; effect on savings, 16; in Japan, 107; in Korea, 38–9; in Malaysia, 136, 169; in the Philippines, 140; in the United States, 44, 57–8, 106, 107; lowering of, 245
International Coffee Agreement, 203
International Development Research Centre, xvi
international trade; evolution of, 41–2, 256
International Trade Organization (ITO), 256
investment, 151; corporate, 67, 270; data, 272, 292–3; domestic, 178, 246, 247
  Australia, 77; Japan, 110; Malaysia, 173–4; Taiwan, 105, 114; Thailand, 149; United States, 2
housing, see housing; investment in developing countries, 40, 178, 198; in Indonesia, 134; in infrastructure, 198; in Malaysia, 138, 173; in research, see R & D investment; in Singapore, 145; in the Philippines, 139; rates of, 31–2, 40, 103, 178; investment, see also foreign investment
Investment Retirement Accounts (IRAs), 49

irrigation systems, 40, 210
Italy, 202, 265, 283

Japan, 1, 8, 179, 213; and Korea, 25, 69, 117; and Malaysia, 64; and the United States, 9, 11, 18–19, 63–4, 69, 95, 106–10, 116, 243
  investment in, 62, 184; trade war, 1, 259–60
budget surpluses, 17, 18, 20, 23, 61; current account surpluses, 107, 118, 171; Economic Planning Agency, 62, 68, 109; economy of, 3, 12, 16, 60–70, 110–12, 220–1, 228
  and world economy, 29, 42, 117, 191, 242, 257; deregulation, 69; postwar growth of, 29, 61, 69
fiscal policy, 66, 108, 109, 110; food imports, 25, 119, 207, 221; government expenditure, 61, 109, 110; import regulations, 68, 207, 221; industrialisation, 11, 111–12; Large-Scale Retail Outlet Law, 67; monetary policy, 109, 110; non-tariff barriers, 68; Overseas Economic Co-operation Fund, 168–9; political issues, 112; trade surplus, 63, 94, 106, 107, 109; voluntary export restraints, 69; *White Paper on the Economy 1989*, 62, 68

Kampuchea, 29
Kenya, 164, 193, 282
Keynes, J.M., *Lord*, 256
Korea, 1, 8, 15, 38, 176, 283; agricultural policies, 40; current account surplus, 4, 17, 20, 23, 97, 113; economy of, 12, 16, 116, 177, 191
  growth, 30–3, 36, 37, 200; liberalisation of, 38–9; trade figures, 215–16, 218–19, 221–2
export assistance, 37, 38; exports, 97, 113, 300 n 12; financial reforms, 39; imports, 97; political issues, 103, 112, 113; textile

industry, 223; trade deficit, 97; trade surplus, 94; voluntary export restraints, 69
Korean War, 69, 234
Krause, Lawrence B., xi, 10, 19, 21, 22, 24, 233
Krueger, Anne O., xi, 8, 16, 22, 27

labour, 29; and education, 39, 40; costs, 98; displacement of, 118; foreign, 146; in agriculture, 193; productivity of, 29, 103; shortages, 105, 142; unrest, 113
labour markets, 40, 247; interventions in, 28
laissez-faire economies, Korea, 39
land tenure, 210
Latin America, 12, 13, 15, 121, 172, 176-7, *177*, 180, 233, 238-9, 264, 268
Latin American Integration Association (LAIA), 267
leisure, 67
liberalisation, *see* trade practices—liberalising
life insurance, 107
Lin See Yan, xi, 9, 155
livestock, *see* meat
living standards, 15, 23, 42, 52, 56, 210; decline in, 193; future reductions in, 44
Louvre Accord, 167

Maekawa Report (Japan), 62, 110
Malaysia, 1, 4, 20, 122, 135-9, 152, 176; and Japan, 64, 65, 157, 168-9; and Singapore, 157, 162; and the United States, 157, 159, 162; balance of payments, 161, 170, 174, *278*, *281*; budget deficit, 17, 23, 136; coffee production, 203; Currency Board, 158; current account deficit, 136, 137, 161, 168; current account surpluses, 17, 136, 138; economy 5, 9, 15, 16, 21, 29, 136, 157-60, 163-4, 177, *277-81*
    recession in, 136, 161, 168; stabilisation measures, 22, 161; trade figures, 215-16, 218-19, 228-9
    fiscal policy, 136, 138, 161, 168; government expenditure, 37, 138, 161, 163; industrialisation, 135, 157, 175, 192; investment in, 12, 136, 191; Malaysian Government Securities (MGS), 178; monetary policy, 136, 137, 170; rubber production, 204; vegetable oil consumption in, 202
manufacturing sector, 190; Australia, 86-90, 92; China, 20; Hong Kong, 28; Japan, 28, 109, 111, 112, 172; Korea, 28, 97, *98*, 172; Malaysia, 20, 138, 139, 168; Singapore, 28, 142; Taiwan, 28, 172; Thailand, 5, 20, 151; United States, 28
markets, 28, 241-2; imperfect, 35; liberalisation of, *see* trade practices—liberalising; *see also* commodity markets
Meade, *Sir* James, 256
meat, 200-1, 209
Messina Conference 1955, 235
metals industries, 204-5, 211
Mexico, 15, 130, 176, 177, 179, 192, 239, 283
Middle East, 121
military expenditure, 18, 240, 246
mining, 86; exports, *see* exports—mining
Monetary Authority of Singapore, 144
monetary policy, 9, 16, 27, 123, 166, 167, 211, 265; public debt and, 58
Montes, Manuel F., xi, xv, 9, 12, 15, 176
Multifibre Arrangement (MFA), 220, 254, 257
multilateralism, *see* economics—multipolar/multilateral

Narongchai, Akrasanee, 23
NATO, 234, 237, 243
Nepal, 177, 282
New Zealand, 3, 12, 179, 283; deficit, 23; economic issues, 16, 17; land

resources, 29; trade figures, 215–16, 218–19, 221, 228–9
Nicaragua, 179, 282
NIEs, 1, 4, 16, 63, 106, 114, 116, 118, 177, 182, 213, 222, 237, 272
Nigeria, 202, 283
North America, 172, 242

OECD, 267, 268
oil consumption, 205
oil crisis, 1970s, 18, 20, 205, 237
oil prices, 20, 96, 97, 102–3, 108, 121, 130, 151, 154, 205–6, 278; see also fuel prices
oil shocks, 21, 108, 121, 141, 146
oilseeds production, 207; prices for, 200–1
Okita, Saburo, 268
OPEC, 253, 267
Organisation for Pacific Trade and Development (OPTAD), 265, 271

Pacific Basin Economic Council (PBEC) 268, 269
Pacific Community Seminar, Canberra 1980, 268–9
Pacific Economic Cooperation Conferences (PECC), 268, 269, 270, 271, 273, 275, 295–7; National Committees, 273; Third Pacific Trade Policy Forum, 270, 296; Trade Policy Task Force, 269
Pacific Economic Outlook, 269, 273
Pacific Trade and Development (PAFTAD) Conference Series, xiii, xv, 263, 266, 268; Eighteenth, Kuala Lumpur 1989, xv, 8, 11, 19; First, Tokyo 1968, xiii; Secretariat, xvi
PAFTAD Conference Series, see Pacific Trade and Development Conference Series
Pakistan, 283; economy, 192; foreign debt, 177; government expenditure, 37; vegetable oil consumption in, 202
palm oil, 201
Panama, 179

Pangestu, Mari, xi, 9, 13, 14, 15, 121
Papua New Guinea, 22, 29, 282
Park, Yung Chul, xi, 19, 93
payments deficits, 23
payments surpluses, 25
pensions, 46
Peru, 15, 176, 177, 179, 282
petroleum, see oil
Philippines, 4, 20, 139–41, 176, 283; budget deficit, 139, 140, 141; coffee production, 203; current account deficit, 139, 141; economy, 5, 12–13, 15, 29, 139, 191, 308
 high debt level of, 28, 122, 139, 177; rescheduling debts, 176; trade figures, 215–16, 218–19, 228–9
 fiscal policy, 139; government spending, 140; monetary policy, 139; structural reforms, 141, 154; tariffs, 140; vegetable oil consumption in, 202
Plaza Agreement 1985, 61, 110, 166, 167, 168
political issues, 233–44; conservatism, 50; instability, 238; liberalism, 50; stability, 23
pollution, 210
population; ageing of, 233; Japan, 110, 119; United States, 248
population growth, 193; fall in, 32
poverty, 33
price controls, 127
price stability, 93, 166; failure of, 211
prices; effect on production, 75; elasticity of, 105; fall in, 69, 203; in Australia, 84–5; in Korea, 113; in Thailand, 148; modelling of, 293–4; prices, see also fuel prices, grain prices, oilseed prices etc
primary product exports, see exports—agricultural, exports—mining
private ownership, see free enterprise
production; costs, see costs; factors of, 36, 73, 117; levels in Australia, 74, 77; monopolies, 36; quotas, 206

productivity, 23; increases in, 29, 42, 57, 208
profit; and investment, 76, 77; incentives and, 36; rates of, 86
protection, 18, 23, 90, 128, 199, 231; and profitability, 36; for trade in services, 42; vs deregulation, 69; *see also* agriculture—price protection schemes
public expenditure, *see* government expenditure
public works, 105

R & D (research and development); investment, 1, 198; in agriculture, 40, 193
recessions; 1980s, 121, 152, 157, 161, 163; 1970s, 121
resource allocation, 123, 127, 154; and exchange rates, 160; and high wages, 73; and government regulation, 28, 40; resource gap 178-90
regionalism, 10, 243, 252, 253, 261-73
restructuring of industry, *see* industries—restructuring of
revaluation, *see* currencies
rice, 209, 221, 227
Rockefeller Brothers Fund, xvi
Rome Treaty, 264
rubber, 203-4, 210, 221, 278

savings, 16, 17-18, 33; and investment, 29, 127, 178, *179*, 250, 252
  in Australia, 72, *81*; in Korea, 97, 98, 100-2; in Malaysia, 137-8; in Taiwan, 104-5; in the Philippines, 140; in the United States, 44, *45*, 46-9, 53, 245, 250
  domestic, 95, 102, 104, 109, 178, 180, 181; in Australia, 80-3, 90-2; in developing countries, 33, 102, 180; in Japan, 67, 108, 110, 119; in Singapore, 142; in the United States, 245, 248; interest rates for, 32; modelling, 293; net government, 80, 81
self-sufficiency, 21
service industries; Japan, 118; Singapore, 142; trade, 253, 254
shipbuilding; Japan, 118; Singapore, 142
Singapore, 8, 141-6, 152, 283; balance of payments, 142; budget surpluses, 17, 142; Central Provident Fund, 142; economy, 37, 116, 141-2, 146, 153, 177, 191; exports, 30-1, 141, 230; industrialisation, 11, 32, 141; monetary policy, 143; trade deficit, 94; trade figures, 215-16, 218-19, 228-9; trade practices, 4
Smith, Murray G., xi, 10, 24, 253
Smithsonian Agreement, 155, 158
social services, 39
social welfare, 110
Sopiee, Noordin, xi, xiii, xv
Southeast Asia, potential growth of, 43
Southern African Development Council, 267
Soviet Union, 234, 235, 243, 253, 268
spending, *see* consumption
Sri Lanka, 283; foreign debt, 177; government expenditure, 37
steel industry, 222-6, 258; Japan, 118, 225; United States, 225
stock market, 167; Malaysia, 173; Singapore, 145, 173; Taiwan, 114; United States 1981, 47
storage, 142
structural adjustment, 1, 15, 20, 111, 119, 123, 233
subsidies, *see* agriculture—price protection schemes, incentives
sugar industry, 206, 207, 210, 221
Sundberg, Mark, xi, 10, 19, 24, 233
sustainable growth, 23, 210
synthetic fabrics, 222-3, 225
Systema Economico Latino Americano (SELA), 267

Taiwan, 1, 8; current account surplus, 4, 17, 20, 23, 183; economy, 12, 16,

28, 113-14, 116, 177, 191
   growth of, 30-3, 37, 103-4, 112;
   trade figures, 215-16, 218- 19,
   221-2, 228-9
   industrialisation, 11, 32; textile
   industry, 223; trade surplus, 94,
   103, 104
Taiwan Institute of Economic
   Research, xvi
Takenaka, Heizo, xii, 8, 19, 60
tariffs, 257; Australian, 89; Korean,
   39; on industrial commodities, 42
taxation, 18, 153; and government
   deficit, 49; avoidance of, 49, 149;
   corporate, 149; marginal tax rates,
   49, 149
tea, 203
technological; change, 1, 111, 199;
   transfers, 63
textile industry, 223, 258, 270
Thailand, 1, 4, 20, 146-51; coffee
   production, 203; deficits, 23, 146,
   147, 177; Eastern Seaboard Project,
   147; economy, 5, 16, 22, 29, 146-7,
   165, 191, 192
   trade figures, 215-16, 218-19,
   221
   fiscal policy, 146, 148, 149;
   government expenditure, 37, 147;
   income distribution, 23; monetary
   policy, 146, 147-8; rubber
   production, 204; tariffs, 150;
   textile industry, 223
timber, 204, 221, 263; Tropical Forest
   Cooperation task force, 269
tourism, 142, 269
trade, 9, 27, 213-18; blocs, 42, 172;
   contraction of, 4, 164; deficits, *see*
   under names of countries with such
   deficits—e.g. United States; desired
   data on, 272, 290; expansion of, 20,
   214; fluctuations, 16, 20;
   imbalances, 3, 18, 66, 93, 96, 103,
   107, 109, 114, 119-20; intra-
   regional, 1, 117, 214, 227-8, 230,
   261; managed regimes, 260;
   multilateral, 42, 254; negotiations,
   42, 256-61, 267; non-tariff barriers,
   253, 254, 259; practices, 2, 8, 14,
   24, 255-61
   liberalisation of, 4, 21, 23, 24-6,
   39, 42, 114, 116, 117, 150, 227,
   231, 261
   ratios, 32, 227-8; restrictions, 34,
   127, 134, 196; surpluses, 93, 94,
   95, 104; war, 1; *see also*
   international trade, evolution of
trade unions, 145
transport, deregulation of, 40
transportation, 111, 142, 151; costs,
   196
Turkey, 192, 283

UNECLA, 253
unemployment, 6-7; decline in, 32
   Europe, 237
   in Europe, 247; in Malaysia, 163; in
   the United States, 2, 44, 51, 52
United Kingdom, 4, 171, 236, 256,
   283
United States, 1, 20, 166, 179,
   239-40; and Canada, 42; and
   Europe, 237; and Japan, 9, 11,
   18-19, 63-4, 95, 114-18, 240, 243
   trade war, 1, 259-60
   and Korea, 242; and Taiwan, 242;
   and Thailand, 148; balance of
   payments, 2, 240, 244-52; budget
   deficit, 2, 17, 18, 19, 44, 49-51,
   58, 106, 107, 171, 239-40, 246,
   249; budgetary adjustment, 116,
   240; current account deficit, 11,
   14, 17, 24, 29, 45, 52, 53, 55, 59,
   106, 171, 239-40, 250, 277;
   deregulation, 40, 107; economy, 2,
   12, 56-9, 235, 250
   contraction of, 69, 116;
   imbalances in, 43, 44, 120, 175,
   244-52; with world economy,
   29, 44-56, 69, 120, 166, 235,
   242
expansionary fiscal policy, 2, 8, 18,
   14, 108, 166; Farm Bill, 206, 259;
   foreign ownership, 14; government
   spending, 247;
Gramm-Rudman-Hollings

balanced budget act, 49–50, 58, 171, 175, 245–52; imports, 116, 118, 214, 215, 221, 230; inflation, 44, 248; monetary policy, 18, 247, 248; most favoured nation (MFN) treaties, 256; political issues, 24, 51, 55–6, 212, 233, 246, 250, 274; tariff policies, 29, 234–5; trade deficits, 2–3, 8, 11, 52, 55, 59, 64, 95, *96*, 107, 116, 170, 215; United States Agency for International Development, 185; vegetable oil consumption in, 202

Uruguay Round, *see* GATT
USSR, *see* Soviet Union

vacations, 119; *see also* tourism
vegetable oils, 201, *202*, 207, 209, 210, 221
vegetables, 209
Venezuela, 176
Vietnam, 29, 282
Vietnam War, 146, 234

wages; cost-of-living adjustments, 77; increases in, 57, 97; policy, 27 in Australia, 71, 75; in Singapore, 144, 145
real, 52, 57, 71, 248; reductions in, 76, 248; restraint, 145
Warsaw Pact, 234, 243
wealth accumulation of, 48, 114; and income ratio, 47, 48; and interest rates, 246, 247; household, 47
weather and trade, 199, 200, 206
Western Pacific, 23, 24, 42, 242
White, John, 256
Wilcox, Clair, 256
wood, *see* timber
work week; Japan, 110; shortening of, 67, 119
World Bank, 12, 185, 193, 234, 241; risk management program, 198, 211; Structural Adjustment Loans, to Korea, 39

Yamazawa, Ippei, xii, 9, 21, 213
Yokota, Kazuhiko, xii, 9, 213

Zaire, 202, 283